LAWYER TO MAHATMA

Life, Work and Transformation of M.K. Gandhi

LAWYER TO MAHATMA

Life, Work and Transformation of M.K. Gandhi

S.L. MALHOTRA
Formerly Chairman, Department of Gandhian Studies,
Panjab University, Chandigarh.

DEEP & DEEP PUBLICATIONS PVT. LTD.
F-159, Rajouri Garden, New Delhi-110027

were generally excluded from this privilege by orthodox Hindus. Narasimha Mehta who composed Gandhi's favourite hymn 'Vaishnavjan' was the friend of untouchables. The town of Porbandar had several temples and there were two temples near the ancestral house of Gandhi's. The religious atmosphere of Kathiawar was imbued with different religious currents. Karamchand, in conformity with the liberal outlook of the area received the followers of different religions in his house where they discussed their religious beliefs fearlessly. A Jain monk Bechharji Swami was a frequent visitor to their house and after Kaba Gandhi's death his wife turned to him for advice. The Swami was originally a Modh Bania. The religious atmosphere of Kathiawar was impregnated with the teaching and spirit of Jainism and so Gandhi family could not escape its influence. Though not having any religious training, Kaba Gandhi was imbued with that religious culture which was available to every Hindu going to temples frequently and listening to religious discourses. His son remembered that towards the close of his life his father started reading the Gita at "the instance of a learned Brahman friend of the family and he used to repeat aloud some verses everyday at the time of worship." Tulsi Ramayan, too, which his son adored, gave consolation to him to which he listened while lying in his sick bed. Even late in his life Mohandas felt the joy of parental love and believed that his parents surrendered themselves to his love for them. In a reminiscent mood he once told his secretary that his father would never ask any of the servants to do any thing for him but would "insist 'on my doing'—it—He simply doted upon me. Even when the most confidential consultations were going on—he would have me by his side."[3]

What did Mohandas inherit from his mother. The answer is her deep religiosity. For, she was a deeply religious woman who observed the customs and practices associated with orthodox Hinduism. She prayed and visited a temple daily and faithfully kept fasts. As Gandhi remembered she would take the hardest vows and kept them without flinching. "To keep two or three consecutive fasts was nothing to her.''[4] Her piety and religiosity hallowed the atmosphere of the home. Her son later on remembered that though believing in strict discipline "she had such a strain of tenderness and sympathy in his heart that the children clung to her with boundless affection."[5] Those who lived with the 'Mahatma' in his Ashram must have experienced the outcome of this benign trait when they were ill or in difficulty . That accounts for Gandhi's great love and reverence for this mother. His first biographer noticed that "his voice softens when he speaks of her, and the light of love is in his eyes."[6]

While narrating the genial disposition of his mother, the Mahatma used the word saintliness for his mother. But his secretary said that the appropriate word for this trait of her character was austerity. However, Gandhi replied that he had used the word saintliness deliberately for his mother as 'austerity' implies external renunciation, endurance and sometimes even hypocrisy. Saintliness is inner purity of the soul. My mother's austerity was the echo of her inner life."[7]

As the last child, Mohan was the darling of the family, lovingly called 'Moñiya' and was well looked after by his mother who would even take him along with her while visiting a temple or the palace when invited by the queen for her advice. Besides, his elder sister Raliat Behn and a nurse Ramba took care of him. Growing mostly under the care of women added some feminine traits to his character. Possibly the love and care that he received from women around him during his childhood created a niche in his heart for womanhood and raised high in his eyes the qualities of women especially of Indian women who could subdue their men folk through self-suffering and unbounded love. If in his old age his grand niece received motherly love from him, there was hardly anything unusual. For, it was a trait of his character—a part of his mental make-up.

Notes and References

1. Gandhi, M.K., An Autobiography, or the Story of My Experiments with Truth Navajivan Publishing House, 1982 hereafter, Gandhi, M.K. Autobiograph.
2. Desai, Mahadev, Day to Day with Gandhi (Rajghat, Varanasi, 1972), Vol. V, p. 118.
3. *Ibid*, *op. cit.*, Vol. I, p. 61.
4. Gandhi, M.K., Autobiography, p. 4.
5. Doke, Josephy, J., M.K. Gandhi, An Indian Patriot in South Africa (Publication Division), p. 22.
6. *Ibid.*
7. Desai, *op. cit.*, Vol. I, pp. 51-52.

2

Childhood

As a child Mohan was sweet-tempered. But like all children who are given special attention enjoyed doing mischief, such as hiding while others were anxiously looking for him. However, he did not like his elders to keep watch over him continuously. One day he slipped from the house and followed a group of young girls who had adorned their hair with flowers and spent the day with them. A search was made for him and a girl brought him back when it was dark. Curiosity was embedded in the mind of the child and no wonder it had a role to play in his decisions to see new lands later in life.

As a child Mohan was timorous and was affraid of ghosts and snakes. But, according to his own account, he was very truthful. The story of Harishchandra which he read from the collection of his father's books left a deep impression on his mind. Unconsciously throughout his life he appeared to be imitating Harishchandra who sacrificed everything at the altar of truth. Even a few days before his death the conduct of Harishchandra was on his mind in a discussion with a foreign visitor to whom he narrated this story.

As a student, Mohan did not have a distinguished academic record. In his autobiography, he records that he was only a mediocre student in spite of the fact that he sometimes won scholarships. Later in life he even believed that his intellect must have been sluggish and raw at the elementary stage since he had not much to remember of that period. Possibly Gandhi did not keep in view the circumstances under which he had to study during that period. For, his academic career was not smooth as his performance in different examinations depended upon situations on which the child had no control. In Porbandar he was put in an elementary school which was not sufficiently equipped for teaching because it was very near his house, though there were three private primary schools and a Government primary school which had better teaching aids. The boys would learn in this school alphabets by drawing letters on a wooden board on which fine dust was strewn. This was known as 'Dhoolishala' (Dust School). This probably accounts for his bad handwriting which adversely affected all his career as a student. His poor score in geography and history in various examinations was partly due to his bad handwriting. So he learnt the lesson that bad handwriting was a sign of imperfect education.

On the appointment of Kaba Gandhi as the chief Karbari of Rajkot, the family shifted to that town. While Mohan was a school boy, the town grew fast as it was made the seat of political agency. As a result, several schools sprang up out of which the city Taluk school was prominent. However, for first and second standard, Mohan was admitted to the branch school from where he shifted to the city Taluk school. It looks he could not get on well in the second standard, may be because of his serious illness. His performance both in the third and fourth standards, too, was not commendable as he was not very serious about his studies, though he improved his position in the fourth standard. However, at the entrance examination to the high school, he obtained very high percentage of marks (64.25%) the highest being 74%. But he faced great difficulty in following his lessons as the teaching was in English. So he was virtually at the bottom of the class in the terminal examination. But in the annual examination he surprisingly obtained 63% the highest being 64%. He had now improved his English and was placed in section A, to which good students were admitted. Though married while in standard two of high school, he secured 57% marks in the terminal examination. But he could not clear the final examination as he attended the school for 74 out of 222 days. Shocked by this failure he became very serious and in the terminal examination, he secured 65.5% marks and was placed 8th in the class and in the second, he was placed 4th in spite of his absence of 47 days. In the third standard he simultaneously appeared for standard IV and had a leap promotion. Thus he made up the loss of one year of standard II. In the Inspector's report of the fifth standard he secured 62.3% and in standard VI, he obtained 57.4% and stood 6th in the class. In terminal examination of VII class which was the highest class in the school, his performance was poor may be because of the death of his father. In the final examination he simply scrapped through. The standard of the matriculation appears to be very high as is evident from the question papers. A student is required to have good command of English and knowledge of several disciplines. Geometry was beyond his comprehension till his teacher explained it on the blackboard the thirteenth proposition of the Euclid which states that if a straight line is drawn from any point to intersect another straight line the angles formed on that side add up to two right angles. It was an intellectual delight for him when he comprehended it. When a subject gave him enjoyment he took great interest in it and so later in his life he explained some of his own abstruse concepts through geometrical terms. Similarly, later on he developed great interest in Mathematics especially in Algebra as he discovered in it a means of concentration of the mind.[1] He was quite frank about his poor performance in his academic career even when he was looked upon head and shoulders above many topmost leaders and intellectuals of the country. Addressing a gathering of lawyers he said, "I never had a brilliant career. I was all my life a plodder. When I went to England—I couldn't put together two sentences correctly.—On the steamer I was a drone. I did not know whether I would not commit a grammatical mistake or mispronounce a word."[2]

As a child Mohan was shy of company, may be because of his consciousness of his poor physique and his fear that other boys would make fun of him. Normally he would rush back home after the school hours. He has hardly any interest in games. He only once took part in the game of cricket in the high school under compulsion as required by the rules of the school. He never attended a cricket match either in England, South Africa or India. As late as 1931, he did not know what really the game of hockey was.[3] However he knew the rules of the games in vogue among children at that time and would love to act as a referee though he was the youngest and weakest among them.[4] But he loved to walk in the morning while he was in the high school and this habit remained with him throughout his life.

Mohan acquired interest in plants. When the family shifted to Rajkot he had a little garden in the compound of the house.[5]

One special characteristic of the child was his truthfulness. It was his forte, the Mahatma observed. But this quality of the child sometimes landed his playmates in a difficult situation and no wonder if they avoided him. Once the children decided to steal images of gods and goddesses from a temple to play a game. While they were carrying on their plan, the priest awoke and chased the children who threw the images in another temple and disappeared. The priest complained the matter to 'Moniya's' uncle who was a strict disciplinarian and a vaishnava to whom such acts were profane and blasphemous demanding strict action. When interrogated, the boys denied having done so. But when Moniya was asked he told the whole story truthfully. His class teacher, too, was put in an embarrassing position for Mohan's passion for uprightness. The inspector of schools once visited his class and dictated five English words as a spelling test of the class. His teacher noted that Mohan misspelt the word kettle. He threw him a hint to see his neighbour's slate. But Mohan did not take the hint as this was cheating which was not his habit. It induced him to prepare his lessons daily as he could not tell a lie to his teachers for escaping punishment.

To serve his father was pleasure to Mohan. One reason for his lack of interest in games was his desire to rush back home to serve his father after the school hours. Though he had no interest in story books, a chance reading of the story of Shravan while he was in the primary school, carrying his blind aged parents in sling on his shoulders moved him.[6] The scene was depicted in a picture that he saw multiplied its effects. His mother was conscious of child's devotion to his parents and had, therefore, instructed that he alone would press her legs and his father, too, would not accept any service from anybody else. It rankled in his mind all his life that he was not serving his father at the last moments of his life, as overpowered by carnal passions, he rushed to the room of his young wife who was at the advanced stage of pregnancy. His guilt appeared greater to him as the child that was born did not live for more than a few days.[7]

The ideal of filial piety was worthy of emulation for him. But it created a tension in his own family when he discovered that all his sons could not come up to this ideal.

Mohan entered a new phase of his life after the death of his father. For, he was left to himself. He was now to know himself, his resources and his ambition. He was on his way to establish his identity.

Married at the age of thirteen, Mohan was passionately fond of his wife, Kasturba. She was the daughter of a rich merchant of Porbandar, Gokuldas Makanji whose house was close to that of Gandhis. The children might have played together but they were too young to fall in love. Kasturba was brought up in Rajkot which was culturally more advanced than Porbandar. In later years Gandhi referred to his early marriage as a tragedy since it fired his carnal desires at an early age which not only affected his studies but also stood in the way of his service to his father. He remembered that it "took him long to get free from the shakles of lust," and he had to pass through many ordeals before he could overcome it. Possibly his passion for Brahmacharya late in life sprang out of this effort.

It was during this period of his life Mohan picked up friendship with a Muslim boy Sheikh Mehtab through his elder brother Karsandas. Mehtab was three years senior to him. He had certain qualities which Mohan adored but lacked. He was tall, strongly built, was a good athlete and unlike Mohan not afraid of ghosts and snakes and not shy of company of his class fellows. He was, in fact, his alter ego. Mohan tried to emulate him and in this process he picked up several habits which could be considered as sinful in the social environment in which he was brought up. It was Mehtab who persuaded him to take meat on the plea that his poor physique and that of the Indians in general was due to their vegetarian diet as a result of which they have become subservient to the meat eating English. Such arguments appealed to Mohan and so he started taking meat. But meat eating bouts with his friends could not be carried on for a long time as these could be had secretly as Mohan's parents were vegetarian. Moreover, meat delicacies were expensive which the boys could not afford. There could not be more than half a dozen occasions when they took meat. Even then these sessions and other extravagances led his brother Karsandas to fall in debt. The youngest Mohan was persuaded to carve out a small piece of gold from the amulet of Karsandas and sell it to pay off the debt. Though the boy performed this act easily, his conscience was pricked by this guilt. The weight of the guilt on conscience was unbearable for him. So he confessed it to his mother who advised him to confess it before his father. Since he lacked courage to tell it to his father, he scribbled his confession on a piece of paper and placed it before the ailing man and waited for reprimand or punishment. But the result of it surprised the boy. The guilt was washed away by the tears of love that fell from the eyes of his father. It was an experience of unbounded love of his father, though the Mahatma explained it as the supreme lesson of non-violence and truth. The weight of two conflicting compulsions, that is, respect for elders and desire of freedom of action must have been very heavy on the boy's mind and no wonder he toyed with the idea of committing suicide.

Mohan had to suffer some kind of estrangement with his wife as a result of his friendship with Mehtab. For the latter would tell him stories of infidelity of women which fanned the flames of suspicion in the innocent boy about his child wife. His ambition to have full control over her added more tension between them as Kasturba being a self-respecting and freedom loving girl, made it a point to go wherever she liked. Mehtab even led Gandhi to a brothel. This was not his first encounter with sex. He knew what was expected of him on that occasion. But he was so overpowered by the sense of guilt that he couldn't do anything. The woman lost patience with him and showed him the door with insults and abuses which at that time hurt his manhood. He was not free from carnal desire. But there was another feeling that pushed him to the other side. If he could be faithless to his wife, how could he make his wife faithful. Gandhi said later on that he was saved by God from this sinful act. But it was the internal struggle between two forces—desire and ideal that literally paralyzed him.

Mohan had been warned by his wife, elder brother and his mother that Mehtab's company would lead him to evil. But he paid no heed to this warning. He simply satisfied his conscience by assuming that his association with Mehtab would result in reforming his friend. This was delusion. In fact, he was loath to leave some of his habits as he enjoyed them. He tried to cover them up by fine apparels of ideals. Only later on he learnt that true friendship could not be between persons with opposite nature. He wrote, "only between like natures can friendship be altogether worthy and enduring—Hence in friendship, there is very little scope for reform."[8]

In fact, most of the bad habits that the boy picked up had to be abandoned not because they had no attraction for him at that time but because their indulgence involved telling of lies to his elders that pricked his conscience. That also accounts for giving up the habit of smoking which he had picked up before falling into the company of Mehtab. Possibly indulgence was only postponed to some future date when he would not be obliged to explain his conduct to his elders.

After clearing his matriculation examination, Mohan joined college at Bhavanagar. But he fared badly in tests mostly because he could not follow the lectures of the teachers as the medium of all the subjects was English. He therefore, returned to Rajkot in a depressed mood. It was at that time a family friend and chief adviser of Gandhi family, Mavji Dave suggested that Mohan be sent to England for higher studies. The young boy jumped at the idea as he was in no mood to go back to the college. Possibly it was also the intention of Kaba Gandhi to send Mohan to England. For, in a dispute with the ruler of Wankaner over the letter of resignation submitted by Mohan's father, the prince had offered him handsome amount on the condition of making certain amendments in the letter. It was thought that he would fall for this offer as it would fructify his dream of sending his son to England for higher studies. But the proud Dewan rejected this offer.

Initially Mohan wanted to go in for medicine. He even started reading books on anatomy, biology and physiology.[9] But the daily sight of dissection of live frogs and the objection raised by his brother that their father disapproved of the dissection of dead bodies or of live frogs scuttled his plan. Even when he went to England in 1906 he thought of going in for medicine. But again he was prevented from fulfilling this desire by the essential condition of doing dissection and vivisection. There he learnt that two students had given up medical studies because of this rule. There was a case also in the court in England in this connection.[10] Late in his life he felt that if he had followed that profession, he would have risen very high as he was sure of his diagnosis.[11] The attitude for medical profession found expression through his passion for nature cure later on. It was, therefore, decided to send him for the bar which could equip him for the post which his father and grand father had held even without obtaining any academic degree. But the times had now changed with the extension of the control of the British administration over the dominions of the princes in Kathiawar.

However, going to England was not an easy task for Mohan. The difficulties that he faced were likened to the heads of Ravana which were many and which were no sooner chopped off than replaced. For, money had to be arranged as his father had not left enough money; consent of the elders including that of his mother and uncles had to be obtained who were quite apprehensive of sending him to a distant land with strange culture and values that allured young fellows to ways which were considered sinful by the society; his young wife had to consoled who had been nursing his first son Harilal and finally the consent of the caste elders had to be secured who could excommunicate him on the rejection of their advice. In fact, the period of five months before his departure to England really tested his wits and mettle of which he was made. Recording in his diary the magnitude of the problems that he faced at that time, he said,

> "I must write that had it been some other man in the same position which I was in, I dare say he would not have been able to see England. For—I am not a man who would after having any intention, leave it easily."[12]

This is true to a great extent. Before him a journalist Karsandas Mulji was persecuted by his own community for his temerity to visit

England and he died shortly after this visit.[13] Gandhi, too, was jeered by a mob of Modh Banias before he sailed from Bombay to England.

Though his uncle was reluctant to agree to his going to England, he left the final decision to his mother whose permission was obtained by taking a vow in the presence of the Jain saint of avoiding wine, women and meat in England. The money was arranged with the help of his brother. The excommunication by his castemen was courageously faced which was unusual for a youngman of his age. This trait of challenging those whose minds were tied up with traditions appeared at length later in his life when he launched his movement against untouchability.

Notes and References

1. Nayyar, Sushila, Mahatma Gandhi's Last Imprisonment, p. 291.
2. Gandhi, M.K., Collected Works of M. Gandhi (Publication Division), Vol. XLVII, hereafter C.W. p. 317.
3. Gandhi, Prabhu Das, My Childhood with Gandhi (Navajivan Publishing House) p. 28.
4. *Ibid.*
5. *Ibid.*
6. Desai, M., *op. cit.*, Vol. VI, p. 4.
7. Gandhi, M.K., Autobiography, p. 26.
8. *Ibid.*, p. 16.
9. Desai, M., *op. cit*, Vol. I, p. 138.
10. Nayyar, Sushila, Mahatma Gandhi's Last Imprisonment, p. 165.
11. Desai, M., *op. cit.*, Vol. I, p. 138.
12. Gandhi, M.K., C.W., Vol. I, p. 12.
13. Chandran, Devanesen, The Making of the Mahatma, p. 131.

3

Ambition

He was nineteen when he undertook the journey to the unknown land impelled by ambition and curiosity. England at that time was abreast with new ideas which were questioning the validity of current norms and beliefs. They must have trickled into the mind of young Mohandas who was no saint at that time.

Mohan had three major objectives during his first visit to England. First, to keep up the triple vow, second, to equip himself for the legal profession, and third, to improve his English. In the process of attaining them, he got himself acquainted with several new ideas, made new experiments, reformed himself according to the new challenges and needs of the time and became conscious of his latent talents and weaknesses. All this demanded consistent effort, great determination and fortitude. His mettle was tested even during his first voyage. For, his resolve to stick to the vegetarian diet put him to a lot of difficulty and mental tension as he was not a vegetarian by choice or conviction but merely because of his oath which was sacred to him. His poor knowledge of English and the difficulty of adjusting himself to the people of a different culture virtually cut him off from the rest of passengers and compelled him to remain most of the time in his own cabin living on whatever sweets and fruit that he had brought with him. Even as a student he was not very social and was not in the habit of making friends. Most of the persons who came to see him off from Rajkot at the time of his departure were his relatives. It is true Sheikh Mehtab became his close friend. But that friendship he got from his elder brother Karsandas who was Mehtab's class fellow. However the journey did reveal some latent traits of his character. He was capable of appreciating the beauty of stars reflected in the water in dark night or beauty of the sea in a moonlit night. It looks that there was a poet in him which mostly remained submerged under his crowded plans and strifs of his life appearing suddenly like the sun from the clouds on rare occasions. His London diary written in the style of essay by a school boy shows the budding journalist in him. He even had a plan to publish a guide to London for the guidance of young Indians visiting England. But he hardly had any time in South Africa or India to carry it out.

As soon as Mohan stepped on the soil of the new world, his eyes were dazzled by the splendour of the city regarded as the centre of civilization. The Victoria Hotel where he stayed for two days on arrival in London communicated to him the type of culture to which he was exposed. His unfamiliarity with the norms of the new civilization was evident from the clothes that he selected to wear on his arrival. He felt ashamed of himself when he discovered that he was the only person who was wearing white flannel clothes. It was a sight of amousement for Dr. Mehta who met him there for whom he had brought a note of introduction. He initiated him to European etiquette when the young man out of curiosity picked up his top hat and disturbed its fur by passing his hand over it the wrong way. "Do not touch other people's things," 'Do not ask questions—on first acquaintance'; Do not talk loudly; 'Never address people as Sir whilst speaking to them as we do in India as only servants and subordinates address their masters that way.'

Mohan's limited financial resources compelled him to seek ways and means for living economically in London. In this process he learnt to cook his own meals, shifted his apartments occasionally, walked long distances to take his meals at cheap restaurants, maintain accounts of his daily expenditure—the habit that he kept up throughout his life and helped him in keeping strict financial control over the public bodies under his charge. He stuck to vegetarian diet in obedience to the word he had given to his mother in spite of innumerable difficulties that he faced. However, here his vegetarianism acquired sound foundation. For, from a born vegetarian, he became a convinced vegetarian. It signified a new approach to life. For, it meant consciousness of the sanctity of life following from the faith in oneness of life. The vegetarianism of the British was not confined to food. It covered their view of society and their view of human relationship. However, all British vegetarians did not hold the same view in this regard. Radicals and conservatives agnostics, atheists and religious enthusiasts rubbed shoulders in their meetings. They were bound by their compassion and tenderness for all living beings. Among them were such celebrities as Edward Carpenter, Bernard Shaw, Annie Besant, Dr. T.A. Allinson, Henry Salt, etc.

In his search for a vegetarian restaurant, Mohan chanced upon a vegetarian restaurant in Farrington Street while walking from the Inner Temple along Fleet Street. This discovery was a great moment of joy for him. Among the pamphlets and books lying under a glass window near the door, there was 'A Plea for Vegetarianism by H.S. Salt.' He bought it and read it from cover to cover after returning to his room. It roused in him interest in the philosophy of vegetarianism and he avidly went through its literature. Anna Kingsford's 'The Perfect way in Diet' appeared to him equally interesting as it was the product of the experiences of a doctor who claimed that man could transform this world into a 'paradise by working with God and nature'. Now his vegetarianism acquired a rational and scientific basis. He was no more vegetarian because of habit, tradition or vow. He was vegetarian by choice. Narrating the nature of this transformation, he observes in his autobiography, "I had all along abstained from meat in the interest of truth and of the vow I had taken, but had wished at the same time that every Indian should be a meat-eater and had looked forward to being one myself freely and openly some day and enlisting others in the cause."[1]

Besides, this change gave him a mission in life. But as yet it had not been consecrated by any religious motive. He decided to disseminate the message and philosophy of vegetarianism. He founded a vegetarian club in Bayswater where he was living and appointed Dr. Josiah Oldfield as its president, Sir Edwin Anrold as Vice-president and himself as its secretary. It functioned as long as he stayed there and was closed down when he moved to an apartment elsewhere. This was his first experience in organizational work. Experiment in dietetics, which later became his passion, followed from his commitment to vegetarianism. In pursuit of it, he learnt that the "real seat of taste was not in the tongue but in the mind."[2] The London Vegetarian Society that he joined brought him in touch with a number of its members. Among them was Josiah Oldfield, editor of the journal of the society, 'The Vegetarian', a young Oxford theology graduate and a Lincoln Inns barrister. Mohan shared apartment with him for some time. When he went to South Africa he renewed his contacts with Oldfield through correspondence and submitted articles to the vegetarian'. The young editor discovered in Mohan a promising fellow traveller and so encouraged him to attend the International Vegetarian conference where he read his paper which was published in the journal of the society. Encouraged by this success, several more articles followed. 'On Indian Vegetarians' denotes his rational approach to the problems. In the first article he noticed that salt was heavily taxed in India. He launched a powerful movement for its abolition in India four decades later. In another article, he strongly condemned the consumption of alcoholic drink spreading "throughout length and breadth of India hiting hard the poor in the country." In the fourth article he challenged the current view that Hindus were physically weak because they were vegetarians. For, how was it that Kshtriya princes were weak even when they were meat eaters, he questioned. Answering the question, he argued, harmful customs such as child marriage, debauchery prevalent among them, were the real causes for their weakness. Some of these ideas were never out of the mind of Mohan even when he moved towards Mahatmahood and they found place in his programmes for the moral and economic uplift of the people.

Vegetarianism for the young visitor to the new world was an article of faith both for his oath and for its higher moral values. He could even risk his life for it. Once when he was laid up with an attack of bronchitis, the doctor told him that he would die if he did not take beef-tea and meat. But the patient's reply was 'If it were God's will that I should die, I must die but that I was sure that it could not be God's will that I should break the oath."[3]

Mohan's vegetarian circle had a number of religious enthusiasts. Contacts with them opened to him the religious insight of Hinduism, Christianity and Islam. At the adolescent age, he had lost interest in religion and could be taken for an atheist. Though he had crossed the 'Sahara of atheism before coming to England', he was more or less a stranger even to the literature of his own religion. It was in England that he first read the Bhagavadgita in Edwin's translation in verse, the music of which fascinated him. On the insistence of two Theosophist friends he wadded through the original in Sanskrit with difficultly because of his inadequate knowledge of the language. The young Mohan could not imagine at that time that this 'song celestial' that prepared Arjuna to fight by removing his doubts would one day become his 'guiding star' or his 'spiritual dictionary', in his search for truth. It is only when a person is confronted with a situation which Arjuna faced in the battle field of Kurukshetra that the real meaning of the Gita is revealed.

Another work of Arnold 'The Light of Asia' introduced to him the life of the Buddha whose message of non-violence was disseminated to various countries of Asia by dedicated disciples more than two thousand years earlier.

Contacts with the Theosophist brothers brought him in touch with the religious outlook and philosophy of the Theosophical Society. He was introduced to its leaders Madame Blavatsky and Annie Besant and read 'Key to Theosophy by the former, which, according to him stimulated in him desire to read books on Hinduism because of its author's fascination for Hinduism. However, he was not keen to become its member. When pressed hard by the Brothers, he only became its associate member for three months before leaving London.[4] Why did he decline to become its permanent member? The reason that he gave to the Brothers was that he had very limited knowledge of his own religion. But in addition to it, its occultism had no appeal for his rational mind.

He read the Bible but what appealed to him in it was the 'Sermon on the Mount' which, for him, gives the message of supreme forgiveness and non-violence. He did not find any interest in the Old Testament as it did not give satisfactory answer to his questioning mind. 'The Book of Genesis' virtually sent him to sleep. It narrates the story of the creation of the universe by God, making of man in His own image, making of a woman out of the ribs of man and then expelling them from Garden of Eden on tasting the forbidden fruit. What appealed to him most in the teachings of all the religions was the ideal of renunciation and so he believed that all of them communicated the same message. But Gandhi wrote this when he had covered a long journey towards Mahatmahood. Renunciation could not captivate his mind at that stage. He had no time to go deeper into the teachings of religions as he was too absorbed in several other pursuits. Possibly his appreciation for the 'Sermon on Mount' was an after thought which was in accord with his commitment to non-violence. Rather at that time the youth in him prompted him to change his life-style in accordance with the demands of the new civilization to which he was introduced on his visit to England. His guide Dr. Mehta told him that "Indians come to England not so much for the purpose of studies as gaining experience of English life and customs for obtaining access to English society." So in order to act as an English gentleman, he purchased new clothes since Bombay cut clothes were considered as unsuitable for English society. He would spend quite some time in dressing himself, properly arranging his tie and parting his hair in the correct fashion. When Henry Salt first met him at one of the vegetarian teas at central Restaurant he found Mohandas fastidiously dressed.[5] An Indian celebrity who saw him in London at that time carried the impression that the young man Mohan was more interested in fashion than in studies. He started taking lessons in dancing, music, elocution and French which was considered as the Lingua Franca of the continent. But he could not go very far in this pursuit as he had not enough time to learn these things. His judgement that at that time he had no talent for rythmic motions nor ear for Western music or elocution appears to be hasty. For, when he made such remarks about himself all such pursuits had no meaning in the mission of his life. So bidding farewell to all these ventures, he returned to austere living which was the demand of his purse and the purpose of his visit to England.

Mohan's English was weak and that was a perpetual worry to him when he came to England. On the steamer he was virtually a drone. He could hardly put together two sentences correctly. Whenever an Englishman asked him any question, he "stammered and stuttered and shook and could make no reply." During his stay in England he would blush on seeing a lady as he did not know how to speak decently, how to talk". So on the suggestion of a friend he started reading newspapers which he had never done in India. He would spend about an hour in the morning in glancing over the Daily News, the Daily Telegraph and the Pall Mall Gazette. Besides, his decision to appear in the London Matriculation examination was partly responsible for it. It was held twice a year. When he enrolled himself for it, only five months were left for preparation. He worked hard. But having failed in Latin, he could clear the examination only in the second attempt. But he had definitely succeeded in improving his English. For, there is a marked change in his style and expression between his London diary that he wrote on his first journey to England and the articles that he contributed to the vegetarian. Later on he developed great interest in grammar which he considered as the key to the understanding of a language as well as for comprehending the right meaning of every word. He developed so much proficiency in English that even Polak who was an Englishman would not mind the correction that Gandhi made in his language. According to Sushila Nayyar who was his devoted follower, Gandhi even believed that his secretary Mahadev's language had not flowered if he had not come in contact with him. (Gandhi)

Mohan had to struggle very hard to keep up his vow of avoiding sexual relationship with any woman in England. He was young and enjoyed the company of women. From English standard he was of marriageable age. Initially, on the suggestion of Dr. Mehta he started living with a family as it would help him gaining familiarity with English social life. To have a girl companion it was essential for a youngman to pose that he was a bachelor. So Mohan was not keen to disclose that he was married. It was generally customary for the landladies to encourage their young daughters to seduce the young students staying with them as paying-guests. So while staying at Ventnor, Mohan would take out the daughter of the landlady for a walk or for dinner. She gave him advances but he could not respond to them, may be because of his usual sense of guilt that would paralyse his senses. In the company of young girls, he was mostly inarticulate. Once an elderly lady who had helped him in reading the Menu in a hotel invited him to dine with her every Sunday. There she cleverly introduced him to young girls. He enjoyed their company and was therefore reluctant to disclose that he was married and had a son. Quite often he was speechless and confused, may be because of his shyness and nervousness or possibly because of the conflict in his mind resulting from his vow and stress of the youth. It was only when a particular girl was marked out for him for engagement that he could muster up his courage to tell the truth to his host in a letter. The pressure of the youth put him once in a questionable position with the landlady of bad character when he went to Postmouth to attend a conference of the Vegetarian Society. While playing the game of bridge with her, indecent suggestive jokes were exchanged. The landlady gave advances. Just at the moment when Mohan was submitting to her advances, the thought of the vow pulled him out of the lustful situation. While narrating this incident after three decades and a half when Mohan had become the Mahatma, he attributed his escape from this reproachable situation by the grace of God. But, in fact, it was his own will power that asserted itself to extricate him from a situation that would have cast a blot on his character. Self-determination was the major attribute of his character and it was this quality that put to shade all his angularities and weaknesses.

Mohan's main aim of coming to England was to qualify himself for the legal profession. So most of his time was spent for the preparation of Bar-at-Law examination, which, of course, was not difficult. But he took it seriously and worked hard for it. As a result, his studies kept him stranger to many other aspects of life in England. But a few events or his meetings with some persons left a deep impression on his mind and later on removed several cobwebs in his thought and behaviour in his search for truth. One of such events was the funeral of Charles Bradlaugh which he attended. Bradlaugh was known as an atheist. Possibly Gandhi had read his book 'Gospel of Atheism' but did not remember its name while writing his autobiography. Though an atheist he devoted his life to the service of suffering humanity. He was a great friend of India and was popularly known as "the Member for India." Gandhi wrote in his autobiography that Indians were familiar with Bradlaugh's name and his so-called atheism. The use of so-called shows that Gandhi never considered his atheism as devoid of spirituality. In a way Bradlaugh's life and philosophy raised Gandhi's view of truth to a higher pedestal later on.

Apart from visiting Paris for a few days mostly to see the Eiffel Tower and the Great Exhibition which was held in 1890, he remained in England. His constitutional shyness, his vows and meagre financial resources prevented him from coming in contact with different walks of life and various associations that had come into existence as a result of new ideas emanating from changing social and political forces in England. Besides the Vegetarian Society, the only other society that attracted him was Anjuman Islamia, an organization of Muslims in England, which allowed non-Muslim Indians to attend its meetings. But he was only a silent participant in its meetings as his mind would stop working whenever he had to speak before a number of persons. Earlier when he stood up to deliver a speech before the High school boys who give him party on his leaving for England, he says, he could hardly stammer a few words in thanks, although he had jotted down his speech. However, a few words of his speech recorded in the 'Kathiawar Times' tells us that service to the nation was not out of his mind while he was going abroad. "I hope some of you will follow," addressing the boys, he said, "in my footsteps and after you return from England you will work whole heartedly for big reform in India". Again, in a crucial meeting of the Vegetarian Society when he stood up to defend a member, he remained tonguetied although he had written out his view on a piece of paper. His notes were read out by another member with the permission of the president. Before leaving England he gave a farewell vegetarian dinner to a select party of friends. But when he made an effort to address them, according to him, he only succeeded in making himself ridiculous as he could not deliver his prepared speech which was planned as a humorous one. But the mouthpiece of the Society reported that "At the close Mr. Gandhi in a very graceful though somewhat nervous speech welcomed all present, spoke of the pleasure it gave him to see the habit of abstention of flesh progressing in England." At that stage an impromptu speech was an impossibility for him. He could overcome this drawback later on in South Africa. However, he made a virtue of this weakness, though at that time it must have been quite annoying to him. It taught him the economy of words and led him to cultivate the habit of restraining his thought and observing silence as a part of discipline for the votary of truth.

As a student of law, Mohan's mind was troubled by the fear that his limited knowledge and lack of acumen would not make him a successful lawyer. He thought of seeking the advice of Dadabhai Naoroji who was approachable. But he restrained himself from troubling him as, in his view, the grand old man of India was too big a person for a petty demand of a student. But on the suggestion of a friend he met Frederich Pincutt who discovered that the stock of general reading, essential for a successful lawyer, of the youngman was disappointing. He, therefore, advised him to read more books on Indian history, psychology and physionomy since a lawyer is expected to read man's character from his face. Though he did not find the books suggested by Pincutt interesting or useful for the practice of law, his general advice that honesty and industry were enough for the success in this profession reassured him, for, he thought he had a fair share of these qualities.

Mohan completed the requirements of Bar-at-Law on June 10, 1891. He was placed 34th in a group of 109 out of whom 77 passed in the Bar final examination. He received the news on 12 January 1891. But he had to complete the remaining three terms for which he had to stay on for six months more. He was enrolled in the High Court on 11th and sailed for India on 12th in the Steamship Oceana with mixed feelings. For, he was not happy to leave London as he was getting attached to its intellectual environments produced by its teaching institutions, public galleries vegetarian restaurants etc. But he was glad as he looked forward to see his friends and relatives. He was now a changed man. He was proud to be a vegetarian by choice and was ready to hold discussion on vegetarianism with his fellow passengers and was even prepared to deliver a speech on vegetarianism to the unsympathetic audience as there were only two vegetarians on the ship.

A shocking news awaited him in India as his mother had passed away only a few days before his arrival. Though the shock was very great for him, he did not give himself to any wild expression of grief. He even checked his tears. He was now a responsible barrister. He was proud that he had stayed in England for about three years without breaking his vows and had become an important member of the Vegetarian Society of England. He had realized his ambition besides having done many things which he could not do in India. He was bubbling with self-confidence.

On reaching Bombay, he had to perform certain acts as a matter of expiation which consisted of taking a bath in the sacred river at Nasik and giving a caste dinner for his readmission to his community. Though he did not like it he agreed to perform these ceremonies to please his elder brother whose will was command for him and his boundless love for his youngest brother. He scrupulously avoided hurting the feelings of his castemen by respecting the caste regulations about excommunication. So there was no occasion of his confrontation with his caste fellows though a section of them could not be reconciled to his readmission.

It was a great moment of his life when on his return from England he met Rajchandra, who, in Gandhi's view, was a great intellectual prodigy and spiritual giant. He was a partner in the firm of jewellers. But he was continuously absorbed in his search for God even in the course of his commercial transactions. Mohan was deeply impressed by him. In South Africa whenever his mind was afflicted by religious doubts, he turned to this godly man for advice.

Mohan's stay in India for about two years after his return from England was full of stress and strains. His life style had changed. Coffee and tea had replaced the ordinary beverages. New China wares and furniture had been purchased to suit the status and position of a barrister. European dress had been added to complete the process of Europeanization. But all these changes had put a heavy burden on the income of the family. So the young barrister was confronted with the problem of earning money. Since Rajkot was not the right place for a lawyer who was conscious of his status but was ignorant of Indian laws, he decided to move to Bombay to acquire knowledge of Indian law as well as to learn the way cases were conducted in the High Court. An illiterate Brahman was engaged to prepare food for him. So in Bombay he would daily go to the High Court. But he hardly felt any interest in the cases because of his ignorance of Indian legal system. So it was not unusual for him to doze off in the Court. Since he was against paying commission to the touts which was the general practice observed even by the flourishing lawyers, he remained briefless for a long time. However compelled by the mounting expenses of living in Bombay, he took up a case in the small cause Court where he appeared for the defendant, an old lady. But he failed miserably as soon as he stood up to cross examine the plaintiff's witnesses. As usual his head started reeling and his heart 'sank into his boots'. He couldn't ask any question. It was too much for a sensitive youngman. He was ashamed of himself and in disgust returned the money to his client. Bewildered and disappointed, he applied for a teaching job. How could he get it. For, he was not a graduate which was the basic qualification for getting into the teaching profession. He had no choice but to move to Rajkot where he was mostly occupied with drafting applications and memorials. All these cases came to him from a firm in which his brother was a partner. He now compromised with his principle of not giving commission to the Vakils and touts who briefed him. But here, too, another humiliating experience was in store for him. His elder brother Laxmidas had annoyed the political agent for his alleged advice to the young prince of Porbandar to remove some jewels from the state treasury without authority. Mohan had picked up a little acquaintance with the political agent in England. So his brother asked him to speak to the political agent in his favour. Unwillingly he sought an interview which was readily granted. But on entering his office, the young barrister realized that the officer on vacation in England was entirely different from the officer on duty. As soon as he opened his lips to say a few words in defence of his brother the political agent warned him not to abuse his short acquaintance. When Mohan persisted in arguing the case of his brother, the officer angrily ordered the door keeper to remove the young lawyer from his office. Insulted so badly by the political agent, Mohan threatened to proceed against him in the court. He consulted Pherozeshah Mehta, one of the topmost lawyers of Bombay, in this connection. But he dissuaded him from moving the court on such matters as these, in his view, were common in India. So he had no choice but to pocket the insult which was nothing short of swallowing a poisonous pill. But it left a lasting lesson with him, that is, never to place himself in such a false position by any attempt to exploit friendship. It also changed the course of his life. For he realized that he had no future in Rajkot as it was not possible to carry on his practice there since most of the cases would be in the court of the political agent who was now prejudiced against him. Intrigues in the courts of petty states suffocated his mind. He again thought of a job. But it was difficult to get a good job without powerful backing. For some time he held the post of a companion-tutor of the prince of Porbandar. But it did not give him any job satisfaction as he soon discovered that he neither had any use for the prince nor for his subjects in view of the arbitrary and bureaucratic attitude of the officers, both English and Indian. It is at this time an offer came to him that turned the course of his life. A Muslim Indian firm Dada Abdulla & Co which had a claim for about forty thousand pounds in South African courts offered him employment for a year on payment of 105 pounds and first class fare to advise Dada Abdulla in a law suit and also to handle the correspondence of the company. It was not a suitable job for a barrister. Dada Abdulla had his lawyers in South Africa. But there was a communication gap between him and his lawyers as he was not keeping his accounts in English. It was more or less a clerical assignment. But Mohan jumped at it. For it was an opportunity to get away from the humiliating atmosphere of working in the petty Indian states.

Notes and References

1. Gandhi, M.K., Autobiography, p. 41.
2. *Ibid.*, p. 48.
3. Hunt, James D., Gandhi in London (New Delhi, Promila & Co., 1978), p. 22.
4. Desai, *op. cit.*, Vol. V, p. 103.
5. Quoted in Hunt, Gandhi in London, p. 29.

4

Destiny

Destiny has mysterious ways of working out its plans. It may produce hope out of frustration, good out of suffering and selfless service out of personal ambition.

Like his first voyage, Mohan's second voyage, too, had various motives, ambition, escape from the demoralising atmosphere in his home country, gaining new experiences, earning his livelihood and seeing a new land. In his autobiography he wrote:[1]

> "I had gone to South Africa for finding an escape from Kathiawar intrigues and for gaining my own livelihood. But I found myself in search of God and striving for self-realization."

However, this time he did not feel the wrench of separation which he had experienced at the time of leaving for England since his mother was dead and he had already gained some experience of living in a foreign country. Of course, he felt the pang of parting with his wife but it was not unbearable.

Mohan sailed for South Africa in April 1893. The young barrister could not get a first class ticket and he felt below his dignity to travel on the deck. However, by making a special request to the captain of the ship, he was allowed to travel by sharing latter's cabin who wanted a companion to play chess with him in the long and dull journey. The captain developed fascination for him. But this worked to the disadvantage of the young innocent lawyer who was virtually pushed into the den of sin where his own frame of mind alone could save him from committing an undesirable act. At Zansibar where the ship halted for more than a week, the captain took him and an English gentleman to a brothel and pushed him into the room of a Negro woman where he remained in a quandry as he did not know what to do. He stood there dumb with shame till the captain called him and he came out morally unscathed. This time he knew where he was being led to. But as yet he had not become a master of himself and lacked courage to say 'no' to a person who had been so nice to him on board the ship. From Zansibar the passengers were to be transferred to another boat. It reached Durban towards the close of May where Dada Abdulla received him. Seeing his employee in frockcoat and turban that distinguished him from all other Indians, it disturbed him. For, he was afraid that the young barrister might prove to be a white elephant for him. Abdulla Seth was unlettered but he had picked up just sufficient English for conversational purpose. Practically there was no work for Gandhi in Durban as the case was in Pretoria in Transvaal. However, after a few days, the Seth started appreciating the young lawyer's qualities of sincerity, devotion to work, desire to learn and most of all his sense of self-respect. It is this quality that gave him the first shock of racial discrimination in this strange land which at the same time introduced him to Natal where for most of the whites he was an unwelcome visitor. He had noticed on watching the people coming on board to meet their friends that Indians were not held in respect in Durban. But since he himself was queerly dressed—wearing European clothes and a turban, he was distinguished from other Indians and was an object of curiosity. But when he was taken to the court by his employer, he had an unpleasant experience. For the judge ordered him to remove his turban in accordance with the prevalent practice and norms of the court. For every person had to remove his head gear on entering the court room. Mohan refused to do so and left the court in protest as he viewed the order as an insult to an Indian. He defended his action in the local press which raised a heated controversy that gave him some publicity. There does not appear to be any fault of the judge who ordered him to remove his turban. For, Mohandas was entirely a stranger there as he had no case. Possibly his employer took him to the court to make him familiar with the procedure of the court in South Africa.

The young lawyer was totally ignorant of the conditions in South Africa. At that time the Union of South Africa had not yet been born. There were several geographical divisions having different political status. Natal was a Crown colony of Britain with Durban as the chief port. The

Cape Province was self-governing colony under the British-flag. The Transvaal and Orange Free state were independent Boer republics. But all of them pursued a policy that would keep the hegemony and interests of the whites in tact, though the rigour with which it was enforced varied from time to time and place to place.

Initially most of the Indians went to South Africa under a contract as the English settlers in Natal required a hard working labour force to work on their plantations. For, the native population of Negroes could not be induced to work constantly and efficiently throughout the year. The first batch of Indian labourers known as the indentured labourers reached Natal in November 1860 under the terms of contract. They were to work for their employers for five years after which they could return to their home country or settle down in Natal as free persons. Indian traders followed the Indian labourers capturing not only the trade among the Indians but also among the Negroes because of their courtesy greater business acumen and frugal habits. Thus by the time Gandhi reached Natal, there were 44,000 Indians of whom 16,000 were indentured and 25,000 ex-indentured or free Indians in a population 47,000 Zulus and 45,000 Europeans. From Natal the Indian traders moved into Transvaal and Orange Free State ruled by the Boers who were of Dutch descent. Indians were divided into several classes and groups. Muslims were comparatively affluent and they would call themselves Arabs to acquire a better status in the eyes of the Whites as a large number of labourers were Hindus who were contemptuously called Samis a Tamil suffix occurring after many Tamil names which is a perverted expression of Sanskrit word Swami which, of course, means a master. In fact, all Indians were addressed as coolies and Gandhi was called a cooli barrister. There were some Parsis who were mostly employed as clerks. Some of the Indians had become converts to Christianity and most of them worked as bearers in the hotels. They distinguished themselves from other Indians by wearing European dress. Gandhi was not aware of these distinctions. The Muslim merchants were allowed to wear turbans in the courts. When Gandhi was asked to remove his turban in the court, he felt that the order was tantamount to insult to him as an Indian. In order to avoid any controversy, he was ready to wear hat in place of turban. But his employer dissuaded him from doing so on the grounds that it would not only compromise the position of Indians in Natal but he would be pass for a waiter.

However more humiliating and horried experiences were in store for him when the young barrister was sent to Pretoria in Transvaal to help his employer's counsel in the case for which he had been called from India. Before leaving he made efforts to pick up some knowledge of book-keeping and accounts with the help of books and his employer's clerks. In terms of his status he set forth with a first class ticket. Dada Abdulla came to the station to see him off. He advised him to get a bedding on reaching Maritzburg, the capital of Natal by paying five shillings. But Gandhi did not pay heed to this advice as he was carrying his own bedding. At this station a servant asked him whether he required a bedding. On his refusal another official came and asked him to go to the van compartment irrespective of the fact that he had a first class ticket when a European on entering the compartment reported that a black skinned person was travelling in the first class compartment. On his refusal he was thrown out of the compartment followed by his luggage. It was a bitter cold night. In a dark waiting room he shivered as his top coat was in his luggage and he dared not to go in search of it lest he should be insulted. One thought that haunted him throughout the night was whether to return to his home country in order to avoid such a humiliating treatment in a foreign country or to fight for his rights as an Indian. It might have passed through his mind that in his home country, too, there was hardly any respectable place for him as a lawyer. However by morning he had made up his mind to continue his journey as it would be unmanly for a barrister like him to surrender to injustice. This was the most momentous decision in Gandhi's life. A few decades later in a chat with an American missionary who asked him about his most creative experience of his life, Gandhi stated that the struggle in his mind in the dark waiting room of Pietermaritzburg was the most revolutionary experience of his life. For some biographers, a new Gandhi was born on this night. Is it true? It was certainly new in the sense that it gave a new turn to his life. But it did not mean a revolutionary change in his character. For, self-respect was his natural trait and it was unmanly for such a person to submit to injustice simply because of the colour of his skin. More indignities were awaiting him during this journey. At that time there was no direct rail-road link between Durban and Pretoria. So part of the journey had to be covered by coach up to Johannesburg. Racial discrimination was more rigorously observed in Transvaal. Dark skinned passengers were not permitted inside the coach. So Gandhi was given a seat outside on the coach box. In the course of the journey, the leader of the coach asked him to sit on a sack cloth on the footboard as he himself wanted to sit on the coach box to enjoy the fresh air. Nothing could be more humiliating for a proud barrister to sit at the feet of any person. He refused and so blow after blow from the hefty leader of the coach started falling on him till other passengers intervened and agreed to accommodate him inside the coach. On reaching Pretoria, he called a meeting of the Indians living there through a Muslim merchant, Tyeb Sheth, his opponent in the law suit, in order to make them aware of their deplorable condition in a foreign country and explore methods for raising their position. Most of those who attended it were Muslims as there were very few Hindus in Pretoria. The burden of his speech was that in order to raise their status in South Africa, Indians must observe truthfulness in business dealings, cultivate cleanliness and sanitary habits as they were the repository of India's honour in a foreign country, for "the conduct of a few Indians was the measure of that of the millions of their fellow country men."[2] He urged them to form an association to bring their hardship and disabilities to the attention of the authorities. Whatever he said was not something spectacular. All his suggestions were commonplace which his audience must have heard a number of times. But it shows young lawyer's practical approach to the problems of Indians in South Africa. For, in his view the first step for the Indians for raising their status in a foreign country was to disabuse the minds of the whites that the Indians were as a matter of habit untruthful, dirty, untrustworthy and so could not become a part of the main stream of the cultural life of South Africa.

This was his first successful public meeting addressed by him. He had overcome his usual nervousness while speaking to strangers. May be because of his consciousness that most of the persons attending his meeting were uneducated or the organizer of the meeting had already communicated to the audience the status of the speaker.

Gandhi's stay in Pretoria was important as he was for the first time called upon to delve deep into the teachings of major religions as a result of his encounter with Christianity. For, Dada Abdulla's attorney in Pretoria, A.W. Baker was a devoted Christian. He had built a church in Pretoria with his own money where he preached regularly on Sundays and held a prayer meeting every afternoon. He looked upon the new comer as a possible convert and so started making efforts in that direction. Gandhi was, therefore, introduced to several Christians in Pretoria especially to Michael Coaste—a Quaker and two elderly spinsters Miss Gabb and Miss Harris. He was invited to afternoon prayer meetings which he attended. The ladies gave him standing invitation to evening tea on every Sunday. Possibly his favourable response to the offer of friendship by the whites Christian was motivated by his personal interest as it would make his stay comfortable in a country where most of the

Whites were not well disposed towards the Indians. However, this encounter with devout Christians seeking his conversion placed him in a very difficult situation, for he had very little knowledge of religion whether of his own or of any other religion and it would be totally irrational on his part to move from one religion to another without knowing any of them. So his mind turned to Rajchandrabhai for guidance. In a letter to him he asked him several questions about God, Moksha, Arya Dharma, Bhagavadgita, Vedas, animal sacrifice, theory of incarnation, Christianity, Buddhism, etc. He also opened dialogue through correspondence with Christian friends in England especially with Edward Maitland who sent him his book 'The Perfect Way' which was a repudiation of the current Christian beliefs. He also sent him 'The Interpretation of the Bible'. Tolstoy's 'The Kingdom of God is within you' came in his way at this time that impressed him most. Most surprisingly the new approach to Christianity with which he came in contact strengthened his devotion to Hinduism.

A feeble attempt was also made to impress upon him the superiority of Islam over all other religions which brought him in touch with Muslim religious books. In all he read about eighty books mostly on religion during his stay in Pretoria. As a result of this study and encounter with Christianity, he received his own religion free from accretions and overgrowth that had settled on it over the centuries. For, he accepted only that part of Hindu religion which was in accord with reason and the spirit underlying all religions. Fortunately, he came in contact with non-conformist Christian sects whose approach to religion did not offend or undermine reason. He read the books suggested to him by such Christian friends who had an open mind and was impressed by the moral appeal of some of them. Though his rational mind was repelled by the narrow exclusiveness of the missionaries and their claim that God was accessible only through their religion, their stress on personal holiness and deep faith in their religion left a deep mark on him which found expression through his new look at Hinduism.

Being a lawyer, he examined the claims and arguments that challenged his beliefs and faith. He exploded the arguments of those Christian Brethren who claimed the superiority of their religion on the grounds that by merely holding faith in Christianity one is automatically redeemed of all the sins since Jesus suffered and atoned for the sins of mankind.[3] A dialogue with devout Christians and study of religious books of different religions strengthened his view that conversion was futile since the spirit underlying all religions is the same. It is because of this conviction that he claimed towards the end of his life in an interview with the Governor of Bengal, Casey that he was better acquainted with Christianity than most Christians, better acquainted with Zoroastrianism than most Parsis, with Islam than most Muslims.[4] In fact, he saw through new lenses—the lenses provided by his training as a lawyer, the Hindu tradition of looking at all religions as leading to the same goal and the situation in an alien country that demanded unity of Indians.

Gandhi's professional work in Pretoria did not require hard work as his employer had already engaged a very competent attorney. His main job was to sort out facts in support of the case of his client. Though the facts supported his client, he was equally sure that the prolongation of litigation would ruin both the parties. He favoured settlement outside the court by arbitration. It was arrived at with the help of the court. After the settlement he returned to Durban where his employer arranged a farewell party on his departure from South Africa. Just at that time his eyes fell on a paragraph in a corner of a page in a newspaper that he was reading. It was about the bill before the Natal legislature seeking to disfranchise the Indians. On enquiring from the persons attending the meeting about it, he was amazed to learn that all of them were ignorant of it. His host Dada Abdulla expressed the helplessness of Indians in all such matters as most of them were uneducated and a few who were affluent were depending upon the European attorneys who would never enlighten them about such matters. Gandhi while explaining to them the importance of a right to vote warned them that this bill when passed would strike at the root of their self-respect besides making their lot difficult in South Africa. On the insistence of all the persons attending the party, he postponed his departure for a month and immediately started taking steps to prevent the passage of the bill. A meeting of the Indians was held the next day and it was decided to oppose the bill by submitting a petition to the Assembly as it was in the third stage. The drafting of the petition put his legal skill to test. The submission of the petition was followed by letters to the editors, Memorial to the Natal Premier and a petition to the Governor. All these show high degree of erudition. He appears to have worked hard to justify the claims of his clients. He made full use of the researches of European Indologists and western admirers of democracy and liberty to support the claim of Indians for franchise. He appears to be familiar with the writings of Mill, Burke, Bright, Henry Maine, Hunter, Maxmuller, Schopenhaur as well as the contemporary bureaucrats and heads of governments who had come in contact with the Indians.

His main arguments were:

I. That the treatment meted out to the Indians in South Africa was contrary to the teachings of Christianity.
II. That the Indians were the British subjects and the treatment meted out to them was against the British sense of justice.
III. That the Indians made substantial contribution to the economy and welfare of the colony (Natal).
IV. That the Indians were cultured and so can exercise the right to vote judiciously.

Though he could not prevent the bill from getting into the statute book, his efforts did create awakening among the Indians in South Africa and a stir among the whites in Natal. The young lawyer was conscious that the mission undertaken by him was far beyond his ability and position. But there was hardly any choice. For, according to him, he was the only available person to undertake it. A regular organization was needed to carry on the struggle against continuous hostile moves of the whites against the Indians in South Africa. As a result, Natal Indian Congress was founded. Abdulla Haji Adam was elected its chairman and Gandhi its honorary secretary. It was mostly a middle class association as a vast majority of Indians in South Africa were labourers who could not afford to pay its £ 3 annual membership fee. However, when the struggle of the Indians against discrimination in South Africa became fierce and intensive, it started enrolling even those persons as members who could not pay subscription but could work for the programmes of the association. Initially a member was required to have a working knowledge of English but it was not strictly enforced.

A small committee was formed to carry on its day-to-day work. It was not a political party as it had no aim to capture political power in South Africa. Its main objective was to raise the social, political and economic status of the Indians in South Africa. Thus, the Natal Indian Congress was different in its working, structure and objectives from Indian Nation Congress functioning in the last decade of the last century. For, unlike the latter it was working continuously throughout the year and holding its meetings frequently to carry on its work. The name Congress that Gandhi gave to this body was symbolic of his regard for the leaders of the Indian National Congress especially Dadabhai Naoroji who presided over its session in 1893. But it was an intelligent decision as by allying his association even symbolically with that of the home country he hoped to win the support and sympathies of the Indians for their brethren fighting against injustice in a foreign country. By a happy chance Gandhi's ignorance of the working of the Congress in his home country produced better results in the process of creating an organizational set-up to carry on the work of the association.

Gandhi's short experience of constitutional fight with the Natal Government brought home to him that he would be needed in South Africa for a longer period to guide the Indians' struggle against racial discrimination in South Africa. He needed regular income corresponding to his style of living as a barrister. The merchants in Natal were ready to support him financially. But it was below his dignity and against his sense of public service to accept any remuneration for this kind of work. He liked to be a retainer. This could raise his position as a lawyer in South Africa and would enable him to earn his living even when the public cause did not require his services. Then about twenty merchants agreed to retain him for legal advice for a year which would yield £ 300 a year. Henry Escombe, the attorney general of Natal suggested to him to live in a bungalow next door to his in an exclusively European quarters near the sea. Dada Abdulla paid its rent and fully furnished it. His employer must have been very much impressed by him. The young barrister was not a Mahatma at that time. He had self-respect and pride in the cultural heritage of his country. He wanted to live with dignity which, in his opinion was essential for fighting for the cause of Indians in a foreign country. He wrote:[4]

> "I also had the idea that I could not add to the credit of the community unless I lived in a style usual for barristers."

It looks that he believed that living in the style of Europeans would raise his status as a barrister. Such arguments could serve both his personal and public interests. This kind of approach was contrary to his view when he took long strides towards Mahatmahood.

Settled in Natal, he decided to apply for admission as an advocate of Supreme Court. He was able to obtain the certificates of good character from two European merchants which had to be attached to the application according to the rules. Henry Escombe agreed to present the application. But it was challenged by the Law Society of Natal which incidently gave unexpected publicity to the young lawyer. It looks that the European lawyers of Natal were afraid that the new young barrister would make an encroachment upon their legal practice by becoming friendly to Indian merchants involved in any law suit in Natal. However, Gandhi succeeded in obtaining the admission as the chief justice ruled that the law did not make any distinction between the whites and the coloured people. This was his first victory. But he was advised to remove his turban on entering the court according to the prevalent practice of the court in Natal. He agreed to submit to the rules of the court as he was now a lawyer of the court, though Dada Abdulla and other friends did not appreciate his submission which could be interpreted as a weakness. The young lawyer defended his decision with all his dialectical skill but failed to convince his friends. It looks that he took this decision on pragmatic considerations. For, he did not like to exhaust his energy on a trivial issue as he could foresee a long drawn struggle on the vital issue of the rights of the Indians in South Africa. Submission to the rules of the court was equally essential for carrying on his practice in the court. Gandhi looked at things from different standpoints in different situations. This approach was noticeable in the development of Satyagraha later on.

Though living in style, Gandhi was always ready to help the poverty stricken Indians whenever he found them in difficulty. Once an indentured Tamilian labourer who was heavily belaboured by his European master made an appeal to him for relief. The young lawyer was moved by the piteous condition of the poor labourer. He immediately got the injured person examined by a European doctor and after obtaining his certificate, he took legal action against the employer who agreed to transfer the indentured labourer to another European employer as according to the law in Natal no Indian could employ an indentured labourer. By such actions Gandhi became the messiah for the poor Indians in an alien country. So within a short span of time Gandhi established himself as a hard working lawyer who would diligently examine the facts of a case and would argue without fear that sometimes locked him in legal exchanges with the judges which gave him good publicity in the press. In reality facts were his guide to truth and he would insist on his clients to tell the facts honestly to him. However most of his work was confined to his chambers conveyancing and arbitrating.

He had tremendous energy which is evident from his multifarious activities in Natal. Besides representing his clients in the courts, he was engaged in protecting the interests of the Indians in the various spheres of life, promoting the cause of vegetarianism and carrying on his religious pursuits. He launched a fierce campaign against the pole tax levied on every free Indian which was reduced from £ 25 to £ 3 partly as a result of his agitation and partly on the intervention of the Viceroy of India. But

£ 3 was still a heavy burden on poor Indian families and so he carried on his agitation against it through petitions and memorials to the authorities.

His religious pursuits really refurbished his energy for public work as he came to believe that self-realization could be attained only through service to his fellow human beings. His contacts with Christian friends whetted his appetite for religious knowledge. Besides reading the Upanishads in translation, he made an intensive study of Tolstoy's books especially the 'Kingdom of God is Within You', 'The Gospel in Brief' and 'What to Do' whereby he began to realize the infinite possibilities of universal love. He had acquired so much proficiency over Christian literature that he could cite biblical sayings in support of his contentions and was in a position to ask the supporters of racial discrimination to 're-read your New Testament.'[5] He renewed his contacts with his Theosophist friends in England, Edward Maitland and Anna Kingsford. He became the agent for the Esoteric Christian Union and London Vegetarian Society and sent an advertisement to the Natal Mercury for the sale of books of Esoteric Christian Union. In a letter to the editor of the paper he claimed that the system of thought expounded by these books is not a new system but recovery of the old presented in a form acceptable to the modern mind. It is a system of religion which teaches universality. It reconciles other religions with Christianity.[6] His vegetarianism, religious quest and his curiosity took him to the Trappist monastery as he had read about the missionary zeal of the Trappist in Anna Kingsford's book 'Perfect Way in Diet'; as a student in England. It was situated sixteen miles from Durban in a picturesque locality. It had one hundred and twenty brothers, sixty nuns and about twelve hundred Zulus. Mohan was impressed by the simplicity of its members. They observed strictly the principle of liberty, equality and fraternity. For, there was no distinction between the whites and the blacks. The brothers lived on vegetarian diet. But the sisters were allowed meat four days because of their belief that women were more delicate than men. Most of other devoted inmates would get up at 2 a.m. and devote four hours to prayer after which they were given breakfast with bread and coffee. Dining at twelve, they had supper at six or seven before going to bed after an hour. The settlement had various workshops, that is, of blacksmiths, tinsmiths, carpenters, shoemakers, tanners, etc. where Zulu boys were given training besides education in English and Zulu languages. They grew many kinds of tropical fruits on the farm making the settlement almost self-supporting. But the most important feature of the settlement was that one could see religion everywhere. Every room had a cross and on entrance a small receptacle for holy water which every inmate would reverently apply to his eyelids, the forehead and the chest.[7]

After his stay in Natal of more than three years, Mohan decided to bring his family there on his realization that the struggle would not end soon. On a suggestion of his colleagues in Natal, he decided to avail himself of his visit to India to seek the support of the Indian leadership for his struggle in South Africa. This was a good strategy which paid high dividends later on. But before leaving he assured the members of the Natal Indian Congress that he would endeavour to persuade a number of good Indian barristers to come to Natal.[8] True to his word, he tried to persuade Taleyarkhan, a barrister who returned to India from England with him by the same steamer, to accompany him to South Africa where, in his view, there was "much fight ahead which alone was sufficient to absorb the attention of two men—if full justice is to be done to the cause."[9] He offered him partnership on terms that would assure him moderate income at least for six months. However he told him that the amassing of money was not their aim in South Africa but fighting for the cause. However, Taleyarkhan did not oblige him and on returning to Durban, he realized that it was good both for him and his friend in view of anti-Indian feeling in Natal and strict quarantine regulations. Nevertheless he continued pressing on Indian barrister to set up practice in South Africa which, in his view, could accommodate six Indian barristers.[10]

On reaching India, he published a pamphlet which came to be known as the 'Green Book' for its green cover that he wrote during his voyage from Natal to Bombay wherein he described the wretched condition of Indians in South Africa. The burden of the essay was that "sufferance is really and sincerely the badge of the Indians in South Africa"[11], on account of deep hatered against the Indians in South Africa especially in Natal "which has been crystallized in legislation" putting innumerable legal disabilities on them. As a result, they could not leave their houses after 9 o'clock without a special pass, could not walk on the footpaths; could not travel in first class in a train; had to stand up on footboard in the trams; had been denied franchise by a special law; had to pay a special poll tax of £ 3, etc. The object of all such disabilities "is to drive them out of South Africa." Thus he is allowed to exist there as pariah, as an indentured labourer at the most 'a free labourer' but he must not aspire high.[12] In the Transvaal "the Indians cannot own landed property; they can be ordered to reside in locations. They are made to pay a special registration fee of £ 3. They cannot as of right walk on the foot path in Pretoria and Johannesburg. The railway officials in South Africa treat the Indians as beasts.

Besides distributing the pamphlet which ran into second edition because of great demand, he delivered lectures at several politically prominent places, met eminent Congress leaders such as Pherozeshah Mehta, Tilak, Gokhale, etc. Pherozeshah Mehta seemed to the young lawyer great like the Himalaya, unscaleble because of his great stature and Tilak vast and immeasurable like the ocean. But Gokhale appeared to him "an adorable and amiable leader who like holy Ganga invited every devotee to consecrate himself or herself by taking a dip into it." This was young lawyer's way of showing his preference for a leader without indicating any disrespect for others. May be, Pherozeshah Mehta and Tilak had not accorded him due consideration as they had not been able to size up the magnitude of the inner being of the young man who was still a novice in politics and had approached them with folded hands for help in South Africa. But Gokhale extended him the loving hand of an elder statesman well appreciating his sincerity and devotion to a public cause.

Mohan stayed in India for five months and his efforts had the desired result as he received the support of most of the Indian leaders for his struggle in a foreign country. He set sail for Natal in December with his wife two children and the only son of his widowed sister. Dada Abdulla's agents made arrangements for his second voyage to South Africa. At that time European style of living was the badge of civilization for the young lawyer. So he opted for Parsi dress for his wife and children as it was nearest to the European style, though it took them sometime to get used to that dress. When the steamer was near the port of Natal, it was overtaken by a storm and for about 24 hours the steamer rolled and tossed to such an extent that it appeared as if it would capsize any moment. So God appeared to be the only hope. But when the sky became clear every body took a sigh of relief. However, for Gandhi another storm was awaiting him at Durban which virtually threw him at death's door step. It was the result of a wrong reporting of the contents of his Green pamphlet by Reuter. For, it was reported that its author had stated that Indians in Natal were robbed and assaulted and treated like beasts and are unable to obtain redress. But its author, on the other hand, had made a balanced and reasoned statement in the pamphlet which he had substantiated several times in his statements and letters in the press, in Natal earlier. Even the pro-White papers in Natal had expressed their appreciation for his approach to the problem. For instance, the Natal Mercury, the government organ, wrote referring to his open letter: "Mr. Gandhi writes with calmness and moderation. He is as impartial as every one could expect him to be and probably a little more so than might have been expected considering that he did not receive any just treatment at the hands of the Law Society when he first came to the colony."[13]

The wrong report infuriated the Whites especially the youth who blamed Gandhi for spoiling their reputation in India. This gave an opportunity to the colonial patriotic Union aiming at the expulsion of the Indians in South Africa to mobilise the Whites for the attainment of their goal. Unfortunately, another ship owned by the Persian Steam Navigation Company carrying Indian passengers also arrived at the port which led to the rumour that Gandhi was bringing with him a large number of Indians in Natal for immigration. As a result, a large number of European hot heads gathered near the port to prevent the landing of Gandhi. The Government tried to prevent any clash by imposing quarantine on the ships on the grounds that Bombay had been declared the 'plague port' when the ships left. But the landing could not be stopped for an indefinite period. So it had to be allowed after a few days. Gandhi's family and all other passengers landed safely. But there was the problem of bringing him to the shore as he was in no mood to land stealthily. So one of Dada Abdulla's legal adviser, F.A. Laughton, offered to accompany Gandhi to his destination. But on his way, the young Indian lawyer was recognized and was separated from Laughton by the crowd that attacked him. He was belaboured mercilessly. Brickbats, stones and rotten eggs rained on him followed by kicks and blows. He would have been lynched had not the wife of the police superintendent intervened and saved him by opening her parasol and standing between Gandhi and the crowd that checked the fury of the mob as it was difficult for them to 'deliver blows on him without harming' the European lady. He was taken safely to the house of Rustomji by the police where his family had taken refuge. But the house was besieged by the demonstrators who were after Gandhi's life. The superintendent of police, fearing serious disturbance and forcible entry of the house by the crowd which could cause damage to the life and property of his host had not Gandhi been removed to the police station disguised as a police man. It is difficult to decide as to what motivated him to move out of the house in disguise especially when he was ready to face fearlessly the infuriated crowd on landing. Many ideas must have passed through his mind while accepting the suggestion of the superintendent of police to leave the house in disguise which was contrary to his own principle. For, it was a form of untruth. It was a crucial moment in his journey towards Mahatmahood. Possibly he did not want to put in danger the property and family of his friend who had given him and his family a refuge in an explosive situation. Possibly the Mahatma in him had not as yet gauged the dimensions of truth. It was after a long journey towards truth that he felt that any kind of secrecy was violation of truth.

The Secretary of state took a serious view of assault on Gandhi and so instructed the Natal Government to punish the offenders. But when Henry Escombe, the Defence Secretary of Natal approached Gandhi for identifying and prosecuting the offenders, he refused to do so on the grounds that the assailants could hardly to be blamed as their leaders had misled them by giving them wrong reports of what he had written about the Natal Europeans in Indian. This was certainly a very wise step as the prosecution of the alleged assailants would have taken a long time besides accentuating acrimony between the Whites and Indians in Natal. On the other hand, his refusal raised his image among the Whites and won for the Indians' struggle against racial discrimination many White sympathisers in Natal. In place of taking legal action against the individuals, he submitted a long Memorial to the Secretary of State on behalf of Indians in Natal wherein he rubbed in point that behind the incident, there was a clear intention of the White Government in Natal to force the Indians to leave South Africa. All the statements made by him were supported by evidence. He showed his forensic skill and industry as he marshalled facts and arguments in support of the cause of his clients. The lawyer in him was in the forefront for defending the interests of the Indians. He had subordinated his personal injury to the interest of the community. No wonder, if the Indians in South Africa looked upon him as their real brother, the 'bhai' of all the Indians there. He was moving towards the stage where individual interest starts losing its lustre and the individual seeks pleasure in the happiness of others.

Notes and References

1. M.K. Gandhi, Autobiography, p. 132.
2. *Ibid.*, p. 105.
3. *Ibid.*, p. 104
4. Manserh & Moon, Transfer of Power (London: Her Majesty's Stationery) Vol. VI, p. 617.
5. M.K. Gandhi, Autobiography, p. 1210.
6. M.K. Gandhi, C.W., Vol. I, p. 137.
7. *Ibid.*, p. 139.

8. *Ibid.*, Vol. I, p. 249.
9. *Ibid.*, Vol. II, p. 85.
10. *Ibid.*, p. 91.
11. *Ibid.*, p. 8.
12. *Ibid.*, p. 17.
13. *Ibid.*, p. 36.

5

On the Road to Mahatmahood

The attack by the White youth had catapulted the young lawyer to an important position in the public life of Natal. His public activities received notice of the White critics that further gave him publicity. His profession progressed and he had enough income to afford European style of living. As his wife and children could not adjust themselves to Western dress, Parsi dress with coat, trousers besides shoes and stocking for boys and sari for his wife was forced upon them.

As the head of the family, he demanded full obedience to his wishes though his plans and life-style appeared irksome to the rest of the members of his family. His social outlook and his multifarious activities sometimes created very embarrassing and comical scenes in the family. Once his wife refused to clean the chamber pot of an untouchable clerk who had become Christian and had started living with him. Being a newcomer he did not know that the chamber pot had to be cleaned by the person himself or herself. Gandhi wanted her to do this work cheerfully. He chided her while tears were dropping from her eyes. In a fit of anger he caught her by the hand and dragged her to the gate threatening to turn her out of the house. By her matchless power of endurance she made him see reason, "have you no shame?" She asked, "Where am I to go"? This melted Gandhi's anger and he realised his mistake.

He could not make any satisfactory arrangement for the education of his children because of his multifarious activities and his new outlook on life for which his children nursed a grievance against him. But what could he do? The greater man in him was pulling him out of the narrow circle of his family. Slowly and slowly it was dawning upon him that the real self of a person was identical with the spirit underlying the universe and so identification with the good of humanity was the only road to 'Mokhsh'. Thus, service to the needy and the poor acquired spiritual meaning. Once a leper came to his door. He gave him shelter, dressed his wounds and later on sent him to hospital. This spirit led him to give his time for a few hours every day working as a male nurse in a charitable hospital opened by his Parsi friend Rustomji. It was more a spiritual necessity for him than a mere social service. However, it brought him in close contact with Tamil and Telugu labourers whose poverty and miserable condition brought home to him that his expensive European life style stood in the way of identifying himself with those whose cause he was championing. The study of religious books deepened this feeling. So he started making experiments in simple living that made him his own washerman, his own barber, though the results of such attempts were initially disastrous as they made him an object of great amusement in the court with the starch dripping from his collars and his hair looking horrible giving the impression to the onlooker as if the rates had been nibbling at it.

After coming in contact with Indians of various walks of life in South Africa, the young lawyer drew the following conclusions from his analysis of their problems:

I. That the Indians were demoralised and were devoid of self-respect, human dignity, awareness of their cultural heritage, self-reliance and courage.

II. They lacked unity as they hailed from different parts of India and followed different religions. Differences in status and professions also prevented them from coming to a common platform for a joint action. The Mohammedan traders mostly hailing from Gujarat, distinguished themselves from the rest of Indians by designated themselves as Arabs. Similarly, children of the erstwhile indentured labourers who had been converted to Christianity would not like to identify themselves with the Indians as they were anxious to move closer to the whites who were Christians.

III. The European traders were afraid of the competition with Indian traders because of their frugal habits and enterprising spirit.

IV. A large number of Indians lacked sense of hygiene and personal cleanliness that gave credence to the charge of Whites that Indians being uncivilized were unworthy of equal rights with the Europeans in South Africa.

V. The interest of the Indian in South Africa was confined only to making money. They had no attachment to the country of their adoption and so would not come to her aid in difficulty.

It was an objective and rational analysis of the problem facing the Indians in South Africa for which he was called upon to seek a solution. He did not absolve the Indians of their responsibility for the policy of racial discrimination followed by the Whites in South Africa. So in accord with his analysis he took several steps to ameliorate their condition in their adopted country.

Firstly, he put in efforts to awaken a sense of human dignity in them which implied awareness of their rights and their duties. Consequently whenever any step was taken by the Natal Government against the Indians in violation of the principle of equal citizenship, he led them to challenge such an action through representation to executive authorities or by filing appeals against them.

Secondly, with a view to forging unity among them and to bring them on a common platform, he tried to involve the diverse sections of Indians in common programmes and issues. Even those who could not pay high membership fee of the Natal Indian Congress were associated with its programmes by allotting to them manual or other kinds of work.

Thirdly, he founded the Natal Educational Association in order to develop self-confidence in the Indians besides creating awareness among them about current problems. In addition, he brought to the notice of the authorities both in England and South Africa the apathy of the Government of Natal towards the Indian educational institution in Natal.

For claiming equal status for Indians in a colony of the British, it was imperative and logical for the young lawyer to demonstrate that Indians in Natal were no less loyal to the British Empire than the Whites. So he left no opportunity to sing the song of the blessing of 'munificent British rule'.[1] It was a matter of pride for him that India was viewed by the British as the brightest jewel in the British Empire. No wonder he sent a message of congratulations to the Queen on behalf of the Indians in South Africa on her eighty-first birth day[2] and on her death he advised his friends and colleagues in Natal to close their business premises as a mark of personal grief and join in a profession of Indian mourners through the streets of Durban. In fact, he looked forward to the development of the sentiment of imperial Brotherhood in South Africa. He planned to distribute among all the Indian children in schools in Natal of a souvenir bearing a photograph of Queen Victoria with an extract of her proclamation of 1858 to the people of India at the top and six dates in her life in relation to India in 1901 showing in its entirety as British possession.[3] When the Boer War broke out in 1899 between the British and the Boer, he persuaded the Indians in Natal to help the British in the hour of their trial to remove the impression of the British that Indians lacked courage and were merely a drag on the White colonists. He organized the Indian Ambulance corps to take care of the wounded soldiers in war with the object of convincing the colonists that the Indians were the worthy subjects of the Queen. He could even ask the Indians to enlist themselves as soldiers. But they couldn't do so as they had no training in handling arms. Nor could they be trusted by the Whites. Even when Gandhi and his colleagues offered the services of Indian Ambulance corps, it was first refused. But when the British suffered serious reverses in war, they accepted the offer. Gandhi also collected money and goods from Indian merchants in Natal for the help of soldiers engaged in war. All such activities of the Indians under the leadership of Gandhi was well appreciated by the British generals. Gandhi and thirty-seven other Indian volunteers were awarded the war medals. He also organized a meeting of Indians and Europeans in Durban which was well-attended to congratulate the British generals Lord Roberts and Sir George White for their splendid feats and victories in this war. As a practical man and a shrewd lawyer, Gandhi had realized that in the British colonies Indians could obtain fair treatment only as British subjects as their own country was a part of the British Empire. For, he knew that the British authorities would be replaced in an awkward position if they openly refused protection to the Indians in the colonies controlled by them. There was no international body like the League of Nations or the United Nations to whom appeal could be made for the violation of human rights in a foreign country. The British Empire was the only substitute of a world organization.[4]

When Gandhi was deeply occupied with looking after the interests of his countrymen in Natal, he heard a very sad news of the death of his spiritual guide Rajchandrabhai. But where was the time to mourn his death? He wrote to a friend "I got the letter while I was at my desk. Reading it, I felt grieved for a minute and then plunged immediately into office work."[5] Such is the lot of those who take up public work as a moral duty and religious act. For, he had enough time to lead a procession in Durban to lay a wreath on the state Queen Victoria and write letters to his friends in other towns in Natal to do the same. But he had no time for himself. Service to the community was the only way to see God face to face.

After the Boer war Gandhi felt that his work in South Africa was over as the local leadership which he had created in Natal was competent enough to carry on the struggle if any hostile White Government denied them their rights. Friends and relatives at home were pressing on him to return to his country. So he decided to leave Natal but not without a promise to the local leadership that he would return within a year if he was needed by them. Farewell meetings were held at several places in Natal where costly presents were given to him and his wife. One of the gifts was a gold necklace worth fifty guineas meant for his wife. It set him thinking as to whether he and his family had the right to keep with them such costly gifts which were given to them as a reward for service to the community. The presents in place of giving him satisfaction created a conflict in his mind and his family. There was a fierce struggle in his mind that gave him sleepless night over the question of acceptance of the gifts. He remembered his state of mind even decades after the event. "The evening I was presented with the bulk of these things," he recalled. "I had a sleepless night. I walked up and down my room deeply agitated but I could find no solution. It was difficult for me to forgo the gifts worth hundreds, it was more difficult to keep them. And even if I could keep them what about my children? They were being trained to a life of service, and to an understanding that service was its own reward. I had no costly ornaments in the house, we had been fast simplifying our life."[6] How then could we afford to have gold watches—then I was exhorting people to conquer the infatuation for jewellery[7]—Mohandas was making efforts to shed attachment to worldly possessions which, in his view, was a condition for becoming an instrument of the Great Soul dwelling in all human beings. So he decided to create a trust of the gifts he had received with Parsi Rustomji and others as its trustees to be utilized by the Natal Indian Congress in dire need. But this decision generated great tension in the family as his wife felt that she had been unjustly deprived of the costly presents. To make his wife abandon her claim to the presents, he carried the children with him who agreed to plead with the mother not to insist on keeping the presents as they did not need them. What a clever move to disarm his wife who had her own view of life? When the discussion started, the wife argued "your children may not need them but what about my daughters-in-law. They will be sure to need them." The torrent of arguments went on, reinforced in the end by tears'. But the budding Mahatma was unmoved. She then retorted 'You are trying to make Sadhus of my boys from today and firmly said that the necklace would not be returned. "Is the necklace given you for your service or for my service," the lawyer rejoined. "But service rendered by you is as good as rendered by me. I have toiled and moiled for you day and night. 'Is that no service', she asked. Arguments could go on. But since Gandhi was determined to return the ornaments, his wife yielded but remained unconvinced of the propriety of the action of her husband.

Gandhi left for India with his family towards the close of 1901 and reached Bombay on December 19 just in time to attend the annual session of Indian National Congress held at Calcutta. He left his family at Rajkot and returned to Bombay where he tried to contact Pherozeshah Mehta to seek his help for getting a resolution passed at the forthcoming session in support of the struggle of Indians in South Africa. But the young lawyer could not have an easy access to one of the topmost leaders of the Congress and a legal luminary of Bombay. He could see him only for a few minutes in his separate saloon while he was travelling from Bombay to Calcutta to attend the session. In Calcutta he was put up with Tilak and other delegates in the Ripon College. It was a good occasion for him to meet several Congress leaders. The President of the session, Mr. Wacha, had appreciation for the young lawyer for his enthusiasm and his work in South Africa. He was taken to the Subjects Committee meeting by Gokhale where he was given only five minutes to speak on his resolution and before he could come to the main subject, the bell rang and he returned to his seat. The bell had only warned him that he had two more minutes to speak. But he was not aware of the procedure. He obtained some experience of the working of the Congress when he offered his services to the secretary to the Congress session who assigned him some clerical work. In sheer humility, young Gandhi offered even to button the shirt of the secretary which function was normally performed by a bearer. However, after enquiring about the credentials of the young lawyer, the secretary was sorry for having given minor assignment to him.

The working of the session disappointed Gandhi as most of the resolutions were passed by the delegates without even reading them. He observed that the volunteers lacked training. English occupied an important place in the working of the Congress and this made him unhappy. He noticed that the working of the Congress at that time was not in accord with his view of the working of a national organization.

For, very few delegates and leaders had any idea of the importance of public work. The Natal Indian Congress founded by him worked entirely on different lines.

Gandhi prolonged his stay in Calcutta with a view to promote a deputation to the Viceroy through Mr. Turner, President of the Bengal Chamber of commerce.[8] After staying at the India Club for a few days, he moved to the apartment where Gokhale was staying. This turned out to be a very fruitful occasion for him. Not only he got closer to Gokhale and won his appreciation for his devotion to public work, the Congress luminary introduced him to several Indian leaders. He met Babu Kalicharan Banerji who was taking keen interest in the Congress, to honour his promise to Christian friends in South Africa that on reaching India he would acquaint himself with the condition of the Christians in India. On meeting him at his residence, the young lawyer dressed in Parsi coat and trousers, was pleased to observe that unlike many Christians in India, Babu Kalicharan had not given up his Bengali 'dhoti' and shirt. Though keen to see Devendranath Tagore, father of Rabindranath Tagore and the leader of Brahmo Samaj, he could not meet him as no interviews with him were allowed. But he received an invitation to a celebration of the Samaj at Devendranath's house where for the first time his ears were entertained by fine Bengali music that made him a life long lover of Bengali music.[9] He went to the 'Belur Math' to see Swami Vivekananda but was disappointed as the ailing Swami had been removed to his house in Calcutta. Gokhale introduced him to P.C. Ray whose erudition and simple life made a deep impression on the mind of the Mahatma in the making. The visit to the temple of Kali was a painful experience for him as he saw flowing rivers of the blood of goats to appease the goddess. He also made use of his stay in Calcutta to have a flying visit to Burma where he was impressed by the spirit of independence of Burmese women.

It was during his stay at Calcutta, he took the decision to go round the country in third class just to have a feel of the hardships of the third class passengers. This was the demand of his ideal of public service. He was looking forward to the emergence of a new crop of leaders in India who would identify themselves with the masses. For, after attending the session of the Congress, he felt that there was a vast gulf between the outlook of the masses and the life style of their leaders as a result of which there was communication gap between the two. It is in this context he even raised an objection to the use of his own horse carriage by Gokhale in place of tram car for local travel like ordinary people. Possibly his readiness to serve even as a personal attendant to the secretary of the Congress session was motivated by this attitude. For he believed that for a public servant no public work could be viewed as menial.

At first Gokhale dissuaded him from undertaking this kind of journey in the train. But when he insisted on it, he admired him and took the trouble of coming to the station to see him off. Gandhi experienced tremendous hardships in the train journey which was the lot of all those travelling in third class. He avoided the mail trains which were less crowded but more costly. He spent hardly thirty-one rupees including the fare in this journey to Rajkot. On his way he halted at Varanasi, Agra, Jaipur, etc. for one day in each of these cities staying in dharmashalas or with pandas like ordinary pilgrims. At Varanasi he visited the temple of Kashi Vishwanath, the atmosphere of which appalled him. There the stinking mass of rotten flowers spread over the marble floor hurt his aesthetic sense. Hypocratic atmosphere of the temple touched him to the quick and he created a comical situation by offering only one pice to a panda who at once swore at him and threw away the offering but pocketed it afterwards. Cogitating over such experiences after two decades he felt that the only way to improve the condition of third class passengers was that educated persons should travel in third class and inundate the authorities with complaints if the conditions were not satisfactory.

He started his practice at Rajkot and his performance in the three cases that were passed on to him by his old acquaintance was encouraging enough to infuse confidence in him to start his practice in a big city like Bombay in accordance with the advice of Gokhale who felt that Bombay could be the right place for Gandhi to carry on his public work. So he moved to Bombay and set up his office on receiving over Rs. 3000 from Natal. He rented a fine bungalow in Santa Cruz and started living in style. He travelled first class on his way to the court and took pride in being the only first class railway passenger in the compartment. For, he believed that a barrister must keep his dignity and prestige.[10] It had not yet dawned upon him that voluntary poverty was a road to salvation both for him and for his country, though he was happy to rub shoulders with the poor who looked upon him as their 'bhai' or brother. In Bombay, the young lawyer solicited Mehta's blessing for his new venture. But the former discouraged him as, in his view, Gandhi would be wasting his small savings in a city like Bombay. The response of other solicitors whom he met to seek briefs was equally disappointing. However he received good response from the clients and started getting good income to maintain himself in Bombay. His South African clients often entrusted him with some work which was enough to enable him to pay his way.

But scarcely he had settled down in Bombay, he was confronted with a situation which put his faith in God and vegetarianism on trial. His second son Manilal who was ten years old and was weak because of an attack of small pox a few years earlier, was down with typhoid. A doctor was consulted who advised eggs and chicken broth for recovery. The father showed his inability to administer this diet because of the religious conviction of the family. He tried Kahne's hydropathic treatment. It was a dangerous undertaking as for sometime the life of his son was in danger since the fever persisted and the patient was quite often delirious. The father was extremely worried. For not only his son's life was in danger, his faith in God and vegetarianism was on trial. He, therefore, looked to God for help. Lo and behold, his treatment started working. The fever came down. Gandhi attributed the success of the treatment to the grace of God. From the medical point of view it was also the right treatment.

When the young lawyer had 'begun to feel his way' in Bombay, he received a cablegram from Natal to reach South Africa to represent the Indian case to Chamberlain who was scheduled to visit South Africa. So he left for Durban in compliance with his promise to his friends in Natal, though he was not feeling strong enough for the mental strain that the visit involved. Hoping that the work there would keep him engaged at best for a year, he left his family in India.

This time what he discovered in South Africa really shocked him. The real face of Imperialism was slowly and gradually unveiling itself before his eyes. He saw that after the Boer War, the lot of Indians had become harder in all parts of South Africa. The old laws such as the License Act, the Immigration Restriction Act, Restrictions on Indians in getting admissions to Government Schools, etc. were being enforced with greater rigour. The lot of Indians in Transvaal was even harder.

Gandhi first led a deputation to Chamberlain at Durban. But the Secretary of State was in no mood to listen to the disabilities of the Indians in South Africa. For, his main mission for his visit to South Africa was to get a loan or a gift of thirty-five million pounds from South Africa to repay to the British treasury for the cost of the war. The success of his mission depended upon his ability to win the hearts of Englishmen and Boers in South Africa. So the lengthy memorial drafted by the young lawyer for the occasion and his pleadings fell on deaf ears. The only reply the deputation received was that Indians should win the hearts of the Europeans in South Africa if they had to live there happily.

The young lawyer followed the Secretary of State to Pretoria. He procured a permit to enter Transvaal with the help of his old friend Alexander, Superintendent of Police in Durban to lead a deputation in Transvaal, too. But the chief of Asiatic Department in Transvaal refused to accept his permit as valid on the ground that it must have been issued by mistake and so ordered him to go back. It was an insult to him. This was the easiest way to exclude him from the deputation in spite of several requests from the Indians in Transvaal to allow him to represent their case. The result was the same. The deputationists were disappointed.

What could the young lawyer who had decided to serve his community in South Africa, do in such a situation. He was determined to fight. He, therefore, decided to settle down in Transvaal, though the life there, in his own words, was no bed of roses. He applied for admission as an attorney in the Supreme Court which was easily granted as no one opposed because of his friendship with several lawyers in Johannesburg. At the same time he founded the British Indian Association to fight for the rights of the Indians in Transvaal. Fortunately his dedication to a cause attracted a few Whites who were ready to join his office without giving much consideration to monetary rewards. Among them were Miss Dick from Scotland and Miss Sonia Schlesin of Russian-Jewish origin. About the salary, the latter replied, "I am not here to draw a salary from you. I am here because I like to work with you and I like your ideals."

Besides an Indian clerk, there was also an Englishman, Louis Walter Ritch, a successful businessman who agreed to attend to his office. This man was Theosophist and through him Gandhi came in contact with several Theosophists of Johannesburg. The young lawyer had to manage a big household as he treated the members of his staff as members of his family.

Notes and References

1. Gandhi, M.K., C.W., Vol. III, p. 200.
2. *Ibid.*, p. 74.
3. *Ibid.*, p. 178.
4. *Ibid.*, p. 136.
5. *Ibid.*, p. 193.
6. M.K. Gandhi, Autobiography, p. 184.
7. *Ibid.*, p. 185.
8. Gandhi, M.K., C.W., Vol. III, p. 236.
9. *Ibid.*, Autobiography, p. 198.
10. *Ibid.*, p. 208.

6

Search for a Strategy to Fight Racial Discrimination

In Transvaal Gandhi was in the thick of the fight as the struggle against anti-Indian legislations had become more intense than he expected. For, the Indian traders who had been previously trading in Johannesburg were being denied licences as a result of which they had to close their stores in spite of the fact that they had large stocks. The Asiatic Office which had been established with the object of helping the Indians in Transvaal had become a terror for inventing new methods for harassing Indians. Respectable Indians were ordered to get out of footpaths. Indian traders were compelled to trade in separate locations euphemistically called 'Bazaars'. Gandhi first tried to win the confidence of the authorities by his offer of co-operation and his readiness for a compromise. For instance, in the case of the law about separate locations, he was ready to co-operate for the success of the system provided it was applicable only to the new entrants and Indian trading centres were located in the central business section of any town and the Indians were allowed to purchase property subject to building and sanitary regulations. Similarly, he restricted the present struggle of the British in Transvaal only to the protection of the rights of those who were already settled there. This was done to remove the apprehension of the Whites that Indians were aiming at swamping the colony with Indian immigrants. But all such offers were of no avail. So the young lawyer had to adopt his old technique of writing letters to the press about the problems and difficulties of the Indians, and by putting pressure on the Government of India through the Indian leadership to intervene in the matter. He invoked the proclamation of the Queen of 1858 assuring equal rights to all her subjects in her Empire. This technique also involved sending deputations to the authorities both in South Africa and England for the removal of disabilities of the Indians in South Africa. At the same time he made a fervent appeal to the affluent Indians in South Africa for funds to carry on propaganda in India for the amelioration of their condition in their adopted country. His strategy did work to some extent. For he put the British statesmen both in England and India on the defensive. The Viceroy Lord Curzon had to act on the side of the Indians in South Africa on the grounds that the Indians were the subjects of the British Empire and any discrimination against them in a colony under the control of the British Crown would compromise the British position. The Supreme Court in Natal, too, had to take a similar position as it declared in its judgement in a case that His Majesty's Government was trustee of Imperial interests including those of Indian subjects of the Crown. This decision put the administration in Transvaal in a quandary as it could not freely put restrictions on the Indians.

However, such decisions did not raise the status of Indians in Transvaal as their condition there was worse than that of the Indians in Natal. For, Transvaal was a Boer Republic before the war and they did not owe any responsibility towards any power beyond the frontiers of their dominions. So the Boer authorities were free to impose any number of restrictions on Indian immigrants. Though after the war Transvaal administration came under the control of the British, they were not keen to restrain the erstwhile Boer administration with regard to their policy towards the Indians especially when in their own Crown colony a similar policy was pursued by the Whites. Moreover, the number of Indians in Transvaal was very small. There were hardly twelve thousand Indians as against one lakh Europeans in Johannesburg where Gandhi had decided to settle down. Most of the Indians were illiterate. With a view to giving wider publicity to the cause of Indians and to create understanding between the Indians and the Europeans in South Africa, he started a weekly 'Indian Opinion' in June 1903 and practically invested all his savings in this project. Initially it was multi-lingual but was later on reduced to bilingual on practical considerations. Its object was to educate the people, both Indians and Europeans and to seek their support for the cause of Indians in South Africa. It was to serve as an interpreter between the Indians and the Europeans to bridge the gulf between them. In the very first issue he set forth the vexatious laws and disabilities under which the Indians suffer in different colonies of South Africa. The prejudice against Indians had become much toned down in Natal,[1] while it was highest in Transvaal. Five hundred complimentary copies of the issue were sent to important persons in South Africa, India and England. The subsequent issues further highlighted the difficulties of the Indians and the unsympathetic attitude of the authorities in South Africa.

The young lawyer now realized that it would not be possible for him to leave South Africa early as the struggle in Transvaal would be fiercest and long as the Government was rather thinking of modification of the existing laws to the disadvantage of the Indians. The struggle was now shaping the course of his life, preparing him for a new role in life, creating in him a new vision and purpose of life and determining his priorities and values. He was working more than twelve hours a day and most of his time was occupied by public work. He lived with utmost simplicity in a single room next to his office. The walls of his office were adorned with pictures of Christ, Ranade, Mrs. Besant and W.W. Hunter. At his home there was a picture of his father and a large photograph of Dadabhai Naoroji. He adored Christ for his selfless suffering for humanity. He held Ranade, Mrs. Besant Dadabhai Naoroji in high esteem for their dedication to public work. Hunter had impressed him for his works on India and for upholding the rights of Indians in South Africa in the 'Times'. His devotion to his father sprang from Indian tradition.

In Johannesburg the young lawyer was in close contact with a number of Theosophists with whom he had religious discussion. On his first sojourn to South Africa it was contact with Christian friends that kept alive his interest in religion. But this time his association with Theosophists led him to delve deep into religious literature especially of Hinduism since Theosophy drew its strength from Hindu religious thought. He read Vivekananda's Rajyoga and Patanjali's Yoga Sutras. He committed to memory the whole of the Bhagavadgita by reciting two or three verses in the morning every day while brushing his teeth. He would stick on the wall slips of paper on which were written the verses and would try to memorize them. Thus, the Gita became his spiritual guide or spiritual dictionary which he would consult whenever he was confronted with a conflict situation. The ideals of 'aparigraha' (non-possession) and Samabhav (equability) fascinated him. How to act according to these ideals was his main problem. How to divest himself of all possession created a dilemmatic situation for him. For, his books, his property even his family could be considered as his possession. Did it mean to give up all? The lawyer in him found all the answers in Snell's equity. If all these were treated as a trust, then one could lose all attachment to these things. This meant true 'aparigraha'. Thus he found religion in jurisprudence. Surrounded by unsympathetic people and insolent bureaucracy in an alien country, Gita's ideal of equability gave him comfort and solace. He was striding towards Mahatmahood.

Though as a lawyer he had built up good reputation in Johannesburg, he was losing interest in personal comforts and material things of life. He was earning between four and five thousand pounds a year. He invariably took the fee in advance from a person not known to him. But he never filed a suit against anybody for default of payment and conducted deserving cases gratis. In his legal practice he demanded truthfulness from his client and more than one occasion he threw over his brief if he discovered that his client had given him false information. He never relied upon his client's statements. He cross-examined him, criticized him and squared with him. He once saved his friend and co-worker Parsi Rustomji, who would quite often resort to smuggling, from going to jail by asking him to admit his guilt to customs officer and by paying penalty equal to twice the amount he had confessed to have smuggled[2]. However, he was losing interest in his income. The more he earned, the more he was drawn towards simplicity, austerity and spirituality and public work. He allowed his insurance policy to lapse which he had taken when he had established himself as a lawyer. But his new ideals and commitment to the service of the community created a serious misunderstanding with his elder brother Laxmidas who was relying on the savings and remittance of his younger brother for the well-being of the family which had suffered a lot for sending him to England for higher studies. This misunderstanding with his elder brother pained Mohan most. In reply to his letter he wrote:

"I do recognize your (right to a) share in all my savings. But since there is no such thing as an income for me now, what can I send you?— I am not spending your share (on myself). If anything is left over after what has been used for this purpose, I would like to send you all of it, not just your share of it." For, whatever he earned, it was for the community and God gave him all the money for the people."[3] Mohandas was moving towards 'Moksha' which in his view, could be obtained by the elimination of ego. It is only then an individual can claim to 'prevail into everybody'. The first step in this direction is "intense experience that I am unhappy when others are unhappy and happy when others are happy."[4] Could his brother be won over by such arguments. For, he had not reached the stage where family ties fall asunder. So he stopped all communications with Mohandas. He died before the younger brother returned to India. But it was a great relief to Mohandas that on his deathbed Laxmidas understood the mind of his younger brother and commended his sons to his care.

So much faith he had now in God that he would undertake any dangerous mission for the good of his fellow human beings. Thus when in 1904 Pneumonic plague broke out in the Indian location in Johannesburg, he immediately took action on learning the suffering of the Indians. The municipal authorities were unable to diagnose the disease and so did not take any precaution though Europeans and Kaffirs were also affected by it. Indians suffered most because of unhiegenic environment and lack of resistance power as a result of poor diet. He set up a temporary hospital for those who were affected by it as Pneumonic plague was highly contagious. But he moved fearlessly among the patients while nursing them relying entirely on God's benevolence. His Indian clerks followed in his footsteps. Move by his selfless service the municipal authorities and some Europeans offered help. Dr. William Godfrey who was practising in Johannesburg ran to the rescue of the patients. His dedication to the suffering humanity also won for him the friendship of Henry Polak who on reading his letter to the Press holding the municipality responsible for the outbreak was anxious to see him. The two met at the vegetarian restaurant. Just at the time the young lawyer was making efforts to re-orient his life in terms of his ideals, Polak passed on to him Ruskin's 'Unto This Last' at the station when he was going to Durban to make certain decisions about the management of 'Indian opinion' as its editor had decided to return to India and its publication was becoming a heavy drain on his financial resources. The title 'Unto This Last' is taken from a biblical parable that narrates the story of a virtuous man who pays the same wages to all the labourers in his vineyard irrespective of the fact whether a labourer has been hired at the first hour or the eleventh hour. This book of eighty pages published originally in 1860 in the form of series of articles gripped him during his twenty-four hours journey from Johannesburg to Durban. He couldn't sleep for the whole night. in Ruskin's economics, profit is not the only motive of human action. Happiness must be measured by things other than money. Its miraculous effect on him was that it worked to crystallize some of his own ideas which had accumulated in his sub-conscious mind as a result of his experiences in his public life and his aspirations. But two decades after this event, Gandhi wrote that he learnt mainly three lessons from it. Firstly, that the good of the individual is contained in the good of all. Secondly, that a lawyer's work has the same value as the barber's in as much as all have the same right of earning their livelihood from their work. Thirdly, that a life of labour, i.e. the life of the tiller of the soil and the handicrafts man is the life worth living. He admitted that he had long been aware of the first, dimly recognized the second and had never grasped the third. However, it is doubtful whether Ruskin himself clearly favoured the life of handicraftsman or tiller of the soil. It looks Gandhi read into the Ruskin's some of his own ideas. Possibly he was never conscious that he was transmitting his own ideas to a book that impressed him. In fact, this book brought out his latent thoughts. It served as a catalyst. In Gandhi's life thought and action go together. He would immediately act as soon as any idea appealed to him. So on reaching Durban, he bought a piece of land from a land owner at Phoenix near Durban for a thousand pound. The place was without any habitation. There were sugarcane fields around the land and the station was used as a centre from where the sugarcanes were carried. Gandhi's settlement was two and a half miles from the station. The land acquired was uncultivated and snake infested. Except for a piece of land two or three acres in area, it had never been ploughed. Beyond the settlement no buildings were to be seen except a few small Zulu farm huts about two miles away. There was no shopping centre and all the articles had to be procured from Durban. But life close to nature attracted Gandhi. Even as a child he took some interest in tending to the plants. In South Africa when he visited the shop of a relative at Tonagat, a little garden behind his shop received his special attention and he even suggested to the owner that it would have been much better for him if he had converted his shop into a small orchard.[5]

On acquiring the farm at Phoenix, the printing press was shifted there. Sheds and small dwelling places were built there. All the inmates in the new colony were to live a community life. The settlers were divided into two classes. The schemers and the paid workers. A schemer was granted an acre or more of the estate where he or she was to build a small house with corrugated iron sheet. However, Gandhi's original idea was to have mud huts thatched with straw like those of ordinary peasants in India. But this idea had to be abandoned as it appeared to be more expensive and time consuming. In addition to the land and a house all were to draw £ 3 a month for working for the 'Indian Opinion' with the right to divide the profits. Other class of workers were simply paid wages for their labour. Gandhi's quarters were no different from the others, except they were larger. Gandhi was satisfied with the name Phoenix for his new settlement as it referred to the Greek legendary bird that had the qualities of purity, sacrifice and immortality. For, it is reborn from its own ashes.

Among the settlers were Gujaratis, North Indians, Tamilians and Europeans. His European friends West and Polak joined the settlement. After his marriage West brought his wife and mother-in-law who willingly participated in the community life. Later on, Polak was called back by Gandhi for attending to his legal work. The plan of its founder was to settle there and earn his livelihood by manual work like other settlers. But he could stay there only for brief periods because of his more pressing engagements in Johannesburg. Some arrangement was made for teaching the children in the settlement. The elders including Gandhi whenever he was there, performed the duties of teachers. The number of children in the school of the settlement varied from time to time. When Satyagraha was launched in South Africa, some of the children of the Satyagrahis were sent to the settlement and they were billeted with the settlers. This policy besides subjecting some families to great mental tension, created a comical and hypocritical situation. For instance, when Muslim boys had to be accommodated with Hindu families that had not as yet risen above their orthodox traditions, the ladies were put to very awkward situation as they were accustomed to purifying the brass utensils used by Muslim boys by putting them into the fire.[6] Gandhi's dietary experiments in the settlement also created some difficulties for the inmates especially the children as they initially resisted to the proposal of a saltless diet. They were made to agree to it by the allurement of a spicy diet on every Sunday to which they looked forward anxiously throughout the week. To Gandhi's eldest son Harilal this experiment only bred hypocrisy as some of the inmates accepted it only in deference to Gandhi and not out of conviction. However, his father at that time did not feel that he was imposing his will on those who had not reached his level of awakening. This happens with all reformers who are in a hurry. They become oblivious of the mental make-up and habits of the people around them in their zeal for raising the society to a higher level.

The young lawyer, tried to change his life style even at Johannesburg in terms of the Phoenix ideals to set an example before others. His wife and sons except his eldest son Harilal reached Johannesburg sometime in the beginning of 1905. Polak and his wife were also living with him as members of his family. Simplicity, austerity, physical labour and self-reliance were the chief attributes of his new way of living. Unleavened whole meal bread was to be prepared at home for which wheat was ground with hand mill by the children and other members of the household to have good flour for baker's bread. Though a servant had been engaged he was treated as a member of the family and so all were expected to help him in carrying on daily household chores. The young lawyer was 'Bapu' to his large family while his colleagues affectionately addressed him 'Bhai' (brother). The young lawyer generally walked to his office in Johannesburg which was six miles from his house, though for some time he used the bicycle. He never used a Rikshaw as he abhorred the idea of man pulling another man. His sphere of public work by this time had widened. He had started taking interest in the conduct and problems of the Chinese labour and Negroes. He was pained to learn the cruelties done to the Chinese labour working in the mines in Transvaal. He appreciated the work of Associations of the Chinese in Johannesburg. He was equally in deep sympathy with the Negroes who were known as Kaffirs. They had been doing good work for the whites in Natal. Though they were loyal subjects of the king, they were denied their rights in the land of their birth. However the young lawyer had not as yet become conscious of the need of identifying himself with the cause of all non-whites and mobilising them all to fight for their rights in South Africa. Loyalty to the Empire was still his foremost belief and concern. Thus, when the so-called Zulu rebellion broke out in April 1906, the Natal Congress at his suggestion made an offer to raise Indian Ambulance Corps for service with the troops. He even encouraged the Indians in Natal to enlist themselves like the whites in the army if the offer was made to them. It was their duty. In a way he was performing the role of Lord Krishna encouraging Arjuna to perform his duty as a Kshtriya on the battlefield. Practical considerations were at the back of this advice. For, he was aware that all the Indians in South Africa had no faith in non-violence and consequently if they kept themselves away from enlistment in the militia they would be considered as cowards and disloyal to the Empire. Since the Natal Government did not make any offer of enlistment of Indians in the militia, he organized the Ambulance Corps with twenty-four volunteers consisting of nineteen ex-indentured men, one Pathan and four Gujaratis. Faith in the British Empire prevented him from examining the act of the Natal Government against the Zulus in proper perspective. On reaching the scene of the so-called rebellion he discovered that it was merely a no-tax campaign and therefore, he developed sympathies with the Zulus. The Ambulance Corps did not face any danger or risk since the Zulus were in no position to attack the white soldiers. Attending to the wounded Zulus who had been mercilessly beaten by the white soldiers eased his conscience to some extent as no White nurse was ready to attend to the wounds of the blacks. "I could see", he later on observed "that but for us the Zulus would have been uncared for."[7] However weighed in the scale of Ahimsa there could not be any defence for his conduct in doing even Ambulance work as he drew no distinction between those who wielded weapons and those who did Red Cross work as both participated in war and advanced its course. But the young lawyer was no Mahatma at that time and had not fully understood the implications and universal significance of non-violence. He adopted a course which under the circumstances in his opinion would advance the cause of his community. He was only a patriot. His first biographer, Joseph J. Doke gave the title to his biography written in 1909. M.K. Gandhi—An Indian Patriot in South Africa and it looks that he approved of this title as he sent a copy of this biography to Tolstoy. He had the satisfaction that such acts of service by the Indians would help in lessening racial distinction in South Africa since the Indian stretcher bearers were all well treated by the white soldiers.

Since service of the community had become a passion with him, it did not take him even a minute to break up his large household and send his wife and children to the Phoenix settlement without any consideration of their inconvenience. His wife submitted to all such decisions as a matter of her duty. In the light of his commitment to the service of the community, a more serious question arose in his mind. Could he serve the suffering humanity whole heartedly, if he were engaged in the pleasures of family life and in the rearing of children? Or precisely was it possible to "live both after the flesh and the spirit?" Or could he devote himself completely to the good of the community had "his wife been expecting a child"? After giving a deep thought to all such questions he arrived at the conclusion that without the observance of 'Brahmacharya' service of the community would be inconsistent with service of the family. Abstaining from sexual pleasure was essential for checking the expansion of his family as he abhorred the use of artificial methods of birth control. So he took the vow of 'brahmacharya' after discussing it with his friends. He was 37 at that time, an age when a restless man is likely to make a radical change in his life. However his mind, had been working on this line for a long time and in a way he had been observing sexual abstinence since 1900. But in the middle of 1906 when he was in the midst of strenuous physical and mental work in connection with Zulu rebellion he finally made a resolve to accept 'brahmacharya' as a way of life and intimated it to his wife who did not demur even for a moment. Though it was public service that led him to take the vow of 'brahmacharya', he subsequently felt that the exercise of self-restraint that it involved, distinguished man from the brute. Possibly it was based on his belief that Brahmacharya would generate tremendous physical energy in him for carrying on his strenuous struggle. Young Mohandas was very careful about his health. He was conscious of his weak constitution but very indomitable spirit. The technique that was developing in his mind for fighting against racial discrimination was rooted in these two traits of his character.

His resolve of life of poverty and 'brahmacharya' equipped the young lawyer with wherewithal to carry on the struggle against racial discrimination which was becoming more and more severe with the consolidation of the British power in South Africa. For the harsh laws and regulations of the Dutch Government in Transvaal were extended to all Asiatics including the British Indians in Transvaal. On August 22, 1906, the Transvaal Gazette Extraordinary published a new ordinance which was applicable to Indian settlers. It enjoined upon every Indian 'coolie' Arab and Turk of eight years or upward, entitled to reside in Transvaal must register his or her name with Registrar of Asiatics and take out a certificate of registration. It required noting down important marks of identification upon the applicant's person and also the finger and thumb impression. Any person failing to comply with it was to be severely punished. Gandhi on reading all the sections of it was horrified as it showed nothing but hatred of the Indians. It seemed to him that if the ordinance was passed and the Indians meekly accepted it, absolute ruin was in store for the Indians in South Africa.[8] He translated the draft ordinance in Gujarati and published it in the 'Indian Opinion' to make Indian settlers aware of the gravity of the situation. He led a deputation to the Colonial Secretary on behalf of the British Indian Association who in reply vouchsafed that Government would consider its suggestion. But nothing was done and bill was introduced on September 4 in the Assembly. Gandhi called a meeting of the Indians in Transvaal to oppose the proposed legislation. It was held in the Jewish Theatre in Johannesburg. About 3000 delegates from different parts of Transvaal attended it. It was presided by Abdul Gani, Chairman of the Transvaal British Indian Association. A number of resolutions were passed. But the most important was the fourth resolution by which the Indians present there solemnly decided not to submit to the ordinance in the event of it becoming a law in the teeth of their opposition and to suffer all the penalties to such non-submission. The implications of this resolution was explained by the speakers in Hindi, Gujarati, Tamil and Telugu. One of the speakers Sheth Haji Habib went so far as to say that they must pass this resolution with God as witness. It is this suggestion which, in Gandhi's opinion, attached great significance to this resolution and so while explaining its significance to the delegates he proposed that it meant a separate decision or sort of a pledge by every individual since only those who took this pledge of God as witness could be bound by it. So all of them took the oath while standing with upraised hands. In Gandhi's view, it was this fact which changed the complexion of the movement against the proposed legislation. It became a religious movement or a struggle for the freedom of conscience which brought a number of non-conformist clergymen in South Africa into the thick of Gandhi's movement, such as Rev. Joseph J. Doke, Revs Perry, Howard & Ross. The association of the sympathetic Christian missionaries with his movement raised his image among the whites in South Africa and strengthened his resolve to carry on the movement by means of self-suffering which appeared to the conscientious clergymen as emanating from the Gospel. No wonder if a devout Christian found in him the traits of Christ.

Notes and References

1. Gandhi, M.K., C.W., Vol. III, p. 315.
2. *Ibid.*, Autobiography, p. 308.
3. *Ibid.*, C.W., Vol. VI, p. 432.
4. *Ibid.*, C.W., Vol. XCV, p. 180.
5. Gandhi, Prabhu Das, My Childhood with Gandhi, p. 34.
6. *Ibid.*, p. 56.
7. Gandhi, M.K., Autobiography, p. 264.
8. Gandhi, M.K., Satyagraha in South Africa (Ahmedabad, Navajivan Publishing House), p. 92.

7

Attributes of the New Weapon

Gandhi now started thinking of a technique corresponding to his principle for fighting injustice. Initially his struggle against the oppressive laws was given the nomenclature passive resistance with which the Europeans were acquainted as it was used by the Non-Conformists in England under the leadership of Dr. Clifford against the Education Act and by the Suffragists who campaigned for women's right to vote in England. During his visit to England in 1909, Gandhi met Clifford through Rev. F.B. Meyer who was president of Free Church National Council and a member of Passive Resistance Committee. Gandhi once told a missionary convention in London that he remembered Meyer fondly for his respect he showed to Hinduism. In Meyer's opinion Gandhi's familiarity with the passive resistance movement in England helped him in developing methods for his Satyagraha.[1] A number of Indians in South Africa, too, were familiar with passive resistance movement in England as Doke, who was to serve as a judge in the essay contest on the topic of the 'Ethics of Passive Resistance'.[2] No wonder if the sympathetic Europeans viewed satyagraha as a form of passive resistance movement. However, Gandhi never considered satyagraha as a copy of the Suffragette movement. He rather drew a sharp distinction between their methods and those of his movement. Similarly he was quite uncomfortable with this nomenclature. For, it hurt his national pride for using a foreign phrase for his struggle against the oppression of the Europeans but most importantly it did not fully explain the distinct character of his struggle. For, passive resistance was generally taken as a weapon of the weak while to Gandhi their struggle sprang from the spirit or soul which could not be equated with weakness as soul force, in his view, was far superior to brute force. Thus, in order to find out the right name for his struggle, he offered a nominal prize to the readers of the Indian opinion for suggesting a suitable name for the movement launched by him. Maganlal Gandhi, his nephew, who had been living in the Phoenix Settlement and was associated with the working of the weekly, suggested the word Sadagraha and Gandhi changed it to Satyagraha which means holding on to truth. Maganlal was aware of the working of the mind of his uncle because of his long association with him and his identification with his cause and life style. In fact, his suggestion gave expression to what was latent in the mind of his uncle. For, Gandhi was drawing strength from within, from his conviction that he was fighting for truth which in social life, in his view, takes the form of justice and so he was sure to triumph over untruth or evil. But an action based on truth must eschew untruth, violence, receipt or secrecy. Non-violence in this context is the only means for getting nearer to truth. It is the only weapon with which a person committed to truth must fight. Such a person does not submit to untruth or evil but suffers to sustain truth. Thus, for the author of this weapon, non-violence was active force. It was a powerful weapon which was designed not to cause suffering to the opponent but to oneself with a view to make the opponent realize his mistake and desist from committing evil.

Nevertheless, the lawyer in Gandhi felt that all existing constitutional remedies be exhausted before using the new weapon as it also involved suffering. Since Transvaal was a crown colony and the Imperial Government was responsible for its legislation and administration, it was viewed as pertinent to send a delegation to England to persuade the British Government to withhold assent to any discriminatory legislation passed by the Transvaal legislative assembly. Gandhi and H.O. Ali constituted the delegation. The former made use of this journey to England for learning Tamil, the language of a large number of poor ex-indentured Indian labourers and hawkers in order to communicate with them directly. In London he stayed in India House for two days and had long talks with Symjikrishna Varma, the founder of India House as a centre for Indians in England for study and propaganda. He also started a monthly journal, the *Indian Sociologist*. He had criticised Gandhi's action of organizing Ambulance Corps during the Zulu rebellion in his journal. There was a peculiar trait in Gandhi. He never hesitated to face his opponent of any decision in order to convince him of the justification of his action. May be the combination of the saint and lawyer in him prompted him to make an effort to convert his opponent to his view because of his conviction of the purity of his motive and moral soundness of his cause. However, on finding the place unsuitable for his mission, he shifted to hotel Cecil, the biggest and the most luxurious hotel in London, may be for practical reasons, as he was to contact important British leaders in order to seek their support for the cause of Indians in South Africa as well as to maintain his dignity.

He started working vigorously for his mission on reaching London. A typist was engaged and quite often Gandhi worked till 1 a.m. or even 3 a.m., since a large number of communications had to be sent in addition to writing to the press. The extent of the work can be judged from the fact that five thousand penny stamps were used for the work of the Delegation. The number of notices issues to a member of parliament was alone 2,000. The Delegation received support and sympathy from various quarters. A meeting of the Liberal, Labour and Nationalist members of the house of Commons under the Chairmanship of Henry Cotton passed resolution in support of the objects of the Delegation.[3] As a result of his efforts, the organ of public opinion in England, *The Times*, opened its columns to discuss the case of the Indians in South Africa. The young lawyer by his propaganda had put the British Government in an embarrassing position by invoking the principles with which the British had tried for decades to give a pleasing face to their imperialism while attacking the discriminatory laws being passed by the Transvaal Government. *The Times*, in one of its eloquent moments remarked, "As a nation we have little reason to be proud of the treatment being meted out to our fellow subjects in the Transvaal."[4]

Gandhi's strategy was to seek the support of all the parties in England, whether in opposition or in power to the cause of the Indians in South Africa. He also tried to approach the editors of all the important newspapers both Conservative and Liberal. As a result of his efforts a number of important persons in England agreed to introduce the Delegation to Lord Elgin, the Secretary of State for the colonies. Among them were Sir Lepel Griffin, a former British administrator in India and for many years chairman of the East India Association in London, Lord Stanley, Sir Gorge Girdwood, Sir Henry Cotton, Dadabhai Naoroji and Sir M. Bhownaggree. On November 8, the deputation headed by Sir Lepel Griffin waited on Lord Elgin. Introducing it to the Colonial

Secretary, he made a forceful plea for doing justice to the Indians in Transvaal who were the British subjects and had rendered valuable service to the British during the Boer war and Zulu rebellion. What Indians asked, he said, "that the whips which the Boer have inflicted upon us may not be changed into scorpions wielded by the British Government."

Like a good lawyer Gandhi was quite tactful in presenting the case of the Indians. His approach was not entirely negative. He recognized the fears of the Whites in Transvaal and suggested positive measures to mitigate them. He proposed the appointment of a Commission to investigate whether a fresh legislation was required to safeguard the interests of both the Whites and the Indians in Transvaal. Besides pleading the case of the Indians before the Secretary of State, he formed in England the South Africa British Indian Committee with L.W. Ritch as Secretary with a view to consolidate the work of the Delegation. This body did a useful work after his return from England.

The Secretary of State was non-committal. He neither wanted to displease the Whites in Transvaal most of whom were English nor did he want to take any action which would appear contrary to the British claims of treating all their subjects as equal in their Empire. He tried to meet the situation by a subterfuge of which Gandhi realised later on. For, on their way back the Delegation learnt that the Secretary of State had refused consideration by His Majesty's Government of the proposed legislation. But all their hopes of the redress of their grievances were dashed to the ground when Gandhi reached Johannesburg. For, he discovered that the Colonial Secretary had, in fact, assured the Transvaal Government that the 'Black Act' would not be disallowed when it was passed by the Transvaal legislature constituted after the grant of responsible government which was to be conferred on Ist January 1907. For Gandhi, it was a breach of faith as Lord Elgin by his assurance in advance of royal assent to the oppressive law encouraged the Transvaal Europeans to carry on their anti-Indian programmes. It is unfortunate that while Gandhi trusted the Secretary, the historians called him unreliable undistinguished, lethargic, pedestrian as a Secretary of Colonies and as Viceroy of India 1894-99.[5] The speeches by the candidates during the election of the legislative assembly on the grant of responsible government clearly indicated that the Asiatic Amendment Act would be passed by the new legislature without much ado. Thus the original ordinance was rushed through all its stages at a single sitting on March 21, 1907 in the new legislature. The Act was proclaimed to take effect from July 1, 1907 and the Indians were called upon to apply for registration under it by July 31.

The number of Indians in Transvaal was not very large. It did not exceed 13,000 at any time, though when Gandhi launched his movement the number varied between 7000 and 8000[6] against the White population of 2,80,000. Most of the Indians were living in Johannesburg and Pretoria as traders and hawkers. Majority of them were illiterate and some of them had only the working knowledge of several Indian languages and could communicate with Indians speaking different languages. Gandhi's technique and strategy of meeting the challenge of a powerful White Government developed out of this peculiar situation. Truth and non-violence became the mainstay of his struggle. The success of the movement depended upon the dedicated and committed volunteers, the pressure of public opinion and the sympathies of the liberal Whites. He was sure that the hatred of the Whites was rooted in certain misgivings and wrong information. So he took pains to avoid hurting the sentiments of the Whites while fighting against invidious laws and acts of the White Government. It was like tight rope walking. That is what the situation demanded. Thus, when the decision was taken that Indians must refuse to register themselves according to the new law, he posted volunteers near the Registrar's office to dissuade the Indians from going in for registration by making them conscious of the harm done to the community by this Act. Special instructions were given that no force be used to prevent registration. 'Indians Opinion' turned out to be a powerful weapon for building up public opinion for the success of the campaign. For, a struggle of this kind, "which chiefly relies on internal strength could not be carried on without a newspaper" as in its absence its leader could not perhaps educate the local Indian community nor could keep Indians all over the world in touch with the course of events in South Africa in any other way. So he decided to do away with advertisement and increase the number of subscribers in order to make it entirely the mouthpiece of Satyagraha campaign. This plan worked well as the number of subscribers rose to 3500 from 1100 before the launching of the movement which was quite remarkable as the reading Indians population in South Africa was hardly twenty thousand.[7]

Through it he dolled out regularly information about the state of the movement, the strategy followed and the legal position in various situations in the course of the struggle besides issuing words of encouragement to the volunteers whom he advised to read the columns of 'Indian Opinion' carefully. As the name Satyagraha had not yet been coined when the struggle was forced upon the Indians in Transvaal, a separate body under the name 'Passive Resistence Association, was formed, although there was in Transvaal British Indian Association with a large membership which had been established earlier to protect the interests of Indians in Transvaal, may be because a number of members of this body were not inclined to challenge the authorities directly. This was a tactful act as by this decision he averted a rift in the community as he observed later on "If I had made the blunder of dragging the BIA into the agitation, I would have cut the Association into pieces and there would have been no South African victory." Moreover, the Passive Resistance Association had been assigned many other social and political functions besides organizing resistance to obnoxious laws. Special care was taken to avoid any step which could cause rift in the community. Volunteers were instructed not to be rude to any person taking out a permit. So much so people were informed by announcements at every public meeting that if any one desirous of taking out a permit was afraid of the pickets, he could ask the workers to detail a volunteer to escort him to the permit office and back. It was an intelligent move. For, he disarmed the authorities from taking any action to divide the community by coming to the aid of those who were ready to comply with their orders. To avoid any kind of a violent clash with the authorities, volunteers were instructed to behave with the police with due respect and suffer peacefully if violence was used against them. Any person charged with breaking of the law was neither to offer bail nor pay fine. But the leader assured that he would appear in defence gratis and offer himself for punishment for encouraging people to break the law. Secrecy was ruled out of the movement. All programmes and policies were published in the Indian Opinion. As a result, the officials started relying on the information about the movement given in the Weekly. However, the practice of publishing the names of those who took out permits was neither in accord with this policy nor with his view of non-violence as developed subsequently since it injured the feelings of the opponents besides forcing them to refrain from doing something by creating a fear psychosis. Nevertheless, he succeeded in carrying the community with him. It was reported that not more than 500 Indians took permits in spite of the special arrangements made by the authorities to issue permits clandestinely at night at the houses of those who were ready to take out permits to save themselves from any hardship but were afraid of losing the goodwill of the community. Gandhi was proud to inform the readers of the Indian Opinion that at Pietersburg the boycott of the new law was cent per cent.[8] The 'Star' reported on 6th July that very careful and complete passive resistance had been organised by the Indians and not a single Asiatic had registered until then.[9] Another paper, the 'Transvaal Leader' commented that even after sixteen days had passed not a single Indian resident in the capital had troubled the authorities to ask for registration.[10] The Government was left with no choice but to start arresting the leaders of the movement to suppress it. Some of them were served with the notice in late December of 1907 to appear before the magistrate. Since registration was applicable to all the Asiatics a leader of the Chinese residents in Johannesburg, Mr. Quinn was also served with this notice. In this way the Chinese who were not more than 400 in Transvaal were brought into the ambit of the movement. Among the Indian leaders Tahambi Naidoo, a Tamilian born in Mauritius and M.K. Gandhi were served with similar notices. None of them defended himself of the charge of violation of law in accordance with the general policy of Satyagraha. So Gandhi was sentenced for two months' simple imprisonment though he asked for three months with hard labour as given to his compatriots participating in this movement. This was his first experience of jail going. He was not sure about the outcome of his struggle. For, the strategies of the movement were evolving under the pressure of the circumstances and the policies of the opponents. Thus, when the sentence was pronounced against him, he felt depressed for a moment.[11] Several thoughts crossed his mind. He could think of the possibility of Indians not courting imprisonment in large number in his absence or succumb to the pressure of the authorities. It was natural for him at such moments to seek inspiration from the ideals and deeds of Socrates or Thoreau or Sein Fein movement in Ireland etc.

To avoid any complications or confrontation with the authorities in jail, Gandhi had advised all the volunteers to observe the jail regulations strictly so long as they were not inconsistent with their self-respect or religious convictions. They were to wear jail dress according to regulations. So he accepted the dirty clothes given to him without any remonstrance as this was a test for his self-control and perseverance. Though he was not accustomed to the diet served to them in the jail, he and his compatriots reconciled themselves to it shortly. After his arrest a number of Indians, mostly traders and hawkers offered themselves for arrest and so the number of prisoners rose to 150, though their leader had calculated that at least half of the Indian population would be arrested. However, they had not to stay in the prison for a long time as only after a fortnight of Gandhi's arrest a settlement was arrived at between him and General Smuts through the good offices of Albert Cartwright, editor of Transvaal leader, an able and broad-minded person who was known to Gandhi. As a result all Satyagrahis were released. Gandhi had been assured that the Black Act would be repealed if Indians agreed to register themselves voluntarily. This was not a surrender on the part of Gandhi. For the Indians had offered voluntary registration on 29 March, 1907 long before the new Act was implemented. Similarly, the British India Association had telegraphed the Secretary of State on April 7, 1907 that the Indian community was willing to co-operate in a programme of voluntary registration.[12] In fact, the Indians did not so much object to re-registration as they did to the compulsory issuing of new certificates with ten digit finger printing. In June 1907, Gandhi had made it clear that the requirement of giving finger prints was only one of the objections. But thumb impression could be given if insisted[13] on. So the crucial point was compulsory registration under the law.[14]

On his release Gandhi reached Johannesburg at 9 p.m. after borrowing some money from Smuts' Secretary. He contacted chairman Yusuf Mian at his residence and sent a notice of the meeting which was held immediately between 11 and 12 p.m. where he explained the terms of the settlement to a gathering of one thousand Indians. He exhorted them to register voluntarily to show that we do not intend to bring a single Indian into the Transvaal surreptitiously or by fraud. But some members were doubtful about the settlement as they feared that General Smuts might betray them and the law might not be repealed after the Indians had voluntarily registered themselves. A Pathan Mir Allam raised his voice against the agreement on the grounds that their leader had compromised the principle by agreeing to registration by giving finger prints. "It was you," he thundered, "who said that the struggle centred round the finger prints. How does all that fit in with your attitude today?" There was some force in Mir Allam's arguments and Gandhi tried to assuage his feelings by assuring that those who objected to giving fingerprints would not be compelled to do so and promised all possible help to any person who wished to register without giving finger prints. But this did not pacify Mir Allam who swore that he would kill any person who would first register himself by giving finger prints. There were about fifty 'pathans' staying in Transvaal and some of them were Gandhi's clients including Mir Allam. They had fully participated in the struggle and none of them had submitted to the new Act. But they were unsophisticated and credulous. They were carried away by the rumour that their leader had sold the interest of the community to General Smuts for fifteen thousand pounds.

As the principal party responsible for the settlement, Gandhi felt that it was his clear duty to take the lead for registration by giving finger prints. Thus on February 10, 1908 when he proceeded to the office of the registrar with his friends, Mir Allam and his associates followed him and near the office of the registrar, Mir Allam asked Gandhi what he intended to do. "I propose to take out a certificate of registration by giving the ten finger prints," replied Gandhi. "If you go with me, I will first get you a certificate, with an impression only of two thumbs, then I will take one for myself giving the finger prints." But before he could finish his last sentence, he was hit with a heavy stick by Mir Allam. Others accompanying Mir Allam showered blows on him. He became unconscious. Thami Naidu and Essop Mia tried to protect him and were also hurt. The policeman caught the assailants. Several Europeans had been a witness to this scene. He was removed to the house of Rev. Doke, where he was nursed by him and his wife after the doctor had stitched up the wounds. Doke was a Minister of the Johannesburg Baptist Church. He became Gandhi's intimate friend in South Africa and wrote the first biography of Gandhi and edited the Indian Opinion during the absence of Gandhi and Polak who were in prison in 1911. On regaining consciousness, he asked the Registrar of Asiatics who had accompanied him to Doke's house, to issue the first certificate to him by taking his ten finger prints in accordance with the declaration that he had made at the meeting after his release. After this he wired the Attorney General that he did not want any action to be taken against Mir Allam and his companions as he did not hold them responsible for this action. However, Mir Allam and one of his companions were sentenced to three months' hard labour as some Englishmen who had witnessed the attack on him wanted them to be prosecuted thought he was not summoned as a witness in this case. Gandhi and Mir Allam were known to each other. The action of latter may appear rash. But former's consent to the requirement of giving finger prints strengthened his belief that their leader had betrayed the community. For, he had a number of times raised his objection to the giving of finger prints in his weekly and in his memorials to the authorities. However, he had made it clear that the question of finger prints was not the fundamental issue, though its demand by the authorities was highly objectionable.[15] Highly emotional and credulous person like Mir Allam could not understand the difference between the two situations and there was nothing unusual for such persons to give credence to rumours deliberately circulated that their leader had betrayed them. There appears to be a deeper conspiracy to eliminate him and Mir Allam and his friends might have become tools in the hands of those who had a design on the life of Gandhi. Thus, when he went to Durban to seek support for his movement from the Indians in Natal, his supporters apprehending an attack on him, formed a ring round him at the meeting to save him. A story was current that when Gandhi and Mrs. Polak came out of the hall after the meeting was over, a man was noticed lurking in the shadow. Gandhi went up to him, linked his arms in his and talked in a low voice. The effect was magical. The man took out his weapon and handed it over to him and went away. Keeping in view the danger to his life, his supporters followed him to his Phoenix settlement and guarded him at night as he had the habit of sleeping in the open. Their fear was not baseless. Later on the chairman of the British Indian Association in Natal, Essop Mia was assaulted and seriously injured by a Pathan because of the Asiatic compromise. Possibly the kingpin in this conspiracy was one Mohammad Shah, a Pathan and a fanatic Muslim who had once wired to Jinnah that 700 Muslims were displeased with the compromise.[16] Gandhi had even received letters from some Muslims deprecating the compromise.[17] Mir Allam might not have been directly in touch with Mohammad Shah. But some persons who were not well disposed towards Gandhi's leadership were giving currency to undesirable rumours and news to damage his reputation. For, some affluent persons were afraid of associating themselves with Gandhi's movement in view of the risk involved in incurring the wrath of the Government in a foreign country. Even a Muslim leader Ally, who had earlier accompanied Gandhi to England to persuade the British Government not to allow the Asiatic Amendment Ordinance sent a telegram to Ammer Ali, a member of the South Africa British India Committee expressing his opposition to Gandhi's continued campaign against the Asiatic Registration Act on the grounds that it would ruin thousands of his co-religionists who were all traders as against Hindus who were mostly hawkers. Such ideas and fears, howsoever groundless, encouraged the authorities in South Africa to intensify propaganda to divide the Indians on religious lines. This policy was given a boost by officers who had served in India and had stayed on in South Africa after serving in the Boer War as they were accustomed to weakening any nationalist Indian movement by fomenting communal differences. In a similar vein General Smuts circulated a story that Gandhi was charging two pounds a piece only from the Mohammedans for legal work done for voluntary registration applications. It was not true. Rather he was charging the same amount from all whether Hindus or Muslims as it required a lot of work besides filling up the applications. However, the number of such applicants did not exceed[18] 235. No doubt, the Muslim traders had a greater stake in opposing the Government as most of them were owning large stocks and property as they could be deported and their property confiscated. But it was their competition with the White traders which was mostly the cause of the trouble as the Whites were putting pressure on the Government to force the Indian traders to leave the country by restricting their activities or by humiliating them. However, by a tactful handling of the situation, Gandhi kept the majority of the Muslims with him and important Muslim leaders vigorously campaigned for the success of his movement. In spite of the small number of Indians in the Transvaal, their leader's character, spirit of self-sacrifice and intelligent moves put the Colonial Government on the defensive and his struggle held the attention of the entire British Empire. Some discordant voices against the compromise not withstanding, practically all the Indians got themselves registered in terms of the agreement. General Smuts admitted that 9158 Indians out of their population of less than 12,000 applied for registration and that only 70 had refused to allow their finger prints to be recorded. Gandhi claimed that even the rest would have registered themselves if the Government had not halted the procedure on May 9, 1908.[19]

Initially the compromise was interpreted even by the White press as a gain for the Indian community. Rand *Daily Mail* commented on February 1, 1908, "it is certain that the compromise now agreed upon differs in no material respect from that suggested by the Indians themselves in May last and it is just as certain for this reason that every Indian regards the compromise as complete victory over the Government in spite of the very generous and exemplary attitude adopted in public by Mr. Gandhi himself."[20] Two cartoon appearing in a paper represented the general feeling of the Whites in South Africa about the outcome of the movement. One appearing during the Satyagraha represented the Transvaal Government as a steamroller which was up against an elephant, the Indian community. After the compromise, the paper published a sequel showing the wrecked steamroller and General Smuts lying on the ground amidst the ruins of his chair-miserable looking unhappy at the elephant.[21]

Nevertheless the compromise was not the end of the road. The fears of those who smacked of foul play in this compromise turned out to be true. For, it became clear after a few days that the Transvaal Government was in no mood to repeal the Asiatic Law Amendment Act in terms of the settlement as interpreted by Gandhi. Rather the Government of

General Botha went on passing discriminatory and oppressive laws against the Indians even when Gandhi and his associates were busy in honouring the agreement. Thus, by the Act 35 of 1908, Indians were prohibited from dealing in precious metals. They could not hold or sublet property on proclaimed ground, nor could they reside on proclaimed ground. Similarly, there was a disguised form of attack on Indian merchants by the Shop Hours Act of 1908. In addition to all these restrictions Smuts started laying down new conditions for the repeal of the Act. He wanted the consent of the Indian leadership in Transvaal for prohibiting the entry of the Indians in Transvaal who had been residing there before the Boer War as well as all those Indians who cleared the education test. This was clear violation of the principle of equality of all subjects of the British empire which was the main demand of Gandhi. So he commenced his struggle for claiming the immigration rights of the educated Indians. A few educated Indians from other parts of South Africa were advised to enter Transvaal and thereby challenge the Immigration Restriction Act. Accordingly Sorabji came from Charlestown and entered without permission. He was tried and sentenced to one month's imprisonment with hard labour. The next move was to advise the Indian traders in Transvaal to carry on trade without licences. So important Indians such as Essop Mia, chairman of British Indian Association of Transvaal, Gandhi's eldest son Harilal, Abdul Cadir Bawazeer, Chairman of Hamida Islamic Society and Naidoo, offered themselves for arrest[22] by hawking without licence. They were sentenced to imprisonment with hard labour. Their arrest was followed by closing of all Indian business establishments throughout Transvaal. This was the beginning of 'Hartal' which later on became an effective weapon in Gandhi's armoury of Satyagraha or a non-violent war. Generally mass meetings were held on the arrest of an important leader. About hundred persons had been arrested and sentenced for imprisonment for various terms.[23]

However the struggle reached its climax when Gandhi decided that all the registration certificates taken out voluntarily be burnt as neither the Government was ready to repeal the Act nor the Supreme Court of Transvaal was permitting the withdrawal of their applications for voluntary registration. He had given prior notice to General Smuts of this programme.[24] At a meeting outside the Hamida Mosque in Johannesburg some 3000 Indians from all over the Transvaal gathered to witness a conflagration that intended to mitigate their humiliating status in the country of their adoption. It was their leader's reply to what he considered as a breach of faith. A large three legged pot was filled with registration certificates about 1000 in all and about 500 trading licences. Parafin was then poured in and the certificates set on fire amidst scene of wildest enthusiasm. For Gandhi, it was a 'yajna' and so he invoked the blessing of the almighty and appealed to all to trust God in their fight for their rights.[25] A British journal compared the bonfire with that of the Boston Tea Party that led to the American War of Independence. This act was, in fact, a master stroke to quicken the flagging zeal of the Indians. There was a drama in the whole affair, and every one present there was touched by the scheme. Some of those who still withheld their certificates brought them to the platform to be consigned to the flames. Mir Alam who had made a murderous attack on Gandhi had been just released from jail was also present at this meeting. When he handed over his certificate, there was an emotional scene. Gandhi clasped his hand, pressed it with joy and assured him that he had never harboured in his heart any illwill against him. He actively participated in the Satyagraha and wrote emotional poems to inspire the Satyagrahis.

Though both the Generals, Botha and Smuts, were ready for some concessions, the Indian leadership was not prepared for any compromise without the repeal of the Asiatic Amendment Act and Immigration Act. In fact, the merging of the immigration and registration issues was inevitable as any Indian who failed to register or to produce on demand a registration certificate in effect became a prohibited immigrant requiring his expulsion from Transvaal according to law. However, Gandhi had no desire for a large scale immigration of Indians and Chinese who could claim no pre war residence. This was a pragmatic approach and he had reiterated this point in a number of communications to the authorities and articles. But he certainly wanted the right of the Indians to immigrate on the basis of equality with Europeans.

Consequently, Gandhi was arrested on September 29, 1908 while returning from Natal for not producing his certificate which had been consigned to flames. He was sentenced to pay a fine of 25 pounds or to go to jail for two months with hard labour. He preferred jail like his compatriots who had been arrested and jailed either for not producing the certificates or for hawking without licence. He was removed to Volksrust prison and was drafted to work in digging earth, attired in the prison garb. He was later on transferred from Volksrust to Johannesburg jail. On reaching the railway station, "this small, slim dark complexioned man with calm eyes and serene countinance clad in the convict clothes putting on a small military cap which did not protect him from the sun descended from the train attended by a prison warder in uniform."[26] He chose to walk three quarters of a mile in broad day light carrying his bundles like other convicts. He was lodged in a ward of dangerous convicts where he had to keep himself awake all night as he was not sure of the conduct of other prisoners. At this time he received a letter from a friend that his wife was seriously ill. He was very much perturbed. He could get his release if he paid fine. But he was not ready to do it; for that meant betrayal of the cause. So he wrote an emotional letter to his wife assuring her that even if she died, he would not remarry and would take the death of his dearest one as a sacrifice for a righteous struggle. After his release he immediately went to Durban where his wife had been undergoing treatment under the care of a doctor and his wife who were friendly to him. But he was shocked to learn that their patient had been administered beef tea. After consulting his wife who vehemently opposed the taking of beef tea as a part of her treatment, Gandhi removed her to Phoenix where he put her to his hydropathic and nature cure treatment. As a part of nature cure treatment, Gandhi suggested the giving up of salt and pulses. But his wife flatly refused to accept this suggestion on the plea that no individual could give up such articles. But she yielded when her husband swore that he himself would not take salt and pulses at least for a year. His wife pleaded with him to take back the vow. But he could not withdraw a vow seriously taken. The restriction on salt he continued for ten years as he considered it unnecessary for vegetarians. He looked after his wife with great care and devotion administering lemon juice, fruit and milk to her. Kasturbai returned to health and this strengthened Gandhi's faith in nature cure as Kasturbai's diseases was looked upon at that time as a fatal disease.

On his return to Transvaal Gandhi was rearrested twice for non-production of registration certificate. Arrests and imprisonment became normal for him. Rather he considered it as 'the height of good fortune to be in the jail in the interest and good name of his country.' Besides, daily life in jail appeared to him more comfortable as it offered greater opportunity to him to pray to God and attend to the need of his soul. He read the works of Mazzini, Ruskin, Tolstoy, Emerson, Thoreau, Carlyle, in addition to Hindu religious works such as Manusmriti, Patanjali, Yoga Darshan, the Upanishads, the Gita. The Indians in Transvaal followed him. More than two thousand out of a population of six thousand during the struggle had a taste of the prison life. The movement acquired significance in view of prospective union of the colonies on the insistence of the Europeans in South Africa. Smuts and Botha were ready to concede some concessions on that account. But were opposed to giving equal treatment to all the subjects of the British empire which was the main demand of the Indians. Both the Generals were scheduled to visit London to carry on negotiations for the creation of the Union of South Africa. Gandhi immediately suggested to his compatriots to take advantage of this demand of the Europeans and send a deputation to England to press on the British Government to settle the Indian question in South Africa before conceding the demand of the Europeans for the union of all the colonies. This suggestion was accepted. Gandhi and Sheth Haji Habib, a Memon merchant from Porbandar constituted the deputation that left Cape Town on June 23, reaching London on July 10, 1909. This assignment kept Gandhi in London for four months. This time he preferred to stay in a hotel that catered to middle class clientele. For, he had to meet several English politicians and statesmen besides correspondents of influential papers. He addressed meetings and wrote letters. He met the Secretary of State, and the Colonial Secretary. But the delegation could not make any headway. The two Generals of South Africa were ready to concede only minor concessions to Indians in South Africa in their talks with the British statesmen, and the British administration was in no mood to press them to consider sympathetically the fundamental demand of the Indians. This position was made clear by Lord Ampthill to the delegation. Sheth Haji Habib, the other member of the delegation was ready to yield to whatever was being offered claiming that he represented the majority of the community that held the major portion of the community's wealth in South Africa. But Gandhi while admitting the truth of the statement made by his colleague strongly dissented with this view on the grounds that they were fighting not only for practical relief but for principle as well.

Though the mission of the delegation remained unsuccessful, Gandhi had certain experiences that kept his mind agitated and occupied during his return journey. His humility and life style once created an amusing and for some an embarrassing situation during this visit to London. Some Indian students in London had organized a gathering of Indians in England and were in search of an important Indian as a main speaker at their function. At that time very few could recognize Gandhi. Since no other person was ready to do this job, a leader of their group, T.S.S. Rajan approached Gandhi who consented on the condition that the dinner to be served to the participants would be vegetarian. The organizers engaged a hall and decided to cook Indian dishes themselves. They entered the cellar and started working for preparation of the dinner. Lo and behold at about 2 p.m. a small, thin wiry man with a pleasant face joined them and offered to do the washing of plates and cleaning of vegetables. All of them were happy with this new comer whom they did not know. Then the man who had contacted Gandhi turned up and all were stupefied when he announced that the stranger washing the plates was no other person but the speaker of that evening.[27] He continued washing the plates even after his introduction to the organizers. Several revolutionaries studying in England were present in that meeting. Savarkar had his seat by the side of Gandhi. Another revolutionary Virendranath Chattopadhyaya also attended the meeting. B.C. Pal was in the chair. Gandhi delivered a speech on the Ramayana since the meeting was in connection with the Vijyadashmi or Dussehra. He dwelt upon the personal qualities of Rama, the suffering of Sita etc. But Savarkar in his speech highlighted that Rama could destroy evil represented by Ravana only through violence. In fact, the story of Rama led to a dialogue between violence and non-violence.

Notes and References

1. Hunt, J.D., Gandhi & Non-Conformists Enclouers in South Africa (New Delhi, Promila & Co.), 1986, pp. 119-20.
2. *Ibid.*, p. 52.
3. Gandhi, M.K., C.W., Vol. VI, p. 46.
4. *Times*, Jan. 7, 1908, quoted in Hutten Gandhi in South Africa, pp. 182- 83.
5. Quoted in Hunt, *op. cit.*, p. 69.
6. C.W., Vol. VII, p. 319.
7. Gandhi, M.K., Satyagraha in South Africa, p. 142.
8. C.W., Vol. VII, p. 164.
9. Nayyar, Sushila, Satyagraha at Work, p. 92.
10. *Ibid.*, p. 96.
11. Gandhi, M.K., Satyagraha in South Africa, p. 149.
12. Hutten, *op. cit*, p. 179.
13. C.W., Vol. VI, p. 362.
14. *Ibid.*, Vol. VII, p. 27.
15. *Ibid.*, p. 175.
16. Nayyar, Sushila, Satyagraha at Work, p. 270.
17. C.W., Vol. VIII, p. 97.
18. *Ibid.*, p. 262.
19. Hutten, *op. cit*, p. 191.
20. Nayyar, Sushila, Satyagraha at Work, p. 226.
21. *Ibid.*, p. 275.
22. C.W., Vol. VIII, p. 366.
23. *Ibid.*, p. 451.
24. *Ibid.*
25. *Ibid.*, p. 459.
26. Shukla, Chandran Shankar, Incidents of Gandhi's Life Fits Published in 1949, Bombay, Vora & Co., p. 242.
27. *Ibid.*, p. 260.

8

Hind Swaraj

Gandhi had several encounters with the revolutionaries and had long and heated discussions with them over the question of use of violence for the attainment of self-rule or Swaraj. In his earlier visit in 1907 he had discussions with Shymaji Krishna Varma who had opened India House where he (Gandhi) had stayed for a short while. Vinayak Savarkar virtually took charge of India House when Shymaji Krishna Varma left for Paris. Madan Lal Dhingra who shot Curzon Wyllie in London shortly before Gandhi's visit to London this time also had stayed there. These revolutionaries must have emphasised the futility of non-violence in fighting oppression and imperialism. But Gandhi while admiring the spirit that animated the Indian revolutionaries was fundamentally opposed to their creed of violence. Reflecting on Dhingra's deed, he observed "those who believe that India has gained by Dhingra's act and other acts in India make a serious mistake. Dhingra was a patriot but his love was blind. He gave his body in a wrong cause." He was returning from England empty handed as he had failed to get justice from the British statesmen for the Indians in South Africa. Sitting in his cabin on board S.B.S. Kildonan Castle, his mind was seized with very serious questions which the partisans of violence had raised during his discussions with them. He also had a discussion with his friend Pranjivan Mehta who must have laughed over his views about Swaraj, civilization, use of violence. Later on Gandhi recorded that he wrote the entire *Hind Swaraj* for his friend Pranjivan Mehta. The question that agitated his mind was "What is the efficacy of his own method in the light of the present attitude of the British and South African authorities? What is at the root of oppression and exploitation of one nation by another or miserable existence of those whose hard work supports luxurious living by a few in a community?" Is the system at fault or the individuals are so depraved. What is real Home Rule or Swaraj for which the Indians had been fighting? His mind was crowded with currents and cross currents of ideas some of which did not fit into his view of life and his methods of attaining his objectives. In order to unburden his mind of the answers of these questions and to reassure himself of the rightness of his approach to the problems that confronted him in South Africa he started putting them down in black and white. He worked day and night for about ten days and wrote on the steamer's stationary 30,000 words covering 271 pages in Gujarati. When his right hand was exhausted, he wrote with left hand as if he was seized by some kind of spirit. His ideas about, swaraj, ends and means, religion, Hindu-Muslim relations had by this time taken shape and therefore the flow of ideas was unbroken. The main issue of the discussion was swaraj or the nature of Indian Home Rule. So the title of the essay or booklet was Hind Swaraj or Indian Home Rule. As to what constitutes Swaraj or Home Rule takes him to the fundamental question of the test of true civilization which, in his view, is not material progress not its railways, progress in medical science industrialisation but its tendency and competence to elevate the moral being. On this criterion the western or the modern civilization, in his view, is satanic. It is a disease, for, it neither takes note of religion nor of morality. It caters only to the needs of the body at the cost of demand of the soul. The ills of the English people follow from the modern civilization. Their parliament which is believed to be the mother of parliaments, is like a sterile woman and a prostitute for, it has not done a single good thing and like a prostitute it is always under the control of ministers who change from time to time. His own experience in South Africa of the working of democratic institutions was not very happy. He had observed how a small minority of the Whites could use democracy to oppress the large majority of the natives and Indians. The railways have done no good to India. For, it has served only as an instrument of tightening the control of the British over India besides causing epidemics, recurrence of famines by the easy export of local products. Doctors and hospitals though claiming to fight disease, have worked only in the opposite direction by encouraging people for self-indulgence which is at the root of all diseases. The objective of the doctors is not service of the people but only enriching themselves. Similar is the case of lawyers whose professional interest demands greater dissensions among the people. No wonder they accentuated communal dissensions in India and have confirmed the authority of the English by upholding the English law and English law courts. So is the case of the system of education. To give millions merely knowledge of English is to enslave them. English knowing Indians have not hesitated to cheat and strike terror into people. For seeking justice in the court one has to employ English language as a medium. Is this not a sign of slavery. True education, on the other hand, is not merely learning of English language or of Western sciences but that which builds up the character and enables a person to bring his senses under subjection. For that our ancient school system, in his view, is enough. The real swaraj for India does not mean imitation of the Western civilization which the British rule has introduced into India but the removal of the civilization that has been brought by the British. 'Swaraj' means self-rule which can be attained only if Indians follow their own civilization which tends to raise the spirit and points out to man the path of duty. So the fault does not lie with Englishman but with the system under which they work and which they are introducing into our country. It is that which is enslaving us. If Englishmen cater to real needs of India on the basis of Indian civilization, then they should be welcome. For, real patriotism is not to drive out the British from India but to rid people of the crushing hold of men in authority whether they are Indian or English. "My patriotism, he reminds us all" does not teach me that I am to allow people to be crushed under the heel of Indian princes just as that of the English. By patriotism I mean the welfare of the whole people and if I could secure it at the hands of the English, I should bow down my head to them.

For him, India means its teeming millions on whom depends the existence of princes and all others, whether lawyers, politicians and the rest. But the crux of the whole problem is how India can attain self-rule or how her millions can get rid of their miserable existence or how an unjust law or any law repugnant to our conscience can be resisted. Two courses are open before the resisters. One, to take up arms against the unjust authority the other is passive resistance. The first represents brute force and the second soul force. It is an all sided sword; it blesses him who uses it and him against whom it is used. It is not the weapon of the weak. For, it requires the highest type of courage. He, who keeps death always as a bossom friend, or he who controls the death of others is a true warrior. The sacrifice of self is infinitely superior to sacrifice of others. Fearlessness is the quality of a passive resister.

On practical grounds, too, armed resistance to the British for self-rule is not free from many problems and dangers. For, they are splendidly armed and to pit Indians against them in arms, will take many years. Moreover to arm India on a large scale is to Europeanize India which means acceptance of Western civilization which is virtually the negation of self-rule. Consequently, those who are well-trained in that civilization will dominate over the rest of the Indians who will then fight for a few rights. If India selects the way of violence, then violence alone will rule. Peace and happiness will not be established. We can reap what we sow. Our means are likened to a seed and the end is the tree and there is just the same inviolable connection between the means and the end as there is between the seed and the tree. One is not likely to obtain the result flowing from the worship of God by laying oneself prostrate before Satan.

At the end of the discussion, he dwells upon the most controversial question, that is, the role of machinery in human life. He had to explain his position on this issue throughout his life and even his most devoted followers could not fully endorse his views on this issue. He condemns machinery as it is the symbol of modern civilization. For, it has made workers working in the mills slaves. There is hardly any difference between Indian mill owners and English mill owners. For, all rich men flourish through immorality. In India they support the British rule because of their own interest. Craze for machinery will make our country unhappy. It is the mill industry which has destroyed our sacred handlooms which supplied cheap cloth to millions of our people. It is the installation of big machines that have led to the rise of big cities with its concomitants tramways and railways that pose a big threat to the health of the people. So he concludes that there is no single good point in favour of machinery.

Hind Swaraj appeared serially in the 'Indian Opinion'. It was later on published in the form of a booklet covering twenty chapters. The Bombay Government prohibited its circulation when it attracted some attention in India. Gandhi replied it by publishing its English translation. But it did not impress all Indian leaders. Gandhi's own 'political guru' on reading it, looked upon it as so crude and hastily conceived that he remarked that Gandhi himself would destroy the book after spending a year in India. But that did not happen. Rather even after spending more than six years in India and at a time when he was at the height of his popularity he refused to withdraw nothing from it except one word-prostitute, in deference to a lady friend. He sent a copy of it to Tolstoy who in reply showed great interest in author's commitment to passive resistance which he considered not only of importance for India but for the whole humanity.

It is written in the form of a dialogue between the Reader and the Editor, who is the author himself. The reader represents any intelligent Indian who held current views on Indian politics, economics and the state of Indian society. The dialogue form is selected to drive home Gandhi's views on the solution of current Indian problems. He must have been impressed by Plato's style some of whose works he had read with great interest and appreciation.

The essay which is viewed by some as Gandhi's manifesto is a product of the amalgam of a lawyer and a prophet. As a lawyer the author exposes the weaker or the dangerous aspects of the case of the other side. And whatever he says is true if it is not weighed along with its stronger or its positive aspect. For instance, railways, at least in India, were not built for the good of the people. The motivation or urge behind it was commercial and political. So it became an instrument of imperialism and capitalism to exploit the resources of the country. If some good followed from it that was incidental. No doubt, it increased mobility but no one can deny that with that diseases and epidemics became more mobile. Today when the fear of Aids is shaking every individual all over the world, one can understand that easy and enhanced mobility cannot be accepted without reservations. The prophet in Gandhi warned us the health hazards of our dependence on locomotion. But as a lawyer he has not pointed out the advantages of railways and easy mobility. For it also served as an instrument for forging national unity and mass mobilisation for driving the British out of India. Similarly, if its use resulted in spreading diseases, it also made it easier to meet the challenge of epidemics by concerted efforts of the whole nation.

We are now faced with the problem of pollution resulting from the indiscriminate use of machinery for the exploitation of natural resources and mass production and use of automobiles transmitting noxious gases. The prophet in Gandhi warned us much before the world became conscious of it. It is true that he went too far in the condemnation of machinery in his zeal for pulling down the industrial civilization following from his consciousness of the dangers of our craze for machinery. But he forgot that the handloom or the bullock cart was also a machine. It was later on he explained that what he condemned was not the machine as such but only our craze for machinery which has led us to employ machines without any consideration of its utility to the society as a whole. When he was engaged in the reconstruction of Indian society, especially the rural society, he recommended several kinds of machines useful for rural society.

Similarly, he judges the doctors by a criterion which should be applicable to all professions. Very few join any profession for the service of society. Doctors can be no exception. It is certainly a matter of great comfort to a patient if the doctor attending on him is inspired by a missionary zeal. But such persons are rare in a society where we value material possessions more than ethical norms. But as a prophet he has told us that it is better to seek the prevention of a disease through self-control than seek a medicine for the cure of an ailment resulting from self-indulgence. Whatever he has said about the lawyers is true to a great extent. For, they will starve if there are no disputes in society. But who will fight for the rights of those who suffer under an unjust system? As a lawyer he himself made efforts to protect the rights of the poor and helpless Indians in South Africa.

Hind Swaraj is considered by several admirers of Gandhi as the quintessence of his philosophy. It is so if one keeps in view the spirit underlying it. For he was in search of a social system which ensures maximum freedom to an individual, makes him self-reliant and enables him to satisfy both his material and spiritual needs in co-operation with other members of society. With experience he realized that neither parliament, nor railways nor all the industrial establishments had to be given up. But individual freedom can be protected if individual is never lost sight of in the process of development. The core of the Hind Swaraj is still valid for the whole humanity. For it reminds us that the measuring rod of a civilization is morality. But the propelling force of industrial civilization "is hunger for wealth and greedy pursuit of worldly pleasures." Another point that the Hind Swaraj lays emphasis on is that a country is not merely a geographical configuration but it consists of its people both rich and poor and patriotism means welfare of all the people.

Notes and References

1. C.W., Vol. LXXI, p. 238.
2. Most of the references are from the Hind Swaraj.

9

Power of Satyagraha

On his return from England Gandhi was pushed into a grim struggle. The White Government was bent upon breaking the backbone of the movement by employing all possible harsh measures. About 2500 had been sentenced to hard labour. About a thousand had been ruined and a thousand had left the colony. However, one concrete gain of the struggle was that it caught the attention of the nationalist India. Gandhi became an object of admiration and reverence. He was held in awe by some leaders for his devotion to public work and his life style. His name was even suggested for the Presidentship of the Congress by the Bengal Provincial Congress Committee in 1909.[1] At its session at Lahore in December 1909, Gokhale, while paying tribute to him, referred to him as "a man who may be well described as man among men, a hero among heroes, a patriot amongst patriots and we may well say that in him Indian humanity at the present time has really reached its high watermark."[2]

Money started pouring in for the help of the Satyagrahis in South Africa from all the communities in India—Hindus, Muslim, Parsis. Even when Gandhi stepped on the soil of Capetown on his return from London he received the cable that the great Indian industrialist Ratanji Tata, had sent Rs 25000[3] for the Satyagrahis and in January next year it was followed by another donation of the same amount.[4] The Nizam of Hyderabad sent Rs 2500[5] and the Aga Khan collected Rs. 3000[6] for the Passive Resistance. The Congress also sent money for the cause. But all these contributions were not sufficient to meet the needs of the Satyagrahis. The struggle was becoming a heavy financial burden on

Gandhi's dwindling financial resources as his preoccupation with it hardly left any time for his legal practice. The struggle became more vexatious and prolonged on coming into existence of the Union of South Africa by the merging of all the colonies into one political union, in 1910. For, the intensity of the struggle that had varied from time to time in the four colonies of South Africa became a central issue of the new Government of the Union, though the conflict continued to be centred in Transvaal where Gandhi was heading the struggle. In such a situation it became imperative for him to think of a plan to provide some kind of subsistence to the families of those who had been engaged in the struggle. Financial aid in the form of monthly allowance in cash was beyond his financial resources. It appeared more economical to him if all the distressed families lived together. He had the Phoenix settlement where the Satyagrah families could be lodged. But it was very far from Johannesburg where the struggle at that time was at its height. In this predicament his friend Kallenback, a German architect who had thrown his lot in Gandhi's struggle, came to his rescue. He purchased 1,100 acre farm twenty-one miles from Johannesburg and gave it rent free for the use of the Satyagrahis. Both Gandhi and Kallenback stayed there. It was a pragmatic decision. But it gave Gandhi another opportunity of making an experiment in community living. This estate was Christened as the Tolstoy Farm—a tribute to the Russian philosopher whose 'Kingdom of God is within You' and the 'Gospel in Brief' had left a deep mark on Gandhi's view of religion. This was the time when letters were exchanged between them and Tolstoy admired Gandhi's non-violent struggle "as the most important of all the work now being done in the world."[7] Tolstoy Farm had one thousand fruit bearing trees and a small house at the foot of a hill with accommodation for half a dozen people. New structures of corrugated iron were put up on the farm and the Satyagrahi families were invited to settle there. The number of residents of this settlement varied between fifty and seventy five. They hailed from different parts of India and followed different religions. In a way it was a mini India inhabited by people speaking different languages and following different religions. The efforts of both Gandhi and Kallenback were to make it self-sufficient. All were served by a vegetarian kitchen, though Gandhi initially gave choice to the inmates to have non-vegetarian food. But in consideration of Gandhi's faith, they all agreed to have vegetarian food. All were required to do manual labour. The kitchen was under the charge of women. Among them were some well-to-do persons who were not accustomed to doing manual labour. But they readily adjusted themselves to the new situation. "The weak", observed their leader, "became strong on Tolstoy Farm and labour proved to be a tonic for all."[8] Kallenback learnt the art of shoe-making in a German Catholic monastery and taught it to Gandhi and other inmates of the Farm. Efforts were made to make all requirements, from boxes to benches, on the farm as self-sufficiency to Gandhi was a condition for the success of the struggle. For, in his view, they could carry on the struggle for an indefinite period if they could make the farm a busy hive of industry and self-supporting. Life, on the farm, therefore, was very hard and Gandhi wanted all to share this hardship in order to train themselves for Satyagraha. Kallenback who had been brought up in the lap of luxury, readily accepted this way of life. He was head of the carpentry department of the farm. He also assisted Gandhi in providing education to the children on the farm. Gandhi made an experiment with co-education. The class that he taught had children of all ages, boys and girls from seven years of age to young men of twenty and young girls of twelve. He divide the class into two sections, the Gujarati section to be taught through the medium of Gujarati and the rest through English. He was teaching through the narration of stories. However, some knowledge of history, geography and arithmetic was also imparted. No text books were used. For, the main objective of education was building of character.

Experiment of Tolstoy Farm was another milestone in the lawyer's spiritual growth. Voluntary poverty appeared to him as the right road towards spiritual happiness. Sudhama, a poor Brahmana playmate boy of Lord Krishan who preferred virtuous life to the life of luxury even when his friend was a king, and Narasimha Mehta became his ideals. He had practically abandoned his legal practice and had converted the Phoenix Farm together with buildings and machinery valued at about five thousand pounds into a trust. The fee of three hundred pounds sent by a client for fighting his son's case was also used for public purposes.[9]

On learning the cruel treatment accorded to cows in Calcutta in extracting the last drop of milk from them, he along with Kallenback gave up milk and both of them restricted themselves to a diet of olive oil and fresh dried fruit, raw groundnuts, bananas, dates and lemons. This was understandable as it could be argued as the right step for preventing cruelty to the cows. But the lawyer in Gandhi was on a slippery ground when he, later on, argued that cow's milk was not permissible to a vegetarian because it was the essence of beef. For it could be argued that all children were cannibals as mother's milk could be viewed in the same way as the essence of human flesh. This is how young

Radhakrishnan as a teacher of philosophy showed the hollowness of his argument on his first meeting in Madras when Gandhi advised him not to drink milk.[10] Both Gandhi and Kallenback gave up cooked food and to demonstrate that this change in his diet had no effect on his health and efficiency, Gandhi would walk forty miles a day.

The hard life of the Tolstoy Farm was a training ground for Satyagrahis. However, efforts were afoot in the year 1911 for some kind of settlement between the Union Government and Gandhi. Letters were exchanged between him and Smuts and provisional settlement was arrived at. The Union Government was ready to repeal Act 2 of 1907 and the exclusion of the Indians was to be effected not on the basis of racial discrimination but by providing a rigorous education test. As a result, all the Satyagrahis were released on June 1. At home the Indian National Congress put pressure on the Government of India to abolish the system of indentured labour. Gandhi had been requesting Gokhale to visit South Africa in order to examine the situation himself. So in consultation with the Secretary of State, he went to South Africa in October 1912. The former had in the mean time informed the Union Government of the high position held by Gokhale as a member of the Imperial Legislature which assured him official co-operation and facility during his journey in South Africa. Gandhi planned a heavy programme for the Indian dignitary and acted as his secretary during his tour in South Africa. The Union Government offered warm hospitality to him and placed the state railway saloon at his disposal. The meetings he addressed were attended both by Indians and Europeans. The Mayor of Johannesburg placed his car at his disposal during his stay in the city. At the meetings addresses were showered on him. At one of the meetings in Johannesburg, Gandhi made an unusual request to Gokhale that made him laugh. For, he asked him to speak in Marathi which he would translate into Hindi as there were several Konkani Muslims and some Maharashtrian Hindus among the audience. For, Gokhale had no appreciation for Gandhi's knowledge of Hindi and Marathi and his offer of translating Marathi speech into Hindi was quite amusing to him. But Gandhi without claiming any proficiency in these languages assured him that he would be able to communicate the substance of the speech in Hindi. Gokhale agreed and this experiment worked well at a number of places during Gokhale's tour of South Africa. It catered to the national pride of Gandhi since Indian languages had been given some importance in South Africa. Gokhale also visited the Tolstoy Farm where he stayed for four days from 2nd to 4th November. Gandhi and Kallenback attended on him. The former nursed and cooked for him and ironed his scarf. At the end of the tour, the Indian dignitary had a conference with the Ministers of the Union Government. On his return from the meeting he told Gandhi that their demands would be mostly conceded. The Black Act would be repealed, the racial bar would be removed from immigration law and three pound tax would be abolished. So he advised Gandhi to return to his country as he would be no more needed for carrying on the struggle. But Gandhi had his own apprehensions, for, he knew very well the types of politicians and statesmen he was confronted within South Africa. Possibly Gokhale carried the wrong impression because of the conciliatory tone of Smuts and other Ministers of the Union Government. Gandhi, too, had been expecting some steps from the Union Government for the removal of certain disabilities from the Indians. May be Smuts and his party were unable to resist the pressure of diehard Europeans in South Africa who were not ready to tolerate the Indians in their country at any cost or condition. Gandhi's fear, therefore, turned out to be true. The repeal of three pound tax was not honoured. Nor was any vacation taken to lighten the disabilities on the Indians. Rather a decision of the Supreme Court about the legal validity of Indian marriages made all Indians in South Africa nervours. A Muslim resident of Port Elizabeth Hassan Esop had married in India Bai Mariam in 1908. He returned in 1909 without her. He again went to India in 1912 and returned with his wife. But the immigration officer refused her immigration and ordered that she be sent back to India. The application of the husband restraining the government from deporting his wife was refused by the Supreme Court on March 14, 1913. The government refused to intervene on Gandhi's request to find a way out of this provocative situation. In his view the meaning of the judgement is that "every Hindu and Mohammedan wife is in South Africa illegally married and, therefore, at the mercy of the government whose grace alone can enable her to remain in the country." In other words, all marriages which had not been celebrated according to Christian rites were invalid. It implied that all women whose marriages had been according to Hindu, Muslim or Parsi rites were only concubines. This was an intolerable situation for Indian families and this brought the Indian women into the Satyagraha struggle in South Africa. So at a mass meeting held at the Hamida Islamic Society's hall in Johannesburg on March 30, 1913 Gandhi declared while referring to this judgement of Justice Searle "It will become the bounden duty of the Indian community, for the protection of its womanhood and its honour to adopt passive resistance."[11] The Indian leader selected a very emotional and sensitive issue for his next phase of struggle. So the Transvaal Indian Women's Association informed the Minister of the Interior that they would offer passive resistance and suffer imprisonment rather than suffer the indignity to which the Searle judgement subjected them. With a view to broaden the base of his struggle and make his demands clear and definite, he listed the following demands:

(i) Abolition of three pound tax,
(ii) Acceptance of the legal validity of all monogamous marriages performed according to Indian rites,
(iii) Retention of the right of South Africa born Indians to enter the Cape by the reason of birth,
(iv) A declaration that existing laws such as the Transvaal land Township Act, the Licensing laws of the Cape and Natal and the Immigration Act shall be administered in a liberal spirit and with due regard to vested rights.

In fact, the major issues of the struggle this time were the three pounds tax and the recognition of monogamous Indian marriages. In this way he kept the doors of compromise open. In fact, he carried on negotiations for an honourable compromise till the launching of the struggle.

Though Gandhi was ready to start his movement with a small trusted band of followers and associates (16 at best), he was sure that the struggle this time would enfold all the Indians in South Africa. He, therefore advised the Indians in Natal and Free state to prepare themselves for struggle by making arrangements for the families of those whose members would offer themselves for arrest.

The strategy, initially, was the same which was employed during the earlier struggle. But the author of Satyagraha knew that it could take a new turn and develop into a mass movement of the Indians in South Africa with the participation of women in the movement. The Satyagrahis were either to enter the border of any province without permits or to hawk in the streets without licences and offer themselves for arrest. They then would refuse to give particulars of their names and addresses which was another offence. Women Satyagrahis were advised that if they were not arrested on entering Natal, they should move to New Castle a great coal mining centre in Natal where the majority of labourers were from Madras and appeal to them to go on strike. A pioneer party from Phoenix consisting of twelve men and four women including Gandhi's wife

Kasturba tried to enter Transvaal. They were arrested at the border and sentenced to three months imprisonment. A second batch went from the Tolstoy Farm of eleven persons to enter Natal. They were not arrested and according to the plan, women moved to New Castle where the workers struck work on the appeal of women. This made the authorities nervous and harsh. Seventy eight workers and women Satyagrahis were arrested. As a result Indian workers in other collieries went on strike. The owners of the mines stopped the lights and water of the quaters where the workers were lodged. Notices to quit were given to many workers as the tenements were built by the owners. Gandhi rushed to New Castle and the workers in large number came to him. He asked them to join his movement and live with him so long as the strike lasted. The number of strikers went on increasing. The leader was now at the end of his tether as the government was in no mood to arrest them and he had not sufficient money to provide food and shelter to such a large number of workers who had struck work and joined his movement. His own financial resources were at the lowest ebb and money had not yet started coming from India. The Indian traders in Natal were afraid of openly offending the owners of the mines by supporting the movement because of their trading relations with them. There was war of nerves. Transvaal border was at a great distance and there was no money for railway fare. So the choice left to the leader was to march on foot with the army of 2,037 men, 127 women and 27 children (5000 according to Gandhi, though he was not sure about the exact number) from New Castle on November 6, 1913 to Charlestown, close to the border of Transvaal, a distance of 36 miles on a ration of a pound and a half of bread and an ounce of sugar for each, though Gandhi anticipated replenishment of their ration on the way by the Indian traders. The marchers were strictly instructed not to touch anyone's property on the way and not resist if they were flogged, abused or arrested by the officials. They were to continue marching even if their leader was arrested. Gandhi showed great courage in leading this army of illiterate persons who were not accustomed to the discipline of Satyagraha. There were threats from certain ultra militant white groups. But the non-violent army of Gandhi passed through the 'dangerous zones' peacefully. Rather his patience and good will for the Whites produced dividends. The European bakers agreed to supply bread to the marchers at the usual rates of excellent flour and Gandhi viewed this offer as a great success of Satyagraha that rouses the dormant feeling of love in the opponents. On reaching Charlestown the marchers were looked after by the Indian traders. No untoward incident happened during the journey except a child fell from the arms of his mother while crossing a small stream and drowned. On crossing the border of Transvaal Gandhi was twice arrested but bailed out and he was able to join the strikers. He applied for bail with a view to guide the campaign. Everything moved in accordance with his plan. His aim was to take the marchers to Tolstoy Farm if the Government failed to arrest them. But he was rearrested, tried and fined sixty pounds or nine months' rigorous imprisonment under the Natal Indenture Law. But he chose to go to jail. However, during the campaign, he continued making efforts for an honourable compromise. But he was rebuffed . Even before starting the long march he responded to the invitation of the mine owners at Durban for the exchange of views.

After the arrest of their leader, the Government came down heavily on the marchers. They were all arrested and sent back to Natal where they were tried and sentenced for rigorous imprisonment. The authorities hit upon an ingenuous plan of keeping the mines working by declaring the mine compounds as out states of Dundee and New Castle jails where the Europeans were appointed as warders and the work in the mines by Indian prisoners was declared as part of the sentence. When the prisoners refused to observer this order, they were brutally punished. Gandhi, too, was put to great hardship in the jail. He was made to dig stones and sweep the compound in the Volkshurt jail. The hard life of the prison had its own reward. For, he acquired great facility in writing with his left hand, too as he was quite often so tired after day's hard labour that he could not move his right hand. The warder shouted at him incessantly when he returned to his cell. His whole body was so stiff with pain that he could scarcely move. In Pretoria jail he was lodged in a small dark cell, was denied a bench and refused permission to walk in the cell. He was marched to the court with handcuffs and monacles. He faced all these indignities with great patience. Rather he had happy memories of Bloemfontein jail where the medical officer tried to provide him with all kinds of fruit as he was on fruitarian diet and tried to make his stay in the jail comfortable to the annoyance of the jailer.

However, this blood and iron policy of the Government boomeranged as the news of the harsh treatment meted out to the Indians in the jails in South Africa agitated the Indian labourers in South Africa who struck work in sympathy with the satyagrahi prisoners. The government tried to meet this challenge by opening fire upon the striking workers. In India, Gokhale broadcast the news of these outrages from his sick bed. Even the Viceroy felt indignant and identified himself with the sentiments of the Indians. In a speech in Madras, he severely criticised the South African Government and defended the action of the Satyagrahis. It raised his image in India that shocked the South African Government that unsuccessfully pressed on the British cabinet to recall the Viceroy. Gokhale sent C.F. Andrews and Pearson to South Africa on learning that all the persons guiding the movement had been arrested. Andrews was an English missionary who came to India in 1904 and taught at St. Stephens in Delhi. He fought against the British attitude of exclusiveness. Though completely devoted to Christ, he considered service of the poor, servile and the down trodden as true missionary work. "The true way, 'he said is to empty ourselves of the west to be the citizen of no country' but Christian pure and simple like the first disciples."[12] As a priest and missionary, he impressed the Viceroy Lord Hardinge and no wonder if behind the Viceroy's famous speech at Madras expressing his sympathy with the Indians in South Africa was the mind of Andrews. He had already administered many shocks to a number of diehard British administrators in India by his active sympathy with the aspirations of Indian nationalists.

Both Andrews and Pearson had not seen Gandhi earlier and their first dramatic meeting with the Indian leader in South Africa raised a controversy in South Africa. On their arrival, many Indians including Gandhi and Polak had come to receive them. Andrews noticed Gandhi in the crowd but did not move towards him thinking that he was an ordinary Indian Sadhu as Gandhi was dressed like an ordinary labourer wearing a kurta and a loin cloth and without foot wear, the dress that he imposed upon himself as a penance on learning the shooting of innocent labourers during the strike. But being keen to meet Gandhi he asked Polak about him who smilingly replied, "you have already met him" and pointed his finger towards that Sadhu. With reverence, Andrews moved towards that Sadhu and touched his feet. The Whites watching this scene were shocked. For, a European had bowed to a man who was in their eyes belonged to an inferior race. The White Press in South Africa attacked him for this so-called blasphemy. But more shocking must have been Andrews rejoinder "I saw Christ in Gandhi, a renunciation incarnation."[13]

The British press and the Secretary of State showed sympathy with the struggle of the Indians in South Africa. The Union Government was caught in the net of their own. To wriggle out of it, the Government appointed a commission with Justice Sir W. Solomon as its chairman to inquire into the causes of the Natal Indian strike. The Commission called upon the Government of India to give evidence and recommended the release of Gandhi, Polak and Kallenback who were set free on December

18, 1913. Many had lost their lives during the Satyagraha and the leader, therefore, as penance adopted the dress of an ordinary Indian labourer. Among those who died during the struggle was Harbat Singh aged seventy five who died in jail. A young girl Valliamma died within a few days of her release. Gandhi visited her when she was confined to bed and was touched by her pride in dying for the country. On her death Indians resolved to erect Valliamma Hall in her memory. However, Gandhi was not satisfied with the personnel of the Commission since in his opinion its two members were known to have anti-Indian bias. So he wrote to Gokhale that it was a packed body intended to hoodwink the public in England and India. But as a practical measure he did not seek their removal but only wanted the co-option of some impartial persons on the Commission. He also sought the release of all Satyagrahi prisoners. He threatened to boycott the Commission and start satyagraha again by courting arrest if his demands were not complied with. Gokhale was annoyed at this attitude of Gandhi. But Andrews removed the irritant in the relation between the two by reasserting Gandhi's stand that Satyagrahis were bound by a pledge to which "no exception can be taken" and his pledge was at the root of Gandhi's threat of boycotting the Commission.

Just at a time when Gandhi was contemplating to commence the march to Transvaal again as a part of Satyagraha there was great strike of the European employees of the railways of the union. This appeared to many persons as a great opportunity for the Indian Satyagrahis to embarrass the Government and snatch a few concessions. But Gandhi refused to take advantage of the difficulty of the opponent. This decision was a great act of statesmanship. For, it earned for the leader of the Satyagrahis sympathy and goodwill for him of the Europeans in South Africa as well as people of England. Lord Ampthill congratulated Gandhi on this decision. It created favourable atmosphere for a settlement. General Smuts agreed to grant an interview to Gandhi. Though he was unwilling to co-opt another member holding the confidence of Indians in the Commission, he was inclined to appreciate the position of the Indians. This short interview was followed by many more interviews and exchange of letters. The negotiations reached a deadlock over the insertion of a phrase in the settlement by Smuts to which Gandhi would not agree. Situation became very critical as Gandhi received a telegram that his wife was seriously ill in Durban. But he refused to go to Durban to see his wife at that moment when his public duty demanded his presence some where else. Just at that time Andrews overcame all hurdles to the settlement by finding an alternative phrase which was acceptable to both Gandhi and Smuts.[14] During the talks Pearson noticed how hard was meek and self-effacing Gandhi. For, he felt that no one could change his mind or no amount of discussion could change the decision he had taken. Thus when the talks had reached a crucial stage Gokhale was seriously ill in India. He was sending him telegrams every day to sign the pact with Smuts. Gandhi knew that his refusal might hasten Gokhale's death. But this had no effect on him. However when affairs had been finally arranged he should have hurried back to his wife. But not at all. He refused to go till he had signed the pact with Smuts. When Pearson told this story to Romain Rolland, the latter remarked "he has turned out to be a stone thrown into the duck pond."[15] The result of the negotiations was the provisional settlement which conceded some of the major demands of the Indians. In the meantime the Commission of Enquiry also made certain recommendations for the removal of some of the grievances of the Indians. The Indian Relief Act was passed by the South African Parliament in pursuance of the recommendations of the Commission and the provisional settlement. The three pound tax on the ex-indentured labourers was abolished; marriages performed according to Indian rites were legalized. A domicile certificate bearing the holder's thumbs impression was to be considered as sufficient evidence of the right to enter the union of South Africa. According to the settlement certain outstanding difficulties were to be removed by an administrative action. Assurance was given that government would create no impediment to the entrance into the Union of existing plural wives of domiciled Indians. A discharge certificate would be issued to all indentured or reindentured Indians upon completion of their period of service. Bonafide passive resisters would not in the future have their convictions used against them by the Government. Educated Indians were to be allowed to enter the Cape Province. However there remained many more irritants and restrictions on the Indians. The system of location continued by which the Indians were forced to live and trade in separate localities. Similarly the Gold Law, trade licensing laws, the bar on the purchase of landed property continued embarrassing the Indians. Gandhi did not insist on the abolition of all the restrictions on the Indians at that time as Satyagraha had been started with a limited objective. So in that limited context, the movement was a success. For, according to its leader, it was against the principle of Satyagraha to enhance the original demands during the struggle or on its successful termination. Nevertheless he hoped that the spirit of goodwill which pervaded the settlement created by his

European in South Africa as well as the quality of life that he experienced there impelled him to know himself. It is this quest that led him to understand his deepest convictions, his own religion and its relations with other religions, his responsibility as an Indian in a country where most of his countrymen were subjected to humiliation and his role and duty as a subject of the British Empire. It is this pursuit that led him search for his own identity and in the process he realised that his identity as a separate being was merely an illusion and that his real would surface when he "is free from the sense of I and mine and is unconscious of his duality as a separate being," More specifically his self-realisation was rooted in his realisation of the relationship of his self with other selves. In this process he discovered that to have a glimpse of the universal he must reduce himself to zero as an individual. It is this endeavour that led him to surrender gradually his worldly possessions and to move from the circle of his family to a bigger circle of human relationships. In this process of enlightenment the pursuits and achievements of his own forefathers or of his family fell off in his eyes. He was more or less an agnostic when he left India in 1893 and was transformed into a unique spiritual figure when he left the shores of South Africa in 1914. When he left India, he considered it below his dignity as a barrister to travel in any class other than first class, though he was to work in South Africa more or less as a clerk of a firm. But when he left South Africa after about two decades of stay and struggle there, he was proud to travel as a third class passenger, though he was no ordinary passenger as he was known to the topmost politicians and statesmen in South Africa, England and India. His journey from an ordinary lawyer to a Mahatma was long and arduous. For a long time he was the 'bhai' (brother) of the fellow Indians in South Africa, when he was in the thick of the battle, he was 'Karmavir Gandhi'. He was 'Bapu' to all those who lived with him as members of his family. Finally, his sufferings and sacrifices for others, his preference for the life of poverty, his unique character and spiritual mission held every body in awe and he was viewed not an ordinary soul but a great soul a 'Mahatma'. Thus, South Africa forged Mohandas a patriot, an author of a unique technique for fighting injustice, a lover of mankind and a unique religious leader whose religion embraced all religions of the world.

Accompanied by Kasturba and Kallenback, he had a pleasant journey to England. The steamer supplied them the fruitarian diet and provided them ample facilities during the voyage. Kallenback must have realized that to travel with a Mahatma was not so easy. For he had to throw into the sea his seven pound binacular as Gandhi argued with him that to possess such an expensive article was not in accord with their ideal of simplicity. On reaching London Gandhi discovered that Gokhale whom he was anxious to see, had been stranded in Paris as war had broken out two days before he reached London. So he decided to wait for him there. In the meantime some Indian leaders who happened to be there organized a reception for him which was attended by some of his British admirers. The chairman of the reception committee was Bhupendranath Basu, head of the Indian National Congress deputation to the India Office. Other notables were Sinha, Lajpat Rai, Ameer Ali, Jinnah, etc. Anand K. Comarswami and Jinnah paid tributes to him for his heroic fight in South Africa. Sorojini Naidu's first meeting with him produced a dramatic and comic situation as the two were cast in different moulds. She in her mid-thirties, was wearing a costly sari and was bedecked with jewels. After half an hour effort she located his lodging in an obscure part of Kenisgton in London. Seated on the floor on a black prison blanket, he was eating "messy meal of squashed tomatoes and olive oil out of wooden prison bowl. Around him were ranged some battered tins of parched groundnuts and tasteless biscuits. It was virtually impossible for her to restrain her laughter on seeing this small man with shaven head. She was amused. It must have crossed her mind "Is this man whom Gokhale described as a man who makes heroes out of clay, or a crusader who waged a non-violent war against Smuts". But the little man was not surprised. He welcomed her with a smiling face. The poetess discovered a strong man in the frail body when he talked to her. The involvement of England in the war upset Gandhi's programme of returning to his motherland as early as possible. Though committed to non-violence, he felt he had the responsibility of sharing the burden of an Empire of which he claimed to be a member and getting his food in war time in London because of the protection provided by the English Navy. He, therefore, decided to organize an ambulance corps to nurse the wounded in the war, though he was fully conscious that even this act of first aid amounted to supporting war and violence. In pursuance of this decision, a circular letter was sent to the Indians who were in London suggesting that they should place their services unconditionally at the service of their motherland and the Empire. An unconditional service during war could not be reconciled to his commitment to non-violence. It is true that the only service he could render was nursing of wounded since he was incapable of handling a gun. But what about others? They could be asked to enlist themselves in the army and given training in the handling of arms. However, the Mahatma was saved from the official drift of the arguments of unconditional service as the authorities in England could understand what he meant and assigned to his men only the task of nursing of the wounded. But he did confront this situation after some time during the war.

Some of his admirers in South Africa were surprised by this offer of their hero. But he defended his decision like a good lawyer. The burden of his arguments was that pure non-violence was possible in a state of perfection and so long as he was imperfect and was depending upon political authority for his life and comforts, he had the responsibility of sharing its burden.

Though such arguments have their pitfalls at the logical plane, it was a practical approach of a person who was trying to carry the society with him in his search for a non-violent order. However, in 1928 in a mood of self-introspection he told a correspondent who had questioned his participation in the world war, that he was prompted by mixed motives in his offer to the British at that time. The first was to win over the British people by making them feel that he was their friend and it was an important condition for the success of non-violence. For, as an individual opposed to war, "I had no status for offering effective non-violent resistance which can follow real disinterested service, the other was to qualify for Swaraj through the good offices of the statesmen of the Empire as at that time he was a believer in the Empire."[20] Here Gandhi was more a patriot than an apostle of non-violence, more practical than a seeker of an ideal. He was a unique combination of a patriot, prophet and a lawyer. He could make a case for all his moves which could surprise his friends and followers.

The authorities in England well appreciated the offer of Gandhi. The members of his ambulance corps were given six weeks' training in first aid. Indian women volunteers including Kasturbai and Sorojini Naidu were assigned the task of making clothes for the soldiers. Gandhi's health was delicate mostly because of three weeks fast that he had to undertake at Phoenix as penance for the ethical fall of some of the inmates in his settlement. But he did make some efforts to undergo the military training which the members of the ambulance corps were required to have according to the rules. He looked elegant in the European dress with topcoat and hat. However, he fell ill and was confined to bed for several days. The doctors diagnosed pleurisy and his condition worsened because of his dietetic experiments. He was completely avoiding milk, cereals, pulses. His diet consisted mostly of groundnuts, bananas, lemon, tomatoes, olive oil and grapes. However, on Gokhale's persuasion, who had returned to England, he agreed to take the food prescribed by the doctors except milk and meat. But there was no improvement in his health and so on the advice of friends and the under-secretary of state Mr. Roberts he decided to return to India. Kallenbach who had come with him to England to accompany him to India could not get his passport being a German in spite of Roberts' request to the Government of India. On December 19, 1914, he sailed for India with his wife in second class as third class passage was not available on P.&O. Steamers.

Notes and References

1. Tendulkar, D.G., Mahatma (Life of Mohandas Karamchand Gandhi), (Publication Division), Vol. I, p. 111.
2. *Ibid.*, p. 112.
3. *Ibid.*, p. 111.
4. *Ibid.*, p. 112.
5. *Ibid.*
6. *Ibid.*
7. *Ibid.*, Vol. I, p. 123.
8. Gandhi, M.K., Satyagraha in South Africa, p. 238.
9. C.W., Vol. XI, p. 61.
10. Quoted in S. Gopal, Radhakrishna, A Biography, p. 28.
11. Tendulkar, *op. cit.*, Vol. I, p. 133.
12. Chaturvedi, and Sykes Marjorie, Charles Freera Andrews first published in G.B. 1949 reprint in India, 1971, p. 91.
13. Nayyar, Sushila, *op. cit*, p. 704.
14. Reminiscences of Andrews (unpublished) quoted in Karjorie Sykes, *op. cit.*, p. 97.
15. Romain Rolland and Gandhi Correspondence (Publication Division), 1976, p. 16.
16. Tendulkar, *op. cit.*, Vol. I, p. 150.
17. Gandhi, Prabhudas, *op. cit.*, p. 181.
18. C.W., Vol. XII, p. 438.
19. *Ibid.*, Vol. XII, p. 461.
20. C.W., Vol. XXXVIII, p. 196.

PART II

THE GREAT TRANSFORMATION

10

Political Apprenticeship in India

The Mahatma landed in Bombay on January 9, 1915. He was given a hero's welcome. Dressed in Swadeshi clothes—a Kathiawadi cloak, turban and dhoti, he would have been taken as a Gujarati Bania, had his return not been widely publicized. He had one front tooth missing on the left side. Possibly because of his food habits, his teeth started giving trouble to him and even in his early thirties some of his teeth had to be removed and by 1936 his toothless laugh was an amusing sight for his admirers. Several functions were organized to honour him. Topmost Indian leaders such as Pherozeshah Mehta, Jinnah, Tilak, etc. welcome him. At one of the meetings on January 27, he was described as 'Jagat Vandaniya Mahatma' in a Sanskrit address.[1] But all this did not turn his head and divest him of his characteristic humility. At one of the meetings Tilak was invited to attend but he said he would do so only if Gandhi had no objection to his presence as it was likely to embarrass the loyalists attending the meeting. But Gandhi not only welcomed him when he came but got down from the platform and embraced him in the Indian fashion and seated him in the chair on the platform. At another meeting, the Mahatma fell prostrate at the feet of Pherozeshah Mehta in accordance with the ancient Indian practice of greeting elderly persons. In fact, Gandhi made no distinction between the followers of the father of Indian urest (Tilak) and those who claimed to be loyalists and regarded the British rule as a divine dispensation, while paying tributes to the Indian leadership. He valued the contributions of both the sections of the Indian

National Congress, known as the Extremists and the Moderates.

His replies to the welcome addresses also revealed his humility. For, he mostly reiterated that he could not do any thing without the sacrifices made by the thousands of Indians in South Africa who participated with great enthusiasm in all the movements launched by him. Though uneducated and unknown, they were worthiest of all for their love of their country and sacrifice making him feel at home amongst them. At a special reception given by the Gujarati community in Bombay, he replied in Gujarati, though most of the speeches delivered in his honour were in English. This showed that as a leader he was cast in a different mould. In a way he had opened his campaign for the use of Indian languages in a gathering where the audience was familiar with an Indian language. The use of English language as a medium of communication was, in his view, violation for the principle of Swadeshi with which most of the leaders of the Congress were committed. Commitment to Swadeshi, in his view, obliged the Indian leaders to learn as many Indian languages as possible. He himself started learning Tamil while he was in South Africa since a large number of his volunteers understood only that language. On his arrival in India he sent his son and nephew to Madras to acquire proficiency in Tamil in order to teach it to the students in the Ashram.

His technique of fighting injustice by non-violent action also obliged him to remain in touch with the Government hierarchy in order to avoid any misunderstanding with the Government in any conflict-situation. He, therefore, met the Governor of Bombay Lord Willingdon who advised him to contact him first before taking any action in which his Government was involved. In his meeting with the Viceroy, Lord Hardinge, he paid tributes to him addressing him as a noble Viceroy for his valuable help in the struggle of the Indians in South Africa.[2]

After attending several functions and meetings at Bombay, he left for Poona to meet his mentor Gokhale where he was entertained with fruits and nuts. Gokhale wanted him to join the servants of India Society and Gandhi, too, was equally anxious for it. But this proposal divided the society. When the issue of his admission was under discussion, several members made it plain that they were poles apart from him in several vital matters and the Mahatma, according to Sastri, sat there like a man rebuked. He withdrew his name as he never wanted to embarrass the colleagues and followers of the person whom he claimed to be his political 'guru'. Srinivasa Sastri who became President of the Society after Gokhale's death while opposing his entry to the Society, expressed his feeling thus "Still our hearts trembled as well as grieved when we told him that it was best for both of us to remain apart and pursue our several courses."[3]

During Gandhi's absence from his mother country, political conditions in India had changed enormously. New political alignments had taken place. The Moderates headed by Pherozeshah Mehta, S.N. Bannerji, Gokhale did not represent the spirit that was agitating the minds of the youth. The leader of the Extremist group, Tilak had spent long years of exile in Mandalay and had been released only a few months before Gandhi's arrival in India and his close associate Aurobindo Ghosh had retired to Pondicherry in search of the spiritual vision which the Indian sages of the yore had seen. Mrs Besant was advocating Home Rule for India. Jinnah and Lajpat Rai were in agreement with her approach. She had stirred the minds of the younger generations by her forceful voice. However, the war which was threatening the existence of England as a great power had thrown under the carpet all the seeming differences of leadership of different shades and hues as all of them were declaring their loyalty to the British Empire, for it was viewed as a road to freedom. This was the right moment for bringing on the common platform both the Extremists and the Moderates and Mrs. Besant's efforts bore fruit after a temporary set back. Gokhale was aware of Gandhi's ignorance of the political currents blowing in India on his return to India. So he took promise from him not to express his opinions on political matters in India at least for a year. During this period he was advised to move round India to feel the pulse of political India. So from Poona Gandhi went to Rajkot and Porbandar to see his relatives and to console the widows in the family whose maintenance had become his responsibility. His nephew Magan Lal had arrived with a party of 28 inmates of the Phoenix. They were first sent to Gurukul under the charge of Swami Sharaddhananda who had been introduced to Gandhi by Andrews even before his arrival in India. Later on these boys were sent to Tagore's Santiniketan. From Rajkot, he went to Santiniketan along with his wife on February 17. At this stage he made some changes in his dress. He gave up using the scarf, the turban and the cloak and wore a cap. But the poet was on tour and in his absence he was welcomed by the teachers and students of the institute. The visit was fruitful as he met there his future colleagues and admirers Kaka Kalelkar and J.B. Kriplani. The former was teaching Sanskrit there and was known as Brahmachari Dattatreya. Kriplani who was struck by the intensity of the character of Gandhi was introduced to him by Kalelkar. He appeared to him to "be a man who could, if need be stand alone, provided he was convinced that the course of action he was following was the right one." He was austere and puritanic but he was not censorious. Though he admired Gandhi, he did not surrender his judgement to the Mahatma. For, when Gandhi sent the prospectus of the Ashram for his comments, Kriplani could not accept Gandhi's view that husband and wife should consider themselves as brother and sister.[4]

Gandhi had to cut short his visit to Santiniketan on learning Gokhale's death. He immediately went to Poona to participate in the mourning of his hero and guide. As a mark of respect to his memory, he gave up wearing sandals for a year.[5] After Gokhale's death, he had to depend upon himself for his future course as he could not find anyone in India who could take Gokhale's place. So to understand India and her people he decided to travel third, dressed like a poor passenger. He wore shirt, dhoti and put on a cheap Kashmiri cap. He stayed at Calcutta on his way to Rangoon. On his return he visited Santiniketan again where Tagore welcomed him. It was a great moment for both of them as well as for the students and staff of the institute. Gandhi went into the drawing room where Tagore was sitting. The latter rose from his sofa and offered him a seat beside him. But the visitor decided to settle down on the carpet on the floor and his host followed suit. It was an amusing sight when they met. The tall, stately figure of the poet with silvery hair and long beard was confronted with a small, thin and lean figure of Gandhi in his dhoti barely covering his legs, his simple shirt and his Kashmiri cap. But physical appearance shrinks into insignificance before a person whose eyes are in search of inner greatness and beauty. So the poet saw in the puny frame a great soul. In April Gandhi went to Hardwar to witness the Kumb festival where the Phoenix party led by Maganlal was already there to assist the volunteer corps of the Servants of India Society to help the pilgrims. Gandhi joined them in their social work. But he was appalled by the hypocrisy and slovenliness of the pilgrims and the Sadhus who descended there in thousands and were no different from the ordinary people. They were there to enjoy good things of life. There were, of course, pious souls surrounded by hordes of hypocrites. The visit to Hardwar in this atmosphere was sinful. He thought of imposing on himself an act of self-denial in atonement for the iniquity prevailing there. So he took the vow of taking five articles of food during the 24 hours.[6] This would also save his hosts from unnecessary trouble who used to entertain him lavishly. He took this opportunity to pay his regards to Shraddhananda for accommodating his Phoenix inmates on their arrival in India. In fact, he was more interested in meeting Shraddhananda than in attending the Kumb festival when he decided to visit Hardwar. In his characteristic humility he touched the feet of the Swami. The inmates of the Gurukul presented an Address of Welcome and Gandhi was addressed as Mahatma in the Address. This meeting led to close friendship between the two 'Mahatmas' and later on Gandhi sought the Swami's guidance in setting up his Ashram at Ahmedabad.

From Hardwar, Gandhi went to Madras accompanied by his wife where he was warmly received. He was the guest of Natesan. Addresses were showered on him at several largely attended meetings. At a Madras Law Dinner, while proposing a toast of the British Empire, he expressed his deep loyalty to the Empire on the grounds that every individual in it had the freest scope possible for his energies and honour and under this government one 'is governed least' which, in his view, is the hallmark of a 'best government'. At another meeting he stated the rationale of his loyalty to the Empire as follows:[7]

> I ally myself to the British Government because I believe that it is possible for me to claim equal partnership with every subject of the British Empire I today claim that equal partnership I do not belong to a subject race—But there is this thing; it is not for the British governors to give you, it is for you to take the thing . . .''

He went to Adyar to meet Mrs. Besant and visited one of the 'Panchama' school. While on tour he was keeping with him the Tamil primer to carry on his study of Tamil language. No doubt, Gandhi had given promise to Gokhale that he would not open his mouth on political matters at least for a year. It is true that he did not express his views on current controversial issues. But what was political and what was non-political, he alone had to decide. Loyalty to the British Empire and condemnations of political terrorism were political issues and he had expressed his views on such subjects. Quite often he was critical of the conduct of the contemporary leadership and the people and some of his speeches gave the impression that he was at war with the contemporary leaders. For, his view of Swadeshi transcended the contemporary practice of Swadeshi as the word Swadeshi, he observed, was written in English. Though rich tributes had been paid to him for his heroic struggle in South Africa at several meetings organized to honour him, most of the contemporary leaders were not impressed by his life style. His conversational style without any rhetorical flourishes and gestures was in sharp contrast to the eloquence and histrionic of Surrendranath

Bannerji. Srinivasa Sastri who saw Gandhi for the first time on January 9, 1915, was not impressed by "his retiring speech and felt that if he did not drop his 'anarchic' views, he would eschew politics and become an exclusively social worker." Similarly when he visited the Gujarat Club, which was the rendevous of lawyers and business men of Ahmedabad, to enlist the support of its members to his scheme of national schools, Vallabhbhai Patel hardly took notice of him and went on playing bridge. To young J.L. Nehru he appeared very distant and different and unpolitical when he saw him first at the Lucknow Congress in 1916. Undoubtedly the Mahatma appeared queer to the educated westernized elite for his attire, his unconventional habits and his opposition to western culture and English education. The year of apprenticeship in India for him only meant that he should equip himself with the knowledge of the conditions in India. But he could not be an apprentice to any leader. For he was far removed from contemporary view of life of public men.

In addition to travelling through the length and breadth of the country, he had before him the immediate task of setting up his 'Ashram' for training young boys for the service of the country besides accommodating the inmates of the Phoenix and Tolstoy Farm who had accompanied him to India. He first indicated his intention in this connection to Gokhale who assured him financial help for this project. After his death, he had to depend upon his own skill and efforts to carry out this programme. Swami Shraddhananda suggested to him to settle in Hardwar. Friends in Calcutta recommended Vaidyanathdham. Others favoured Rajkot. But Gandhi decided to settle down in Ahmedabad on the grounds that being a Gujarati, he could influence people there through the mother tongue. Moreover, Ahmedabad being the richest trading centre could provide adequate financial support for this purpose. A barrister friend Jivanlal Desai, offered to let his one storied bungalow in Kochrab, a small village near Ahmedabad, and Gandhi agreed to establish his Ashram there. There were in all twenty-five persons who were to be accommodated. Out of them thirteen were Tamilians, five of them had accompanied him from South Africa and the rest came from different parts of the country. It was given the name Satyagraha Ashram which conveyed its goal and method of service as the creed of the inmates was devotion to truth and their business was 'the search for and insistence on truth.' All were to live as one family. All of them were to do manual labour either by working on the land or on the wheel. Gandhi himself used to work nearly over four hours on the loom when the Ashram was set up. He kept account of every penny received or spent. But as soon as the Ashram started functioning, Gandhi was faced with a very critical situation when he admitted an untouchable family consisting of Dudabhai, a teacher in Bombay, his wife Danibehn and their daughter Lakshmi. It created and uproar among the orthodox Hindus of Ahmedabad as well as the inmates of the Ashram including his wife. This was certainly an attack on the citadel of caste system, whether Gandhi was conscious of it or not though he had defended the caste system in some of his speeches on his arrival in India. He could not give a suitable reply to a correspondent who asked him to which caste the untouchables would be taken in if the four-fold caste system was to be retained. However, eradication of untouchability was a fundamental question for him and his faith was on the anvil. The first difficulty arose with regard to the use of well which was the main source for supply of water to the Ashram as the man incharge of the well would treat all the Ashramites as if all of them were untouchables and would shower curses on them when they came to use the well. His wife Kasturba and his nephew Maganlal who was managing the Ashram were not well disposed towards the untouchable family. Things came to such a pass that Gandhi had to tell his wife one day either to observe the Ashram rules or to leave the Ashram. She relented and reconciled herself to the new conditions created by her husband on the plea that a woman following in her husband's footsteps incurs no sin. His elder widowed sister whose maintenance was his responsibility gave up her plan of staying in the Ashram when Gandhi adopted Lakshmi as his own daughter.[8] Maganlal was sent to Madras to save him form the predicament of either leaving the Ashram or living with an untouchable family. His cousin Khushal Chand was sorry for having permitted his sons to live in the Ashram where the untouchable family was taking food in the common kitchen.[9] So deep was the prejudice against the untouchables in Gujarat that even in 1918 when Gandhi was to open a temple in Walpakhadi, the municipal colony near Mazagoan, it was reported that no millionaire Hindu friend of Gandhi would give him his car for the visit to that Bhangi colony.[10] All financial help to the Ashram was stopped by friends and sympathisers and things came to such a pass that Maganlal informed him that all the funds were exhausted and there was nothing left for the next month. But it was against the grain of Gandhi to surrender in matters of principles. He was by nature tenacious. To his critics and opponents he appeared to be obstinate. Whatever he was, instinctively he would do whatever was the demand of his conscience which he considered as the voice of God. So he decided to shift the establishment to the untouchable quarters and earn their livelihood through manual labour. But a dramatic event averted this eventuality. A car stopped outside the Ashram gate and Gandhi went out to see the stranger who asked a straight question to him, "would you accept money from a stranger for the Ashram?" He did not disclose his name. On hearing 'yes' from the head of Ashram, he immediately left and appeared next day with a bundle of currency notes and handed it over to the Mahatma. The stranger had parted with 13,000 rupees. The financial crisis of the Ashram was over at least for a year.

Just at that time Gandhi received appreciation for his services from the Government and as a token of it he received Kaiser-i-Hind medal (June 26, 1915). But he was not at peace with himself on receiving this medal. For, it was an attempt of the alien Government to lure him into their net. For, by this act they had put him into the rank of loyalists who were sharply distinguished from those who were undergoing hardships to free their country from the thraldom of the alien Government. Gandhi was aware of it. On the arrival of the medal, Kalelkar made the following observation: "Bapu you have given a lot of help to the Empire and your loyalty has won you this medal. I am afraid the Government are ought to lure you into their net." "Oh you, too, believe that, do you, was Gandhi's comment. He was, in fact, in search of an opportune moment to throw away this badge which came to him when he was ordered by the magistrate of Champaran to leave the district. While returning it to the Viceroy, he wrote, "Since Government did not trust him enough to let him do public service in Champaran, it would not be proper for him to keep that medal."

Gandhi after the termination of the year of apprenticeship was still groping in the dark about his mission in his mother country. For the millions in India, he was 'Mahatma' whose darshan meant spiritual satisfaction. But the consciousness that he was far from it pained him a great deal. For he was in the process of cultivating essential attributes of a 'Mahatma' such as 'daya' (forgiveness or magnanimity), 'akrodha' (rising above anger), 'aman' (rising above the desire to be respected). He was sometime losing temper even with his wife which meant he did not have adequate self-control.

One programme that was uppermost in his mind on his arrival in India was to bring together Hindus and Muslims on the common platform. He had his experience before him of his struggle in South Africa where he was successful to a great extent in this regard. He was therefore, hopeful of succeeding in this mission in India, too. But he had not yet realized the different conditions in the two countries that determined the relations between the two communities. However the burden of his speeches during the year of his apprenticeship was the importance of communal unity. Of course, there were winds of change in Muslim politics that favoured his programme of Hindu-Muslim unity. Young Abul Kalam Azad through his paper *Al-Hilal* and Mohamed Ali were bringing about a change in Muslim's attitude towards the Congress and national unity. A large number of Congress leaders including Gandhi and Mrs. Naidu attended the Muslim League session of 1915. On the initiative of Jinnah the Muslim League started preparing a scheme of political reform for India in consultation with the Congress leadership. The political atmosphere in the country was full of hope. Surendranath Banerjee felt that since both the League and the Congress aim at self-government within the Empire, their joint demand would become irresistible. At Lucknow both the Congress and the League held their annual session and hammered out a join scheme of political reform. The Congress leadership in their enthusiasm for seeking the support of the Muslims for the political advancement of the country yielded to the Muslim demand of separate electorate jettisoning their fundamental principle of joint electorate which was the bedrock of their view of nationalism besides agreeing to the principle of weighted representation of minorities. Gandhi had no hand in all the confabulations of the leaders of both the parties resulting in the Lucknow Pact. The leaders were Tilak, Annie Besant, Jinnah and B.C. Pal. The Pact, in fact, could not receive the sanction of the Congress without the powerful support of Tilak who, it appears had yielded to the communal demands under the erroneous impression that by this act Congress would be able to replace the extra-territoral loyalty of the Muslim leadership. Thus the year 1916 turned out to be a landmark in the political history of India. Though the League and the Congress had decided to work together for the political advancement of the country, the demand of the separate electorate which the Congress conceded, permanently divided the two major communities of the country and resulted in the partition of the county.

Notes and References

1. Keer, Dananjay, *op. cit.*, p. 212.
2. C.W., Vol. XIII, pp. 1-2.
3. Rao, Kodanda, P., The Right Honourable, V.S. Sastri, p. 17.
4. Shukla, Incidents of Gandhiji's Life, p. 122.
5. Keer, *op. cit.*, p. 214.
6. Gandhi, M.K., Autobiography, p. 325.
7. Tendulkar, *op. cit.*, Vol. I, p. 166.
8. Prabhudas, *op. cit.*, pp. 19-20.
9. C.W., XCVII, pp. 27-28.
10. Kanji Dwarkadas, *op. cit.*, p. 90.

11

Preparation for Swaraj

The expiry of the year of apprenticeship in India coincided with the invitation that he received to the foundation ceremony of the Benaras Hindu University, the foundation stone of which was laid by the Viceroy Lord Hardinge whom Gandhi hailed as a noble Viceroy on his return to India. Many Indian leaders and princes had been invited to this function. So very strict security measures had been taken. The pomp and show of the occasion was completely in contrast to Gandhi's life-style. On the dais were sitting several princes bedecked with jewels and wearing costly costumes. The Maharaja of Darbhanga was in the chair when Gandhi clad in a short, coarse dhoti and Kathiarwadi cloak and turban rose to speak. His speech revealed the working of his mind and the type of leader he was. The speech was mostly addressed to the students and the common people to whom he assured that it was not merely a speech but it was an attempt to think audibly. "I do not want to make a speech and if you find me this evening speaking without reserve, pray consider that you are sharing the thoughts of a man who allows himself to think audibly."[1] Undoubtedly he spoke without reserve that pleased the youth and displeased the elite and bejewelled gentry. The burden of his speech was that India's salvation was not possible without bidding farewell to the existing methods. He said, ". . . I do venture to suggest to you that we have now reached almost the end of our resources in speech-making, and it is not enough that our ears are feasted, that our eyes are feasted, it is necessary that our hearts have got to be touched and that our hands and feet have got to be moved."[2] He was sorry that he had to speak in

English since this was not the language through which the masses residing in innumerable villages could be mobilized. So English could not become the national language of India. It was necessary to use and develop our own languages for national development. For, English was a handicap on the nation. In his view if we had been receiving during the past fifty years education through our vernaculars—we should have today a free India. For the salvation of the country could not come through rich landlords, lawyers and doctors but only through farmers who understood only the language that they spoke. The youth attending the meeting must have been surprised by the rare fearlessness that his speech exuded, for he could openly tell the bejewelled audience that the poverty of India could not be removed unless they stripped themselves of their jewellery and held it in trust for the people. He was equally critical of the security arrangements for the Viceroy, for it showed, the inability of the British rulers to win the hearts of the people. It was his way of telling the British that the imposing structure of their Empire stood on slender foundations. He referred to the activities and objectives of some young men known at that time as anarchists who relied on violence and sporadic murders of British officers. He had a word of praise for their love of the country and bravery. But he told them plainly that "there is no warrant for such methods in any scriptures." Thus, he exposed the hollowness of the existing methods for attaining political objectives and thereby suggested that the leadership must search for new methods for the salvation of the country. While he was dwelling upon the misdirected zeal of the 'revolutionaries', Mrs. Besant could not contain herself and said 'please stop it'. But there were cries from the audience 'Go on' and the chairman politely said 'explain your object'. In fact, his words were falling like sharpnels on the organizers. But the ears of the youth present there were having a rare feast, for the speaker was not sparing anybody. Lack of sense of hygiene among the people in this holy place also received his admonition. There was commotion on the dais as the galaxy of the 'rajas' and the distinguished guests including the President could not swallow all that the tongue of this simple man was pouring out. They left the hall. It was quite an unusual sight. For quite often audience leave the hall out of sheer boredom or the speaker is made to sit down by the audience. But rarely the president leaves when the speaker is still addressing the audience. So the meeting ended abruptly. According to Bhagwandas who was present in the meeting, the patience of the Rajas was at their "tether end when the speaker compared them with a troop of monkeys who would invade fields in Gujarat when the crops were ripe and left the hall in anger leaving Malaviya in great predicament."[3] Several leaders including Mrs. Besant came down heavily on Gandhi for this speech. Their main charge was that Gandhi encouraged the cult of violence while admiring the patriotic fervour of the youth that indulged in terroristic acts. But this was the least he was expected to do being a devotee of non- violence. In a letter to the Maharaja of Darbanga he explained thus, "My sole object in referring to the Viceregal visit was to express the very strong views I hold against all acts of violence and so-called anarchy," for, "my mission in life is to preach and assist in securing the utmost freedom for my country but never by violence to the person of any human being, even under the greatest provocation."[4] Later, he stated that had Mrs. Besant not interrupted, he would have concluded his speech in a few minutes and "no possible misconception about my views on anarchism would have arisen." He did not agree with those that his speech was not well organized and well considered and well-weighed. In fact, his forthright expression of his views which appeared unconventional to the ears of the contemporary leadership and the elite shows that the 'Karmavir' Gandhi of South Africa had acquired confidence and had no fear of the authorities. He could feel the pulse of the audience and was fully aware of the effect of his speech on the students present there. However, the police commissioner ordered him to leave the city immediately against the wishes of Malaviya who had invited Gandhi to the function. So he left Benaras. Gandhi now went round the country and openly expressed his views. But he mainly dwelt upon the immediate need of eradication of poverty, propagation of swadeshi and close communion between the leaders and the masses. Addressing the students of economics at Muir College Economic Society, Allahabad, he pointed out that the "test of orderliness in country is not the number of millionaires it owns, but the absence of starvation among its masses." For, the poor, he believed, 'were the custodian of moral progress as they would advance struggle of passive resistance which was real test of moral advancement'. He put the whole blame on the English educated classes for losing touch with the masses and by an almost fatal departure from the 'swadeshi' spirit. For our English educated classes were incapable of reacting upon the masses.

Gandhi attended the Congress session of 1916. But his role was mainly confined to speaking on South African Indian question. Quite often he pleaded for the use of Hindi in the Congress session. But his visit to this session turned out to be a landmark as it introduced him to the conditions in Champran in Bihar. Rajkumar Shukla, an agriculturist from Bihar who had been agitating for a long time against exploitation of peasants in Champran by the European planters pressed on Gandhi to do something to alleviate the condition of the suffering peasantry in that area. Gandhi had not heard even the name of this area much less its geographical position. Shukla took the help of Babu Brij Kishore Prasad, a well-known lawyer of Bihar who represented that area at the Congress session, to explain to Gandhi the real situation in Champran. But the latter was not impressed by the lawyer wearing alpaca coat and black trousers and so suggested to Shukla to carry the matter to the Congress session. It ended in Congress passing a resolution in requesting the authorities to institute a commission of enquiry consisting of officials and non-officials. But such pious resolutions could not touch even the fringes of the power and influence of the factory owners and land lords. So Shukla implored Gandhi to visit the place and see things with his own eyes. The latter agreed. Shukla followed the Mahatma and ultimately on his visit to Calcutta took him to Patna on his way to Champran.

Gandhi and Rajkumar Shukla dressed in peasant attire had some unpleasant experiences in the house of Babu Rajendra Prasad who was out of station. The servant did not allow them to use the well or the laterine inside the house as their dress and demeanor showed that they did not belong to a higher caste. Gandhi and his guide then boarded the train to Muzaffarpur to see Maulana Mazharul Huq, whom Gandhi first met while studying in London and later on in Bombay in 1915 where he had extended him an open invitation to stay with him whenever he visited Bihar. At the station he was received by Kriplani and a large number of students who dragged his carriage as a mark of adoration and admiration. He stayed in the family quarters of Government college staff with professor Malkani whose principal warned him that he had lodged a dangerous person in his house. However this dangerous persons turned out to be an interesting company for Malkani's wife and his two little daughters who played with him. He was, in fact, a queer guest who was using a two-anna aluminium glass as spittoon and another two-anna dibia (small box) with a bit of mirror, containing a cheap soap inside as his shaving kit and a two pound tin containing groundnut butter and some fruits and his food.[5] In the morning Gandhi had a talk with the lawyers. Brajkishore Babu and Rajendra Prasad had also arrived. Gandhi found the situation in Champran much more serious that he had imagined. For, he discovered that the condition of the peasantry there was worse than the Indians in Fiji or Natal. It reminded him of the struggle that he had in South Africa. It demanded from him greater sacrifice. For, it was the land trodden by Rama and Janak and so sacred for him.

Champran is situated in the north-western corner of Bihar. The two important towns in Champran at that time were Motihari and Bettiah. Ninety-eight per cent population of the area was living in villages, most of them were Hindus speaking Bhojpuri, dialect of Hindi. Indigo cultivation in this area had been going on for more than a century. Europeans had captured the indigo cultivation. The peasants had been forced to cultivate indigo in three-twentieth of the land and supply it to the factories manufacturing indigo as a part of rent. The land owners of the planters flourished at the cost of toiling peasantry who were subjected to many illegal exactions known as 'abwaos' wherever the land owner purchased a car or an elephant, attended a festival or married his daughter. This kind of oppression had been going on for several decades in spite of agitation by the oppressed peasantry because of the apathy of the Government towards their grievances. In fact, the relations between the landlords, tenant zamindars and peasants were strained to the breaking point. Further, certain developments about the indigo trade had aggravated the situation. For, indigo cultivation had lost its lustre as a result of competition with synthetic indigo in the European market. The land-owners started playing tricks with the ignorant tenants by offering to free them from the imposition of indigo cultivation on payment of increased rent. But this trick was found out and the peasantry started an agitation against it. But of no avail. Some tenants took recourse to law courts for relief. But no substantial relief could be obtained as the cases lingered on for several years and the poor tenants had to pay high fees to the lawyers. Rajkumar Shukla had made several efforts to obtain the help of the Congress leadership to secure justice. But they were so absorbed in their struggle for the attainment of their political goal that they could not afford to pay sufficient attention to the grievances of a section of peasantry in Bihar.

After the discussion with the lawyers, Gandhi came to the conclusion that recourse to law courts for relief would be of no avail as it was beyond the resources of the poor ryots. His experiences as a lawyer had revealed to him that facts bring to light the truth and so justice would always be on the side of the party which had facts on its side. So what he needed from the lawyers was not their legal acumen but only clerical assistance for collecting facts by recording the statements of the peasants who had been subjected to oppression. This meant an open enquiry into the problem. But before starting it, he met the commissioner of the district and the secretary of the Planters' Association in order to know the point of view of the opponent and the Government. But they either bullied him or questioned his bonafides to hold any enquiry into the problem as he was an outsider. He brushed aside commissioner's objection on the grounds that he had been receiving letters from the people of the area complaining about the conditions of the indigo workers and so he wanted to see the conditions with his own eyes. He was not representing any organisation, not even the Congress, for it was a body which was, at that time, more or less a debating club of the English educated Indians who had as yet not identified themselves with the peasants. It was a practical decision. For, had he sought the assistance of the Congress, he would have been put to a lot of difficulty by the Congress leadership who had as yet no experience of challenging the alien bureaucracy on any issue concerning the common people living in the villages. He proceeded with the enquiry. He also sent an intimation to the commissioner along with a letter of some prominent Congressmen requesting him to hold some kind of enquiry to find out the truth of the problem. But in return a notice was served on him by the Deputy Superintendent of Police to leave Champaran immediately. So a clash with the authorities became inevitable on his refusal to comply with this order. Gandhi apprehended arrest any time. He, therefore, prepared a plan for the guidance of those who were to carry on the work in his absence. Telegrams and letters were sent to Congress leaders about the developments in Champaran. Malaviya expressed his willingness to come. Rajendra Prasad was asked to come with volunteers. Andrews came and made an unsuccessful attempt to see the collector. The news of Gandhi's trial spread like a wild fire in Motihari, the headquarters of the Tirhut division of which Champaran was a district. A large number of peasants' collected outside the courtroom where Gandhi was to appear before the magistrate. Several people witnessed an amusing and strange sight. For the police was seeking Gandhi's help in controlling the mob. It was an unusual friendship between the accused and the authorities. To Gandhi, it was the result of the operation of the power of Ahimsa. The people had for the moment, he observed, "lost all fear of the punishment and yielded obedience to the power of love which their new friend exercised."[6] That day in Champaran was an unforgettable event in his life and a red letter day for the peasants.

Legally Gandhi was on trial. But it looked as if the Government was on trial that day. The Mahatma's fearlessness had an electric effect on the unsophisticated and rustic peasants that infused into them the spirit of fearlessness. The magistrate was at a loss as to what to do with the strange person on trial who was protesting against the refusal of the prosecutor to postpone the trial. He pleaded guilty and was ready to accept punishment. The magistrate was in a fix and after seeking the advice of the lieutenant Governor, he withdrew the case. In fact, it was his support to the British war efforts that had turned the table against the bureaucracy since the higher authorities were not in a mood to punish him and so he was allowed to carry on his movement for the redress of local grievances. He was allowed to hold the enquiry and local officials were instructed to give him facilities. He and his colleagues worked hard and recorded more than ten thousand statements. As a result the Government appointed a commission in which Gandhi was to represent the ryots. With the help of facts in his possession, it was not easy for anyone to misguide the commission. Thus while examining an important witness, Mr. W.S. Irwin, manager of the Motihari limited, a concern consisting of six factories of Indigo, Gandhi showed his investigative skill by making him accept the charge that he had indulged in oppression. By an adroit handling of the discussion he made the planters agree to twenty-five per cent compensation to the tenants while initially he had demanded fifty per cent compensation. He proposed the abolition of 'tinkhatia' system and cancellation of 'sharah basti' or the enhancement of rent in lieu of 'tinkhathia' which was the main demand of the tenants. The Commission accepted it. The lieutenant Governor in spite of planters' protest sponsored a bill giving the recommendations the force of law. This experience confirmed his view that the facts were the real road to truth. Gandhi's regard for truth sometimes surprised or even irked his colleagues working with him for the collection of facts. For instance, once a Government employee provided Rajendra Prasad and his colleagues with a copy of the report secretly that he had sent to the Government. They took it to Gandhi who refused to read it as it had come to him in a secretive manner.[7] Facts in his view, provide a steel frame to a just cause. However the real gain of Champaran struggle was that it stirred a new life among the so-called rustic and illiterate people. Champaran, therefore, was a red letter day in Gandhi's life. For it brought him face to face with the realities of village life in India which was hitherto based on theoretical observations. He saw for the first time the ignorant, poverty-stricken, under-nourished and superstitious villagers living in the environment full of dirt and disease. It was for the first time that he challenged the British authorities in India and had declared that the British had no right to prevent an Indian from pursuing the welfare of the Indians and fighting for their rights. He was becoming conscious of the fact that political salvation of the country could not be pursued in isolation. It had to be integrated with the social and economic uplift of the people. Thus Champaran experience entered into the very fibre of his public life. It contributed a great deal to the development of his philosophy of constructive programme. He became conscious of the gulf between ideal and reality. For, poverty and disease stricken villages of India could not provide a sound foundation of a free and happy India. According to Rajendra Prasad the great national movement led by Gandhi today is only a development, on an immensely vaster scale of what was begun in Champran "—Whatever the Non-co-operation Satyagraha Movement has achieved or proposes to achieve is foreshadowed by this movement."[8]

So he felt that his mission in Bihar did not end with providing relief to the peasants of Champaran. For the real need of the country was to build up character of the people so that they could resist any oppressive regime. What the unlettered villagers, in his view, needed was self-reliance which could be inculcated through proper education and training. He picked out six villages in Champaran and opened primary schools in each. The teachers were to be maintained by the local people in order to involve them in their own uplift. So he discouraged financial help from outside Bihar. It was a sort of community project for the development of Indian villages. However, since it was difficult to find good local teachers who would work for a bare allowance or without remuneration he appealed for volunteers from outside Bihar which received good response. A number of them came as far as from Gujarat. Among them was Mahadev Desai in whom Gandhi discovered the man he wanted, to whom he could entrust all his work and on whom he could rely with confidence. As Gandhi's secretary, he served him with rare devotion till his death in jail in Aga Khan Palace while providing company to the Mahatma. Gandhi also summoned his wife and some inmates of the Ashram to carry out his constructive programme in Champaran. Some of those who came had nothing more than a bare knowledge of Gujarati and his wife not even that. What was required in a teacher, in his view, was moral fibre and not merely literary attainments. But among them were also highly cultured and educated persons like Avantika Bai Gokhale and her engineer husband Babban Gokhale who had forsaken the comforts and luxury of their home to live among rustic villagers to make their environment clear and healthy. For, what they were to teach the children was not grammar and three R's but cleanliness and good manners. They were to give practical lessons in hygiene to village folks by cleaning their wells and roads. A medical doctor offered his services to guide the volunteers working in the villages. They concentrated their energies on cleanliness. They swept the roads and the court yards, cleaned out the wells and lovingly persuaded the villagers to raise volunteers from amongst themselves to carry out the programme. While working among them, Gandhi witnessed poverty in its nudity which left a lasting impact on his mind. He was on a visit to a small village accompanied by his wife. He saw some women dressed in very dirty saris. When his wife asked one of them as to why she did not wash her sari, she was told that she had only one sari which she could neither wash in her hut as it was occupied by several persons nor outside. How difficult it was for him to build up the new India where the vast majority of the people were deprived of the bare necessities of life, "if they spin and weave in their own hut wont they have better life." Such thoughts must have passed through his mind. It was the last man, the poorest of all that he had to keep in view while planning for the uplift of all.

Some planters or their agents tried to put hurdles in his way in order to discourage him or his volunteers in carrying out his constructive programme. A hut made of Bamboo and local grass used for school building under the charge of Gandhi's wife was set on fire possibly by the agents of the planters. Though no harm came to the occupants, it was decided to build 'pucca' houses for schools. Besides rural education and sanitation work, Gandhi also envisaged a programme of dairy development including cattle breeding, improvement of stock and human treatment of bullocks. All these programmes received great importance in his plan of village developments later on.

However, the constructive programme in Bihar could not find at that time permanent roots as the volunteers had come only for a temporary period. The whole project, therefore, came to an end as soon as Gandhi and his party left Bihar. While the Mahatma was busy in Champaran, plague broke out in the village where his Ashram was situated. This alarmed him. It was a sufficient notice to him to change the site of his Ashram. He was in search of a place which was at a safe distance both from town and village, and yet at a manageable distance from either. With the help of a merchant friend who had been in close contact with the Ashram, he selected a site on the bank of Sabarmati river near the Sabarmati central jail which could be a permanent reminder to the Ashramites that 'jail-going was their normal lot'. There was no building or tree there. A friend told Gandhi that his new Ashram stood at a place where the Ashram of the mythical sage Dadhichi stood who supplied to

Indra, the king of gods, his bones to be forged into weapons in the war against the demons. Possibly it might have occurred to the Mahatma that destiny had contrived a similar role for him. The Ashramites, whose number had now grown to forty, men, women and children, started living under canvas till permanent houses could be built there. The place was infested with snakes and the general rule which Gandhi had been observing since his Phoenix days was not of killing a snake, though it was no small risk to live with children under such conditions. A snake was generally caught without killing it by a rope fixed in a special manner to the end of a stick and let off in the middle of a river. Gandhi wrote in his autobiography that by the grace of God no incident of snake bite took place in his Ashram. Once, of course, an inmate saw a snake moving on the back of Gandhi's body of which he was not conscious. He kept sitting without moving and slowly and slowly the reptile moved away.

At this time two very serious developments took place in Gujarat that widened the scope of Satyagraha and kept him occupied for some time in his own province. One problem concerned the peasants that brought him in confrontation with the Bombay Government and the other involving the industrial workers and the mill owners of Ahmedabad who had been financially helping him for his various programmes. Both the problems occurred simultaneously. So no breathing time was in store for him. The first problem occurred when excessive rainfall in Kheda district in 1917 led to the failure of crops which involved the postponement of the payment of revenue in accordance with the land revenue rules under which the cultivators could claim suspension of the revenue assessment for the year if the failure of the crops was four annas or under. But the officials insisted on immediate payment of revenue as according to them it was not less that four annas. As the president of the Gujarat Sabha which had taken up the case of the cultivators, Gandhi suggested the appointment of an impartial commission of enquiry to assess the loss. But the officials were in no mood to listen to this advice. So Gandhi had no choice but to fix up his quarters in Nadiad to mobilise and guide the peasants for the struggle. He was assisted by several prominent persons such as Vallabhabhai Patel, Shankerlal Banker, Anusuyabehn, Indulal Yajnik, Mahadev Desai, etc. Though the struggle was local, its fall out according to Gandhi, would have wider significance. For, if the people submitted to the high handed attitude of the authorities, "then for a long time the people of India will not be able to stand up." In other words, its success would carry the country towards the road to freedom. Since the author of the Satyagraha had to depend upon the determination of the people involved in the struggle to carry on the movement he asked them to take the pledge that they would not voluntarily pay the revenue or any instalment thereof. This is what the author of Satyagraha did while starting the movement in South Africa. Thus, Satyagraha started on fairly large scale after the pledge had been taken. The officials replied by confiscating the property or attaching the crops causing great suffering to the peasants. Gandhi accompanied by his close associates visited several villages to raise their morale. All his meetings were well-attended. It appeared quite unusual to his audience when he appealed to them not to be discourteous to the officials or harass them in spite of the fact that they were suffering great hardships at the hands of the latter. With a view to raising the tempo of the movement and the drooping spirit of the peasants, he hit upon an ingenious strategy. There was no occasion for the officials to arrest those who were not paying revenue. Gandhi, then, advised one of the leaders of the campaign to remove onion from a crop attached by the officials for non-payment of revenue and thus court imprisonment. So under the leadership of Mohanlal Pandya, a lawyer, some of the volunteers removed the onions. They were convicted and sentenced to brief imprisonment. This generated fresh enthusiasm among the peasants of the area. The government was cornered. It could not afford to lose the sympathy of the people during the war. So the struggle came to an end abruptly as the authorities decided to suspend the collection of revenue only from the poor peasants. Possibly Gandhi's participation in the war council and his plea that the Government must make a congenial atmosphere for recruitment had some effect on the authorities to modify their policy. The word must have come from the Viceroy to the Commissioner as the former was looking for Gandhi's support for Britain during the war. Gandhi's strategy of fighting for redress of grievances of the poor peasants without alienating the Raj was paying dividends. At times his moves were very astonishing. For, on the one hand he was asking the simple, unsophisticated and unlettered peasants to defy the orders of the mighty Raj and on the other hand, he was ordering his rebel army to be courteous and polite to their tormentors.

What was the result of Kheda Satyagraha?

How far was it a success?

For, both the parties accepted the termination of the agitation without any fuss or excitement. Both believed that they had made some gains. The Governor of Bombay gleefully reported to the Viceroy that Gandhi had taken a fall over Kaira business.[9] No settlement had been made with the leaders of agitation. The Government quietly changed its policy without arriving at any agreement with the leaders. The authorities themselves prepared two lists that is, of those who were in a position to pay. Gandhi was asked by the officials to advise those who were in a position to pay to comply with the orders. No doubt the poor were granted suspension of payment of tax which was the main demand of the agitators. But very few could get the benefit cf this concession as the authorities alone were to determine who was poor and who was in a position to pay. Possibly Gandhi, too, was not very keen for prolonging the struggle as he felt that the people were exhausted and therefore he hesitated to let the unbending be driven to utter ruin. So he was looking for some graceful way of terminating the struggle.[10] But the campaign definitely created an awakening among the peasants of Gujarat besides compelling the educated public workers to establish contact with the actual life of the peasants and identify themselves with the latter. However, it raised the image of Gandhi in Gujarat and gave him many valuable colleagues who became key figures in his many subsequent campaigns. It brought him close to Patel who put all his energy and practical sense in his political and social movements. To a devoted follower Gandhi once said, "Look here, in Vallabhbhai I have found such an extraordinary man that if he alone tries to know me truly and follows my path much that I wish to do in Gujarat, will be done by him—."

The Satyagraha on the issue of the dispute between the mill-owners and mill-workers was unique in character for the way it was carried on. Gandhi believed that there was absence of bitterness and ill-will in the campaign.[11] For, not only the leader maintained good relations with the mill-owners who were his opponents in this campaign, but also the sister of the leader of the mill-owners stood on the side of the workers. There was good humour between the two sides and so Gandhi declined the good offices of Mrs. Besant for a settlement who happened to be in Ahmedabad as a guest of the leader of the mill-owners. The cause of the dispute lay in the grant of bonus to the workers on the outbreak of plague in Ahmedabad. But they decided to withdraw it when the city was free from the epidemic. However, the workers claimed the enhancement of wages on account of the rise in prices during war. But on Gandhi's persuasion they agreed for a settlement through an arbitration. Gandhi, Patel and Shankarlal Banker acted as the representatives of the weavers and Sheth Ambalal Sarabhai together with Jagabhai and Chandulal Chimanlal represented the mill-owners. Mr. Chatfield, the Collector, was chosen to act as an umpire. Unfortunately when the deliberations of the board of arbitration was in progress, some mill-hands struck work which gave an excuse to the mill-owners to withdraw from the arbitration board. They unilaterally offered 20 per cent enhancement of wages and threatened to dismiss those who refused this offer. They declared lock-out as most of the workers were not satisfied with the offer. On the other hand, the workers' representatives on the board suggested 35 per cent increase after giving full consideration to the interests of both the parties against the workers' demand of 50 per cent. A stalemate followed. The workers then gathered under the babul tree on 26th February and on the advice of Gandhi took a pledge not to resume work until 35 per cent increase was obtained and to carry on the struggle peacefully. They were not to bear any ill-will or grudge against their employers in spite of the suffering involved in the struggle. As a part of the programme the workers would gather under the same tree every afternoon where Gandhi would address them to keep their morale high by telling them of his experiences of workers' strike in South Africa as well as reminding them of their pledge. Leaflets were issued daily to guide the workers who would march through the streets with banners inscribed Ek Tek- Keep the pledge. To strengthen their resolve, he assured them that leaders themselves would not eat or dress themselves without providing food and clothing to those who had been reduced to destitution during the struggle. He also suggested to them to find alternative occupations during the period of struggle. At the same time Gandhi was making all possible efforts to open the channels for negotiations in order to reduce the suffering of the workers. To the surprise of many, the leader of the mill-owners Ambalal Sarabhai dined with him at the Ashram during the struggle. But in a letter he warned him that the success of the mill-owners in the struggle will have serious consequences for the whole society. For the employers' real success, he reiterated lay in earning the good will of the workers by meeting their demands. But the mill-owners remained adamant. On the other hand, some of the workers began to show signs of flagging after remaining steadfast for two weeks. It had its effect on their attitude towards the blacklegs. There was apprehension of rowdyism or eruption of violence. The attendance at the meetings also began to dwindle. It was reduced from ten thousand to two thousand. Despondency and despair was writ large on the faces of those who were attending. At this moment the mill-owners made a clever move to outmanoeuvre Gandhi. For, they decided to withdraw the lock-out on March 12 and expressed their willingness to take back all those workers who would accept twenty per cent increase. The strike thus entered a dangerous phase. For a violent clash between the strikers and those accepting the offer of the employers could not be ruled out in spite of Gandhi's strong appeals to the strikers to keep their cool. But his own patience was at the end of his tether when his cousin reported to him the following talk among some of the workers:

"What is it to Ansuyabehn and Gandhiji? They come and go in their cars; they eat sumptuous food, but we are suffering death agonies; attending meetings does not prevent starvation." This showed the mood of the workers. But to the Mahatma, pledge was a sacred resolve. It was taken with God as a witness. So breaking of it was an irreligious act, an annihilation of dharma and dharma could be sustained only by suffering. That was the situation that he faced in South Africa that gave rise to his Satyagraha. Consequently, he announced that "he would not take any food or use a car till the workers get their increase." A leader must share the suffering of his followers. That was his creed; and that is what he had already demonstrated in South Africa. This was the mainstay of his campaign there. He had undertaken fasts a number of times before. But this was the first time that he undertook fast for a public cause. This act of self-sacrifice raised the spirit of workers. "They, according to him, " "awoke to the reality of their soul, a new consciousness stirred in them and they got strength to stand by their pledge". This act put the mill-owners on the defensive. There was a wave of sympathy for Gandhi and workers. Patel and Maganlal Gandhi started looking for alternative jobs for the workers so that they were not starved into submission. Conferences were held to save the life of Gandhi and after some deliberations a formula was found out that virtually conceded the demand of the workers but allowed face-saving to the mill-owners. They accepted that final settlement would be through arbitration. But the workers on joining the duty would get 35 per cent increase, 20 per cent next day as offered and for the rest of the days till the award was given $27^1/_2$ per cent. The award given by the arbitrators would be adjusted against $27^1/_2$ per cent, that is, if the arbitrators gave more than $27^1/_2$ per cent, the employers would give the increase and if the award was less than $27^1/_2$, the employees would refund the excess.

To Gandhi, this settlement not only upheld the honour of the workers but also vouched for the efficacy of arbitration in all disputes. Recollecting the result of his fast, he observed that it generated an atmosphere of goodwill all round. For it touched the hearts of the employers who set about discovering some means for settlement. The house of the sister of Ambalal became the venue of discussion. But it looks that Gandhi was not sure whether the fast caused coercion or conversion as he observed "Before I took the vow I knew that there were serious defects about it.

For me to take such a vow in order to effect in any shape or form the decision of the mill-owners would be a cowardly injustice done to them—I know that I ran the risk of being misunderstood I could not prevent my fast from preventing their decision."[12] Further, "There are hardly any acts of human beings which are free from taint. Mine, I know, was exceptionally tainted but I preferred the ignominy of having unworthily compromised by my vow the position and independence of the mill-owners rather than it should be said by posterity that 10,000 men had broken a vow."[13]

Addressing the Ashram inmates on the day of settlement he said, "Deny it as emphatically as I may, the people cannot but feel that the mill-owners had acted under pressure of my fast and world at large will not believe what I say." But to him it was not true since he did not admit his opponent's surrender as his victory. For he allowed the mill-owners to concede only his original modest demand of the acceptance of the principle of arbitration, though they were ready to concede every demand of the workers for his sake. Very likely the decision for undertaking fast was determined by his apprehension of the impact of its failure at the all-India level, for "it would never again be possible, in his view, to raise the worker's issue in spite of the sufferings undergone by ten thousand mill-hands for more than twenty days." Its failure would be construed as the failure of his technique which he distinguished from that of Tilak and Malaviya or for that matter from the current techniques to which the elite and people were accustomed. In fact, Gandhi had an eye on something spectacular and sensational to raise the spirit of the participants. He had done that in South Africa. In the Kheda Satyagraha, too, he hit upon the programme of onion stealing. Commitment to truth and non-violence did not prevent him from giving a surprise to his opponent by adopting a new course. His strategy grew out of the situation. He could invest any normal move in the struggle with spirituality. For, power, for him, flows from the spirit. It is the spirit in every man that has to be awakened.

Though all the three struggles were local in terms of the involvement of the people and the issues involved, for Gandhi, they had all-India significance in terms of struggle for Swaraj. For, they, in his view, demonstrated the power of the people over their Government. Participation in them was a training for Swaraj. "So addressing the people during the Kheda Satyagraha, he said, "Through this struggle we want to bring home to the Government that it ought to yield to the people. No king can remain in power if he sets himself against the people. I have taken it as the chief mission of my life to prove this—."[14]

But an individual has to free himself from all kinds of controls whether of his passions, bad habits or social evils before he can claim and attain political Swaraj. This was the creed of the new leader. "Government of the self is the first step" towards political Swaraj. The ancient Indian concept of Swaraj meaning self-rule and bearing spiritual connotation was the foundation stone of political emancipation. In this context the demand for 'Swaraj' would become irresistible when the people living in the villages or workers working in the factories understood its meaning and become worthy of it by freeing themselves from all social evils like untouchability and unhygienic habits. It was, therefore, not enough to petition the Government for the acceptance of their demand for swaraj. But the real need of the hour was to 'direct the torch inward' and remove our own weaknesses. Thus, Swaraj was not to be wrested from unwilling hands but to be cultivated. It is not a condition of the rise or development of a nation but the consequence of the self-rule attained by each individual in a nation.

Gandhi was now emerging as a unique leader. He was rubbing shoulders with the topmost political leaders of India. For him, there was no leader who was unapproachable or unscalable like Himalayas or awe inspiring like a vast ocean. At the Gujarat political conference he could make Tilak, the idol of millions of India to speak in his mother tongue, Marathi and Jinnah to move his resolution on Congress-League scheme in Gujarati.[15] The new leader was leaving everybody guessing about his moves and solutions to the problems facing the country. Was he a mixture of opposites? That is what appeared to many who watched him from a distance. One admirer while introducing him to the people described him as a man who cared nothing for sensual pleasures, nothing for riches nothing for comfort or praise or promotion, a man who was simply determined to do what he believed to be right. For a ruler such a man could be a dangerous and uncomfortable enemy. For, his body which one could conquer, gave one little control over his spirit from which flowed his power.[16] Wasn't it a strange political behaviour that while declaring faith in the British Empire, he was fighting with British bureaucracy for the right of the 'ryats' with such tenacity and courage which was the dream of any revolutionary or extremist. Once the Secretary of the Viceroy told Andrews that Gandhi was a very difficult man to get on with. He was agitating against the British officers for the redress of local grievances but at the same time evincing great loyalty to the British Empire. The Indian leaders were struck by a streak of authority behind his simplicity, humility and spirituality. Even one of the topmost leaders prophesised that "This man will overreach all other leaders.[17]

Wasn't it an unusual political phenomenon that while he was in the thick of Kheda Satyagraha, he was invited to Viceroy's War Council when Tilak, Annie Besant and Ali Brothers were ignored? Though attendance of the war council and supporting the official resolution in the absence of all such leaders appeared to him some what compromising his position, he tried to retrieve his reputation by taking an assurance from the Viceroy that the political reforms embodying the main principles of Congress-League Scheme was on the cards. Besides, he got his permission to speak in Hindustani in the conference which was certainly an unusual act. For, it was the first time that an Indian leader could use an Indian language in the presence of the Viceroy. However, he left the conference with his conscience pricking and so immediately sent a letter to the Viceroy through Reverend Ireland of the Cambridge Mission wherein he expressed his regrets for the exclusion of Tilak and Ali Brothers from the conference and stated the reasons for supporting the official resolution. The burden of his arguments was that ungrudging and unequivocal support to the Empire in the hour of its danger would take us to our goal of becoming equal partner in the Empire which was equivalent to Swaraj. So he argued, "We can but accelerate our journey towards the goal by silently and simply devoting ourselves, heart and soul, to the work of delivering the Empire from the threatening danger— We must perceive that, if we serve to save the Empire we have in that very act secure home Rule."[18] With the permission of the Viceroy, he published this letter to remove any misgivings in the minds of nationalist India about his position in her struggle for freedom. In line with this outlook was his strong condemnation of the action of Governor of Bombay stopping Tilak and Kelkar of expressing themselves in the meeting called by him and it was like walking on the edge of a naked Sword to support the two forces opposed to each other—that is, nationalist and imperialist forces. The Mahatma in Gandhi held fast to the belief that the opposites could be synthesized and fashioned into a better arrangement for human progress. However, his support to war efforts was hedged in by innumerable difficulties both logical and practical. For it involved assistance for recruitment to the army which could not easily be reconciled to his commitment to non-violence. No-doubt earlier, too, he had offered his help to the British in war. But that was confined to helping the wounded. But a case for enlistment in the army posed one of the biggest problems of this life as an apostle of non-violence. But the lawyer in him hammered out a new formula that reconciled the two opposite concepts of actions. To one of his European disciples he wrote, "Before I can make him feel the virtue of non-killing, I must restore to him the arms he has lost. I have always advised young Indians to join the army but hitherto refrained from actively asking them to do so, because I did not feel sufficiently interested in the purely political life of the country or in the war itself. But a different and difficult situation faced me in Delhi; I felt at once that I was playing with the greatest problem of life in not taking the question of joining the army seriously. Either we must renounce the benefits of state or help it to the best of our ability to prosecute the war. We are not ready to renounce. Indians have double duty to perform. If they are to preach the mission or peace, they must prove their ability in war—A nation that is unfit to fight cannot from experience prove the virtue of not fighting.[19] I do not infer from this that India must fight. But I do say that India must know how to fight. Ahimsa is the eradication to injure or kill. It is personal courage that is absolute necessity. And some will acquire that courage only after he argued, "Ahimsa is the renunciation of the highest type. A weak and effeminate nation cannot perform this act—It may look terrible but it is true we must by a well-sustained conscious effort regain this power and then if we can only do so, deliver the world from travail of 'himsa' by a continuous abdication of this power."[20] In fact, the nationalist in Gandhi had taken over the apostle of non-violence. To a reporter, who failed to understand this logic, he said, "to one who comes for the advice whether it is right to fight or not, I would distinctly say no, it is not. But to one who comes with the clear conviction in his pocket that fighting is right, but is doubtful whether it is right on a particular occasion, I would advise him that the present is the right moment."[21] This, of course, was a more logical approach which he maintained till the end of his life. It is not possible to observe complete non-violence in a political and social system based on violence. One can move towards non-violence gradually. Though Gandhi's argument that for preaching the mission of peace one must prove one's ability in war may not appeal to the head, for, he himself never proved his ability for war when he undertook to propagate non-violence, he appears quite practical when he maintains that those whose view of life is based on violence have the duty to fight when their society is in danger. He rightly replied to his close associate C.F. Andrews who doubted the justification of his recruitment campaign "that his call for enlistment to army was for those who did not believe in non-violence. For, he could best spread the "gospel of ahimsa, or satyagraha by asking the 'himsk' (militant) men

had an attack of dysentery as a result of rigours of the campaign and his food habits as his food in those days consisted of groundnut butter and lemon. Initially the trouble was not very serious but his lack of faith in allopathic treatment coupled with his vow of avoiding milk made his recovery difficult. He lost all hope of life and felt as if he was at death's door. Possibly it was a nervous breakdown due to extreme weakness or may be because of depression resulting from the failure of his mission. He was in deep distress. For, his conscience was pricking him for having taken up several projects after his return from South Africa but had to leave them unfinished. Lying helpless and surrounded by his friends and followers, tears rolled down his eyes and he cried like a child. A little later he composed himself and said, "These tears have brought some peace to my mind. What God wills will happen?"[32] To fight the disease, he tried his own naturopathy or Ayurvedic treatment. But it failed to give him any relief. He declined to take any injection or allopathic medicine. It was at this time he learnt the defeat of Germany and consequently the end of his recruitment campaign which gave him great mental relief. But his physical ailment deteriorated as he suffered from Fistula. A doctor was consulted who prescribed milk diet and injections of iron and arsenic for building up his body which was essential for operation. He agreed to the injections but refused to take milk. His wife hit upon an idea. She argued that since at the time of taking the vow, he was keeping in view only cow's or buffalo's milk, he could take goat's milk which would save him from the breach of pledge. He yielded to this suggestion but not without a strain on his conscience. For, his commitment to truth demanded that a vow taken be fulfilled both in spirit and letter. In fact, it was not the issue of milk but of vow which had raised a row. For, some of his admirers questioned the value of vow when its observance caused so much suffering. One of his European disciples asked him why should the children of God who is the loving father take burden upon themselves which they are not asked to carry. The value of vow can be questioned on pragmatic grounds. For taking a vow means determining one's future in the light of the present. It is like anticipating one's own future or making one prisoner of the present and restricting one's freedom of action in future to meet the new situation. Consequently, it became difficult for him to reconcile his action of taking goat's milk with his vow. He tried to answer his critics by his own interpretation of the vow. To a friend he wrote after the operation "It appears to me that I should allow myself as much freedom as is consistent with a very liberal construction of my vows. I will not admit that, though the freedom I have allowed myself I am in any way violating my vow, even on the strictest view of it. The medical experiment of a milk diet I was making may indeed receive a great setback, but an experiment in medical science is no affair of the spirit."[33] But reflecting on this issue later on, he admitted that by accepting the goat's milk he bypassed the spirit of the vow and kept only its form. So he wrote "My intense eagerness to take up Satyagraha fight had created in me a strong desire to live, and so I contended myself with adhering to the letter of my vow only and sacrificed its spirit . . . the will to live proved stronger than the devotion to truth, and for once the votary of truth compromised his sacred ideal by his eagerness to take up the Satyagraha fight. The memory of this action even now rankles in my breast and fills me with remorse, and I am constantly thinking how to give up goat's milk. . ."[34]

However, Gandhi always maintained that vows were of great value for the spiritual development of an individual. For, it results in the purification and expression of the soul. Its value lies in bringing the body under subjection and using it for the expression of the spirit.

During the period of four years since his return from South Africa, he applied his mind to most of the major problems of the country. But his solutions were distinct corresponding to his distinct personality. It was clear to him as well as to his contemporaries that he could not fit into existing political patterns. He took up any problem that came to him without working out all its possible deduction or its implications to his entire satisfaction. That is what he wrote to Andrews:

"I did not work out the possibilities in Champaran, Kheda or Ahmedabad nor yet when I made an unconditional offer of service in 1914. I fancy that I followed His Will and no other and He will lead me 'amid the encircling gloom.'[35] He was fully aware that his solutions about the problems of the country were not shared by a number of leaders.[36] For, he was not in favour of a patched up truce between the Extremists and the Moderates. Nor could he approve of Tilak's policies which he summed up as 'Tit for Tat' in spite of their hold over the educated classes.[37] It appeared to him that he was ploughing a lonely furrow. He, therefore did not attend the special session of the Congress in August 1918 because of his differences with Tilak and Annie Besant over the question of war recruitment and Montagu-Chelmsford Reforms which were the issues before the Congress leadership. His active involvement in the recruitment campaign also prevented him from attending that session. Similarly, while opposing the British bureaucracy in his Champaran and Kaera Satyagraha, he put in all efforts to make the issues apolitical. But that was not the approach of the contemporary leadership. His failure in the recruitment campaign left a lasting lesson for his future programmes and policies. He learnt that a leader howsoever selfless and dedicated to the good of the people could not turn the tide of time or go totally against the public opinion. His leadership was limited to imparting concrete meaning and design to their amorphous aspirations and desires and showing them the way for their fulfilment. But he could not wipe out all the impressions engraved on their minds as a result of their experiences through the ages. Neither the rustic peasantry nor the educated urbanes could forget the tremendous hardships they had suffered at the hands of the British. It was only when the British turned their face against the Indians in spite of their ready co-operation during the war by passing the Rowlatt Act, Gandhi realised the pent up feelings of the people against the British and he girded up his loins to give a battle to the British by his non-violent strategy and weaponry.

Notes and References

1. C.W., Vol. XIII, p. 211.
2. *Ibid.*
3. Shukla, *op. cit.*, p. 16.
4. C.W., Vol. XIII, p. 218.
5. Malkani, N.R., Rumblings and Reminiscences of Gandhiji (Navajivan Publication House) 1972, p. 4.
6. Gandhi, M.K., Autobiography, p. 343.
7. Prasad, Rajendra, At the Feet of the Mahatma.
8. *Ibid.*, p. 26.
9. Quoted in, Nanda, B.R., Gandhi, Panislamism, Imperialism and Nationalism, p. 162.
10. Gandhi, M.K., Autobiography, pp. 365-66.
11. C.W., Vol. XIV, p. 268.
12. *Ibid.*, p. 285.
13. *Ibid.*, p. 286.
14. *Ibid.*, p. 329.
15. *Ibid.*, p. 68.
16. Desai, M., *op. cit.*, Vol. I, p. 134.
17. Diwakar, R.R., My Encounters with Gandhi, p. 10.
18. C.W., Vol. XIV, p. 378.
19. *Ibid.*, pp. 462-63.
20. *Ibid.*, p. 485.
21. Desai, M., *op. cit.*, Vol. I, p. 103.
22. C.W., XIV, p. 444.
23. Keer, Dhananjay, Lokamanya Tilak, p. 392.
24. *Ibid.*,

25. Prasad, Madho, A Gandhian Patriarch (Bombay, Popular Prakashan, 1965), p. 168.
26. Gandhi, M.K., Autobiography, p. 371.
27. Desai, M., *op. cit.*, Vol. I, p. 193.
28. C.W., XIV, p. 473.
29. *Ibid.*, 493.
30. *Ibid.*, Vol. XV, p. 28.
31. *Ibid.*, p. 17.
32. Prasad, Rajendra, At the Feet of the Mahatma, p. 80.
33. C.W., Vol. XV, p. 74.
34. Gandhi, M.K., Autobiography, pp. 378-79.
35. C.W., XV, p. 4.
36. *Ibid.*, p. 15.
37. *Ibid.*, p. 26.

12

The Great Transformation

The Rowlatt Act invested the Government with extraordinary powers to suppress any kind of political agitation. It provided for the trial of seditious crime by special tribunals consisting of three judges without juries and assessors and without preliminary commitment proceedings or appeal. It denied the accused the right of defending himself with the help of a counsel. It also provided for the arrest, confinement of or detention of any person without showing any cause. All such drastic measures were summed up in the slogan na apil, na dalil, na vakil (no appeal, no argument, no lawyer). As soon as the Rowlatt Bills were introduced in Viceroy's legislative council, Gandhi declared that he would start satyagraha if they were passed. For, the contents of the Bills stirred him to very depths. Though he had not yet left his bed, he could not watch easily the progress of the Bills, lying in the bed. He had been operated for piles and was unconscious as a result of chloroform administered to him before the operation. Kanji Dwarkadas who saw him in that state heard him saying 'Government must remove salt tax and it must nationalise milk'.[1] The prospect of a brush with imperialism revived his desire to live. His mental depression and gloom following the failure of his recruitment mission and serious illness gave way to the zeal for direct encounter with imperialism. The Mahatma in the making was a strange mixture of a pacifist and a crusader or a fighter. Prospects of a fight with a powerful adversary worked as an elixir for him. He immediately called a meeting of his co-workers at his Ashram where he was convalescing. Among them were Vallabhbhai Patel, Sarojini Naidu,

Horniman, Umar Sobani, Shankarlal Banker, Anusuyabehn. On Gandhi's suggestion it was decided to form Satyagraha Sabha to start agitation for the repeal of the Act. It was conceived as a temporary body for a specific purpose. It was a pragmatic step as Gandhi had at that time no hold over the existing political bodies such as the Home Rule League for Indian National Congress. For, he had openly expressed his differences with Home Rule leaders and both sections of the Indian National Congress. He had joined the Home Rule League and after Besant's resignation he became its president. But the differences arose with other leaders when he changed its name to Swaraj Sabha (Hindi equivalent for Home Rule). Jinnah, Jayakar and Dwarkadas resigned from the League denouncing Gandhi's methods as dictatorial. Moreover as an author of Satyagraha, he alone was competent to give guidance. According to the rules of Satyagraha Sabha, a volunteer was to take satyagraha pledge which committed him 'to sacrifice his all for his honour'. But before taking such an extreme step he must be fully convinced that the "Rowlatt Bills were unjust, destructive of elementary rights of an individual and subversive of the principle of liberty." So the summary of the Bills was issued by Gandhi so that the contents were known to the participants. Students and persons below the age of 18 were excluded from signing the pledge. Another step that he took was to write to the Indian members of the Viceroy's council to resign from the Select Committee or even from the council if the Government insisted on having what he called 'a piece of devilish legislation.'

Though still very weak, he went round the country to seek support for Satyagraha campaign. He could hardly stand to address the audience and quite often his speeches were read out by others. In most of his speeches he laid stress on the essential qualities of a Satyagraha which included courtesy to the opponent, toleration of his views, strict adherence to truth and non-violence. However, there was practical difficulty of working out an effective and definite programme of opposing or disobeying this particular law. For, the ball would be always in the court of the government. One could disobey it only if the Government gave once an opportunity for it. It was for the Government to take action against a person on the basis of this law. So the question before Gandhi was whether other laws could be civily disobeyed to force the Government to repeal this Act. If so which law could be disobeyed without causing much inconvenience to the people or to the law and order machinery. Such questions were always before him whenever the situation compelled him to offer Satyagraha. Gandhi claimed that the programme for resisting the 'Black Act' occurred to him just in a dream while he was staying with Rajagopalachari in Madras and having serious discussion about it with all the friends around him. "The idea came to me last night in a dream that we should call upon the country to observe a general hartal. Satyagraha is a process of self-purification and ours is a sacred fight and it seems to me to be in the fitness of things that it should be commenced with an act of self-purification. Let all the people of India, therefore, suspend their business on that day and observe the day as one of fasting and prayer."[2] Thus Gandhi was making it a religious fight and not merely a political agitation. In South Africa, too, he converted agitation against racial discrimination into a religious fight when those attending the meeting took a vow with God as witness. The programme was welcomed by Rajagopalachari and others. However, the idea was not new. Nor was it the result of any intuition. In his struggle in South Africa the hartal by Indians occurred sometime spontaneously and Gandhi found it quite effective in mobilising the people as well as communicating to the Government the feelings of the people about certain laws. His mind was occupied with this question and the rational process for the search of an effective programme was going on in his mind when he fell asleep. It was not a message from God. His inner voice was his own voice crystallized and purified after the elimination of conflicting choices through a rational process which works imperceptibility even when one is asleep. Moreover, hartal or the suspension of business as a mark of protest against an unpopular measure was not new to the Indians. But the idea of fasting and prayer added a new dimension to it, for, even women and children could observe it and thereby identify themselves with the national cause. It signified the will of the people to make some sacrifice for their country. By this method, Gandhi had enlisted to his cause the support of millions who had hitherto been bypassed or left in the dark by the leaders about any issue affecting them. So he wrote to Mazharul Haque on March 20, 1920 that he was making collective fasting and prayer a science which would do immense benefit to this country.[3]

Besides this, he issued an unregistered newspaper 'Satyagraha' as a part of civil disobedience. For, till then he had no paper of his own and he had to depend upon other papers for the publicity of his programme. In Bombay, the plan of action also included distribution of proscribed literature. Copies of the 'Hind Swaraj' and 'Sarvodaya' which had been proscribed were printed in large number and were distributed at the monster meeting in Bombay. Though all the copies were sold out, the government did not take any action against anybody on a lame plea that the proscribed copies had not been sold. The reprint was held to be a new edition of the books that had not been proscribed and to sell them did not constitute an offence under the law." Since the publication of Bombay Chronicle had been suspended which had become more or less Gandhi's mouthpiece, the author of Satyagraha was left with no means to maintain direct communication with the people. In fact, publicity for any campaign undertaken by him was an essential component of his technique. In South Africa he virtually staked all his savings for starting the 'Indian Opinion'. He requested Lord Ampthill to write the introduction to his biography by Doke and bought the whole lot about 700 copies for distribution. So his friends Umar Sobani and Shankarlal Banker who were controlling the weekly 'Young India' offered its editorship to him which he readily accepted and converted it into a bi-weekly. But when Bombay chronicle resumed publication, 'Young India' was restored to its original weekly form. Similarly, Indulal Yajnik who was conducting the Gujarati monthly 'Navajivan' placed it at his disposal since it was not possible for him to maintain contact with the non-English speaking people through 'Young India'. So a powerful instrument for carrying his message to the masses fell into his hands which filled the gap of 'Indian Opinion' through which he could carry on Satyagraha in South Africa. These papers became his mouthpiece for educating the people for Satyagraha and uplift of the nation. However, their circulation varied from time to time depending upon the fate of this movements launched by him at different times. During the Rowlatt Act agitation their circulation rose rapidly and Gandhi even thought of starting weeklies in Urdu, Hindi and even Tamil as the press for Gandhi was a powerful vehicle for mobilising the people. He, therefor, wanted every inch of the space of his papers for this purpose. That accounts for his opposition to advertisements in his weeklies. Writing for the paper was a serious work for him, a sort of meditation or penance in the pursuit of truth. He, therefore, wanted all information to be fully screened and records examined before an opinion is expressed on any issue. He wanted a journalist to be a scholar. He advised his editorial staff to go through the works of great scholars on a subject, Government records and blue books before arriving at any conclusion. He was an investigating journalist. His famous Green pamphlet, according to him, was the result of extensive reading of all the blue books and writings of authorities on the subject. As a writer of an article or of as letter to the Government authorities, he was very cautious not only about the choice of words but also of grammar. Once while addressing a letter to the Viceroy before launching his Salt

Satyagraha, he wrote the words 'so charged'. His secretary felt that it was typographical error and preferred the word surcharged. Mira who was sitting there when this letter was being discussed agreed with Mahadev. Gandhi told them that it was no mistake as he had deliberately used this word and gave a discourse on English language and grammar. So far as the sentence was concerned 'so charged' appears to be correct as Gandhi wanted to communicate that "there is every danger of independence itself coming to us so charged as to be of no value." The policy of minutely examining facts and records before expressing his opinion, he maintained while examining the actions of the authorities during the martial law period in the Punjab. The lawyer in him was at its best while commenting on the judgements given by the Martial Law regime. He maintained a balanced outlook while pointing out the injustice done to those who were tried by such courts.

During the suspension of Satyagraha, he was keen to go to the Punjab to assess the situation himself as the authenticity of the events and brutal suppression by the Government could not be easily verified because of the restrictions imposed on the press. The news trickled down to him only through Punjabis visiting him in Bombay. But he had to postpone his visit to this province till October as the Government allowed him to enter Punjab on the appointment of Hunter Committee to hold an enquiry into the disturbances in the province in April 1919. The Indian National Congress, however, boycotted the official committee and appointed its own sub-committee to investigate facts leading to the disturbances. Resides Gandhi the Committee had Motilal Nehru, M.R. Jayakar, C.R. Das and Abbas Tayabji as its members. But most of the work was assigned to Gandhi on whom devolved the responsibility of organising its work as well as of conducting the inquiry at most of the places in the province in addition to drafting the report. The people around him were astonished by his analytical skill. He was a rare combination of a lawyer and a Mahatma. For, without transgressing the bounds of truth, he could win over his opponents through his sincerity and rational analysis of facts. J.L. Nehru, who saw a great deal of Gandhi during this inquiry was impressed by the way he argued his point. He observed, "Very often his proposals seemed novel to our committee and it did not approve of them. But almost always he argued his way to their acceptance."[4]

Gandhi's strategy during the Rowlatt Act agitation was to provoke the Government to arrest him or his followers so that he could start a movement to fill the jails. But the Government tried to scuttle all such moves. Initially March 30 was fixed for general hartal but subsequently it was changed to April 6. But the original programme was observed in Delhi as the information of its postponement did not reach there. Delhi had not witnessed the hartal of this kind. There was a great spectacle of the fraternization of Hindus and Muslims in Delhi and Punjab. In Delhi a procession led by Swami Shraddhananda was fired upon causing a number of casualties. It was followed by a reign of repression. The same attitude of the Government was witnessed in Lahore and Amritsar, the principal cities of Punjab. The programme was implemented in Amritsar with enthusiasm under the leadership of Dr. Saif-ud-Din Kitchleu and Dr. Satyapal on 30th March and 6th April. A mass meeting was held on 30th March. Processions and meetings were held in Lahore and several other towns of the Punjab. The authorities were shaken. They saw in all these programmes a conspiracy to destroy the government. This assumption led them to let loose a reign of terror in the province. Gandhi was arrested at Palwal on his way to the Punjab and was sent back to Bombay. The two doctors of Amritsar were deported on 10th April. This ignited the political atmosphere in the city. An impromptu procession was formed that moved towards the Deputy Commissioner's bungalow to protest against the arrest of their leaders. The police resorted to firing as a result of which several persons were killed or injured. This added fuel to the fire. The infuriated mob attacked and killed some Europeans. A few buildings of the Europeans were also burnt or damaged. An English missionary Miss Sherwood was severely assaulted. As a result, the Government became nervous and the city was made over to the army under the charge of General Dyer. To suppress with an iron hand and to teach a lesson to the people of Amritsar with revengeful spirit, he ordered firing on the people gathered at the Jallianwala Bagh on the Baisakhi day as a result of which 400 persons were killed and more than a thousand injured. Besides, Martial Law was proclaimed in the whole of the province and summary courts were constituted to try cases of sedition. Several prominent persons of the province were either arrested or deported. All this was done to overawe the people with the show of the might of the Government.

Violence also broke out in Bombay, Ahmedabad and Viramgar on hearing the news of the arrest of Gandhi. At Ahmedabad one British sergeant was hacked to pieces by the mob. All this disturbed Gandhi who owned the mistake of mob violence. He suspended Satyagraha accepting its commencement as a Himalayan miscalculation. For, he had not fully judged the pent up feelings of the people against the alien and haughty bureaucracy while planning the strategy of this movement. However, in his view, the suspension was no defeat. It was only a step to reconsider the strategy in the light of new developments which he could not foresee at the time of framing his programmes. As a general of his non-violent forces, he needed time to regroup them. The eruption of violence not only left with the opponent an opportunity to suppress the movement with impunity but also weakened his hold over it. The masses and the local leaders could hardly distinguish between the norms and nuances of his Satyagraha and any other direct agitation. For, most of his co-workers did not understand him completely. To a lady co-worker in South Africa, he wrote "I do not know the people here; nor they me."[5]

One reason for the weakness of his hold over the movement was the lack of his own publicity media and consequently absence of direct contact with the local leaders and the masses. He had to depend upon other papers especially the *Bombay Chronical* for guiding the movement. Very few papers at that time were prepared to serve as a link between him and the people for fear of punitive action by the Government. There were very few courageous and impartial editors like Horniman who gave Gandhi full support during his Rowlatt Satyagraha and agitation against Jallianwala Bagh massacre as a result of which he was deported to England on April 26, 1919. *Young India* and *Navajivan* had not been as yet passed on to Gandhi. These papers first appeared in October 1919 under his full control.

Disturbances in the Punjab following the Rowlatt Act agitation pushed Gandhi into the thick of Indian politics in spite of his differences with most of the leaders of the country. His faith in truth and non-violence led him to condemn openly the violent acts of the mob at Amritsar in April even in the face of bitter opposition of the foremost leaders of the Congress. He was even ready to stake the membership of the Congress on this issue. He addressed the audience with words imbued with high idealism: "I agree there was grave provocation given by the Government in arresting Dr. Kitchlu and Dr. Satyapal and arresting me who was bent on a mission of peace at the invitation of Dr. Satyapal and Swamiji (Shraddhananda). But Government went mad at that time; we went mad also at that time. I say do not return madness with madness but return madness with sanity and whole situation will be yours."[6]

In spite of the opposition of several all India leaders to this approach, important leaders of the Punjab like Swami Shraddhananda and Raizada Bhagat Ram of Jullunder endorsed their views that Indians should meet hatred by love and falsehood by truth in accordance with the spirit of Indian culture.

The Amritsar Congress marked Gandhi's deep involvement in the Congress. As he himself records that his attendance "at the previous Congress was nothing more than an annual renewal of allegiance to the Congress. I never felt on these occasions that I had any other work cut out for me except that of mere private, nor did I desire more."[7] Jawaharlal Nehru confirms this change as he observed that the Amritsar Congress was the first Gandhi Congress. Recording his impression of the Amritsar Congress, he said, "Lokmanya Tilak was also present and took a prominent part in the deliberations but there could be no doubt about it that the majority of the delegates and even more so the great crowds outside looked to Gandhi for leadership. The slogan Mahatma 'Gandhi ki Jai' began to dominate the Indian political horizon."[8] In fact, Gandhi's life style and the mode of his functioning had generated new hope in the masses. His approach was novel. Even at the Amritsar Congress he could face the opposition of the old guards over the issue of the acceptance of the Montagu-Chelmsford Reforms. For, he pleaded for the faithful trial to the Reforms without any condition. He proposed an amendment to the Das' resolution to the effect that the words disappointing and inadequate be removed and warmest thanks be offered to Montagu. His amendment was hotly debated for three days. In support of his amendment he appealed to the delegates passionately in the following words: "I suggest to you that Mr. Montagu has extended the hand of fellowship, do not reject his advances. Indian culture demands trust and full trust— If you accept your own civilization, I ask the author of the commentaries of the Bhagavadgita, if he accepts the teachings of the Gita, then let him extend the hand of fellowship to Mr. Montagu."[9] Pyarelal, who was a witness to the whole scene of the tussle between him and the old guards on the dais observes," At the plenary session, he spoke with the fire of conviction and with that passion flung down his white cap on the rostrum and pleaded bareheaded with Lokmanya for the acceptance of his amendment.[10] It had a dramatic effect and a compromise was arrived at which was not fully satisfactory. A rider was added offering co-operation to the working of the Reforms.

A crisis was blown over by this dramatic act of the Mahatma. Drama was Gandhi's forte. He wins over his opponents by some dramatic act. The appeal was made to the devotee of the Gita not because Gita held a direct solution to the problem facing the leadership at that time. But to Gandhi Gita represented the essence of Indian culture and civilization and so the famous commentator of the Gita must honour the hand of co-operation by the representative of the British. Nevertheless Gandhi's policies during this period reveals that he was still uncertain about his role in Indian politics. On the one hand he was in favour of working of the new reforms at the Amritsar Congress. On the other hand his speeches and acts were giving assurance to the masses that he was the right person to lead the people in their fight against the Government. There appears to be mental conflict in Gandhi—the conflict between the co-operative and non-co-operative Gandhi. For, he was still hoping that the British would do justice and the conflict would be resolved. He was, therefore, pleading for giving fair trial to the Reforms. So at the Amritsar Congress his position was close to that of Malaviya and Jinnah.

However, his resolve to co-operate with the British Government gave way to the inflexibility of the British attitude towards the happenings in the Punjab as revealed by the report of the Hunter Commission which appeared on May 28, 1920. It was not unanimous because of the differences between the English and Indian members over the issue whether the outbreak in the Punjab was premeditated revolt or an accidental outbreak. The English members took the former view and the Indians later. Consequently, the English members justified not only the introduction of Martial Law but also exonerated most of the actions of those administering Martial Law while admitting that the administration of Martial Law was marred in particular instances by misuse of power and that General Dyer did not act with such humanity as the case permitted.

Gandhi had sharp differences with the majority report for, he believed that the disturbances were the result of deep rooted resentment of the people of the Punjab against the high handed methods used by O' Dwyer's administration in collecting war loans and recruiting youngmen in the army during the war which were followed by more repressive measures after the termination of hostilities. It was only the wonderfully quick acceptance by the people, he argued, of the principle of Satyagraha that effectively checked the spread of violence throughout the length and breadth of the country. The official report and despatches, according to him, constituted an attempt to condone official lawlessness. The official enquiry, therefore, was nothing but a scandal of great magnitude which could not be tolerated by 'a nation if it had to preserve its self-respect and become a free partner in the Empire'.

So he reminded the nation that the time had arrived when Indians must cease to rely upon mere petitions to parliament for effective action.

"If the parliament fails us, he reiterated " and if we are worthy to call ourselves a nation, we must refuse to uphold the Government by withdrawing co-operation from it. "Gandhi, thus declared his first war without violence against British imperialism. The events in the Punjab not only transformed Gandhi from a loyalist to an opponent of the British Raj but also brought him to the forefront of all-India politics. Earlier he was involved in the local issues. True, the impact of Rowlatt Act agitation was widespread and had communicated to the millions in India the message of Gandhi's Satyagraha. But as yet the Mahatma had not challenged the foundation of British imperialism and relied on the British sense of justice for the redress of the grievances of the Indians.

Notes and References

1. Kanji Dwarkadas, *op. cit.*, p. 96.
2. Autobiography, p. 383.
3. C.W., XCVII, p. 260.
4. Nehru, J.L., An Autobiography (Allied Publishers) 1962, p. 44.
5. C.W., Vol. XV, p. 341.
6. Report of the Amritsar Session of the Congress, p. 66.
7. Gandhi, M.K., Autobiography, p. 405.
8. Nehru, J.L., An Autobiography, pp. 44-45.
9. C.W., Vol. XV, pp. 366-67.
10. Shukla, *op. cit.*, p. 190.

13

Declaration of War without Violence

It was a call to the nation to be ready for a fight against their oppressors with a weapon the efficacy of which was neither known to them nor to their opponents. No other leader could guide them for its effective use. Others could either watch him fighting or join hands with him. He was emerging as the sole arbiter of the destiny of the nation. He had won over important Congress leaders in every part of the country who were ready to carry out his programme. Motilal and his son Jawaharlal Nehru from U.P., Lajpat Rai from the Punjab, Patel from the Bombay Presidency, N.C. Kelkar, Dr. Monje and Abhaynkar from Poona, Rajendra Prasad from Bihar, Rajagopalachari, Rangaswami Iyengar, Satyamurti and Prakasam from the South. He had carried with him the Muslim leadership of the country by his support to the Khilafat issue. Ali Brothers, Azad, Ansari, etc. looked to him for guidance. He counselled to them to withdraw co-operation to the British. The Punjab issue had already stirred the nation. Thus the two issues, one virtually secular but vitally concerning one province of the country and the other religious concerning only one community in India, were joined to attack the citadel of imperialism without using arms. However, initially Gandhi did not favour taging the Punjab question with the Khilafat issue. For, at the Delhi conference he appealed to the Hindus to consider the question of their support to the Khilafat independently of any other issue whether Punjab or cow protection. For, Gandhi believed in trusting people whenever he thought of supporting the cause of any party. This was his main plea at the Amritsar Congress, too, for the acceptance of Montagu-Chelmsford Reforms. By trusting the other party in a case of dispute one is leaving the ball in the court of the opponent. But keeping in view the mood and sentiments of the Punjab Hindus, he yielded to the demand of launching a movement for the redress of the grievances over both the issues. The Khilafat issue both for the masses and most of the leaders of both the communities, was a religious issue. But for Gandhi it had secular connotations. For, it involved breach of trust as during the war the Muslims had been given some kind of assurance by the British authorities that their sentiments would be kept in view while meeting justice to Turkey which had joined hands with Germany during the war. For the Sultan of Turkey was considered by the Mohammedans as the head of their religion (Khalifa). But by the terms of the Treaty of Peace it was clear that the Sultan of Turkey would be shorn of all his political power. The defence of the Khilafat issue put heavy strain on Gandhi's dialectical skill. For, the British political leaders could put him on the defensive by arguing that by this treaty they had only given to the territories under Turkey the right of self-determination which the Indians themselves were demanding for their own country. On a hind sight the reaction of the Muslim leadership on the Khilafat issue was not based on rational considerations. Nor was that of Gandhi. For, the Muslims in Turkey would be shortly fighting under Kemal Pasha for the abolition of Khilafat. So many in India were sceptical about Gandhi's support to Khilafat Issue. But the thrill of Hindu-Muslim unity which it had assured drowned this scepticism. For even Tilak did not oppose support to the Khilafat. In their zeal for Hindu-Muslim unity the Indian leadership lost sight of the rights of the Arabs. Moreover, the Khilafat issue united various Muslim groups under common religious banner. But after the abolition of the Khilafat they disintegrated leaving a lot of confusion in Muslim politics in India as disparate Muslim groups moved in different directions.

Gandhi, in fact, started thinking in terms of non-co-opration with the British at the all-India level even before the Congress met at its special session in Calcutta in September 1920.[1] The Khilafat Conference held at Calcutta on February 20, 1920 had accepted non-co-operation. On March 10, he had issued a manifesto whereby he had advocated launching of non-co-operation non-violent movement. But he was very cautious in framing its programmes as he was in favour of moving slowly as 'to ensure the retention of self-control under the fiercest heat.' It was divided into four stages, the first stage involved minimum of offence to the government and least possible mass action as it entailed only renunciation of titles, honorary posts, resignation of posts in the civil service. Refusal to service in the police was the last item.[2] Refusal to pay taxes occurs in the last stage if the authorities remained adamant. He did not favour the boycott of British goods at this stage to mitigate offence to the British people. He was making efforts to keep his hold over the movement and put volunteers under strict discipline. He had an experience how his plans could go off the rails as a result of the enthusiasm of the masses. So on the Khilafat Day on 17th October, 1919, he appealed to the people to remain indoors and that there should be no processions or public meetings and that mill hands and others involved in essential services should stay at work so that there should be no disorder or violence. He openly denounced the Government for betraying the Muslims over Khilafat issue. He set the ball rolling by returning all the medals that the Government had bestowed on him for his services as a mark of protest for betraying the Muslims over the Khilafat issue. In a letter to the Viceroy he wrote: "The Imperial Government have acted in the Khilafat matter in an unscrupulous immoral and unjust manner—I can retain neither respect nor affection for such a Government.

However, it was not easy for him to obtain the approval of the Congress for non-violent non-co-operation movement. There was sharp division among the provincial Congress committees over this issue. The Andhra Congress Committee and the Punjab Congress Committee recommended the adoption of the policy of non-co-operation but would defer the programme till after the special session. Bengal and C.P. committees considered non-co-operation as the only effective weapon left with the people in the circumstances but did not favour the boycott of new legislative bodies. Bihar, Orissa and Bombay committees only accepted it in principle but had not yet taken any decision with regard to various items of the programme. Madras approved a policy of non-co-operation but voted against Gandhi's programme. The United Provinces approved and formulated a detailed programme adding boycott of the welcome to H.R.H. the Duke of Connaught. At the Gujarat political conference the resolution of non-co-operation could be passed as a result of the efforts of V. Patel and Abbas Tyabji who presided over the conference.[3]

So there was stiff opposition to this programme at the subjects Committee meeting of the Special Session. Gandhi himself observed: "Never perhaps has the Congress witnessed such determined opposition as was offered to the non-co-operation resolution—Again never has there been such united opposition by the noted leaders of the people"[4] like Jinnah, C.R. Das, B.C. Pal, Khaparde, Kelkar, Monje. An imposing phalanx of veteran politicians stood there to torpedo his programmes with a volley of their words. But Gandhi stood unperturbed. Indulal Yajnik recalled later that Gandhi's reply to the debate remained in his memory 'the ablest and most convincing masterpiece to the resolution by his sweet reasonableness, tact and accommodation.[5] He won over a number of veterans of the Congress including Vijayaraghavachari and Motilal Nehru by incorporating the demand for Swaraj in the resolution as originally the object of the movement was redress of the Punjab and Khilafat wrongs. The question of the British connection, that had divided the Congress leadership was kept in abeyance. The British connection was to be maintained if it was consistent with the self-respect and interest of the nation.[6] The boycott of foreign goods was added only to accommodate a few influential leaders, though initially he was opposed to it on practical grounds. He himself recorded, "I am sorry for it. I may not state how it came to find a place there. But as it did not conflict my conscience and in order to show my reasonableness, I undertook to move a resolution whose musical harmony was marred by a false note." "Boycott of foreign cloth was included in Swadeshi. Boycott of all other foreign goods is a senseless proposition if only because it is a virtual impossibility. But if the introduction of the addendum stimulates us to sacrifice our luxuries and superfluities it would have served a good purpose."[7] Practical considerations quite often dominated his mind in framing the programme of the movement. In answer to a question as to why did he not ask for the withdrawal of children from Municipal schools, he said, "I am a practical idealist and so I place before the people only such programmes as can be implemented."[8] In fact, he could not ignore political realities. He had to carry with him the people whose zeal for a fight was unbounded. He was hard pressed by the Khilafatists to put pressure on the British to refrain from taking any action against the Turkish Empire. In a way he was yielding to the demands of his followers to sustain their zeal. The Muslim leaders such as the Ali Brothers were quite often carried away by their own rhetoric. This situation put great pressure on his tact, patience and intelligence.

The resolution was passed in the Subjects Committee meeting by a narrow margin. There were three groups in that meeting. There were those who were supporting the Mahatma whole heartedly. Then there were those who were supporting the programme of NCO excluding boycott of councils, schools and colleges. These included Bengal leaders such as C.R. Das, Bipin Chandra Pal, etc. Then there were those who opposed NCO tooth and nail such as Jinnah and Annie Besant. However, the resolution was passed by a convincing majority in the open session. For it received 1855 votes against 873 for the amendment to his resolution. Possibly there were a large number of delegates who were still wavering and could neither support the resolution as it involved self-sacrifice nor could they oppose it because the mood of the masses was on the side of Gandhi. For the total number of delegates registered at the Congress was 5814 which means that more than three thousand either absented themselves or refrained from voting.[9] Some contemporaries noticed that both at the Subjects Committee meeting and at the plenary session the support of the Khilafatists tilted the balance in favour of Gandhi. The voting at the plenary session revealed that the rank and file of the Congress was with Gandhi. His programme was finally endorsed at the Nagpur session in December 1920 without much difficulty as the issue of Reformed Councils that had divided the leadership at Calcutta was removed after election to councils. It is reported that though C.R. Das had spent a lot of money to send delegates to the Nagpur session to oppose Gandhi's programme wisdom dawned upon him at the last moment and he decided to support Gandhi's programme as the wind was blowing in favour of the Mahatma. There were few who could muster courage to challenge him. He was no more 'Karamvir' Gandhi of South Africa. He was a great soul and could not be treated as an ordinary leader. People flocked to him for his 'darshan'. For a devout it was nothing short of blasphemy to address him as if he was an ordinary person. Thus when Mr. Jinnah addressed him as Mr. Gandhi at the Nagpur session, a large number of his admirers including Mohammad Ali objected. But Jinnah remained firm and refused to withdraw the adjective which he normally used for any good person. This created a furor in the meeting as the devout wanted that Gandhi should be addressed as a Mahatma. The situation was brought under control by Gandhi himself who told the audience that by coercing Jinnah to use a particular choice of word they were not doing any honour to him[10] (Gandhi). Possibly this experience left a deep impression on Jinnah's mind as he felt that he had now no place in the Congress in this kind of atmosphere. The Government of India hoped that the programme of Gandhi would divide the Congress and therefore advised the provincial governments to refrain from interfering with the moves of Gandhi.[11]

The main objective of Gandhi's non-violent non-cooperation was to shake the foundation of the mighty empire that wielded immense power in India simply because of the willing co-operation of the people over whom the power was exercised. He wanted to infuse into them a sense of confidence through a united action of the whole nation. As a young leader who witnessed the change that was brought about by him in the political atmosphere through his courageous actions and pronouncements, Jawaharlal observes "a demoralized, backward and broken up people suddenly straightened their backs and lifted their heads and took part in disciplined joint action on a countrywide scale."

The programme that emerged under the leadership of Gandhi had both negative and positive aspects. The former covered boycott of law courts by the lawyers, boycott of schools and colleges owned, aided or recognized by the Government, boycott of election to the Assembly and Provincial Councils, the surrender of titles, Honours etc. boycott of official functions and boycott of foreign goods. Its positive aspects mostly followed from the void created by the boycott. Thus, the setting up of courts demanded the setting up of popular tribunals or panchayats for administering justice, the boycott of government institutions demanded the establishment of national educational institutions and the boycott of foreign goods required manufacture of cloth by the people themselves by working on the spinning wheels as that was the only machine which the poor people in villages could afford.

Besides, abolition of untouchability and promotion of Hindu-Muslim unity were important items of the programme for fighting the divisive forces within the nation and to purge the nation from all such evils that sapped its vitiality. The campaign against drinking of liquor also fell into this category. Thus, it was non-co-operation in a limited sense. For it also involved programme for the reconstruction of Indian society based on the principles of self-reliance, unity, equality and morality.

Swaraj in one year was the ideal or the goal of this non-violent war. But the meaning of the word Swaraj was left undefined. So it communicated to different people different meanings or different meanings to the same persons at different times or in different moods. It was a parliamentary Swaraj or parliamentary government to Gandhi at a particular stage of India's development. To some it was a state of mind and not a change of government but a change of attitude or a way of looking at things. It meant self-realization or capacity of the people to get rid of any foreign government. To Gandhi, definition was not that important. But what was important was the process through which it was to be attained as during the process its meaning and form would become clear. In other words, if people developed the capacity to resist any kind of injustice by any external authority, they were virtually free from any external control and, therefore, had attained real Swaraj. However, by keeping its meaning undefined he had tactfully prevented a division in the Congress as several important members of the Congress held strong views over this issue.

But Gandhi's programme and the philosophy underlying non-co-operation did not go unchallenged. Some of his friends and admirers both inside and outside the Congress believed that it would result in unbridled violence in the country. But to Gandhi it was the only way to avoid the outbreak of violence since evil system under which India was governed had piled up so much hatred for it in the heart of every Indian that it would burst any day destroying every things good or bad around. But the goal of Swaraj in one year could not be attained without the observance of non-violence by the people and that meant avoidance of violence in any form. R.N. Tagore who had raised his image as the 'Mahatma' or the 'Great soul' in the popular mind was critical of the non-co-operation movement for several reasons. Firstly it was based, according to him on narrow outlook as it was creating a Chinese Wall between the East and the West, while the real need of the hour was co-operation between the two. Secondly, it was negative and inconsistent with the message of Indian culture. Thirdly, it had called upon the students to leave government or government aided schools without making alternative arrangement for their education, both in science and literature.

But to Gandhi non-co-operation was neither opposed to the West nor was it isolating India from the rest of the world. Rather it was "intended to pave the way to real, honourable and voluntary co-operation on mutual respect and truth. It is rather" a protest against an unwitting and unwilling participation in evil. The aspect of negation, he asserted, was not opposed to truth. For, 'rejection is as much an ideal as the acceptance of a thing.' It is as necessary to reject untruth as it is to accept truth. Even the authors of the Upanishads sought 'Brahman' in 'Neti'. So far as the education of the children was concerned, he was of the firm view that the government schools were of no use to the Indians as 'they have unmanned us, rendered us helpless and godless. They have filled us with discontent, providing no remedy for the discontent, and have made us despondent. But the real purpose of education according to him, was to raise our moral character and not merely imparting literary or science education.

According to S.C. Bose, who travelled in the same boat with Tagore from Europe, the poet initially was not opposed to the non-co-operation of the Congress. He was only anxious that there should be more of constructive activity, so that a state within the state could be built up entirely on the co-operation and support of the people. But immediately after his arrival in India he was surrounded by a group of people who were opposed to the non-co-operation movement and who began to point out to him the shortcomings of that movement as well as the personal views of the Mahatma on modern science and modern medicine which had no connection with the political programme of the Congress.[12]

Nevertheless, the differences did not mar the personal relationship between the two. It is at that time Tagore wrote his play *Mukta-dhara* (the free current) wherein the character of Dhananjaya, the saint who led the oppressed people of Shivterrai against the oppression of the ruler of Uttarakut is the portrayal of the character of Gandhi. For Dhananjay's message and personality represents Gandhi's message of non-violence. In fact, in matters of principles Gandhi was unbending. Once he had taken a decision he would put himself in a steel frame. Accompanied by the Ali Brothers he undertook an extensive tour of the country. But the Mahatma was the star attraction. At many a small station people assembled from distant villages and waited with lighted torches for Mahatma's 'darshan'. For his name had penetrated deep into the remote corners of every part of India. At places the crowd was so large that formed a solid mass and "not even a mustard seed if let fall could find its way to the ground."[13] He usually preferred to address the meeting sitting as he could not stand for a long time. There was no music in his voice. But there was ring of sincerity of all that he spoke. He did not raise his voice. It remained at a level. But he strengthened his arguments by facts and reason. A lawyer needs only facts to support his case. Rhetoric and eloquence do not add anything to the strength of the case.

The boycott of cloth gave rise to a dramatic and an exciting programme. All clothes made of foreign cloth were to be burnt as a joint venture. On July 31, Gandhi ceremoniously celebrated the bonfire of foreign cloth at Umar Sobani's yard at Parel in Bombay—a spectacular scene witnessed by thousands of citizens. According to a witness, "when Gandhi lighted the piles a sort of frenzy seized the whole crowd and from all sides foreign clothes rained in heaps upon the burning pile, a sort of divine enthusiasm seized the people."[14] The scene was reminiscent of the bonfire of registration certificates by the Indians in South Africa that heated their passions for self-sacrifice and self-suffering. The bonfire spread all over the country. But it pained Gandhi's very dear friend

Andrews, for it meant to him,[15] destroying in the fire the noble handiwork of one's fellow men and women, one's brothers and sisters abroad. "But Gandhi replied that by this bonfire of foreign clothes he was transferring the ill-will from men to things as the general body of the Indians' are filled with ill-will because they are weak and hopelessly ignorant of the way to shed their weakness."[16]

Tagore's heart was equally filled with remorse on witnessing the enthusiasm of the masses for Gandhi's programme. For him it was nothing short of mass hysteria as people had surrendered their reason and had virtually abdicated their real freedom of the soul in the name of some outward liberty. He questioned the rationale of Gandhi's command 'spin and weave' which for him 'constitute a greater danger for us'. He deplored the blind obedience to Gandhi's call in an article 'the call of Truth' which awakened the poet in Gandhi and in a firm rejoinder dressed in poetic imagery, he wrote, "True to his poetical instinct the poet lives for the morrow and would have us do likewise. He presents to our admiring gaze the beautiful picture of the birds early in the morning singing hymns of praise as they soar into the sky. These birds had their days food and so soared with rested wings—But I have had the pain of watching the birds who for want of strength could not be coaxed even into a flutter of their wings—I have found it impossible to soothe the suffering patients with a song from Kabir. The hungry millions ask for one poem—the invigorating food . They cannot be given it. They must earn it themselves. And they can earn only by the sweat of their brow."

Call for spinning, for him, was the result of reasoned necessity for those who have nothing to cover their nudity and not a morsel to satisfy their hunger and its acceptance is not out of blind obedience. But for the poet and the intellectuals, spinning must be taken as a sacrament. For 'when there is war, the poet lays down the lyre, the lawyer his law reports, "the school boy his books." It was a well thought out reply to the poet addressed to him in his own poetic language. The Mahatma who talked to the people in plain language could talk to the poet in his own language.

But the boycott of foreign cloth could be achieved only if there was sufficient swadeshi cloth to meet the demand of all the people. Looking at the half naked bodies of the people in the South, this idea could strike him, wasn't it possible for the Indians to reduce their demand by covering whatever was essential? Millions had been doing so for ages as they were too poor to cover all their limbs. If a leader claimed to represent all the people, he must first live like the poorest of the poor who had only a loin cloth to cover his nudity. So towards the end of September, he discarded his vest and cap, got his head shaved and wore a piece of Khaddar around his loins. His new dress and new style of living amused and surprised many persons around him. Malaviya was visibly moved when he saw Gandhi in that dress on 22nd Oct. 1921. In fact, the adoption of loin cloth was an effective reply to those who showed their inability to take to Khadi because it was so costly. While Gandhi was on his way to Madura in 1921, he saw in the compartment some people bedecked in foreign fineries. He pleaded with them to use Khadi. They declined to do so on the grounds that they were too poor to buy Khadi which was so costly. It was not the first time that Gandhi showed the depth of his feelings or his outlook in life through the change of his dress. It reflected his inner being. He had dressed like a dandy; he had worn frock coat; the uniform of a sergeant major; the dirty shirt of a Zulu convict in South Africa. When he heard the killing of his two Tamilian comrades as a result of firing in South Africa, he put on the Madrasi dress of a poor man to identify himself with those who were mourning for the loss of their kith and kin. On the death of Gokhale, his political guru, he decided not to wear footwear for a year. When Mohammed Ali was arrested he thought of dispensing with his cap and shirt. But he restrained himself and did not do any such thing at that time. But his new attire of loin cloth could also be a sign of mourning for the arrest of Mohammed Ali.

The organization of the Congress as it existed on the emergence of Gandhi in Indian politics was not suitable for his technique of fighting imperialism. For it lacked mass base which Gandhi considered as the real mainstay of his Satyagraha campaigns. The Congress platform at that time, in his view, was only a seat of long deliberations, speeches, discourses and petitions.[17] So it became necessary for him to reshape the Congress organization. The All India Congress Committee had appointed a committee consisting of Gandhi, N.C. Kelkar, Rangaswami Ayyangar, I.B. Sen and Vithalbhai Patel to examine its constitution. But the task of drafting it fell on Gandhi who restructured it as fighting body drawing its strength from the masses having centralised direction and discipline during critical phases of national life without abandoning democratic methods. For, his view of non-violence and truth could not be reconciled to coercion and suppression of dissent. The draft was sent to all other members and the revised draft was circulated during the Congress session in September 1920 at Calcutta. It was finally accepted and adopted at its Nagpur session which also confirmed Gandhi's programme of non-violent non-co-operation. The new constitution set the goal of the Congress "as attainment of self-government by the people of India by all peaceful and legitimate means. It completely changed the structure of the Congress. It set up an organizational framework from the lowest to the highest level. At the all-India level it came to have its president and working Committee and the All-India Congress Committee. At the provincial level there was the Provincial Congress Committee, the district, taluks, city, ward and village Congress committee with their presidents and office bearers. The Congress provinces were redrawn with indigenous linguistic divisions. The nine Congress provinces of the constitution of 1908 gave place to twenty-one provinces that demanded a change in the composition of the All-India Congress Committee as the number of its representatives could go up to 350. The formation of linguistic provinces stimulated the Congress membership, changed the focus and brought a large new team of provincial and regional leadership. Gandhi now gave a call for mass mobilisation. The target was one crore membership. The new constitution provided adult sufferage as it was open to all men and women subject only to two qualifications, that is, signing of the creed and nominal payment of four annas. The constitution was so framed as to be in a position to carry on work throughout the year. The Congress now became an organisation of the Indian masses including the peasants, the lower middle class, the students and the women. It claimed to be an instrument of dynamic change. In drafting the constitution Gandhi wrote to Kelkar, "I have attempted to give the Congress a representative character such as would make its demands irresistible."[18] It strengthened Gandhi's position in the Congress. For, the new leadership that emerged as a result of its transformation looked to him for inspiration and guidance. He made an effort to prepare a disciplined cadre, a band of workers and future leaders. His Ashram became a training ground for Congress workers. Thus, a new team of Congress leaders like J.B. Kriplani, Rajendra Prasad, J.L. Nehru, Vallabbhai Patel, Rajkumari Amritkaur, Sarla Devi Chaudhrani, Renuka Roy, Kamla Devi Chattopadhaya emerged whose life style was completely changed as a result of Gandhi's influence. But they were not merely 'yes men or women' of Gandhi. Each of them did not lose his or her individuality of identity while remaining in contact with Gandhi. Rather their wit and wisdom sharpened his mind and multiplied his mental and material resources in his search for the solution of any problem. The new members that entered the Congress were not accustomed to the conventional politics that dominated the Congress before the rise of Gandhi in Indian politics. Their place in the Congress hierarchy was determined by their dedication to the cause and their spirit of self-sacrifice which for Gandhi was the right equipment for leadership.

The new A.I.C.C. in its meeting at Bezwada on 31st March and 1st April 1921 resolved to collect one crore of rupees before 30th June for the Tilak Swaraj Fund and to put on the Congress register one crore members and to introduce twenty lakh Charkhas in the cities and villages.

The whole programme of non-co-operation was so framed as to involve every Section of the nation, rich and poor, men and women, old and young; the rich by contributing to the Tilak Swaraj Fund and the young by joining the volunteer corps and women by working on the charkha. According to a conservative Government estimate, there were 345 volunteer corps in existence with 15,186 members and 404 Samitis with 15,269 members in August 1921.[19] For Gandhi non-co-operation movement was no less than war, for it had all the attributes of a war with one difference that it had no scope for brute force or armed might. "As in the usual kind of war, 'he asserted' so in this, too, self-sacrifice, training, planning and so on are indispensable.[20] Similarly in a crisis of this kind people have no time to go to law-courts; the students have to join the struggle for national freedom and look upon their part in it as their studies.[21] 'The qualities he added,' which shine most in such a struggle are firmness and courage." But for the suffering and sacrifice that the participation in this struggle entailed, he put the whole responsibility on the participants themselves. For, they had joined the struggle on the call of their conscience.

Non-co-operation movement spread like prairi fire. The campaign moved with great speed affecting more or less every section of Indian society. Tilak Swaraj Fund was oversubscribed. Contributions came not only from the rich but also from the poor. Twenty-one thousand Textile workers of Ahmedabad raised Rs. 34,000. The drivers of bullock carts in Calcutta presented to Gandhi with a purse of Rs. 10,000. The beggars of Puri, washermen, carpenters, blacksmiths did not remain behind in offering their contributions.[22] According to Hare Krishan Mehtab the contribution of Rs. 23,000 from Orissa to Tilak swaraj Fund was made from door to door collections. Even the copper pice were accepted.[23] However, it cannot be denied that the bulk of financial support came from urban areas, from Gujaratis, Parsis, Marwaris, and Muslim merchants.

The recruitment of members reached nearly half the target. Lakhs of spinning wheels started plying in the villages and cities of India. The programme brought different communities on a common platform and the unity that it accomplished, according to Lajpat Rai, was no mean achievement for "a people so helplessly divided and hopelessly devoid of national consciousness as we were before Gandhi came to the stage."[24]

About boycott, the response to boycott of titles was not encouraging and possibly Gandhi anticipated it. Writing to Andrews in August 1920, after a tour of the South, he said, "I see poor response from the leading class. They do not want to sacrifice anything at all. They expect to gain everything by speeches and resolutions. They (are) keeping back a nation which is ready for sacrifice."

The boycott of educational institutions showed some encouraging response in the beginning. The number of students in the colleges was reduced from 52,482 in 1919-20 to 45,933 in 1921-22 and in secondary schools from 1,281,810 in 1919-20 to 1,239,524 in 1921-22.[25]

The boycott of courts, too, received modest success initially in some provinces. A Tilakite colleague of Kelkar from Noyth Karnatak wrote to him in early December 1920 that no lawyer who had not given up his practice could appear in public; the people just did not want to listen to him.[26] Bengal led in this programme with 300 lawyers suspending their practice followed by U.P. with 116 and Andhra 108. But a number of them resumed their practice after some time in the absence of alternative employment to support their families. The author of Satyagraha was aware that he would not be able to carry with him a large number of lawyers for a long time, for it was difficult for most of them 'to give up the arm-chairs and motor cars.'

However, the boycott of election to the Reformed Councils was met with success. A large number of persons qualified as voters did not register themselves. In Amritsar out of two hundred and thirty-nine persons, only six presented themselves for registration as voters. In Lahore only 3.5 percent of the total registered voters exercised their right to vote in non-Muslim urban constituencies. The effect of the boycott of foreign cloth was felt throughout India. It attained considerable success in Bengal, Bombay, Madras and the United Provinces. The boycott of liquor had the effect of reducing excise revenue. In the Punjab, Bihar and Orissa and Bombay the reduction was respectively 33, 10 and 6 lakhs of rupees.

The Government tried to meet the situation by repressive measures. All public meetings were banned by Seditious Meeting Act. Congress and Khilafat volunteers organisations were declared unlawful. Several arrests were made all over the country. Mohammed Ali was arrested and prosecuted for calling upon the Muslim soldiers to abandon service as it was religiously unlawful. Gandhi replied it by issuing an appeal to the Muslims to repeat the formula of the Ali Brothers regarding the duty of soldiers and invite imprisonment. On October 4, he convened a meeting of leaders in Bombay, to issue a manifesto stating clearly that "it is contrary to national interest for any Indian to serve as a civilian and more especially as soldier, under the Government." The manifesto was ratified by the A.I.C.C. held at Delhi. The committee authorised every province to start civil disobedience. But Gandhi appealed to the people to first wait and watch the C.D. campaign to be led by him at Bardoli, for "mass civil disobedience is like an earthquake, a sort of general upheaval on the political plane." The train on which he was going to Bardoli was filled with enthusiasts who were singing 'Bardoli is India's Thermophyle.' It looks Gandhi had been very much impressed by the heroic resistance of Spartans to the Persians under Xerxes (480 B.C.) at the pass of E.C. Greece. For he used the heroism of the Spartans at this fight more than once. On his way to Bardoli, he stopped at Bombay when the Prince of Wales landed there. The general hartal greeted the royal guest. For, in Gandhi's view, it had been arranged by the Government of India to "make their hold of India tighter." A large number of people had gathered at Parel, to participate in the bonfire of foreign cloth. While he was addressing the audience riots broke out in the city. The Parsis who had joined in the demonstration of welcome to the prince were attacked by the infuriated mob. Their foreign caps and foreign clothes were seized and consigned to flames. A number of policemen were assaulted by the mob. Gandhi went out to give succour to the injured. On his arrival on the scene he saw a policeman lying prostrate and unconscious. He sprinkled water on his face, nursed him and made arrangement of his removal to the hospital. He was filled with remorse and despondency.[27] For, it made him conscious that his message of non-violence had not gone deep into the hearts of the people, though he suspected that it could be the handiwork of skilled hands. It must have occurred to him that if riots could be engineered by the opponents, then how risky it could be to launch C.D. movement all over India. He suspended the launching of the movement at Bardoli. Penance for madness of the mob was the only course left to him. This was the only way to appeal to the almighty abiding in him to show him the way. "I must draw upon God he said," for further credit to enable me to transact his business. I could only do so by humbling myself, crawling in the dust before Him, denying myself the food He has given. "The penitential fast was broken on November 22 on the restoration of peace in the city."

Earlier, too, Moplah rising in Malabar had marred Gandhi's programme of Hindu-Muslim unity and non-violent non-co-operation.

The Moplah or Mappila Islamic community was the oldest in India. Their ancestors were the Arab traders who had settled at Malabar coast in the 9th century. Most of them were very poor and the British land tenure system had reduced them to the position of serfs under the Hindu landlords who had been earlier rent collectors. The system was so oppressive that the Muslims quite often rebelled against the landlords assuming the fight as a Jihad. Between 1836 and 1898, 31 outbreaks were recorded.[28] The victims were mostly Hindus. The outbreaks were essentially agrarian, though it took the form of religious wars. The Khilafatist and non-co-opration propaganda started spreading from February 1921 in Kerala. The Khilafatist meetings intensified religious feelings. The rising of the Moplahs was initially anti-British that took the form of religious war. A number of Hindus too, suffered as the rebels viewed them as supporters of the Government. Terrible atrocities were committed by the poor and ignorant Muslims under the influence of Oazis and Maulvis against the administration. The rising was suppressed with heavy hands by the Government. It revealed to Gandhi the complexity involved in the Hindu-Muslim relations. These two outbreaks made the General of non-violent war cautious. But the tempo of the movement went on rising. As a precautionary measure for preventing such outbreaks the Congress Working Committee under his guidance decided to raise a volunteer corps the members of which were to take a pledge of non-violence in word and deed and inculcate the spirit of non-violence in others. The campaign gained greater momentum when the government started arresting leaders and volunteers. Gandhi was pleased to hear the arrest of all the important leaders as this in his view was the most enduring contribution to the national cause. For, the spirit of sacrifice, fearlessness and courage that they had shown would be contagious and would become a part of national character essential for winning the battle of Swaraj. On hearing the news of the arrest of his eldest son Harilal in Calcutta, he felt exulted and sent a message to his youngest son Devadas to be ready for arrest.

In this atmosphere of hope, exultation and fear, the Congress met in Ahmedabad. The Congress camp was named Khadi Nagar as pure Khadi was used in its construction. Nearly two thousand Khadi clad volunteers looked after two lakh delegates and visitors. The Congress decided to launch individual and mass civil disobedience and appointed Gandhi as its executive authority to decide the time and the manner of civil disobedience. In the meantime an effort was made by Malaviya, Jinnah and several other leaders to bring about a rapprochement between the Government and the Congress. But it failed as both sides had adopted tough posture. While Gandhi insisted on the release of Ali Brothers and other Khilafat prisoners before the holding of a Round Table Conference for the settlement, the Viceroy and the bureaucracy went on pursuing the policy of browbeating the Congress. Gandhi then, decided to launch the C.D. movement from Bardoli. All other parts of India were advised to co-operate in the Bardoli Satyagraha by refraining from civil disobedience of aggressive character and waiting for their turn. But unfortunately a tragic event occurred at Chauri Chaura, in Gorakhpur district that upset all the programmes of Gandhi. A mob harassed by the police party attacked a police station where a number of policemen had taken shelter and set fire to the building as a result of which all policemen were burnt alive. Initially the short news item about this incident that appeared in the morning paper of 8th February 1922 escaped Gandhi's notice as his mind was occupied with the preparations for civil disobedience. It was pointed out to him later on during the day by V.J. Patel in the discussion. He immediately called for the paper and on reading it, he was extremely agitated. Violent incidents had occurred at other places also in connection with his movement. But Chauri Chaura appeared to be the last straw. He decided to suspend the movement, though a day earlier he had hurled defiance at the Government in his rejoinder to Lord Reading's communique about the former's Bardoli ultimatum. However this decision appeared sudden to the world. But, in fact, it was the culmination of the fears that had bedeviled his mind. A few days before he had been apprised of the report that Gorakhpur alone had enlisted 34 thousand volunteers. But hardly one fourth were observing the Congress discipline about the use of Khadi.[29]

The suspension of the aggressive part of the non-co-operation movement caused great consternation in the nationalist camp. Motilal and Lajpat Rai wrote angry letters to him. C.R. Das was beside himself on hearing this decision of their leader. Gandhi's secretary Mahadev Desai wrote that the C.W.C. resolution had absolutely unhinged him. Most of the Congress workers were disappointed by this action of their general. It was the force of his personality and faith of his followers in his insight that made them yield to his decision. However, this decision offered a field day to his critics. Both militants and opponents to his Satyagraha charged him with bungling. The former for letting them down in the midstream. At the A.I.C.C. meeting at Delhi there were bitter attacks on him. Dr. Moonje moved a resolution asking for the correct and right definition of non-violence, that is, where is the line that could be drawn between violent and non-violent action in such situations. Several eminent leaders joined in this chorus. Amidst the heated debate, Hakim Ajmal Khan who was presiding, retired because of indisposition and requested Gandhi to take the chair. He conducted the meeting in such a way that the sting of the attacks was removed. For, he allowed his opponents to speak to their hearts content. But did not allow his supporters to defend his action. The resolution was put to vote and was thrown out with an overwhelming majority.

The Mahatma remained unmoved in spite of bitter attacks by eminent persons of his action as he was sure of the soundness of his decision. In an article in *Young India*, he wrote:[30]

> "The drastic reversal of practically the whole of the aggressive programme may be politically unsound and unwise, but there is no doubt that it is religiously sound and I venture to assure the doubters that the country will have gained by my humiliation and confession of error."

However the expression 'religiously sound' was used in a special sense. It communicated his faith in non-violence. He had earlier warned the enthusiasts of non-co-operation that violent and non-violent movements could not go side by side, for, he was sure that ultimately violence would overtake non-violent movement causing a reign of terror and anarchy in the county besides pushing out the non-co-operation movement from the political scene. Expressing his grief over the assassination of an English Deputy Commissioner by a Muslim, he said, "If violence broke out, the people would not be able to keep up non-co-operation. There would be reign of terror all over the country and the people themselves would get panicky. No one would then go with non-co-operation."[31] So his decision to suspend the movement was not sudden and instinctive. He had been meditating over the state of non-co-operation for some time as the disheartening and alarming news of the unruly conduct of non-co-operators were pouring in and being passed on to him. At places ignorant people had started non-payment of taxes to the Government and dues to the Zamindars without the sanction of the Congress Working Committee.[32] Some clever and self-styled leaders had given the impression to the peasants that Gandhi would soon announce the distribution of land among the landless and would remove zamindars. But in Gandhi's programme of non-payment of taxes was the last stage in aggressive civil disobedience and could not be resorted to without adequated preparation. In fact, as Gandhi's secretary during the course of the movement, Krishandas noted that the advocates of violence were gathering strength under Mahatmaji's aegis and unless they were isolated it was difficult to keep the movement non-violent.

In a situation when most of the leaders were in jail, it had become difficult to restrain the people in view of the reign of terror unleashed by the Government through its policy of suppression. What Gandhi feared most was mob violence as it would not distinguish friends from foes. The Moplah rising was a ready reminder, for, the Khilafat enthusiasm led the ignorant masses to turn their swords against the Hindus. So he argued, "suppose the non-violent disobedience of Bardoli was permitted by God to succeed and the Government had abdicated in favour of the victors of Bardoli, who would control the unruly elements that must be expected to perpetuate inhumanity upon the provocation."[33]

Jawaharlal Nehru who was quite upset in jail on hearing the news of the suspension of the movement, revised his views about it later on. Reflecting over this decision he wrote:[34]

> "As a matter of fact even the suspension of civil resistance in February 1922 was certainly not due to Chauri Chaura alone, although most people imagined so. That was only the last straw— At that time our movement, in spite of its apparent power and the wide-spread enthusiasm, was going to pieces. All organisations and discipline was disappearing, almost all our good men were in prison and the masses had so far received little training to carry on by themselves."

The Mahatma himself explained to R.R. Diwakar who was with him in jail for a few days that the reason for the withdrawal of the movement "was not a question of merely violence at Chauri Chaura, but the calculated act of brutal atrocity by trained Congress volunteers against armed constabulary. The Government would have been justified if they had clamped Martial Law— If that had happened there would have been demoralisation of high order for years. Today we are in a position to declare that we have the capacity to forge a powerful weapon, at the same time we have the stern discipline to withdraw its use."[35] Gandhi had the information that at Chauri Chaura the procession was deliberately formed by Congress volunteers and wickedly taken in the direction of Thana (police station). He believed that it was equally easy for such a large number of volunteers to have effectively prevented the atrocious murder of the constables.[36]

Nevertheless, there was a flaw in the objectives of the movement.

It was not easy to join the Khilafat and the Punjab wrongs with its main goal of Swaraj. For the Khilafat was a religious issue which had touched the emotions of the Muslim masses. For the Muslim leaders, it was the most effective method for accomplishing Muslim solidarity in India. It had created awakening among the Muslims in India even before the arrival of Gandhi on the Indian political scene and even when Mustafa Kemal abolished Khilafat in Turkey the Muslim leaders kept its shadow to maintain Muslim solidarity. But it was not easy for Muslim zealots to work under the straight jacket of non-violence since Islam, in their view, allowed them the use of violence for the protection of their religion. So quite often their leaders' rhetoric left the impression with their audience the validity of violence. Could Gandhi's programme of non-violence succeed in this situation? Moreover, Khilafat was a Pan-Islamic issue. But the Mahatma and several Muslim leaders such as Ansari, Azad, etc. believed that the Pan-Islamism as represented by the Khilafat could be reconciled to nationalism which ultimately would bring Muslim masses into the main stream of national movement. But that did not happen and the result was that most of the Muslim leaders who had jumped on Gandhi's bandwagon under the impression that it would serve the cause of Islam moved towards communal politics.

Gandhi's decision to withdraw the aggressive non-co-operation at that stage was a very bold step. For it could lead to the total political eclipse of a lesser mortal. But Gandhi showed great moral courage in taking of very unpopular decision. A votary of truth may have to shed his personal glory to vindicate truth when events demonstrate the error in his judgement. He rises morally while his social or political stature goes down in the eyes of the world. History may vindicate the soundness of his decision which eludes the eyes of his contemporaries. Gandhi was not apologetic after the withdrawal. We find him writing very forceful articles in support of his decision. He did not evade the accusations of his critics. But faced them with his head erect. For, in his view, the violence that erupted at Bombay, Madras or Chauri Chaura was avoidable if the volunteers and the leaders had observed patience and self-restraint. He had not given halt to the movement when there occurred the outbreak of violence at Malabar by the Moplahs. For, they were neither co-operators nor committed to non-violence. Moreover, it was a war, though without the use of lethal weapons and in every war a general has to change his strategy in view of his own resources, the strength or weakness of his forces, the moves of his opponents, new developments in his own camp or those in the camp of his opponent. By suspending the aggressive part of the programme, he had only changed the strategy and had not thrown in the towel, though frustration was felt in his own camp by this move. For the movement had not yielded the desired results. The mass hysteria which Gandhi's call created and the enthusiasm among the masses generated by his assurance of Swaraj within a year could not create a disciplined non-violent army. For, it was only a slogan. Nor could his speeches and writings carry with him all those who had acquired vested interest in the existing system of Government. However his movement had transformed the character of the nation which henceforth would not like to be ruled by an alien power and would continue to struggle hard to throw away the foreign domination. The Congress which had spearheaded the movement penetrated every nook and corner of the country. The myth of the might of the alien government with which it had kept its hold over the vast country was destroyed. The fear of imprisonment gone, any unjust order of the Government could not go unchallenged. Though political Swaraj had not been achieved as the fiat of the foreign power ran the administration, the politically conscious people had become free from the fear of the Government and for Gandhi this was real Swaraj as it would enable the people to resist any unjust authority. As the scale of the popularity of the Mahatma after the suspension of the aggressive part of the Movement slumped the Government decided to arrest him. Originally this action was to be taken on 13th February. But on the advice of Tej Bahadur Sapru, the law member of the Viceroy's Council it was postponed for some time. He was charged with sedition on the basis of his three articles in the *Young India*. The publisher Shankar Lal Banker was also tried with him. The trial took place in the court house of Ahmedabad before justice Brownfield. The trial was historic. Not only because the eyes of the nation were riveted on it. But also because of its effect on all the persons present in the court including the prosecutor and the judge. Both the accused and the judge showed maximum courtesy to each other. Sarojini Naidu who was present in the court at that time felt that the only parallel of his trial was that of Jesus of Nazareth. The charge against the Mahatma was preaching disloyalty and disaffection towards the Government. He made the task of the prosecutor easier by pleading guilty of the charges. Concluding his statement he said, "I hold it to be a virtue to be disaffected towards a Government which in its totality has done more harm to India that any previous system. Holding such a belief, I consider it to be a sin to have affection for the system—In fact I believe that I have rendered a service to India and England by showing in non-co-operation the way out of the unnatural state in which both are living.

He thus, invited the highest penalty that could be inflicted upon him. In a way he turned the accuser into an accused before the higher court of moral justice by pleading that the British rule had caused immense suffering to the people of India. As observed by a contemporary "The state trial was not so much trial by the state as the trial of the state itself." However, the judge while admitting that the accused in the eyes of his countrymen was a great patriot and a great leader who was looked upon even by his opponents as of high ideals, sentenced him to six years imprisonment as "the law is no respecter of persons". Gandhi while acknowledging the sentence as very light thanked the court for extending great courtesy to him.

After the judge and officials left the court he was surrounded by his friends and admirers, some of them with tears in their eyes and all anxious to touch his hand and feet. Others who had been most intimate simply ran away from the scene lest they should break down under the swelling emotions that were agitating them. "But the Mahatma was in high spirits and was all the time smiling. Looking at Shankar Lal who was sitting beside him, he said," so you are seated near me to give me your support in case I break down, he jested with the happy laugh. Looking around at the host of familiar faces, who had come to see him at this historic moment, he said, "This is like a family gathering and not a law court."

Notes and References

1. C.W., Vol. XVIII, p. 107.
2. *Ibid.*, pp. 74-76.
3. Gandhi, M.K., Autobiography, p. 415.
4. C.W., Vol. XVIII, pp. 259-60.
5. Quoted in Nanda, *op. cit.*, p. 234.
6. C.W., Vol. XVIII, p. 262.
7. *Ibid.*
8. *Ibid.*, p. 335.
9. Quoted in Nanda, *op. cit.*, pp. 235-36.
10. Chaudhry, Ramnarayan, Bapu as I saw Him (in Hindi), Navajivan Publishing House, pp. 15-16.
11. Quoted in B.R. Nanda, Moti Lal Nehru, p. 120.
12. Bose, S.C., The Indian Struggle, p. 88.
13. Krishan Das, Seven Months with the Mahatma, p. 26.
14. *Ibid.*
15. C.W., XIII, p. 188.
16. *Ibid.*, Vol. XVIII, p. 3.

17. Brown, Judith M., Gandhi's Rise to Power in Indian Politics (Cambridge University Press, 1972), p. 316.
18. C.W., Vol. XVIII, p. 316.
19. *Ibid.*
20. Nanda, Gandhi, Pan Islamism, Imperialism and Nationalism, *op. cit.*, p. 262.
21. *Ibid.*, In the Footsteps of M. Gandhi, p. 323.
22. Lajpat Rai, Speeches and Writings, Vol. II, p. 144.
23. Bamford, P.C., History of the Non-co-operation and Khilafat Movements, p. 103.
24. Limaya, Madhu, Prime Movers, p. 88.
25. Krishan Das, *op. cit.*, pp. 125-26.
26. Nanda, B.R., *op. cit.*, p. 312.
27. Krishan Das, *op. cit.*, p. 219.
28. C.W., Vol. XXII, pp. 377, 417.
29. *Ibid.*, Vol. XVIII, p. 228.
30. Krishan Das, *op. cit.*, p. 220.
31. Quoted in Fischer, Life of M. Gandhi, p. 198.
32. Nehru, J.L., Autobiography, p. 85.
33. Diwakar, K.R., *op. cit.*, p. 28.
34. C.W., XXIII, p. 1.
35. Montagu Papers, quoted in Nanda, in Gandhi's Footsteps, p. 77.
36. C.W., XXIII, p. 118.

14

Mahatma Bound

After the pronouncement of judgement, he was first taken from the improvised court room to the Sabarmati jail. But was later on shifted to Yeravada jail in Poona where initially he had some unpleasant experiences because of the haughty demeanour of the superintendent of the jail Col. Dalziel. He had been removed from the roll of barristers by the Inns of Court. He was, therefore, treated as an ordinary prisoner. The jail manual was applied to him rigorously. For a number of days he was subjected to search like other prisoners daily before lock up. His blanket was searched and the jailer would even touch his groins as he had only loin cloth on him. He even touched his pot with boots. This was very irksome to him. On the first day he was neither allowed to carry his spinning wheel nor his books. Banker was not allowed to stay with him in spite of the special request made by him. However, the spinning wheel was restored to him next day as he undertook semifast since working on the spinning wheel was a religious matter with him. He was also allowed to keep his books with him and after some time Banker, too, was allowed to stay with him. He was made to stand during the interview as no prisoner was allowed to sit in the superintendent's office while meeting his visitors. His son Devadas and Rajagopalachari had first meeting with him in jail on Ist April. The former broke down on seeing his illustrious father standing in the superintendent's office. However, the Mahatma remained unruffled as jail life was no new experience for him. In South Africa he had three convictions to his credit and was treated like a dangerous criminal. He remained in jail therefor five months and three weeks. But things changed in Yeravada and his stay there became comfortable when Col. Jones took over as the superintendent on Col. Dalziel's promotion as acting Inspector General of Prisons. He treated Gandhi with great consideration and transferred him to the European ward along with his companions where they had greater comfort. His physical needs were well attended to. He was allowed to choose his own diet. He was supplied adequate quantity of goat's milk and butter. He was also supplied oranges. The superintendent even wanted him to take more nutritive diet and suggested the intake of butter and immediately arranged the supply of goat's butter. Since it had to be mixed with something, twenty pounds of flour were also issued. But after a few days Gandhi felt that he could not make use of the large quantity of flour supplied to him. So he requested the superintendent to remove it on the grounds that it was a waste of public money. There was an incredulous smile on the face of the superintendent on hearing this plea of his prisoner. Noticing it Gandhi pressed home the point. Surely it is my money "the prisoner asserted." How much have you contributed to the public treasury "was the quick retort from the superintendent." You contribute only a percentage out of the salary you get from the state whereas I give the whole of myself, labour, intelligence and all," Gandhi replied. There was a loud suggestive laughter. But the prisoner remained unruffled, for, he argued that a labourer like him "labours for the state, for mere maintenance, more to the state than a Viceroy who receives twenty thousand together with royal residence and contribute only a percentage of his salary if it is not tax free." The superintendent was facing a lawyer and not an ordinary criminal.

On Banker's discharge, Manser Ali and later on Indulal Yajnik were transferred to his ward to give him company. After a hectic life of non-co-operation days, jail now provided him with an excellent opportunity for rest reflection and reading. He enjoyed what he called perfect peace. During the period of less than two years in jail, he read 150 books. Getting up at 4 a.m., he would commence his studies at 6-30 a.m., devoting 6 hours to it every day. Besides literature of various religions that fuelled his spiritual yearning, he read books on history, literature, social and natural sciences. Most of these books he found in the prison's library. Among them were, Christianity in practice, Bible view of the world, the Quran, Mirza's Ethics of Islam, Shibli's life of the Prophet, Ameer Ali's History of the Sarcens, Kidd's Social Evolution, Brierly's Ourselves and the Universe, Spencer's Elements of Sociology, Hopkin's Origin and Evolution of Religion, Lecky's European Morals,

Natural History of Birds, Haeckel's Evolution of Man, Gibbon's Rise and Fall of the Roman Empire, Guizot's History of Civilization in Europe, Well's History, Motley's Rise of the Dutch Republic, Shaw's Man and Superman, Goethe's Faust, Lord Rosebury's Life of Pitt, Stories from the History of Rome, etc. He noticed that while Gibbon traced the decay of a mighty empire, Motley extracted from little Republic the life of his hero. So Gibbon's heroes are subservient to the story of a mighty empire, Motley's story of the state is subservient to that of one single life. He marked in faint pencil in Gibbon's work anything in support of his view of non-violence.

He also studied Hindu religious works such as Bhagavadgita, the Mahabharata, Tulsidas' Ramayana, the Upanishads, Vivekananda's Rajyoga and Patanjali's Yogadarshan that furnished him with greater insight into Hindu religion. This knowledge gave him an edge over the orthodox Hindus who questioned his efforts and campaigns to remove the overgrowth of superstitions and pernicious customs on his religion which was essential for adjusting Hinduism to the new age dominated by reason.

He acquired a deeper knowledge of Sikh religion and history since, according to him, the contemporary Sikh struggle could not be comprehended and appreciated without understanding their previous history and the lives of the 'Gurus'. He studied the voluminous work on Sikh religion by Macauliffe, History of the Sikhs by Cunningham and Transformation of Sikhism by Gokal Chand Narang. Each of these works he found good in its own way. Macauliffe's was good for its sumptuous printing, for the biographical sketches of the Sikh Gurus and the copious extracts from their compositions. But its fulsome praise for the English rule and its design to represent Sikhism as a religion having nothing in common with Hindu religion had reduced its importance. In Cunningham's work he found a sympathetic record of events in the Punjab while Narang's work appeared to him equally valuable.

The study of historical works strengthened his view that the dividing line between fact and fiction is very thin and that even facts have at least two sides, or as lawyers say, facts are after all opinions. In that case a nation is happy that has no history. If the ancestors of the Hindus ignored history as it is understood today they did not lose anything. They rather built on slight events their philosophical structure like Mahabharata which, in Gandhi's view, is superior to the works of Gibbon.

It is true that facts communicate different meanings to different persons at different times. So facts become opinions of different persons.

In other words, past can never be perceived or retrieved since our understanding of the past is coloured by our present interest, understanding and attitude of the mind. Our judgement on the past is always in the framework of the present. But a nation without the memories of achievements or sufferings in the past stands on slender foundations. For its glorious achievements in the past sustain or maintain its fabric in the present and prepare it for greater achievements in the future. But history does not mean merely history of the rise and fall of kingdoms or empires, of wars and revolutions. It can be history of civilization, the development of human mind that finds its manifestation in art, architecture, philosophy. Possibly when Gandhi claimed the superiority of the Mahabharata over Gibbon's work, he was keeping in view the continuous search of the human mind of truth or ultimate reality. For the Mahabharata is not merely a record of events or struggle for power between two royal families. It is a record of the values, mores, attitude towards life, beliefs, metaphysics, political behaviour, etc. of ancient Indians.

Gandhi's first literary achievement in jail was a primer in Gujarati for children which he finished in less than a month after entering the portals of Yeravada jail.[1] He also planned a religious primer which, of course, could not be taken up. He planned to prepare a concordance of the Gita and devoted twenty minutes daily to this task and within twenty months he finished this work and as a result he was able to know where and how often a particular word occurs in it.

He started working on his famous work 'History of the Satyagraha in South Africa' and finished thirty chapters of it dictating it to Indulal Yajnik on his joining him in the jail. It then occurred to him to write his autobiography. The Satyagraha in South Africa is a companion volume of it as it is a mixture of reminiscences, memoirs and autobiography. Besides, he devoted many hours to the study of Urdu and would have acquired a good proficiency in it had he remained in jail for the full term of six years. An incident in jail reported by Indulal Yajnik who stayed with Gandhi in jail for some time, shows the humanity or benevolence of the Mahatma. An African warder with life sentence for murder who was on attendance on him, was bitten by a scorpion one night and he was in intense pain. When Gandhi learnt about it he asked for a knife but it was not available. So he sucked man's poison and relieved him of pain and poison.[2]

His routine in jail was disturbed by his physical ailment. He had severe pain in the abdomen which he initially tried to cure it by his nature cure remedies. But the pain persisted and an allopathic doctor had to consulted. He was suffering from appendicitis but he was initially examined negligently. He was close to dying. Col. Maddock, who was called in great haste diagnosed an abscess on the appendix and so even without asking the Governor's permission urgently took him in his car to Sasson hospital and performed the operation practically in candle light on the night of 12th January, 1924 as during the operation a thunderstorm cut off the electricity and the flash light which one of the three nurses had been holding went out. Before the operation the patient was asked whether he would like to have his own doctor friends present at the time of operation. He asked for Dr. Dalal and Dr. Jivaraj Mehta. But none of them could be contacted. Dr. Phatak reached there to whom a draft was dictated by the patient wherein he thanked the Government for the care that they had taken for him. He refused to give any message to the people since in his view a prisoner was supposed to be civilly dead. He was supposed to have no knowledge of outside events and therefore he could not communicate with the public. When he was shifted to the operation theatre, Sastri sat outside and ruminated over the words of the Mahatma about his opponents and "marvelled at the exhibitions he had witnessed of high mindedness, forgiveness chivalry and love transcending ordinary nature."[3]

The period of convalescence in the hospital was memorable for the affection and reverence that he received not only from his admirers but also from his critics who could not swallow his decision to withdraw the movement. Lajpat Rai who came to Poona to see him could hardly control his tears on seeing his emaciated body. Motilal missed his train to bid adieu to Bapu as he found him asleep when he came to the hospital just before the time of departure of the train.[4] Shaukat Ali took off the covering of Bapu's feet to kiss them. Dilip Kumar Roy came to the hospital and sang for him Bhajans (religious hymns) of Mira and of others that thrilled the Mahatma and all other listeners who were attending on the Mahatma. But it was a surprise to the singer that the austere and ascetic person like Gandhi had an ear for music.[5]

After a few days, Gandhi was released on grounds of health even before the expiry of one-third of his term of imprisonment. He was removed to Juhu on the seashore for convalescence on March 10, 1924. After regaining some strength he resumed the editorial charge of his two weeklies as a first step to guide the nation at a time when the country was thrown into the cauldron of political controversies and communal riots that had reduced to smoke all the political gains made during the years of non-co-operation. While the citadel of Hindu-Muslim unity crumbled, cracks in the Congress organisation occurred over the formulation of the next programme.

Notes and References

1. C.W., Vol. XXIII, (The primer was published in 1951 under the title Balpothi, Navajivan
2. Kanji Dawarka Das, *op. cit.*, p. 282.
3. Tendulkar, *op. cit.*, Vol. II, p. 119.
4. Desai, *op. cit.*, Vol. IV, p. 36.
5. *Ibid.*

15

Fighting the Divisive Forces

It is doubtful that the release of Gandhi on health grounds by the British rulers was entirely based on altruism. Possibly they hoped to gain some political mileage by this release as his presence was likely to widen the gulf between two sections of the Congress that were fighting over the Council entry programme. The Bombay Government which recommended the release of Gandhi had mentioned the possibility of the Mahatma denouncing the Swararjists for their abandoning non-co-operation and thereby weakening their position in the legislatures where they had embarrassed the Governments by throwing out the Government sponsored bills.[1] After the virtual withdrawal of non-co-operation movement and the arrest and conviction of Gandhi a number of top Congressmen under the leadership of Motilal Nehru and C.R. Das resolved to revive political activity in order to raise the sagging spirits of Congressmen by capturing the legislatures. Though this appeared to many Congress men as deviation from the non-co-operation programme of Gandhi they claimed that they were faithfully carrying on the programme of the Master into the Councils by obstructing work there and exposing the true face of the Councils merely as sham parliaments and a mask which the bureaucracy had put on to mislead the Indians. They came to be known as changers. They were opposed by non-changers who in strict compliance with the Master's will, clung to the Bardoli decision regarding constructive programme. They were led by equally eminent leaders like Rajagopalachari, V. Patel and Rajendra Prasad. At the Gaya session in December 1922, C.R. Das as the president of the Congress and Motilal as its secretary put forward their programme of Council entry. But it was defeated by 1748 to 890 votes. Das and Motilal resigned from their respective offices in the Congress and formed the Swaraj Party. It accepted the Congress programme but decided to contest the elections due later in the year. As a result of sharp differences between the two sections, a split similar to that of 1907, was not ruled out as it was believed in Government circles that the repudiation of the Council entry programme by Gandhi would certainly compel the changers to part company with the Congress. The controversy between the changers and non-changers not only divided the Congress but even divided the families of Congress men. The Patel Brothers were ranged in opposition to each other. In the Nehru family father and son were in the opposite camps. Even G.S. Khaparde's family was divided who was the unbending opponent of Gandhian Non-co-operation movement. The policy and programmes of the Swarajists did make some inroads into the citadel of the alien government by capturing the municipalities of important cities like Calcutta, Bombay, Ahmedabad, Patna, etc. But it did not carry them nearer Swaraj. After nearly three months of his convalescence, Gandhi decided to put the Congress again on the rails. So he announced that he would move in the forthcoming meeting of the A.I.C.C. on June 27, in Ahmedabad certain resolutions in strict compliance to the commitment of the Congress to the propagation of Khadi and non-violence. These resolutions demanded from the bearers of the offices of the Congress organisation strict adherence to the Congress creed and programme. Consequently those who would fail to do so would be deemed to have vacated their offices. All of them would be required to spin at least half an hour daily and send the yarn to the Secretary Khadi Board. Similarly, all of them would be required to carry out the various non-co-operation resolutions including the five boycotts, namely of all mill-spun cloth, government law courts, schools, titles and legislative bodies. By another resolution the A.I.C.C. was to condemn the murder of Mr. Day by the late Gopinath Saha.

Das and Motilal objected to the spinning resolutions on the grounds that these proposed a fundamental change in the Congress constitution which the A.I.C.C. was not competent to do and walked out of the meeting of the Working Committee. Their objection was legally valid. But the majority negatived it. However, Gandhi rescinded the penalty clause in order to accommodate the Swarajists. Later after a discussion with them other revolutions were modified. But the shock came to him when the resolution about Gopinath Saha was moved without alteration. Bengal Provincial Congress Committee had passed a resolution paying homage to the patriotism of Gopinath Saha. Das moved an amendment to Gandhi's resolution which mustered 70 supporters out of 148. Tears rolled down Mahatma's eyes. It was a rare sight. For, he had never wept in public. The opposition by Das whom the Mahatma considered as his very close colleague stunned him. Though his resolution was passed, it could carry only a bare majority of eight votes. Recollecting that experience, he disclosed, "I laid bare my heart and let them see the blood oozing out of it. It takes much to make me weep. But in spite of all my efforts to be brave I broke down utterly." Others who spoke after him also sobbed and chocked amidst their speeches. The atmosphere exuded grief and remorse in place of hope for the future, for it was doubtful whether the Mahatma would be able to lead them to Swaraj. Technically his resolutions were carried. But the bare majority that they received and the vehemence with which they were opposed in the meetings was a painful reminder to him of the proceedings of the A.I.C.C. meeting at Delhi before his imprisonment. He felt defeated and humbled. It was now clear that his influence over the Congress had taken sharp curve downward. He even considered retiring from it leaving it entirely under the charge of the Swarajists. But his co-workers dissuaded him from taking any such extreme step in the interest of the country and the Congress. The unhappy experiences of the session chastened him and prepared him for more realistic moves to save the Congress from disintegration.

After several rounds of talks with the changers and non-changers, he took a position which kept both the sections under the umbrella of the Congress. While accepting council-entry as inconsistent with non-co-operation, he was realist enough to recognize that council-entry was a settled fact. He, therefore, tried to arrive at a compromise with the Swarajists in order to save the Congress men from dissipating their energies in working at cross purposes and internecine warfare. So he assured the Swarajists that though he did not agree with their policy and programme, he would not do any thing to weaken their power, nor would like to embarrass them. Accordingly he wrote to Motilal, in August 1924, that he was prepared to facilitate him in securing the Congress machinery. For "he did not like to waste the nation's time in wrangling over getting a majority in an atmosphere such as is prevalent today."[2] Similarly while admitting honest and fundamental differences with the Swarajists, he told them that he "would be no party to putting any obstacle in their way."[3] For, he felt that they were "supplying the felt want and represent a large section of people who want petty relief."[4] He advised both the changers and Non-changers 'to tolerate each other's ideas and practices—and refrain from interfering in the practices of others.' In pursuance of this policy, he suggested a programme which included, *inter alia*, suspension of all boycotts except that of foreign cloth for a year, replacement of four annas franchise by spinning franchise, that is, membership of the Congress be open only to those who would spin regularly and contribute 2000 yds. per month of his or her own spinning to the all-India Khadi Board, and the Swarajists to carry on their activities without any opposition from Non-Changers either directly or indirectly. In other words, the Swarajist Party was accepted as an integral part of the Congress and it was to carry on in the provincial and central legislatures on behalf of the Congress. He favoured surrender to the Swarajists for the sake of unity as it was the condition for winning Swaraj. To a Non-Changer who charged him with forsaking the Non-Changers by this programme he wrote, "I would clear the ground by saying that my own views remain unchanged. I swear by non-violent non-co-operation and all the boycotts that follow from it—But the country as a whole has not understood the non-co-operation that was presented to it—In such circumstances non-co-operation as a national programme must for the time being be suspended." Consequently, the relations between the Mahatma and the Swarajist leadership became cordial. J.L. Nehru noted that as a result of this rapprochement the relations between his father and Gandhi became more affable and his father started appreciating the great qualities of the Mahatma. In a booklet called 'Thought Currents', containing selections from Gandhi, his father wrote in a brief Foreword, " The Thought Currents preserved in this volume have emanated from a man and are things manly. They are illustrative of two great attributes of human nature—Faith and Strength." This shows Motilal admired Gandhi for the strength of spirit in him. He noticed that this little man of poor physique had something of steel in him, something rock-like which did not yield to physical powers, however great they might be."[5] Thus the Mahatma showed his political sagacity in steering clear of the controversy without losing the loyalty of his valuable colleagues. His political prudence is equally evident in shelving a controversy which was likely to strain his relations with Mohammed Ali. For, it was reported in several papers that Ali had said in a Muslim congregation that Gandhi was lower than a most wretched Muslim. As an experienced journalist he felt that in a meeting an opponent of Ali must have tried to corner him by arguing that the Muslim leader had lowered Islam by his worship of Gandhi. In reply to it what possibly he said was that he believed that the religious principles of an adulterous Muslim were better than Gandhi's religious principles. To Gandhi this was only a claim for the superiority of Islam which every devout Muslim had the right to do like his devout Christian friends who wished for his conversion to Christianity because of their faith in the superiority of Christianity.

Gandhi's pragmatism is equally evident from the way he guided the two important Satyagrahas in Indian states, one in the deep South, in the Travancore state and the other in the North, in Nabha, even when he had not fully recovered from his illness. The first known as the Vaikom Satyagraha, was the result of deep prejudice of orthodox Hindus against a section of Hindu society denigrated as untouchables. It followed from the anti-untouchability campaign of the Congress initiated by Gandhi. A road which passed through an area inhabited mostly by Brahmins and close to a temple, was closed to untouchables. The Kerala Provincial Congress Committee decided to launch a peaceful struggle to make it open to all the Hindus including the untouchables. Under the leadership of K.P. Kesava Menon, Secretary Kerala District Congress Committee, volunteers were regularly sent to the prohibited area to assert the right of untouchables to use the road. Menon was in touch with Gandhi and sought his advice in conducting this movement. The state of Travancore had to move in order to maintain peace as the orthodox sections were resisting the entry of untouchables into the prohibited areas. Consequently volunteers were arrested. After the arrest of Menon, Gandhi's Christian friend and follower George Joseph took the place of Menon. Gandhi did not favour a non-Hindu to take part directly in this movement and so telegraphically instructed him to avoid direct participation. But he was arrested before the telegram reached him. Similarly, he did not want Hindus or non-Hindus outside the Madras Presidency to assist the movement directly. Only their moral support was sufficient. For, Satyagraha in this kind of situation, according to him, "is a most powerful process of conversion. It is an appeal to the heart. Such an appeal cannot be successfully made by people from other parts of India flocking to Vykom."[6] A public Satyagraha, in his view, is an extension of private or domestic Satyagraha. Just as in the case of a dispute in the family between parents and children intervention of outsiders only complicates the matter and hardens the attitude of the parties to the dispute, in the case of public Satyagraha, too, outside help prevents a solution by creating certain fears prevents a solution by creating certain fears in the minds of those whose action has caused suffering to others. Similarly any direct participation of the non-Hindus in the movement would harden the attitude of the orthodox section. For, untouchability, he argued, "is the sin of the Hindus. They must suffer for it. They must purify themselves; they must pay the debt, they owe their suppressed brothers and sisters— the silent, loving suffering of one single pure Hindu as such will be enough to melt the hearts of millions of Hindus, but the sufferings of thousands of non-Hindus on behalf of the untouchables will leave the Hindus unmoved, their blind eyes will not be opened by outside interference, however, well-intentioned and generous it may be, for it will not bring home to them the sense of guilt. On the contrary, they will probably hug the sin all the more for such interference. "All reform, to be sincere and lasting, he added, must come from within."[7] Similarly his advice was sought by the Akalis to guide them in their struggle against the authorities of a princely state in the Punjab. An Akali deputation, headed by Sardar Mangal Singh held a week-long discussion with him on this subject. Akalis had given a good account of themselves in their non-violent fight for the management of their religious shrines during 1920-22 especially at the Guru-ka-Bagh Satyagraha while Gandhi was in prison. But this time the issue was not free from political overtones. In the summer of 1923, the young Maharaja of Nabha, Ripudaman Singh was made to abdicate in favour of his minor son. The Akali leadership smelt a rat in this action of the British authorities. For, this could be a punishment for taking interest in the affairs of the Akalis. So the Shiromani Gurdwara Prabandhak Committee (S.G.P.C.) the body of the radical Sikhs engaged in the struggle for the reform of their religious shrines, passed a resolution exhorting the Sikhs to observe September 9, 1923 as the Nabha Day. Consequently the Sikhs of Nabha arranged a non-stop recitation of the Granth Sahib in their Gurdwaras. A 'Diwan' was held at Gangasar in the village Jaitu in Nabha. It was interrupted by the police. A number of arrests were made. The Akali leadership replied to such punitive measures by starting a full-fledged agitation against the authorities of Nabha.

Gandhi's main concern was to keep the Akali struggle non-violent as well as free from political colour. He, therefore, advised the Akali leadership to give no chance or opportunity to the government to use force against the volunteers. So they were advised not to send very large 'Jathas' as the authorities might be compelled to use force out of fear or nervousness. Secondly, the volunteers offering 'Satyagraha' should surrender to the police without any resistance and comply with deportation order. He, therefore, did not favour the Akalis' plan of sending Jathas of

500 each and locking up of the arms of the whole Jatha whenever confronted by the police. This, to him, was nothing short of passive violence as it could force the authorities to use force in order to deport the volunteers from the territory of Nabha. In his view sending of one or two men of undoubted integrity, spiritual force and humility was enough to assert the right of the S.G.P.C. over the Gurdwaras and vindicate their right to perform 'Akhand Path'. But, for their political demand, they should propagate separately.

Gandhi's advice was based on his experience of leading and guiding several non-violent encounters with the authorities. A non-violent struggle, in his view, did not mean merely refraining from the use of physical force. It must not give any opportunity to the authorities to use physical force out of fear or misconception of the motive of the Satyagrahis. Our non-violence, he asserted, must not be a camouflage to cover violence that we harbour in our hearts. Here in this case the authorities of Nabha were not opposed to the holding of 'Akhand Path' but were afraid that it could be a cover for keeping the state in ferment by the Akalis for the realisation of their political demand of the restoration of the rights and powers of the Maharaja of Nabha. That accounts for the policy of the authorities to prevent the entry of large Akali Jathas into the territory of the state of Nabha.

However, Gandhi's advice was not fully adhered to by the Akalis as a number of members of S.G.P.C. did not endorse his view of non-violence. As a result, the sending of large jathas ultimately compelled the Government to resort to violence to meet the situation created by the Akali agitation.

But what weighed most on the Mahatma's mind was the relation between the two major communities of India—Hindus and Muslims. For, after the withdrawal of the non-co-operation movement and his arrest the binding force between the two communities virtually snapped and the tension between them rose to such heights that fierce communal riots broke out in parts of northern India. Some leaders even held him responsible for the deterioration of relations between the two communities. For, he had stirred up the religious zeal of the Muslims by linking the religious issue with the political demands of the nation. R.N. Tagore once told Romain Rollan that by supporting the Indian Muslims in the Khilafat affair Gandhi did not work for the unity of India but for the pride and force of Islam-factors which resulted in violent Hindu-Muslim disturbances.[8] There is no doubt that the Khilafat issue brought to the fore 'Mullahs' or Muslim religious leaders who fuelled the flames of communalism. They blamed Gandhi for leaving them in the midst of a stormy river by withdrawing the movement.

Skirting the accusations of both the sides, the Mahatma dwelt upon the causes and cure of the communal conflicts. He tried to go to the root of the trouble. Loss of faith in non-violence and the distrust between the two communities were the two basic causes of the tension. He denied that the Hindus suffered more during the riots simply because of their observance of non-violence. For, it could not be ruled out that a large number of Hindus did not face the challenge of their opponents not because of their commitment to non-violence but out of sheer cowardice which, according to him, prompted the Muslim bullies to attack and harm the Hindus. It was the mental attitude of avoiding danger that multiplied their suffering during riots. But the remedy was not strengthening their position through 'Akhadas' or gymnasia or 'Sangathan' (consolidation) which the Hindu leadership was propagating. For, it would, according to him, aggravate the situation by proliferating suspicion between the two communities from which sprang their fear of each other. In other words, any programme of preparing one community to fight another was in no way conducive to the promotion of peace between them. It would only give rise to a state of armed peace since the other community would adopt similar measures to strengthen itself. In this atmosphere of suspicion and religious warfare the religious bigots wrote objectionable pamphlets to ridicule the founders of each other's religion. The vernacular press in the Punjab aggravated the situation by multiplying and highlighting such scurrilous writings that led to several communal riots. The real solution to the communal problem, in his view, was the removal of the root cause, that is, removal of distrust between the communities. The first step in this direction was acceptance of non-violence by both the communities in their mutual relations; for, "it is an indispensable condition prior to discussion of remedies for the removal of tension." For, it must be admitted by both the communities that 'neither party shall take law into its own hands' and that "all points in dispute, wherever and whenever they arise, shall be decided by reference either to private arbitration or to the law courts if they wish." A lasting settlement, in his view, was possible only if each party to the dispute would understand that it could not force any solution on the other. This was, of course, a sensible approach to the problem by a lawyer. But very few listened to him. His fears about the baneful effects of the publication of scurrilous literature turned out to be true. For, the immediate cause of riots in Kohat, in the N.W.F.P. that inflamed the passions of both the communities in northern India was the inclusion of an anti-Muslim poem in a collection published by the Secretary Sanatan Dharma Sabha of Rawalpindi and imported by him into Kohat. Hindus suffered a great deal in this riot. 155 were killed and practically the whole Hindu population had to quit Kohat. All these events were unbearable to the Mahatma. Penance appeared to him the only way to wash the sins of his brethren. He undertook a fast of 21 days which was commenced on 18th September 1924 in Delhi in the house of Mohammed Ali. It was a tactful act. For holding of fast in the house of a Muslim leader communicated that the fast was not against any community. However, keeping in view of his emaciated body, his friends and devotees tried to dissuade him as he might not be able to stand the long ordeal. The first week was passed without much anxiety. But at the end of the second week his urine showed dangerous symptoms. Dr, Ansari and Hakim Ajmal Khan urged him to take at least some medicine to control the spread of poison in the body. But of no avail. He only countered their arguments by asking them to wait for another day. His will power worked to wash out the poisonous elements. Religious hymns that were sung daily supplied him the spiritual food that sustained his resolve. Balkoba would sing hymns and his brother Vinoba would recite chapters of the Gita and Kathupinshads. However, the fast caused great anxiety to his friends and followers. They took a sigh of relief when the fast ended on 8th October amidst chanting of 'Mantras' of Upanishads, Sura of Koran and the singing of a hymn by Andrews 'When I survey the wondrous cross on which the prince of glory died.' It was appropriate for the occasion.

The act of penance had some effect on the leadership of both the communities for sometime. It brought the question of Hindu-Muslim unity to the forefront. Separatist movements such as 'Shuddhi' and 'Sangathan' among the Hindus and Tabligh among the Muslims were immediately suspended. The campaign of each community to malign the prophets and religious leaders of its opponents was shamed into silence. The leadership was thrown into a mood of self-introspection by this act of self-suffering of the Mahatma. So a call was given by the leaders of both the communities for an all-India conference for the settlement of communal differences. Three hundred delegates meeting in Delhi on 26th September deliberated for a week over the contentious issues and passed several resolutions calculated to settle the communal differences besides appointing Central National Panchayat or a Board consisting of not more that fifteen persons of both the communities to enquire into and settle communal differences. However, the fast did not yield far-reaching permanent results since many Muslim leaders of the Punjab or N.W.F.P. who were immediately involved in the events of Kohat riots, were cold towards the decisions of the Conference. The enquiry into Kohat affairs which had been assigned by the Congress Working Committee to Gandhi and Shaukat Ali revealed the different perceptions of Gandhi and Muslim leaders about the causes of communal conflicts. It also showed decline in Gandhi's influence over Muslims. But the investigation of Kohat riots by Gandhi made one positive contribution to his understanding of the causes of communal differences. It affirmed his awareness that the causes of the communal riots were not essentially religious, for, he came to the conclusion that the publication of the scurrilous poem alone was not responsible for raising the Muslims against the Hindus of Kohat. Economic factor, too, had played some role in turning the Muslims against the Hindus of Kohat. With a view to ensure the protection of Hindus in Kohat, he made some proposals which, though dressed in his robust idealism, showed his practical insight. For, he advised the Kohat Hindus, who had taken shelter at Rawalpindi, to return to their homes only if the Muslims were ready to assure them protection and were willing to live in peace with them without any regard to the attitude of the Government. For, Hindus in Kohat being in a tiny minority could not live in peace amidst hostile Muslim population. 'A Government,' he said, "can give protection against thieves and robbers, but not even a "Swaraj government will be able to protect against a wholesale boycott by one community or another."[9] Further, our dependence upon the alien government, he argued, for the protection of a minority against a majority would tighten the hold of that government and would nullify our claim for "Swaraj".

Greater responsibility and more hectic life were in store for him when the Congress met at Belgaum for its annual session. He agreed to become the president, which, in fact, was not a feather in his cap, for, he was far greater than the president of the Congress. Earlier he had recommended the name of Sarojini Naidu or of Dr. Ansari for this office. But since the agreement between the Swarajists and the No-changers was in a nebulous state, he agreed to become the president as this would weaken or at least throw under the carpet the opposition to the agreement of both sides. For, he was aware that all the show, fanfare and gala procession associated with the installation ceremony of the president had not much intrinsic value. So while going to Belgaum to preside, he told his secretary that "my state is that of an 'arja' (a jain nun) who before she is initiated, is taken out in gala procession and donned with costliest attire and jewels because she is to leave the world as a recluse.

My presidentship also seems to be a step to turn me out of political life."[10]

At the session after a long discussion in the Subjects Committee meeting and the plenary session, the agreement between him and the Swarajist was accepted, though he was afraid that this acceptance by majority was not out of conviction for the value of spinning franchise but out of regard for him by several members. According to it, any person who had not contributed his quota of hand spinning yarn was debarred from election to any representative body of the Congress. To many opponents of Gandhi, this rule transformed Congress from a political body to only a Khaddar making association. But to Gandhi this would raise the position and prestige of the Congress to great heights. For it would not only make Congress as a well-disciplined organisation by making its each member engaged in physical work like a soldier in the army but would also bring the Congress in touch with peasants and labourers besides creating political consciousness among them. Justifying spinning franchise he said,[11]

"... the Congress expects everyone (member) to spin 2000 yds. per month or get that quantity spun for him by another, therein lies my opinion, the strength of the franchise. It gives the people political education of high type. Now throughout India at the lowest computation, there are at least five million wheels working. These spinners can easily belong to the Congress. Those who are taking work from them can invite them to devote half an hour of their time to the nation by spinning at the wheel for that time."

To a Non-changer, the spinning franchise would reduce the hold of the elite especially urban elite over the organisation. To another, it would go a long way in helping the Congress organisation at different levels in overcoming its financial difficulties besides offering a continuous programme to the Congress for national reconstruction.[12]

During the year of his term as president of the Congress he made strenuous efforts to popularise 'Khaddar' and enrol new members. Initially he was assured of good response by his staunch followers. But shortly he realized that they were simply humouring him. For, even before the expiry of a quarter of the year, reports started reaching him about sharp decline in the membership of the Congress due to spinning franchise. He was now face to face with the hard reality of Indian behaviour. People revered him but paid scant attention to his ideals and programmes. Shouts of 'Gandhi ki Jai' rent the sky wherever he went, but 'instead of a forest of white Khaddar caps' what he saw every where was "the provoking black foreign caps on almost every head." The experience saddened him, though his faith in Khaddar as a deliverer from foreign domination was not reduced. He was aware that the Swarajists had hardly any faith in Khaddar. But he only tried to mend his fences with them in consideration of a political reality. The Council entry had already occurred and its withdrawal could be disastrous. For, it would be interpreted as a weakness both by the people and the alien government. At a time when the Government had launched a full-scale attack on civil liberties and promulgated an ordinance under which it had conducted raids on Congress officials and had arrested a number of Swarajists in Bengal, only a united front of the Congress could meet this challenge. He would have been false to himself, if he had not stood by the Swaraj Party in the hour of its need despite his lack of faith in the efficacy of their methods. He wrote, "Though an uncompromising no-changer I must not only tolerate their attitude and work with them, but I must even strengthen them wherever I can."[13] As a leader, his mind was broad enough to accommodate all genuine efforts towards the common good. He spent one month in Bengal, where the differences between the Swarajists and Non-changers were fiercest because of the style of functioning of C.R. Das, one of the main architects of the Swaraj Party, to bring about settlement between two groups. He told Dr. Ansari frankly that his surrender to the Swarajists was a necessity because of the democratic character of the Congress. For, knowing that he had failed to convince the Swarajists of the error of council-entry and that most of his co-workers and friends had faith in the Swarajists, he had no choice but to throw his weight with them as against other political parties.[14]

The sudden death of C.R. Das created a political void for him. In his obituary article in *Young India* he poured out his heart in an emotional language. "Deshbandhu's death," he lamented, "leaves me in a worse plight. For when Lokamanya left us, the country was full of hopes. Hindus and Muslims appeared to be united for ever. We were on the eve of battle. Now?" This was a big question mark. For there was no glimmer of hope. The nation was in a mood of despondency. He confessed that he realized Das' greatness when he stood by his own conviction and defended his differences with him (Gandhi). In his view, "their differences brought them close to each other as they started appreciating each other's integrity and sincerity to the cause of the country."[15] Both became emotionally attached to each other. He made a fervent appeal for funds for Deshbandhu Memorial. As a tribute to his friend, he put his services at the disposal of the Swarajists for a long time. The climax of that service was reached,

India that two members of the Ahmedia sect had been stoned to death in Afghanistan as a penalty for apostasy, he questioned the morality of the method on the grounds that "every formula of every religion has in this age of reason to submit to the acid test of reason and universal justice if it is to ask for universal assent."[19] This observation infuriated the orthodox Muslim leadership. Maulana Zafar Ali Khan who had been working with him since the beginning of the Khilafat movement and was the president of the Punjab Khilafat Committee in 1924 plainly told him, "that as a Mussalman he would be failing in his duty if he refrained from pointing out to him (Gandhi) that by challenging the right of the Koran to regulate the life of its followers in its own way, he had shaken the belief of the millions of his Muslim admirers."[20]

Gandhi's efforts to reinterpret the old beliefs and doctrine in the light of the experiences of the new age also brought him in conflict with his own people. This was with regard to his view of non-violence. It is an ancient religious doctrine. It had been known to the ancient Indians, Chinese and Christianity. The Upanishads, the Gita and the Mahabharata uphold it. It is the leading doctrine of Jainism and Buddhism. It is stated in the new Testament especially in the Sermon of the Mount. So in his characteristic humility Gandhi did not claim any originality in upholding this doctrine. 'It is as old as the hills', he affirmed. However his exposition of this doctrine has an appeal for the modern mind seeking solutions of social problems. Non-violence for Gandhi is not merely refraining from causing physical injury. But it is absence of ill-will against any one, whether opponent or any living being. In other words, it implies goodwill for all. From this point of view causing physical injury to a person for his good is nothing but non-violence. But very few could appreciate the new meaning that the Mahatma was putting upon the ancient doctrine. It created an uproar in his Ashram when he allowed mercy killing to a calf suffering from the incurable disease even in the face of the opposition of his wife. The surgeon whose advice was sought in the matter had declared the case 'past help and past hope.' He took this decision knowing fully well that it would not go unchallenged in an area around him where Jainism exercised immense influence. He was inundated with sheafs of letters, some of them full of abusive language while others questioning the propriety of such actions on the basis of current values. In reply to a question whether he would apply the same rule to human beings, he replied in the affirmative. But qualified the answer by the condition that such occasions would be rare since in the case of human beings we have ample means to help them besides they had the capacity to think and decide for themselves. Even today mercy killing or Euthanasia and doctor assisted suicide is a debatable issue in the Western countries. Several countries in Europe have taken a liberal view about it in case of terminal diseases like cancer. The object of such an action is to relieve the suffering soul from pain. It is the intention of a person that determines the nature of the action. He could even imagine a situation where the killing of one's own daughter would be considered as 'Ahimsa'. For instance when she is threatened with violation and there is no way by which one can save her. Then it should be purest form of Ahimsa on my part to end her life and surrender myself to the fury of the incensed ruffians. But as an individual the Mahatma had great respect for all life.

Similarly, another controversy arose about his view of non-violence when he gave approval to Ambalal's policy of killing stray dogs. Hindus of Ahmedabad pounded upon him with protests and letters. But he defended his action on the grounds that where the killing of dangerous animals, insects, germs was inevitable, man at that stage of development has no choice but to destroy them. It is violence no doubt. But it only reveals his failing, the weakness of his mind and his civilization. Similarly, monkeys destroying crops have to be eliminated. But man has to go on working for new methods to save his crops with the minimum of destruction of living beings. That some such forms of violence are part and parcel of human life are unavoidable is a fact that we encounter at every step. Absolute non-violence cannot be achieved immediately in the sense of refraining from destruction of all kinds of life. One moves towards non-violence life gradually by cultivating the required discipline, a corresponding way of life both individual and social. Non-violence, therefore, is not a static but a dynamic principle. It is all pervasive. It involves complete self-purification. Any kind of imposition from above whether from the government or from society is a form of violence. From this point of view compulsion is an antithesis of non-violence. Gandhi, therefore, would not object to the formation of a national militia under Swaraj as propel would not be prepared to defend themselves by non-violent means. Non-violence stretched to its logical conclusion, from Gandhi's point overview, means freedom as it involves absence of any kind of compulsion. Non-violence, therefore, does not remain a religious doctrine. It is more a secular way of life or life dominated by universal ethical principles. For, it means absence of "greed, pilfering, untruth, crooked diplomacy or intention to exploit others by withholding what they need for their existence."

During the year of presidentship of the Congress the Mahatma was mostly on tour for the propagation of Khadi, addressing large gatherings, receiving addresses and impressing upon people to shun untouchability as it was a blot on Hinduism. Often he had 22 hours non-stop programme in one day. As his secretary observed, he had no illusions about the intensity of darkness that enveloped him. But his deep faith in God assured him that when the "hour strikes he will shake every one out of slumber." For, people revered him. They were keen to have his 'darshan' or touch his feet only for their spiritual gain. But they were loath to listen to him or follow his programme. His appeal for the eradication of untouchability fell flat on their ears. At places his drive against it created an amusing though deplorable situation. For the caste Hindus were keen to shower addresses on him in public meetings but they were not ready to forgo their prejudice against untouchability. So even at the public meetings organised by the caste Hindus to honour the Mahatma they would set up separate enclosures for the untouchables which sometimes compelled him to go over to the enclosures of the untouchables and receive the addresses from the caste Hindus.

The same attitude of the caste Hindus he experienced at Vykom where he stayed to resolve the dispute between the caste Hindus and untouchables with regard to the use of a road. A meeting with the Nambudris, highest among the Brahmins of the area, who were opposed to the use of the road by the untouchables, revealed the lawyer in the Mahatma. He argued that 'there is nothing in the scriptures to prohibit anyone, because of his birth, from the use of public roads or public places' and asked the opponents to show him any authority in support of their claim. The Nambudris were on the defensive. Though he could not carry with him the orthodox sections among them, he offered them certain solutions as a lawyer. On his suggestion, the caste Hindus agreed to consider referendum or arbitration as a solution of the problem.

Notes and References

1. Nanda, D.R., Motilal, *op. cit.*, p. 151.
2. C.W., XXIV, p. 536.
3. *Ibid.*, p. 413.
4. *Ibid.*, Vol. XXV, p. 149.
5. Nehru, *op. cit.*, p. 129.
6. C.W., Vol. XXIII, p. 478.
7. *Ibid.*, pp. 513-14.
8. R.R. & Gandhi Correspondence, p. 61.
9. C.W., XXV, p. 478.
10. Desai, M., *op. cit.*, Vol. V, p. 264.

11. Tendulkar, *op. cit.*, Vol. II, p. 175.
12. C.W., Vol. XXVI, p. 575.
13. Tendulkar, *op. cit.*, Vol. II, p. 166.
14. C.W., Vol. XXIX, 284.
15. *Ibid.*
16. Nanda, In Gandhi's Footsteps, p. 106.
17. C.W., Vol. XXVI, p. 134.
18. *Ibid.*, XXVIII, p. 263.
19. *Ibid.*, XXVI, p. 226.
20. *Ibid.*

16

Spinner of Destiny

After laying down the office of the President of the Congress Gandhi dedicated himself mostly to the promotion of his constructive programme which to him held the destiny of the country. Though the next president, Sarojini Naidu, was his nominee, he had decided not to stir out of his Ashram at least for some time. His body needed rest as incessant touring had shattered his health. He was under the care of doctors and was taking unwillingly injections of arsenic and iron. He could now devote himself fully to his Ashram as for years he had not been able to attend to it because of involvement in hectic political activities. But destiny had in store for him penance before he could start any new programme. For he had to undergo fast for a week before he could take some steps to improve the life in his Ashram. It was an act of atonement for the lapse of some children of the school in the Ashram. This decision shocked his friends in the country. But for the Mahatma it was not a mere fed or an impulsive act. It was based on his philosophy of education. For punishment was not permissible for any lapse or indiscipline by a student since, in his view, it tends to harden the attitude of the child in place of purifying him. The ordeal and agony had to be undergone by the head of the institution to make the children conscious of their error and reform themselves through suffering.[1]

With the zeal of conviction, he filled the columns of his weeklies to convince the educated classes that his campaign for Khadi was no fad but based on his understanding of the reality of economic and political conditions of the country. For Khadi to him was a symbol of self-reliance and national regeneration as through it he was making an effort 'to revive national cottage industry and to bring about a natural and equitable distribution of the wealth[2] derivable from the largest industry next only to agriculture and thereby stopping the double evil of enforced idleness and pauperism. Moreover, it could break the barriers between the rich and the poor. However, he agreed with a leader of the Punjab that spinning wheel could not be introduced as a subsidiary employment among the farmers in the Punjab whose time was almost fully occupied even with more profitable concerns.[3]

But he was no conventionalist with regard to the use of spinning wheel. He tried to make it more efficient by applying to it modern techniques. He wrote a letter to Sir Harold Mann, head of a technological laboratory, seeking permission for his cousin Maganlal to study different instruments for testing cotton yarn. He gave first priority to the propagation of Khadi and refused to give up daily spinning even at the risk of his life in 1927 as doctors advised him to refrain from doing it for some time. But so far as the nation was concerned he was ready to relent on the clause regarding habitual wearing of Khadi for Congressmen passed at Gauhati session of the Congress on learning that a large number of Congressmen were lukewarm for the support of his Khadi programme. For, in a popular institution, it must be the opinion of majority that must count. In view of his declining influence the Government considered him as a spent force. But to some British pacifists he was a prophet. Eminent pacifists Horace Alexander and Muriel Lester stayed in his Ashram for a few days and were charmed by his religious and social outlook.

After a rest of a year in the Ashram, he undertook a tour for the propagation of Khadi. He toured through Bihar, C.P. and Berar, Maharashtra and U.P. addressing meetings, writing letters and meeting friends, followers and his critics. He had left to himself only three forty-five minutes for three meals (2 hrs. and 15 minutes), one and a half hour for morning and evening walks, a nap for half an hour during the day and finally retiring at 9 p.m. to get up at 4 a.m. next day. Three hours were devoted to correspondence and editing of his papers. Addressing large audiences was a very strenuous work as in those days there were no loud speakers. So the speaker could not reach all the people at a time. He had to address people in front, then those in the rear and then on the side.[4] Moreover, it was very difficult to convince people about the utility and validity of his Khadi programme. Several Congress leaders including both the Nehrus were sceptical about its value in India's fight for freedom as well as for her economic development. For, Khadi, in those days was coarse. It was not easy for the urban affluent sections to wear Khadi clothes. The coarseness of Khadi can be judged from the fact that when one day a large roll of thick fabric Khadi arrived at Rajagopalachari's house, his seven years old daughter Lakshmi asked her father if it was a carpet.[5] Among the critics of Khadi were several eminent communist leaders. On February 5, 1927, the Communist leader Shapurji Saklatwala, M.P. met him at Yeotmal during his tour. His life style was similar to that of Gandhi. He wore a poor English man's dress and had pair of spectacles with one broken pole which he kept in a cheapest steel case and rough and durable shoes that were unpolished . All this revealed his sincerity to the cause of the poor.[6] He talked to Gandhi for four hours. The meeting was followed by an open letter wherein he criticised Gandhi's view of modern civilization, labour-capital relations and Khadi programme. While admiring Gandhi's courage in expressing fearlessly the unexpressed voice of the people, he regretted that the Mahatma had failed in the task of building a new life after making it impossible for the old order to function. He objected to his campaign for Khaddar on the grounds that it was no more non-violent as it 'killed the livelihood of Lancashir.' So he appealed to him to join hands with the Communists for the liberation of the country as well as for the uplift of the labour. But Gandhi was not enamoured of modern civilization as it had crushed under the weight of its despotic regulations the liberty loving patriots. Defending his Khadi campaign, he pointed out that while it was serving the teeming millions in the villages, Saklatwala was keeping in view only the half-dozen cities which were an excrescence and serving at the moment the evil purpose of draining the blood of the villages.[7] He stated that he was neither an enemy of the labour nor of the capital. His effort was directed to taking from the capital labour's due share by educating labour to evolve its own leadership, reform itself by its own action and rely on its internal strength. He was not a faddist about the role of Khadi in India's economic development. Replying to his critics he said, "If even the time comes when the people of this country will have another more honest occupation other than spinning and weaving— then the vow of Swadeshi cloth may serve no useful purpose— My reason cannot conceive such a time ever coming. Whether it comes or not, there can be no two opinions that in our present condition Khadi is the purest form of Swadeshi.

Nevertheless the unremitting tours told very heavy on his health. He had a mild stroke of apoplexy in the last week of March 1927 which could prove fatal had he not taken sufficient precautions on doctors' advice. He was advised to take complete rest and move to a cooler place. He, therefore, went to Nandi Hills in Mysore where he stayed from April 19 to June 5, 1927, practising Yogic Asnas, especially 'Pranayama' Siddhasana, Shrishasana, Sarvaangasana for controlling his blood pressure and overcoming fatigue.[8] His diet was restricted to five articles, i.e. milk, grapes, oranges, figs, home-made bread. Normally he would take 30 ounces of raw goat's milk diluted with boiling water and sometime adding to it juice of 'neem' leaves in the morning or honey.[9] He was taking food as a medicine. 'Svad' or taste had no meaning to him. A person who does not make any distinction between bitter juice of 'neem' leaves and delectable honey has no concept of taste.

After resting at Nandi Hills for a few weeks, he came down to Mysore in the middle of June to continue his tour. Rest was only forced upon him. But it was only technically rest for the body. Otherwise he kept himself in touch with social and political developments in the country since for him there was hardly anything like spiritual or moral apart from work and action.[10] Progress of the soul and the development of the society were interdependent as it could be achieved only through service of society.[11] For him 'moksha' means elimination of ego which is attained when "I feel that I prevail into everybody. When that happens the ego can hardly persist. More precisely true religious life consists in suffering for others. So he advised the Christians that instead of preaching the tenets of the God of history, they should show Him as He lives today through you." For "God did not bear the cross only 1900 years ago but he bears it today and is resurrected from day-to-day."[12]

His visit to Orissa was a painful experience. Nay, it was a lesson for any public man or any religious leader. Was there any meaning of talking religion to such poverty stricken people? Wasn't God to them a heartless creature since He had reduced them to such a miserable condition? For stark poverty had completely wiped out a sense of human dignity among them. What a shocking experience he had there whilst he was talking to Andrews. A man with a half bent back wearing only a dirty loin cloth came crouching in front of them. He picked up a straw and put it in his mouth and then lay flat on his face with arms outstretched and then raised himself folded his hands bowed, took out the straw and arranged it in his hair. On enquiring about this strange behaviour of the visitor he learnt that the man was an untouchable and the straw he had taken in his mouth only to honour Gandhi. This was the custom. Mahatma's Hindus spirit was deeply wounded on witnessing this scene.

For, untouchability had reduced human beings to the position of chattels. The experience, he said, chastened him. The big zamindars and the local police must have compelled the ryots or common people not to go near the Mahatma. Fear had heaped upon them humiliation. So to his critics of Khadi, he said, "come with me to Orissa—to Puri, a holy place . . . within ten miles' radius of Puri you will see skin and bone. With this very hand I have collected soiled pies from them tied tightly in their rags. Talk to them of modern progress. Insult them by taking the name of God before them in vain— What can you do for them?[13]. . ." This was the question he posed to those who complained that Khadi was coarse, heavy and rough. But it was boon for those who were either naked or were in rags.

While touring Tamilnadu for his Khadi campaign, he was confronted with the problem of conflicts between Brahmins and non-Brahmins that called upon him to restate his view of Varna and Caste System. He denied that his concept of Varna had anything in common with existing caste system as it had nothing to do with superiority and inferiority of any caste, or the practice of untouchability. However, his campaign for Khadi had greater relevance for the non-Brahmans since the majority of the workers engaged in Khadi industry were non-Brahmins.

The tour of the South was interrupted for some time by his visit to Delhi as he was called by the Viceroy for talks. He was handed a document by the Viceroy which stated the appointment of the Simon Commission for the purpose of inquiring into the working of the system of Government operating at that time in India. The meeting left him high and dry as the Viceroy had nothing else to discuss with him. In this brief meeting the representative of the British monarch in India could hardly judge the springs of power of the Indian leader who struck him singularly remote from practical politics as "someone who had stepped off another planet on to this for a short visit of a fortnight and whose mental outlook was quite other to that which was regulating most of the affairs on the planet to which he had descended."

From Delhi Gandhi went straight to Ceylon in response to several invitation where he had the opportunity of seeing living Buddhism at close quarters which, in his view, strengthened the bonds between two neighbouring countries. For, the Buddha, he felt, was a "Hindu of Hindus" as he was saturated with the best that was in Hinduism.[14] For Buddhism broadened the base of Hinduism by giving it a new interpretation. He, therefore, advised the Hindus of Jaffna that if they imbued the broadened spirit of Hinduism they would be able to develop harmonious relations with the followers of different faiths surrounding them in that country. Thus by reclaiming the Buddha as a true product of Hinduism, Gandhi paved for strengthening bonds of India with her neighbours having Buddhism as their dominant religion.

The Congress session at Madras in December which he attended partly dampened his spirits. Lack of seriousness among the members and the considerations of his own health kept him away from its business session. The way the exhibition was organized in the session stung him as there was hardly anything Swadeshi in it. Pavilions had been assigned to foreign firms to exhibit their wares in the name of the Congress.[15] It represented, in his view, not rural India but the urban civilization of the West. Ironically the exhibition had the patronage of the Government. Further, he noticed that the resolutions passed during the session were hastily conceived and thoughtlessly passed. But the sharpness of his pen was directed mostly to the resolution on complete independence sponsored by J.L. Nehru. Not that he was opposed to freedom from the English yoke. Rather he was looking forward to the deliverance of all the so-called weaker races of the world through the deliverance of India from the crushing heals of Western exploitation in which England was the greatest partner.[16] But his objection was that before passing it the Congress had not sized up its own strength to implement it as the Congress organization at that time could not claim to be the irresistible force. So all the resolutions, in his view, would remain merely paper resolutions having no response from the people or having no correspondence to the popular wants and aspirations.[17] In fact, his opposition was based mainly on pragmatic considerations. For a fallen India, 'he argued,' to aspire to move the world and protect weaker races is seemingly an impertinence. He looked forward to India coming "to her own which, in his view cannot be better defined by any single word than Swaraj."[18]

His sharp criticism of independence resolution stung its author that brought to the surface the differences between him and J.L. Nehru. The latter not only questioned the propriety of criticising his independence resolution but also challenged the fundamental principles of Mahatma's approach to life, his view of civilization and his solutions of India's multifarious problems. But this declaration of differences by his young colleague did not hurt the Mahatma. For, he honestly believed that no man could claim possession of complete knowledge of truth since like God truth is infinite and multi-faceted. So everyone could claim to be true from his own point of view. He, therefore, appealed to Nehru that their differences must not affect their personal relations. For, he had maintained good relations with leaders like Sastri and Lajpat Rai in spite of their deep differences with him. The young Nehru, too, did not like to carry the differences to the breaking point. For, he was realist enough to understand that the Mahatma still had the power to move the millions in India and anyone whose mission was to carry the country with him for its emancipation could not afford to part company with the Mahatma. A decade later Subhas did make the experiment and found himself in minority.

Another shock was awaiting the Mahatma at this time. His nephew Maganlal who was looking after the Sabarmati Ashram passed away after a brief illness in Bihar where he had gone to help his daughter in a campaign against 'purdah'. He went with Gandhi to South Africa in 1903 and joined the Phoenix Settlement on his uncle's call. The Mahatma had dreamed of and worked for his nephew succeeding him as the head of the Ashram. The immediate result of this tragedy was the additional responsibility of looking after the Ashram fell on him. Unfortunately when the Mahatma was engaged in several problems and controversies, the frequent rise in his blood pressure and his physical weakness caused some anxiety to his friends and followers and raised frivolous speculations in some quarters that his end was near. There was a rumour that he had predicted his death by 12th March 1928. But the Mahatma had no faith in astrology. He knew that he had become weak only because of his experiment with non-milk fruitarian diet. He was quite active. Though staying in his Ashram, his mind was occupied in guiding the struggle in Bardoli where the peasants were fighting under the leadership of Patel whom they had given the well-deserving epithet Sardar. For, the government had imposed Twenty-two per cent enhancement of tax arbitrarily. On Gandhi's advice, the peasants refused to pay the revenue until and unless the enhanced assessment was withdrawn. The Government tried to break the backbone of the movement by terrorizing the people. The officials seized and sold their moveable property, declared the land forfeit and took away their buffaloes. Besides, a rumour was set afloat that the Bardoli Satyagraha did not have Gandhi's support to embarrass Patel as well as to discourage the people to participate in it. But Gandhi denied it. Rather, he asserted that he was associated with it right from the beginning as Patel was seeking his advice frequently and consulting him about its important decisions. If he was not actively engaged in the struggle it was only because of his poor health. However, he was not in favour of the extension of the Bardoli movement to all-

India level as suggested by several leaders. Though dressed in idealistic and religious language, his decision in this regard was based on practical considerations. For, he felt that an all India Satyagraha on this issue would give a political dimension to a local issue involving only the revenue policy of the local Government which would provide the British Government at all levels with an opportunity to crush it with all their strength while the local issue would not be able to sustain the interest of the people of other parts of the country for a long time. The failure of the movement would cause doubts in the minds of the people about the efficacy of the Satyagraha. But if it was confined to the local demand, the Government might yield to it if the people remained resolute and this would yield a psychological gain for the country about the power of Satyagraha. Gandhi's judgement turned out to be true. Under the pressure of public opinion stirred up by the sacrifices of the Satyagrahis, the Government appointed an inquiry committee to judge the validity of new assessment. It recommended 5.7 per cent increase instead of 22 per cent and criticized the assessment made by the revenue officials. The struggle ended. All the Satyagrahis were released and their land and goods restored to them. The major gain of the Bardoli struggle was moral and psychological. For, it raised the moral stature of the nation. "The Dublas (the weak) a name of one of the tribes engaged in this struggle showed unbending resolve and grit which for the poetess (Sarojini Naidu) was 'treasure of the lowly."[19]

While the Bardoli struggle was in progress, the all India political leadership was engaged in framing a constitution for free India in order to demonstrate that Indian leadership was capable of producing a constitution without the guidance and help of Britain. It could be a landmark in India's claim for freedom if this effort succeeded. For, Gandhi both these efforts—of Bardoli and of Lucknow—were essential for India's struggle for freedom. "If the Bardoli victory is a part of history, he said, so will be the victory at Lucknow. Bardoli has shown the way to organic Swaraj—to 'Ramrajya' while Lucknow had opened the gates of constitutional Swaraj. Both things were essential. Whereas learned and political astute leaders were required for the Lucknow, the ordinary illiterate masses served the purpose for the Bardoli Swaraj."

Notes and References

1. C.W., XXIX, p. 291.
2. *Ibid.*, XXX, p. 4.

was fixed). Gandhi yielded to the zeal and demands of younger men in the Congress who were itching for a fight with the 'Raj' for the liberation of the country. A programme was formulated for the members of the Congress to make it a fighting body to carry on non-violent mass struggle. However, it was more or less the same programme which was adopted a decade earlier in a similar situation but with a greater emphasis on activating women to take their due share in nation building. The Mahatma also suggested that Congress members having income more than Rs. 100 p.m. contribute five percent of their income to the Congress for the struggle but it was not made obligatory on the suggestion of some leaders.[2]

Destiny tested the mettle of the Mahatma to lead the nation in a non-violent fight against a powerful adversary which demanded cultivation of equanimity and resignation to the will of almighty. He qualified himself in this test when his grandson Rasik, son of Harilal, died of typhoid just at a time when he was going round the country to prepare his forces for the fight. He received the news of his death when food was being served. He took the meals as usual and carried on his work in Sind where he had gone to collect funds for Lajpat Rai Memorial. In a letter to Mira, he wrote "Have just had a wire saying Rasik passed away yesterday. God's will is our law. My day's work goes on uninterrupted. Whatever I feel is felt for selfishness. . . ."[3]

The impending struggle put a heavy responsibility on him. He undertook long tours which became quite agonizing as he decided to resume third class travelling.

After his tour of Sind, he went to Delhi where he stayed for three days during which he had a chance meeting with the Viceroy at a tea party arranged by Vithalbhai Patel to which the Viceroy and several leaders were invited. This meeting stirred up political speculations in the Press. But Gandhi scuttled them by stating that it was purely a courtesy meeting. To him more important was the meeting of the Working Committee of the Congress to which he had been specially invited by the president. It passed a resolution of boycott of foreign cloth and Gandhi was appointed chairman of the committee to implement it. In pursuance of it, a bonfire of foreign clothes was held at Shraddhanand Park in Calcutta. The authorities took a serious view of it. Declaring it as an illegal act, the police tried to disperse the crowd by lathi-charge. Gandhi was arrested but the prosecution was postponed till it was settled whether the park came under the Calcutta Police Act or not. He was tried and prosecuted on the return of his tour of Burma which had been planned earlier and fined by the Chief Presidency Magistrate of Calcutta. It looks somebody paid the fine without the knowledge of Gandhi. However, Gandhi was sorry for the judgement as in his view he had not committed any illegal act since the park was not a thoroughfare. However, his tour of Burma was satisfactory so far as the promotion of Khadi was concerned. For, he collected one lakh rupees which was a handsome amount in view of trade depression.

He undertook a whirlwind tour of Andhra Pradesh in burning heat for the promotion of Khadi. It gave good return in terms of money as he collected 2,61,463 rupees besides jewels. In August 1929, he met Jinnah on the initiative of Sarojini Naidu, without hoping for any spectacular result from this meeting.[4]

In view of the impending struggle, the overwhelming majority of the Congress offered its presidentship to him. But he declined it on the grounds that at this critical hour a younger man should wear the thorny crown. So at A.I.C.C., J.L. Nehru was elected on Gandhi's suggestion. It was an act of statesmanship. For he satisfied both Motilal who carried weight with older Congress men and the youth in the Congress who adored Jawaharlal. He, in fact, tamed the revolutionary forces by putting the crown of the Congress on Jawaharlal who, he knew, would never go against him. By this action he maintained unity in the Congress as within the organisation there were many who stood for radical action while others were on the side of 'go slow' policy.

Before the session of the Congress, he met the Viceroy accompanied by Motilal. The meeting confirmed his view that the British were in no mood to grant full Dominion Status to India and so he was at liberty to pursue with greater zeal the demand for complete independence in compliance with the compromise resolution of Calcutta session.

At the Lahore session events and discussion moved round him, though J.L. Nehru was the president of the session. For, it was the Mahatma who moved the important resolutions outlining the goal of the Congress and its methods for attaining it. The programmes were mostly on the lines of those of Satyagraha in 1921-22. But the triple boycott was modified on the insistence of some members of the Working Committee who wanted to omit the boycott of schools and colleges and courts as it did not receive adequate response at that time. The students were only encouraged to participate in the movement. Only the boycott of local bodies and legislatures was retained.

However, the management of the Congress was not an easy task for him in spite of his immense popularity with the Hindu masses. For, the resolutions moved by him were not passed without stiff opposition at the A.I.C.C. and the Subnects Committee meetings. To the boycott of councils, an amendment was moved and it was lost by one vote only. Similarly, another amendment moved by Kelkar, for the deletion of the preamble about Viceroy's services towards peaceful settlement, too, was lost by one vote. Again a resolution moved by Gandhi about the reduction of the number of delegates to the session to 1000 and A.I.C.C. members to 100 was lost by 111 against 101 votes. Nevertheless in the open session, he had less difficulty in carrying the Congress with him. However, his resolution deploring the bomb attack on the Viceroy was opposed and was passed by a narrow majority. Amendment was also moved for the main resolution on independence and civil disobedience which was rejected by a considerable majority (802 for and 987 against). Even after the session, the Mahatma remained the star attraction for it was he who had to work out a plan and chalk out a strategy for carrying on the struggle. It was left to him to draft the independence resolution for 26th January. The burden of the resolution was that freedom from the British rule was the question of life and death for the Indians since the British had not only deprived the people of their freedom but had ruined India economically, culturally and spiritually. The plan that was taking shape in his mind was of a fight of "such a magnitude that no one could say as to how it would end." But it must be of such a nature that without causing any destruction it should be large enough to make a great impact. It must bring forth the economic consequences of the British rule especially for the masses who had been reduced to grinding poverty as a result of exploitation. But it must be an issue which could appeal to all classes and religious groups.

In order to judge the attitude of the Government towards his struggle, he made an ingenious move which unfortunately created misgivings among the topmost leaders of the Congress including its young president. He offered his eleven points or eleven demands, the acceptance of which could result in the suspension of the civil disobedience movement. The offer of eleven points was also rooted in the nature of his Satyagraha. For, it involved an offer of peaceful settlement to the opponent. But it was equally a subtle move to keep the Congress united as well as to invite the support of non-Congress leaders to the political struggle of the Congress. For, the eleven demands did not mention the ultimate goal which had kept the leadership divided. The demands were only popular demands that concerned different classes in the country. These included prohibition, reduction of land revenue, abolition of salt tax, reduction of military expenditure, a protective tariff on foreign cloth, discharge of all political prisoners, revaluation of the rupee, right to carry arms, disbandment of C.I.D. It was an adroit move. Reduction of land revenue had fascination for peasants while revaluation of rupee had an appeal for industrialists. Reduction of salt revenue had an appeal for all the poor people of the country. The basic ideas underlying some of these demands became the guiding principles of the fundamental rights passed by the Karachi Congress.

Nevertheless the young president of the Congress felt that the Mahatma had diluted the goal of the Congress by this offer of eleven demands. But to the latter this offer did not mean cessation of the struggle for independence. It only meant lifting the ban on the Congress for attending the Round Table Conference. Moreover, these eleven points, in his view, covered the substance of independence for the masses. For, mere withdrawal of the English, he argued, was not independence. "It means the consciousness in the average villager that he is the maker of his own destiny, he is his own legislator through his own chosen representatives."[6] The nomenclature of the form of government, for him, was immaterial. But it must be government that would obey and carry out the wishes of the people."

However, the eleven points were brushed aside by the British and so the struggle became unavoidable. But as a part of the norms of Satyagraha, he sent a letter to the Viceroy on 2nd March stating reason and programme of his movement. The bearer of the letter was a young Englishman Reginald Reynolds who had come to India a few months before the commencement of the movement and was staying in Gandhi's Ashram. This was a significant gesture demonstrating that the movement was not against the English people but against a system that had caused great suffering to the Indians. So he observed,[7]

> "My indictment is not against the English as men, it is against the Englishmen as the ruling caste. As men they are as good as we. In some respects they are better—but as rulers they are highly undesirable."

He confessed that he owed some good qualities such as punctuality, reticence, public hygiene, independent thinking and exercise of judgement to his association with English friends. In this way he tried to convert his struggle against imperialism not a fight against an enemy but a sort of wrangling between two members of a family because of certain differences in attitudes towards social life. In the same vein later on before starting his Quit India Movement he sent Miss Slade to see the

Viceroy and communicate to him that his call for the British to leave India was in the best interest of both India and Britain. Though the Viceroy at that time refused to see her, he asked her to see his secretary and discuss with him the position. This approach paid dividends in terms of earning goodwill of a section of the British people who earnestly believed that the Mahatma was essentially a man of peace and so the framers of British policy towards India had to keep this fact in view in their dealings with the Mahatma, at any moment of confrontation.

As a general of the non-violent army, Gandhi had to move cautiously. For, he never wanted the recurrence of Chauri Chaura like situation that forced him to withdraw the non-co-operation movement a decade earlier. So he mapped out the course of the movement in such a way that in the beginning the Satyagraha was confined to very trusted and trained persons who could submit to rigorous discipline demanded by a non-violent struggle. It should slowly and gradually fan out to involve more and more people following in the footsteps of trained Satyagrahis. So in the first phase, the inmates of his Ashram who had received sufficient training under his personal supervision would make the first move. The civil disobedience was to start with violation of law about the manufacture of salt. It was an issue that had an appeal for the poorest of the poor in the country. By adopting this issue Gandhi made a departure from his strategy employed a decade earlier when he adopted a religious issue for bringing Hindus and Muslim under the same banner. The violation of salt law was a secular issue and so it had the potentiality, according to Gandhi, of bringing all the communities under the same banner. In a letter to Ansari who did not favour C.D. movement at that time because of Muslims' apathy to the movement he wrote, "I seek independence through a redress of the age-long grievances which touch the masses more than us." Giving instances of the efficacy of secular causes for uniting different communities for a common cause, he drew his attention to the situation created by the flood in Gujarat four years ago that made all without exception to unite to fight the havoc caused by the flood. For, "there was no difficulty about the Muslims seeking the same shelter as the Hindus. The blind orthodox Hindu suspended his prejudice against the untouchable. They discarded his venom for the time being."[8] So he appealed to Ansari to realize the new orientation that he (Gandhi) had given to the struggle. But Ansari who had presided over the Madras Congress in 1927 was not alone in raising doubts about the desirability of launching the C.D. movement at that time because of the general antipathy of the Muslims to the movement at that time. He was the founder of the Nationalist Muslims Party that claimed to keep the Congress flag afloat among the Muslims. However, he jumped on the Congress bandwagon later on and was jailed for some time.

According to his plan, the beginning of the civil disobedience would be sounded by the symbolic picking up of contraband salt by Gandhi at Dandi, a village on the sea coast in Gujarat about 200 miles from Sabarmati. The distance was to be covered in 24 days. The programme was so designed as to enable the party to break the salt law on the historic day of 6th April, the events of which culminated in Jallianwala Bagh massacre on April 13, 1919 as a result of which, according to Gandhi, it had become a day of penance and purification. As a strategist of non-violent fight, Gandhi knew how to make the suffering of the people as an emotive issue to generate zeal and fervour for the fresh fight as well as to give continuity to the struggle for independence. The march of the Satyagrahis from the Sabarmati Ashram was well-planned. The members were to carry their own beddings and simple food was to be provided by the villagers where they would halt. However, the leader was not sure even a day before the commencement of their long journey to Dandi that he would be able to lead the marchers as the air was thick with rumour that he would be arrested shortly. But no such thing happened and at the appropriate time on 12th March the Mahatma started the March accompanied by 78 persons who virtually represented the whole of India, though Gujaratis with 31 marchers toped the list, followed by Maharashtrians with 13, 8 from U.P., 6 from Cutch, 4 from Kerala, 3 each from Punjab and Rajputana, 2 from Bombay, 1 each from Sind, Tamilnadu, Andhra, Utkal, Karnatak, Bihar and Bengal. There was one from Nepal. Among them two were Muslims, two untouchables and one Christian. 12 among them were graduates, 7 of Bombay university, 3 of Gujarat Vidyapith and 2 of foreign universities. Gandhi's son Manilal and his grandson were included in this group of Satyagrahis.

The Mahatma was no novice in organising the march. He had successfully led the long march in South Africa with three thousand rustic labourers who had nothing with them but only faith in their leader. Dandi March shows Gandhi as a master strategist. For nearly four weeks he kept the eyes of his people and the British administrators in India and the statesmen in England fixed on his actions and programmes. With a staff in his hand and the teachings of Lord Krishna and Christ on his lips he was marching like Christ towards his destination. A pony and bullock cart followed him for his use in case he fatigued. But he refused to use any of them. During the march he performed all normal duties. He did not stop spinning. As usual he went to bed at 9 in the night and woke up at 4 in the morning. During all these days he marched more than ten miles every day. The time of rest was utilized to replying letters received during the march. The collector of Ahmedabad noted the religious aura which surrounded Gandhi's journey as he and his followers kept quoting the Gospel—The sale of Bibles to Ahmedabad Hindus shot up.[9] The Mahatma was reminding the whole Christian world that imperialism and the teaching of the Bible could not go together. To him loyalty to a corrupt state was a sin and disloyalty a virtue.

Initially, the programme was an object of ridicule and derision in the official circles. For some of them it was a kindergarten stage of revolution or a fantastic project. For no one could imagine that the British would be forced to give up their most precious jewel in their imperial domain simply because some hot headed Indians had picked up or manufactured salt without their permission. The Viceroy believed that march would peter out in failure and ridicule. But at the same time he felt that the "will power of the man must have been enormous to get him through the march. For he had the information that Gandhi's blood pressure was dangerous and his heart none too good. He had been told that since his horoscope predicted his death that year, he was desperate to throw himself into this kind of enterprize."[10] But the Viceroy did not know that the Mahatma had no faith in astrology. If Gandhi was not arrested before the commencement of the march, it was mostly because the Government believed that the whole project would end in fiasco. But to give surprise to the opponent was an important characteristic of Satyagraha. The salt pans created a revolution in the minds of the people. What escaped from the notice of the British administrators was that the Mahatma was not manufacturing salt but disobedience. They could not imagine that he was releasing tremendous energy in the country through this seemingly innocuous act. As the marchers proceeded there was commotion throughout the length and breadth of the country. It was a holy war or religious act for the Mahatma. The commencement of the march coincided with the publication of his commentary on the Gita entitled 'Anasakti Yoga'. The Mahatma had combined in himself the attributes of both Krishna and Arjuna—the wisdom flowing out of mental equanimity and non-attachment to action and the doer of action. Practically all the inhabitants of the villages came out to greet the marchers. Several heads of the villages resigned on the call of the Mahatma. It was no surprise if at certain places all the villagers were found to be ready for civil disobedience. The heat generated by the zeal of the masses touched the hearts of several members of the Central Legislature who resigned to identify themselves with the movement. The Government was taken aback and it had no choice but to resort to repressive measures to crush it. Several Congress leaders were arrested to check the mobilisation of the masses by Gandhi's supporters. But the pace of the movement remained unchecked. The atmosphere in the evening prior to the lifting of the salt by the Mahatma was solemn and pure. Gandhi addressed the volunteers at the prayer meeting. His speech exuded confidence. While enquiring from the local workers about the arrangement of picking up salt next morning, he humorously remarked that they should not forget the presence of Intelligence men among them as he noticed two sitting in front of him dressed in Khadi.[11]

It looks that the agent of the Government had planned to remove the salt at Dandi which had been left at the shore by the receding waves in order to gain a psychological advantage by propagating that Gandhi failed to pick up salt on the day fixed for it. So there was not much salt when the party reached there and naturally the leader picked up more mud than salt in his attempt to break the salt law. However, picking up or selling and using of contraband was only symbolic of the freedom of the people from alien rule. Since the Government was hesitant to arrest Gandhi he made another provocative but non-violent move to show to the world the hollowness of imperial authority. He planned to take possession of Dharsana Salt works. But before any action could be taken in this direction, he was arrested on the night of 5th May and was removed to Yeravada jail. But there was no abatement in the enthusiasm of the people. No part of India escaped its impact though its intensity varied from province to province. His successor, Abbas Tyabji, ex-justice of Baroda who was to lead a 'Jatha' (a group of volunteers) was arrested along with his followers. Now it was the turn of Sarojini Naidu to lead 2000 volunteers to the salt depots of Darsana for taking possession of them. Columns and Columns of non-violent volunteers moved towards the salt pans, among them Gandhi's son Manilal, completely sure of being beaten down or killed by the flanks of the police carrying five-foot clubs tipped with steel. There was no fight, no struggle, the marchers simply walked forward until struck down and carried to the improvised hospital by the volunteers with heads and limbs broken and blood scattered on their white Khadi clothes. Webb Miller who gave an eye-witness account of an unusual fight noted that there was no sign of wavering or fear on the faces of marchers. They marched steadily with heads up, without the encouragement of music or cheering or any possibility that they might escape serious injury or death. The fight went on for many days. 320 men were injured, many lay unconscious in the temporary hospitals, others lay writhing with pain. Two died. The bureaucracy and the high ups both in India and England were amused without knowing that the blows which were falling on the heads of Satyagrahis were breaking the hard surface of imperialism. Cartoonist in the West had portrayed an impish Mahatma putting salt on the lion's tail. It was a clear demonstration of Gandhi's non-violent war. It was the non-violence of the brave—a perfect thing of its kind. Mrs. Naidu and Manilal were arrested. But with every arrest and repressive measure the chances of reconciliation between the Government and Congress were receding.

Internment was no punishment for Gandhi. Rather it provided him with much needed rest after hectic political life. Not only at night he had refreshing sleep as he was permitted to sleep outside his cell, he could sleep two to three hours during the day, too. However, he maintained the routine of the life in the Ashram. Government had fixed Rs. 100 as the monthly allowance for his food which pained him as he felt that it was a charge on the semi-starved toiling masses. He decided that he would not spend all this money, though particular items of his food had become a physical necessity for him. So whenever it was possible, he dispensed with oranges or other costly items of food. But the persistence of constipation compelled him to take fresh fruits and dry fruits such as raisins, dates, etc. He tried vegetable diet which reduced the cost from 6 annas to 2 annas. For a few days this experience served the purpose as it also solved his problem of constipation. But he had to go back to the diet of dates and raisins because of the trouble in his stomach. Even after his release, he started taking orange peel made into jam in his attempt to give up costly fruit diet.

As against his routine during his imprisonment in 1922-24, when he devoted all his leisure to reading books, he kept himself occupied this time mostly with spinning and carding as he felt that the had not acquired sufficient proficiency in this art. Kaka Kalelkar was transferred to his cell to give him company, though he did not ask for it. However, this gave him good opportunity to improve his knowledge of Marathi and pronunciation of the slokas of the Gita. He made an earnest request to him to treat him as a student proper and not tolerate his mistakes because he was a Mahatma. Similarly, when Pyarelal was transferred to his cell on Kaka's release, he started refreshing his knowledge of Urdu. For he wanted to learn as many languages of India as possible. The leisure in jail also induced him to translate with the assistance of Kalelkar the Ashram Bhajanwali (hymns sung in the Ashram) for Mira in appreciation of her devotion to him and to his ideals.[12] The master and the devotee were trying to excel each other in doing some service to the other as a token of love. Some part of the day was spent in writing letters to the inmates of the Ashram which sometimes took the form of discourses on the fundamental principles of the Ashram.[13]

However, he had a tiff with the authorities over the restrictions imposed on him about seeing visitors. He refused to see any visitor as a protest against such restrictions. Another development in the prison threatened a crisis. Having read in the newspapers reports of ill-treatment of Satyagrahi prisoners in the Yeravada jail, he asked for permission to see them occasionally or to live with them, offering to surrender all the comforts which had been permitted to him. He hinted at serious consequences if his request was not granted. He would withdraw his co-operation as "to the upkeep of his body". However, the crisis was averted when the authorities agreed to allow him to see periodically those whom he wanted to meet.

Nevertheless, he had not to stay in jail for a long time. The Liberal leaders Sir Tej Bahadur Sapru and M.R Jayakar started negotiations for settlement. They met Gandhi on July 23rd and 24th and in pursuit of the negotiations the two Nehrus, father and son, Patel, Sarojini Naidu, Dr. Syed Mahmud, Jairam Das Daulatram were transferred to his jail for discussion. It was virtually conference of the CWC in the Yeravada jail which lasted for three days. But no progress could be made in the negotiations as there appeared to be an unbridgeable gulf between the Congress and the Government. In fact, settlement was no easy task as there were several players in this game of politics. There were the Liberal leaders who were acting as the bridge between the Government and the Congress, the commercial community whose interests were at stake because of the Boycott, the bureaucracy, non-Congress Hindu leaders and the participants in this struggle. The Congress leaders, therefore, had a limited room for settlement. However, the efforts of the Liberal leaders succeeded after a few months. A temporary rapprochement was brought about between Gandhi and the government as a result of which he was released on January 26, 1991. Immediately after his release the Mahatma rushed to Allahabad where his esteemed co-worker and one of the old guards, Motilal Nehru was fighting valiantly his last battle for life. His old friends and colleagues freshly out of prison came to see him. He sat like an old lion mortally wounded and with his physical strength almost gone. The Mahatma remained with him till the end of his life and gave comfort and solace to Motilal's wife and her children. As his son recorded it was above all the wonderfully soothing and healing presence of Gandhiji that helped my mother and all of us to face that crisis in our lives.[14] Motilal's death, of course was no less loss to the Mahatma. He lost a colleague who could mobilize and muster round him the old guards of the Congress.

Gandhi's release was followed by talks between him and the Viceroy for several days. They met eight times. He had enough time to size up the personality of the little man whom Churchill described in an angry mood as a seditious Middle Temple lawyer striding half-naked up the steps of Viceregal palace. But the Viceroy appears to have been won over by the Mahatma's inner being though his outward being did not impress him. He informed the king about the personality of his strange visitor thus "I was conscious of very powerful personality and this independent of physical endowment which is indeed unfavourable. Small wizened, rather emaciated, no front teeth, it is a personality very poorly adorned with this world's trimmings. And yet you cannot help feeling the force of character behind the deep little eyes and immensely active and acutely working mind." Many contemporaries felt that it was a meeting between two Mahatmas, though quite different in their attire, standard of living and the functions that the destiny had assigned to them in the world. It was said that when a member of Viceroy's staff peeped into the Viceroy's study where the two were sitting he found Lord Irwin carefully explaining to Mr. Gandhi the Greek text of a certain passage in the Sermon on the Mount.

But there were many in the British hierarchy who had no faith in Gandhi. The commander-in-chief General Sir Philip Chetwode believed Gandhi to be as cunning as a carload of monkeys.[15] The next Viceroy Lord Wellingdon carried the impression that Gandhi was one of the most astute politically minded and bargaining little gentleman he ever came across. Possibly during the talks the Viceroy Lord Irwin also realized that he was also dealing with a man who was no novice in politics and his religion was not divorced from politics. In an interview with Negley Farson, the American correspondent who was in India in 1930 asked the Viceroy what he really thought of Gandhi "The first time I saw, he said in reply," "I was tremendously impressed by his holiness. The second time I was tremendously impressed by his legal astuteness. The third time I was sure of it."[16] The talks revealed Mahatma's amazing grasp of detail. He was not negotiating a general settlement but insisting on bargaining over a multitude of details. This was too much for the Viceroy who twice during the day arranged for Gandhi to make his points with the Home Secretary in charge of the nation's police and then with the Finance Secretary.[17]

The talks led to the famous Gandhi-Irwin Pact. On March 5, 1931 as a result of which the Congress suspended the movement and agreed to participate in the Round Table Conference with the object of considering the scheme for the constitutional Government of India. The Government assured steps to undo the injuries suffered by individuals during the civil disobedience movement and agreed to withdraw the Emergency Ordinances, release all Satyagrahi prisoners, remit fines not already realised, restore confiscated land and property unless not already sold and pursue a liberal policy in regard to the re-appointment of Government servants and village officials who resigned but apply for reinstatement. It also agreed to allow the people to manufacture salt in areas where it could be collected and made for their use. The right of the people for peaceful picketing without any violation of ordinary laws for furtherance of the replacement of non-Indian by Indian goods or against the consumption of intoxicating liquor and drugs was also conceded provided that boycott of British goods as a political weapon was given up. But, in fact, in material terms the Viceroy did not yield much. It is true that the Mahatma made many demands but the Viceroy showed his inability to accept them on the grounds of a practical difficulties which gave the impression both in India and England that the Government had the upper hand. Both the Viceroy and Gandhi had to do tight rope walking. Gandhi had his own difficulties. For, during the negotiations new points had been raised for clarifications. He had to satisfy the wishes and demands of different groups with different mental make-up and ideologies. J.L. Nehru was insisting that there was no going back on the Lahore resolution. Irwin had his own limitations. The European Association of Calcutta was roaring all the time in tune with Churchill's fulmination in Parliament. A day before signing of the Pact the Government of India sent a verbatim copy of the agreement to be signed. The Secretary of State in a telegram suggested certain modifications mostly of the drafting nature to avoid giving the impression of a treaty, that is, to avoid such expression 'as it has been agreed'.[18]

Gandhi's English friend Reginald Reynolds who had been sent to deliver the letter to the Viceroy before the commencement of the Salt March, was upset on noticing the way the negotiations were moving. He wrote to him from England to know the position of the Congress. Gandhi while assuring him that there would be no surrender on principle, reminded him that Satyagraha "is a method of carrying conviction and converting by an appeal" to reason and to the sympathetic chord in human beings. But the Pact did not satisfy him and he frankly criticised its terms. For, in his view, with the exception of small concession in the matter of salt—no single right or principle has been established. The truce does not even represent the *status quo ante belum* ; it is a partial and patronizing restoration on the part of the Government of its spoils acquired during the struggle but not of any of those rights for which the struggle itself was fought. "Summing up his argument, he said, ". . . to adopt the method of non-violent revolution with all its suffering in order to gain nothing at all—that is a policy I do not understand", "Will India understand?" he asked.[19] The Mahatma published this letter in his paper to give full publicity to the opponent's point of view. However, Reynolds strong criticism of the Pact did not adversely affect their personal relations. For Gandhi, Reynold remained as good as gold and very brave. "But from Gandhi's point of view what Reynold failed to understand was Gandhi's unique approach to the conflict situation. As observed by Nehru, Gandhi was always after psychological change, a breaking of the barriers of anger and distrust, an approach to the other's goodwill and fine feelings."[20] Even if a settlement was a distant reality, negotiations with sympathetic understanding of the point of view of the opponent could at least remove the sting out of the conflict which could pave way for a lasting settlement in the future. Further, Reynolds and many more critics of the Pact failed to notice the psychological gains that the Indians had made as a result of this Pact. For, the negotiations were carried on between two equals. Gandhi representing the Indians and the Viceroy the British. It was for the first time the agent of the British Government condescended to negotiate with the accredited agent of the Indian National Congress on equal footing. There were sharp exchanges between them. The Viceroy did not assume the authoritative role even while not conceding the demands of Gandhi. He only expressed his administrative difficulties in his inability to accept his demands which could not be viewed as unjust. He even admired his salt Satyagraha as a fine strategy. Nor did Gandhi give the impression during the talks that he belonged to a subject nation. So the progress of the talks moved on a snail pace as Gandhi would not accept the use of certain words or conditions in the settlement. For instance, Gandhi insisted on using the word suspension of C.D. as he believed that the C.D. could not be given up finally as it was the only weapon in the hands of the people. But Lord Irwin objected to its use as he wanted some kind of finality about the word. Ultimately, the word discontinued was found out as it represented the position held by both the parties.

Nevertheless, the settlement left many in the Congress including Nehru, Patel, C.R. etc. dissatisfied. But in spite of it, Gandhi's image rose in the eyes of the masses. The Karachi session, observed S.C. Bose, who was a great critic of Gandhi, "undoubtedly represented the pinnacle of the Mahatma's popularity and prestige. It had surpassed even the record of 1921."[21] Gandhi-Irwin Pact was ratified by the Congress and Gandhi was chosen as its sole representative at the Second Round Table Conference. According to the correspondent of the Chicago Tribune, who came to India in the 1930s to cover the independence movement and became a personal friend of Gandhi." At the Karachi Convention of the Congress that year one saw in Gandhi the consummate politician rather than the saint. Several delegates objected to giving full powers to him to negotiate with British on behalf of the Congress. They offered an amendment requiring that any agreement entered into by him in London be subject to final approval by the Congress itself. Gandhi opposing this restriction to his powers admonished his fellow politicians. No one had the courage to say 'no' to what he asked for. The politician in Gandhi was at his best at the Karachi session. The correspondent marvelled during that week in the deadening Indian heat at Gandhi's unflagging energy, his capacity for work, his skill in drafting the wording of the resolutions and in explaining to the delegates what was important.

One question that has been raised again and again is why did Gandhi decide to go alone? Possibly to avoid any division in the Congress over the selection of representatives to be sent to attend the R.T.C. According to Kanji Dwarkadas the CWC met on April 1 and 2 to decide among other things the representatives of the Congress at R.T.C. Most of the members were of the opinion for sending 15 members and the Government was willing to accommodate upto 20. But within 48 hours of the decision Gandhi received applications from about 150 Congress leaders to be included in the Delegation.[22] After his experiences of the talks at the R.T.C. Gandhi observed later on that the task there was so difficult that had he been not the sole representative the Congress would have been torn to pieces.[23]

One remarkable achievement of the Karachi session was the commitment of the Congress to certain fundamental rights and presumably the resolution on this subject drafted by Nehru and revised by Gandhi committed the Congress to certain reforms in free India. This, in Gandhi's view indicated the broad features of Swaraj or Ramrajya. The beauty of this resolution was that for the implementation of most of its articles people had not to depend upon the Government, for, fifteen out of the twenty items of it could be endorsed by the people themselves.[24]

However, the execution of Bhagat Singh, Sukhdev and Rajguru on the eve of Karachi session had some adverse effect on Gandhi's influence especially in the Punjab. For, it was believed that he could persuade the Viceroy to spare the lives of these young patriots. No doubt, the Mahatma made earnest efforts for the commutation of the death sentence in several meetings with the Viceroy during the negotiations and also through a personal letter. On the day fixed for the final interview with Bhagat Singh's relatives, he wrote a personal letter to the Viceroy claiming that "I poured my soul into it but of no avail."[25] While admiring the character of Bhagat Singh as well as of all revolutionaries, he could not endorse their method. So he frankly told revolutionaries ". . . you should accept my testimony that by mixing your method with mine you protract your agony. The belief which I know, some of you hold that an occasional murder of an official helps the cause is wholly unfounded. On the contrary I know that every murder had hampered me in my pursuit."[26]

The period following the Karachi session was full of toil and uncertainty for Gandhi since the settlement was virtually on the rocks because of the unsympathetic attitude of the bureaucracy, local Government, tension between Hindus and Muslims and acts of violence of the revolutionaries. To Andrews, he wrote "Implementation of settlement in the teeth of official sullenness, unwillingness, even opposition is a difficult business."[27] So all through the year he was not sure about his visit to England since it hinged on the solution of Hindu-Muslim problem. For, in his view if the communal problem was solved before the R.T.C. Indians could forcefully speak for their freedom and the British statesmen would have no excuse to delay the grant of freedom. However, the Congress Working Committee held a different view. For, in its meeting on June 9, it passed a resolution asking him to attend the R.T.C. for the presentation of the position of the Congress even if the communal problem defied solution. But the problem weighed so heavy on his nerves that at the A.I.C.C. meeting in Bombay on August 8, 1931, he virtually collapsed while reacting to such news 'as a Mussalman or a Hindu running to cut each other's throat'. On reading an inflammatory leaflet issued by some rowdy elements of Bombay which was full of grossly false statements and deliberate incitement to violence, he said in deep sorrow, "I do not feel like going any where."[28] Moreover, the settlement was practically in ruins as the new Viceroy Lord Wellington being unsympathetic to it, the local Governments were becoming less serious about the implementation of the settlement. He rather felt as 'if the Government was at war with the Congress'. In Gujarat, the trouble spots were Borsad and Bardoli where Gandhi had practically encamped himself to ensure the observance of the truce terms by the cultivators as he believed that Congress had acquired the intermediatory role between the Government and the people. As a logical sequence of this position, any dispute over the interpretation of the terms of the settlement, could be decided by an impartial tribunal. But the Government refused to accept this position and consequently differences with the government reached the breaking point by July 1931. His meeting with the Viceroy did not improve the matter and so on August 13, he wired to the Viceroy of his inability to attend the R.T.C. and this decision was endorsed by the CWC. But the decision was not without inner struggle. For, he had been planning for several years to meet his friends in Europe especially Romain Rolland. It was a big disappointment to him that he would not by meeting his French admirer who was mainly responsible for introducing the Mahatma to Europe by his short biography of Gandhi. However, the events moved very fast and possibly under the pressure of public opinion, an agreement was patched up between the Viceroy and Gandhi in their meetings from August 25 to 27 that changed his decision. It was a sudden development and he had to be taken to Bombay from Simla by a special train. He did not have even half an hour to pack and catch the ship Rajputana, though he had very little hope of any success of his mission. To a friend he wrote "I ought to go to England but I do not feel to be going;"[29] for his 'expectations of the conference were zero.'

On the ship, his daily routine was as usual. In the morning he had a prayer meeting where he would deliver a short discourse. For, prayer had sustained his life and his mental equilibrium. 'Without it,' he said, "I should have been a lunatic long ago— And the more my faith in God increased, the more irresistible became yearning for prayer."[30] His dress remained the same. He was comfortable in his usual loin cloth. Only in England he would add a woollen cloth twisted round his body. This was a poor man's dress and he was going to England to represent the half-naked Indians. As a logical step to this view, he decided to stay in London in Muriel Lester's Kingslay Hall which was situated among the poor of London and dedicated purely to their service where the inmates lived a life of severe simplicity occupying tiny rooms called cells. Four such tiny rooms were vacated by them and placed at his disposal. The rooms were sparely furnished. Beddings had to be borrowed for the use of guests. But since Gandhi and his party were carrying their own blankets they had no use for them. Questioned by a reporter in England, he remarked humourously you people wear plus fours, mine are minus fours. "But in a more serious vein, he said," If I come here to live and work like an English citizen then I should conform to the customs of the country and should wear the dress of an English man. But I am here on a great and special mission and my loin cloth if you choose to describe it, is the dress of my principals, the people of India.[31] In fact, his dress was symbolic of his mission.

It looks that the British authorities in England had taken steps to prevent the Mahatma from receiving any special publicity in England. So the correspondent of the Chicago Tribune who was covering Gandhi's visit to England was refused ticket for the Pullman boat train in which Gandhi would be leaving for London on the grounds that the manager had received instructions from his employers not to issue tickets to the journalists.[32] However, the correspondent received the ticket from Mahadeva Desai accompanying Gandhi. When his party reached London the authorities tried to spirit him away as inconspicuously as possible. For thousands of Indians had crammed into Victoria station to greet him.[33]

Gandhi had a crowded programme in England. For, besides attending the conference and meetings of various committees he was invited to address meetings of several associations where his short lectures were followed by questions-answers session to satisfy the curiosity of the inquisitive audiences surprised by his unusual life style. He spoke twelve times at Round Table Conference—twice before its plenary session, eight times before the Federal Structure Committee and twice before the Minorities Committee. Discussion at this committee not only tired him but made him unhappy as he felt that most of the Muslim members were making fun of him by remarking again and again to concede to their demand as he was a Mahatma.[34] In addition to all this work, many eminent persons from different walks of life sought interviews. So he was always short of time. For days together he did not have even two hours sleep. He met some people while working on his spinning wheel. Among those who met him were Bernard Shaw, Charlie Chaplin, Edmond Demeter, Harold J. Laski, Lord Irwin, Brailford, etc. Winston Churchill avoided meeting him. But Lloyd George had three hours talks with him, at his place.[35] Besides discussion with him, he was amused by the visit of a black cat that sat on Gandhi's lap and did not return after Gandhi left. His visit to Buckingham Palace to have tea with George V created anxious moments for the British statesmen as the Mahatma was to meet the Emperor in his usual dress. The Secretary of State Hoare went to discuss the matter with the king who initially appeared to be annoyed at the suggestion of inviting 'the rebel fakir'. But later on agreed to invitee him without laying down any condition of the dress of the invitee. When Gandhi was introduced to the king, Gandhi's beautiful manners made the course of conversation smooth. But Hoare was horrified when the king uttered the warning that he would not tolerate attacks on his Empire. But Gandhi saved the situation with his grave and deferential reply "I must not be drawn into political argument in your Majesty's Palace after receiving your Majesty's Hospitality."[36]

In his interview with the English dignitaries, Shaw impressed him for his wit, for his love of epigram and paradox with a puck-like spirit and generous ever-young heart. To the Mahatma he was the Arch Jester of Europe. He discovered in him a kindred spirit belonging "to a very small community on earth."[37] Charlie's visit surprised him for he had not heard about him before. What drove the most famous comedian of the cine industry of Europe to the unusual ascetic of Asia? It created a comical situation, apt for Charlie Chaplin. The most modern Mahatma playing on the spinning wheel in England the country that inaugurated the industrial revolution in Europe. But in his talk the Mahatma assured him that he was not opposed to machinery as such but only our dependence on it which had made us dependent on England. The spinning wheel was only a symbol of his dependence or rather a protest against this dependence. Charlie appeared to have been struck by his personality and life style and possibly his next picture 'Modern Times' carried this message of the Mahatma to the world.[38] In fact, in England Gandhi was more interested in his programme outside the conference as the deliberations of the packed body mostly consisting of nominated members known for their communal aspiration and vested interests was not expected to yield anything from the nationalist point of view. The conference consisted of 107 (112 in another account) of these 64 were from British India, 23 from the Indian states and 20 from the British parties. The Minorities Committee of the conference was composed of 6 Britishers, 13 Muslims, 10 Hindus, 2 from the depressed classes, 2 from labour, 2 Sikhs, 1 Parsi, 2 Indian Christians, 2 British domiciled in India, 1 Anglo Indian and 3 women.[39] There was only one nationalist Muslim among them. No one felt that India would get real liberty as a result of deliberations of this conference. The whole exercise of most of the members was to annex a share of power of bureaucracy in India. The Mahatma was a lonely figure in that body from the nationalist point of view. The failure of the conference was a feather in the cap of British statesmanship, for by this failure Britain demonstrated that it " still has, not only the physical strength to uphold its Empire, but also the cunning and statescraft to carry on the imperial tradition." Through the failure of the conference the British tried to show to the world that the Mahatma was only a leader of the caste Hindus; for participating in the conference were separate leaders of the scheduled castes, Muslims, Sikhs, Parsis, Anglo-Indians. The Congress was only one of the parties of India. Then the question arises, why did Gandhi agree to attend the conference if he knew the reality of deliberations? Possibly it was a matter of honour for him. For he had promised to the Viceroy Lord Irwin that he would make every possible effort to participate in the deliberations of the conference.[40] Secondly, since 1926, he had been planning to visit Europe on the invitation of his European friends and admirers but could not do so because of his pressing needs at home. But most of all he wanted to work upon the British public opinion which was the real power behind the Government and Parliament.

While attending the conference, Gandhi's major concern was to prevent further disintegration of Indian nation which had been threatened by the demand for separate electorate raised by Ambedkar. He was ready to stake his life in pursuance of it and the occasion did arise only a few months after his return from England when the British Prime Minister announced his readiness to concede this demand of Ambedkar.

Though the deliberations of the conference did not yield in terms of constitutional advancement of the country, his visit to England did produce some good results by removing from the minds of his western admirers some of their fears and funny notions about him. Though walking the streets in his loin cloth with an old home spun shawl over shoulders to protect him from the chill, the Londoners were aware that he was a special figure. Some of the newspapers had appealed to their readers not to poke fun at his scanty dress. On the day after arrival the *Sunday Times* wrote: "There is in Gandhi's dress and mode of life an invitation to empty minds to regard him as something of a figure of fun. In the interests of common courtesy let those who are so tempted hold their hands."[41] Practically in every public meeting he was asked questions about his views about machinery which gave him an opportunity to explain the rationale behind his opposition to modern craze for machinery and his propagation of the spinning wheel. He told Edmond Demeter that he was not an enemy of mechanism but of organized mechanism which had made man a slave of the machine. However, he conceded to Brailsford that even in free India masses would not do without machinery since only a few would be able to live a simple life without the use of machinery. One thing that confounded the critics was that he consistently maintained for a long time the efficacy of the spinning wheel in the Indian economic situation. He was at pains to show that it was not a fad but a fact rooted in the reality of poor technological advancement of his country. He removed certain misgivings of the workers of Lancashire Textile Industry that the boycott of British cloth was adopted by the Indians only to fight poverty and unemployment. It was not the result of any hatred for the British but was taken for love of the poor in India. Moreover, he explained that the decline in their cloth industry was not totally because of boycott by the Indians of their cloth but because of the competition with the Japanese cloth industry as Lancashire trade with India was hardly 15 per cent of the total production. In his view it was equally the result of the backwardness of Lancashire's cotton industry. He told the correspondent covering his visit that though he was no mechanic he had seen enough up here in three days to show me that the English are using antiquated machinery. It probably explains their inability to compete with other countries. The machinery in the Bombay and Ahmedabad mills is one hundred per cent more efficient.[42] His frankness and sincerity won for him goodwill of the English workers. What he had expected from them was only courteous treatment. But he received from them their deep affection which was evident from the crowds of people lining the streets spontaneously to greet him when he visited their city.

Besides, his visit to England offered him an opportunity to meet his friend Romain Rolland. The Nobel Laureate was living in Villeneuve, in Switzerland. Gandhi and his party comprising his son Devadas, his secretary Mahadev Desai, Pyarelal and Mira, stayed with him for five days on their return from England. Their first meeting reveals Gandhi's deep affection for his French admirer. This is how his host described the meeting,

> "He came to me with a dry laugh, his mouth open, like a dog panting, and flinging an arm around me leaned his cheek against my shoulder. I felt his grizzled head against my cheek. It was, I amuse myself thinking the kiss of St. Dominic and St. Francis."

During his stay there, he delivered lectures explaining his views about God, truth, etc. On the last evening of his stay Gandhi made a special request to his host to play him a little of Beethoven, though he himself had no knowledge of Beethoven except he was a sort of intermediary between him and Mira as it was the love of the music of Beethoven that took the young girl to Romain Rolland who introduced her to Gandhi.

The inhabitants of Villeneuve showed great interest in his visit to the place and offered warm hospitality. Two revered fathers placed their cars at his disposal during the entire period of his stay. A young musician every morning at dawn played the violen under his windows, school children brought him flowers. The Syndicate of Milkmen of Leman had phoned, even before his arrival, to express their desire to supply milk to the 'King of India'. He met his host daily and discussed with him various problems. Besides, he addressed several meetings and in one of the meetings in Church he described his spiritual journey starting from 'God is Love' to 'God is Truth' and finally to 'Truth is God. The Mahatma, in fact had travelled a long distance in his search' after truth changing the proposition from 'God is Truth' to 'Truth is God'. Logically, there may not be any change in the meaning by changing the places of subject and the predicate in a sentence. But for his host this change revealed the boldness and independence of his religious spirit. This marked an extension of his faith. His religion took under its fold even the atheists and the agnostics. For 'Truth is God means that truth itself is of highest category and so some earnest souls in their passion for discovering truth, according to Gandhi have not hesitated even to deny the very existence of God'—from their point of view rightly. He himself came across several such persons and found in them the burning desire to serve humanity.

The diet of the Mahatma did not pose any problem to his host. He was mostly taking boiled goat milk, plenty of grapes, grated apples, hot water with lemon and honey, grated raw vegetables in large quantity especially turnips, raw tomatoes, ground almonds, walnuts, etc. He was avoiding cereals as his constitution was inclined to constipation.

The Mahatma did not miss an opportunity to meet the common people. One day he asked to be driven by car to mountain village where he called on an old peasant woman whom Mira had known when she was still Madeleine Slade and used to visit Villeneuve to see Romain Rolland. Gandhi was drawn to the old woman because she would spin and weave her own garments. He shook hands with her and sat at her loom.[43]

From Switzerland Gandhi went to Rome where he met Mussolini even against the advice of his friends. The dictator was a riddle to him.

For he completely relied on violence and could suppress any opposition without compunction. But he had done some good to the peasantry, though with iron hand. His care for the poor, his opposition to super urbanization, his efforts to bring about co-ordination between labour and capital deserved special attention.[44] in Rome the Pope refused interview to him. May be the refusal was deliberate as many protestant Christians had seen in Gandhi the image of Christ and the Pope possibly did not like to affirm this kind of impression. However, the Vatican galleries were opened for him especially where the art treasure greatly interested him. He spent two hours in St. Peter's. Tears sprang to his eyes as he gazed at the figure of Christ.[45]

A political storm was waiting for him on his return, the rumblings of which he had heard on the deck on his way back home. The new Viceroy had rejected the Congress offer for peace. Nehru was in jail and the arrest of other Congress leaders was on the cards. Gandhi reached Bombay on December 28, and immediately he made an appraisal of the situation. For, he was not in favour of a fiery ordeal soon. Even if there was a single ray of hope, he was ready for negotiations with the Government for an honourable settlement. But the Government under Lord Wellington, the new Viceroy was adamant. Several ordinances were in operation which, in Gandhi's view had been issued to 'to unman a whole race.' He entered into correspondence with the Viceroy and sought an interview without any preconditions. But the Viceroy was not ready to discuss with him the measures which his Government had taken in Bengal, U.P. and N.W.F.P. for the 'preservation of law and order.' Gandhi, in reply declared that the constitutional issues had 'dwindled into insignificance in the face of ordinances. The Congress Working Committee having found the attitude and policy of the Government wholly unsatisfactory decided to resume civil disobedience. Gandhi was arrested on January 4, 1932 while he was staying in the Mani Bhavan in Bombay. A large number of people had gathered there as his arrest was expected. As usual he felt that his arrest was a gift of God and so he welcomed the Commissioner of Police who had come to arrest him with a beautiful smile. He gave a broad smile to his followers and friends who had gathered there. It gave the impression that he was going to a festival. For the jail provided him with necessary rest to his tired limbs.

The Congress president Sardar Patel was also arrested at the same time and lodged with him to give him company. His daily routine in the jail remained the same, that is, writing letters to friends and followers, sacrificial spinning for a few hours, prayer and reading of books. Ruskin's

'Monthly Letters to Factory Workers' impressed him as 'deeply human document'.[46] Books on economics especially on banking and foreign exchange which he read with great interest. He also asked for Dadachanji's Currency of Exchange and Findlay Shirra's book. In fact, he was preparing himself intellectually for his work outside. The company of Patel and Mahadev Desai removed all the drabness of prison life. In reply to Srinivas Sastri who had enquired whether solitude did not create depression in him, he wrote that Sardar Patel was with him and his jokes made him laugh "until I can laugh no more not once but several times a day. According to the Sardar's biographer, there was Shavian flavour in some of Patel's Yeravada repartees."[47] It looks that there were bantering sessions which both of them enjoyed.

However, the repressive measures taken by the Government to crush the C.D. movement and the ongoing events in the country did not allow him peace after some time. He had to stop meeting visitors as a protest against the decision of the Government not to permit Mira (Miss Slade) to meet him as only his family members alone had this privilege. But for Gandhi his family was not confined to his blood relations but extended to all the members of his Ashram as well as to those who were bound to him in the pursuit of truth. Equally disturbing to him was the provisional scheme of minority representation known as the Communal Award announced by Ramsay Macdonald on August 17 which recognized the depressed classes as a minority entitled separate electorate. Gandhi replied to it by his decision to undertake 'fast unto death' from September 20. It was intended to sting the Hindus conscience into right religious action. He skirted all kinds of arguments against this course by his well wishers and detractors by his plea that it was undertaken in obedience to the inner voice. It was the call of God and there was no burden on his mind for its consequences. So he appealed to all his near and dear ones to rejoice with him on this occasion as it was a God given opportunity to serve humanity and affirm truth. However, he declared that his decision "will cease if during its progress, the British Government of its own motion or under pressure of public opinion revise their decision and withdraw their scheme of communal electorates of the depressed classes whose representatives should be elected by the general electorate under the common franchise no matter how wide it is." Patel who was with him at that time had discussion with him over the impending fast. Once the Mahatma had made up his mind over the question of fast it was difficult or rather impossible for any one to make him change his decision, for, it was a religious matter with him. But since the fast over Communal

Award had some political repercussion, he did consult Patel frequently. But the latter failed to change his decision. There were certain matters which were fundamental for Gandhi and an attempt to divide the Hindu society on the basis of caste was one such fundamental matter.

His fast created a lot of anxiety in the country. It bestirred all section of Hindu society including the untouchables to create condition for saving the life of the man who had staked his life to keep Hindu society united. Bhimrao Ambedkar who claimed to represent the interests of the depressed classes was persuaded to give up the demand for separate electorate and join hands with the caste Hindus in order to save the life of the Mahatma.

Born on April 14, 1891, Bhimrao belonged to Mahar family of the depressed classes. His grandfather and father joined the military service under the British. As a student Ambedkar suffered several disabilities and indignities because he belonged to the depressed class. Being hardworking, he graduated and was sent to U.S.A. under the scholarship of the Baroda state where he obtained M.A. & Ph.D degrees. After his return from U.S.A. he joined the service of Baroda State under the terms of scholarship. But as an untouchable he was meted out insufferable treatment by the caste Hindus in Baroda. No inn or hotel was open to him. He had to leave that service and later on joined as a professor of Economics in Syndenham College of Commerce, Bombay. After some time he went to London and joined London School of Economics and Political Science and obtained the degree of Doctor of Science and qualified himself for Bar. On his return he practised in Bombay. He was critical of Gandhi's or of Congress's approach to the problem of untouchability as he wanted to scrap the caste system which, according to him, was mainly responsible for creating a degrading position for the depressed classes in the country. He, for some time, even toyed with the idea of carrying with him all the untouchables to some other religious group in India. The British authorities recognized his position as a critic of Gandhi and the Congress and nominated him as the representative of the untouchables to the Round Table Conferences where he challenged Gandhi's claim to represent the interests of the untouchables. Ambedkar met Gandhi and an agreement known as the Poona Pact was arrived at whereby the major demands of the depressed classes were met within the framework of joint electorate and the British Government withdrew its decision of extending separate electorate to the depressed classes.

After the termination of the fast, the Mahatma initiated fresh efforts to integrate the depressed classes into the Hindu society as equal members.

He planned a campaign to propagate his views in this direction even from the jail. The Government at first hesitated to grant him permission for this purpose but later on relented, may be under the impression, that such moves might open fresh conflicts between Gandhi's supporters and his opponents on this issue. Gandhi was allowed to correspond or see visitors for the removed of untouchability.

Notes and References

1. C.W., XXXVIII, p. 285.
2. *Ibid.*, p. 312.
3. *Ibid.*, XXXIX, p. 431.
4. *Ibid.*, XLI, p. 289.
5. XL II, p. 414.
6. *Ibid.*, p. 469.
7. *Ibid.*, XLIII, p. 265.
8. Quoted in Hassan, Muslims and the Congress, p. 118.
9. Brown, Judith, M. Gandhi and Civil Disobedience (Cambridge Uni. Press, London), p. 105.
10. Limaya, *op. cit.*, p. 27.
11. Shukla, *op. cit.*, p. 215.
12. C.W., XLIV, p. 51.
13. *Ibid.*, p. 55.
14. Nehru, J.L, *op. cit.*, p. 247.
15. Brown, *op. cit.*, p. 180.
16. Kanji Dwarkadas, *op. cit.*, p. 393.
17. Shirer, William, Gandhi—A Memoir (Calcutta, Rupa & Co, 1981), pp. 43-44.
18. Guha, A.C., India's Struggle—Quarter of a Century (1921, 1946), p. 234.
19. Reginald Reynald, To Live in Mankind, p. 87.
20. Nehru, J.L., *op. cit.*, p. 249.
21. Bose, S.C., *op. cit.*, p. 285.
22. Kanji Dwarkadas, India Fights for Freedom, p. 395.
23. Nayyar, Sushila, Gandhi's Last Imprisonment, p. 148.
24. C.W., XLVII, p. 235.
25. C.W., XLV, pp. 333, 351, *Young India*, April 2, 1931.
26. C.W., XLVI, p. 3.
27. *Ibid.*, p. 89.
28. *Ibid.*, XLVII, p. 273.
29. *Ibid.*, p. 164.
30. *Ibid.*, p. 394.
31. Bose, S.C., *op. cit.*, p. 304.
32. Shirer, William, *op. cit.*, p. 136.
33. *Ibid.*, p. 140.

34. Nayyar, Sushila, *op. cit.*, p. 148.
35. Ashe, Geoffrey, Gandhi: A study in Revolution (New Delhi, Asia Publishing House, 1968), p. 309.
36. Kanji Dwarkadas, *op. cit.*, p. 407.
37. C.W., XLVIII, p. 353.
38. Ashe, *op. cit.*,
39. Bose, S.C., *op. cit.*, p. 305.
40. C.W., XLVIII, p. 137.
41. Quoted in Shirer, William, *op. cit.*, p. 303.
42. *Ibid.*, p. 154.
43. Shukla, *op. cit.*, p, 294.
44. C.W., XLVIII, p. 429.
45. Tendulkar, Vol. III, p. 147.
46. C.W., XLIX, p. 278.
47. Gandhi, Rajmohan, Patel (Navajivan Publishing House), p. 217.

18

Gandhi's Hinduism

It is difficult to define Hinduism. For, in its long history it has assimilated the diverse religious beliefs and customs of the communities with which it came into contact. As Valentine Chirol, not very sympathetic student of Hinduism, observed, "the supple and subtle forces of Hinduism had already in prehistoric times welded together the discordant beliefs and customs of a vast variety of races into a comprehensive fabric."[1] Hinduism is, thus, not a creed or dogma or a fixed system of thought. For, it does not believe that divine revelation took place only to one individual at a particular moment of history. Rather it teaches that all individuals are capable of experiencing the light of divinity residing in them. For, Radhakrishnan, Hinduism is not a definite dogmatic creed but a vast, complex but subtle unified mass of spiritual thought and realisation. Its tradition of godward endeavour of the human spirit has been continuously enlarging through the ages.[2] So Hinduism admits that a different people can move towards ultimate reality or can obtain spiritual experience through different ways because of their diverse cultural environment, knowledge, spiritual level, etc. It, therefore, recognizes all methods of worshipping God as valid. They are "all different ways of reaching the same goal like various streams flowing towards one great sea." That way Hinduism caters to the intellectual and cultural levels of different individuals in their endeavour for spiritual uplift. No wonder if in Hinduism one finds highly abstract monism, loftiest monotheism, bewildering polytheism, worship of animals, trees and stones.

However, most of the Hindus hold some beliefs which distinguish them from the followers of other religions. For instance, Hindus accept the principles enunciated in the Vedas, Upanishads and the Bhagavadagita. They believe in the in-dwelling of the spirit in man which means that man has a soul which takes on a body as an instrument for its evolution. In other words, the essence in man is spiritual. The spirit does not die. It is the body that decays and finally comes to an end. The spirit takes on a new body. The incarnation is necessary because the jiva or the individual soul has to go through a long and arduous process before it attains self-realisation or 'Moksha'. But the type of body that it obtains depends upon the past deeds of the body it had cast off or the kind of life that it lived in the previous incarnation. The law of Karma is very rigid and it makes every man responsible for whatever life he lives in the present.

Most of the Hindus believe that at times God takes on a human body to relieve the world of evil. Rama, Krishna were 'avatars' of God Vishnu. From this follows that any individual with exceptional ability represents divine power.

Varnasharma dharma is the distinct feature of Hinduism. It is expected to regulate the life of an individual in society. The four stages of an individual's life are Brahmacharya or the period of training when the individual has to learn without any family encumbrances. The second is 'grihasthya', the period as a householder, third is 'vanaprasthya', or the period of retreat from social bonds and the last is 'Sannyasa', period of renunciation. These stages are not followed these days by all the Hindus. But they do influence their psyche. Varna has assumed the form of caste system and its rigidity has led to innumerable social problems among the Hindus.

Gandhi claimed to be a Hindu not because he was born to Hindu parents but because it was consistent with his spiritual and moral growth; its freedom from dogma as it gives the votary the largest scope for self-expression and enables him "to admire and assimilate whatever may be good in the other faiths."[3] He was proud to call himself a Sanatani Hindu for his belief in the Vedas, Upanishads, the Puranas, Hindu scriptures, avatars, rebirth, varnashrama dharma, protection of cow and no disbelief in idol worship. To him nothing elated him so much as the music of the Gita or the Ramayana of Tulsidas. But Hinduism, in his view, has one distinct feature. It has been ever evolving. It has no one scripture like the Koran or the Bible and its several scriptures are also evolving and suffering additions.[4] As a result, new meanings consistent with the demands of every age have been given to the old concepts. For instance, the Gita has given new meanings to the old concepts of Karma, Yajna, Sannyasa. So he claimed that the Hindu tradition gave him the right to interpret Hindu ideals and its scriptures in the light of his own experiences, reason and modern conditions. It is only then we can derive, he reminds us, full benefit from the study of the Vedas and all Hindu scriptures by "putting them in the crucible of modern conditions, by objective observation, and intense churning."[5] For the Vedas, the Upanishads, the Smritis and the Puranas did not arise at one time. Each grew out of the necessities of a particular period. Hinduism, therefore, "is a growth of ages." So the real test of the validity or authority of any Hindu ideal, custom or tradition is its consistency with truth and non-violence. For the chief value of Hinduism, in his view, lies in holding of the actual belief that "all life is one, that is all life coming from the one universal soul, whatever name is given to it." He, therefore made a fresh interpretation of the Bhagavadgita and some of the concepts of the Upanishads in accordance with his view of truth and non-violence. For the central teaching of the Gita, he asserts, cannot be 'himsa' (violence) but ahimsa (non-violence), for if all life is derived from the same source, wilful destruction of any life cannot be a moral act, whatever may be compulsion of the individuals at any time and given moment. The theme of the Gita, in his view, is self-realization which can be attained only when one rises, above anger, attachment and hatred which generate violence. So he considers the Gita and the Mahabharata as allegorical, stating beautifully an eternal dual going on within ourselves. He views Duryodhana and his party as the base impulses in man and Arjuna and his party, the higher impulses. The field of battle is our own body. An eternal battle is going on between two camps. Krishna is the indwelling spirit within us, ever whispering in a pure heart. The poet seer vividly describes the battle going on in every individual. But scholars in his own time did not agree with his view of the Gita. For, they could cite many verses in the Gita which could not be reconciled to non-violence.

He admitted it but at the same time pointed out that 'it is far more difficult to set the whole of the Gita in the framework of violence'. In fact, the object of the author of the Gita was neither to support violence nor non-violence. His object was to point out how self-realization could be attained without abandoning action in social life. In other words, his purpose was to reconcile seemingly opposite pursuits, that is, desire for salvation or self-realization and worldly pursuits. The answer of the Gita is renunciation of the fruit of action and not renunciation of action. This is how one can be free from the bondage of action. It means the performance of duty without any desire or attachment to the fruit or reward of action. Gandhi agreed to this view and so he called his commentary on the Gita as 'Anasakti yoga' or the selfless action and found in it the essence of his social and political movements. In his view the real message of the Gita is to be found in the second chapter where Lord Krishna speaks of the balanced state of mind or mental equipoise. In 19 verses at the close of the 2nd chapter of the Gita, Krishna explains how this state can be achieved. It is by killing all passions that one can reach that state. The defect of an action, according to the Gita, cannot touch its performer if it is performed with an unattached mind. Gandhi found in the Gita the endorsement of his view of the inevitability of conversion of all human beings. "If all life is one we must treat the sinner and saint alike." He averred.

Undoubtedly, several scholars in recent times have reinterpreted the teaching of the Gita in the light of the new needs of the society and their own experiences. The struggle for freedom became the "Age of the Gita Again". Vivekananda, Tilak, Aurobindo refuted the earlier interpretation of the Gita that favoured ascetism and ultimately renunciation of action for attaining 'Moksha'. It became a spiritual dictionary for all those who were engaged in the struggle for the liberation of the country. The Revolutionaries in India could quote passages from the Gita in absolute honesty and cogency for their terrorists acts. It was no more a religious treatise. But a reservoir of hope for the revival of the glory of India. Valentine Chirol, one of the most virulent critics of the revolutionary movement of Bengal, admitted that the "reading of the Bhagavadgita differentiates the new Indian conception of renunciation, which does not exclude but rather prescribes the duty of service to society from the older conception, which was concerned merely to procure the salvation of the individual by his complete detachment from all mudance affairs." Similarly, Gandhi reinterprets the theory of Karma and Varna. In his view Karma is not intended to kill all reform and all efforts in that direction. Rather its purpose is to prepare or inspire every individual to wash out all evil Karma. Again, he accepted Varna but distinguished it from the existing caste system which he condemned. For, in Varna system, in his view, there is no place for inferiority or superiority of any class or group on which the present caste system is based. Though initially he skirted the question of inter-caste marriages, in later life, he became a great champion not only of inter-varna marriages, but marriages between Svarna Hindus and Harijans.

Though himself not an idol worshipper, he recognized the value of idol worshipping for a large number of people who hanker after symbolism. It is in accord with the Hindu tradition that allows everyone to worship God according to one's own faith or dharma. Temples, therefore, are an integral part of Hinduism. He valued the spirit behind the idol worshipping. For, it is through an image that an idol worshipper Hindus approaches God just as a Christian through the intercession of Mary or Mussalman through his mosques.[6] But he wanted the present Hindu temples be freed from harmful practices and customs. That way the Mahatma was both an idolator and an iconoclast. He wanted to retain in idolatory whatever is in accord with human nature and reason and to destroy all the evils that have grown around idol worship. As a Sanatani Hindu Gandhi held great veneration for cow because it takes the human being beyond his species and the protection of cow means protection of whole creation of God. So, for him cow protection is the gift of Hinduism to the world.[7] But he lamented that cow was subjected to great cruelty by the Hindus themselves, for, "we bleed her to take the last drop of milk from her, we starve her to emaciation ill-treat the calves and castrate the oxen." The cows find their necks under the butcher's knife because Hindus sell them. For him the real protection can be achieved if we maintain our 'Goshalas' in accord with the principles of economics, that is, by making financially self-supporting. In other words, we must develop model dairies and model tanneries. In his Ashram he maintained a dairy and sought the advice of dairy and tanning experts to make it a model dairy. He even sought the permission from the head of Imperial dairy to visit his dairy to learn the modern management of dairies. He favoured the import of machinery for utilizing hides of dead animals as proper treatment of hides in India would save crores of rupees by preventing the export of hides of dead animals to foreign countries. For, in his view, "anything, whether indigenous or foreign which is good and serves our interest is in accord with the principles of Swadeshi."[8] He maintained communication with Harold Mann for his expert advice to carry on his experiment in cattle breeding and dairies.

In fact, Gandhi's mind, habits and approach to life were shaped by Hindu traditions, ethos and myths. At the root of all his struggles for the good of mankind was his belief that desireless and selfless actions lead to moksha or union with God. In his study of Christianity he was impressed only by those aspects of it which were close to Hinduism or Hindus view of life traditions and values. He admired Tolstoy's view of Christianity or of the Quakers or of Esotric Christianity only because of its affinity with Hinduism. The Quakers combined the piety and personal discipline of Non-conformist Evangelicalism with a theology of the spirit which had certain affinities with Hindu philosophy and a peace witness that was akin to Ahimsa.[9] According to Hunt much of 'Tolstoy's philosophy was compatible with Hinduism especially the emphasis on inward growth and the authority of personal experience'.[10] Gandhi's contacts and encounters with Non-conformist Christians helped him to understand the Hindu ideals and practices in the light of the experiences of the new age. The impressions that he carried of other religions especially of Christianity entered his subconscious mind and contributed a great deal in reinterpreting Hinduism as a religion consistent with science and reason. According to his secretary, "The decade and a half following his arrival in South Africa was perhaps the most formative period of his life. Impression absorbed during this period sank deep into his consciousness till their very source and origin forgotten, they became part and parcel of his being."

Thus, Gandhi's Hinduism is Hinduism purified by the elimination of overgrowth of superstitious and, iniquitous customs and nefarious practices that had accumulated over it through the ages. It is Hinduism adjusted to the demands of the new age and consistent with reason. It is broad enough to embrace Buddhism as its elevated branch. It is Hinduism that treats untouchability as excrescence which has reduced a large section of it to the position of chattels. He, therefore, completely identified himself with the cause of the depressed classes and was ready to risk his life if any attempt was made to separate them from the Hindus and kept himself so much involved in the struggle for their uplift in the early thirties that some of his contemporaries even felt that he was on the way of giving up his political struggle. But to Gandhi social life could not be divided into so many watertight compartments. For, in his view, "it is one organic whole."[11] Consequently all his activities sprang from the same source, that is, his passion for vindication of truth and non-violence in every walk of life. So his drive against untouchability like his struggle for the freedom of the country, was a part of his struggle to build social life on the secure foundation of truth and non-violence. He re-christened the depressed or more appropriately suppressed classes as Harijan seizing upon the word used by the poet and saint of Gujarat Narasimha Mehta for an untouchable. Currently they were addressed as depressed or suppressed classes which was abhorrent to him as it signified underdogs in a society. Harijans means children of God and as such they would become indistinguishable from the rest of the classes of the Hindu society as all are the children of God. However, he could not visualize that political consideration and interests would make them a distinct class in Hindu society. A weekly 'Harijan' was started in several languages of the country for the propagation of his anti-untouchability campaign. The first issue in English appeared on 11th February, 1933 with ten thousand copies. It was planned as self-supporting 'for if it could not be so, it had no value' as the object of starting a journal was to carry the Hindus with him in his campaign for the purification of Hinduism. The publication of the weeklies put a heavy strain on him and limited his capacity to correspond with his friends and followers since he had to devote at least two days in a week exclusively to writing articles for the new journal. It served as his mouthpiece of Harijan campaign as a number of issues and questions on the subject of untouchability raised by his correspondents had to be replied, by him. The Government allowed him facilities to carry on his Harijan uplift programme from the jail. Possibly behind this seemingly benevolent act it was looking for political gain. For, it hoped that the Mahatma's immersion in the work would reduce his popularity among caste Hindus, and would arouse strong feelings between the orthodox Hindus and the reformists. To some extent this turned out to be true. Only twelve miles from Gandhi's Sabarmati Ashram, the upper caste Hindus especially the Rajputs of Kavitha boycotted the Harijans and perpetrated untold atrocities on them as a result of which it created a lot of controversies in the country. Ambedkar took this opportunity to criticize the Congress for it. As a result, the Congress leaders of Gujarat especially Patel went to Kavitha to settle the differences.[12]

The major programme in his campaign was the opening of the temples to the Harijans like all caste Hindus. It did not generate much enthusiasm in a large section of the so-called untouchables as they were interested in the programmes for the improvement of their economic conditions. But for Gandhi, it was a fundamental issue as it was expected to remove the stigma attached to a particular section of the Hindu society. It was an indispensable test for the acceptance of the fact that a Harijan was "no longer the pariah of Hindu society."[13] For, "the temple entry prohibition and the consequent segregation that it carries with it constitute the distinguishing bar sinister of perpetual degradation.[14] That accounts for his support to Subbarayan's Bill introduced in the Madras Legislative Council requiring Viceroy's sanction for its inclusion in the agenda and a Private Bill introduced in the Central Legislative Assembly. These Bills, in his view, were permissive in nature as they were introduced to remove a legal sanction that stood in the way of opening of the temples to the Harijans if the people and the trustees wanted to do so.

Nevertheless, in his drive against untouchability, he was cautious enough to avoid an open clash with the caste Hindus. He, therefore, advised his co-workers and followers not to tread on the sensibilities of the caste Hindus. So he did not insist on inter-dining or intermarriage with the so-called untouchables as an essential part of his movement, though such steps were welcomed if taken voluntarily. Similarly for opening the temples to Harijans he desired that the reform be undertaken with the consent of the majority of temple-goers of the area. He even suggested a referendum of the temple goers in the radius of ten miles to ascertain their views on this issue. Even those who objected to Harijan entry into the temples, could be accommodated by fixing certain hours of the day when only 'swarn' Hindus could be admitted.[15] The Mahatma could visualize that a caste or class war would vitiate all his efforts of peaceful transformation of the society if the sentiments of caste Hindus fostered and nourished by religious superstitions and age-long customes were trampled with impunity. He aimed at carrying the caste Hindus with him in his drive to purge the Hindu society of its evils which had been sapping its vitality. He did not like to create a social island in Hindu society by keeping the reformed group as a separate class.

However, the implementation of the Yeravada or Poona Pact had run into difficulties. The caste Hindus of Bengal passed a resolution in the Council denouncing the Pact. It had created political difficulties for the Congress in the Punjab. Several orthodox Sanatanist Hindus denounced Gandhi's Harijan movement as a political stunt and charged him with hypocrisy. Ambedkar had also started a campaign against some items of the Pact.

Besides there were some undesirable incidents in the Ashram that compelled him to undertake self-purificatory fast against the advice of friends. He had been hearing reports of moral lapses of young inmates in whom he had great hopes. His adopted Harijan daughter Lakshmi had failed to come up to his expectation and so had told her "that his proposed fast was for all who are connected with him."[16] He communicated the same message to Prembehn Kantak who had been very close to him. For, the fast, in his view "is a heart prayer for the purification of self and associates, for greater vigilance and watchfulness." For him, it was a panacea to mitigate his mental restlessness."[17] It was a "peremptory call from within." Ranbindranath Tagore, General Smuts and several close friends "appealed to him to reconsider his decision. Rajagopalachari attacked the very basis of his fast in a long discussion with him in jail.

While arguing against it, he said" I feel that you have been brooding over the same thing in jail and so have lost your sense of proportion. You have fondness for conducting experiments. Your are now experimenting with death and you are misguided in it.[18]

To some of his friends his argument that it was prompted by God, was nothing but self-delusion, "a prey to his heated imagination made hotter by suffocation produced by the cramping walls of a prison.''[19] But the Mahatma while explaining his mental state at this time said:[20]

> "The night I got the inspiration I had a terrible inner struggle. My mind was restless I could see no way. The burden of my responsibility was crushing me. But what I did hear was like a voice from afar and yet quite near. It was as unmistakable as human voice, definitely speaking to me and irresistible. I was not dreaming at the time I heard the voice. The hearing of the voice was preceded by a terrific struggle within me. Suddenly the voice came upon me. I listened made certain that it was the voice and the struggle ceased. I was calm. The determination was made accordingly.''

The voice was no voice of God. But it was the voice of Gandhi's own conscience. There were some corners in the conscience of the Mahatma which were entirely exclusive. Friends around him could not judge their intensity and extent of their pressure on his conduct and behaviour. Undoubtedly there are some matters with every individual which are beyond the bounds of cold logic. Decisions on such matters cannot be judged by rational calculations. It is the demand of one's being. Patel, who had been with Gandhi in jail and had been nursing him with motherly care and affection showed his inability to make the Mahatma reconsider his decision since in his view it was a matter of religion for Gandhi and it was a futile effort to persuade him to break a religious pledge. For, in his view, "He (Gandhi) is one person who practises honestly and continuously the Hindu religion."[21]

The Mahatma wrote, "The cause of the Harijans is God's cause. He will throw up men and women as they may be required to do his will—."

The proposed fast was to start from 8th May and would terminate on 29th.... However he was released on its commencement unconditionally as the British never wanted to earn the odium of the Mahatma's death in their custody because of its serious political consequences. He, therefore, stayed in Lady Thackersey's house in Poona during the period of the fast. The civil disobedience movement, too, was suspended. After the termination of the fast, several Congress leaders who were outside the jail met him in an informal conference at his place to decide about their future plan. Most of them were in favour of calling off the C.D. movement unconditionally. But Gandhi did not agree to it. He sought an interview with the Viceroy for an amicable and honourable settlement. On his refusal to start any negotiation without the unconditional withdrawal of the movement, he offered his scheme of individual Satyagraha replacing mass Satyagraha. This was the only way to keep the movement going as the Congress leadership appeared to be tired. For, in the case of individual Satyagraha one has not to wait for others to give any direction or consent. Nor weakness of one can have its effect on others since each acts independently on his own responsibility. But doubts were expressed about the suitability of his programmes and strategy from two opposite points of view. V.S. Srinivasa Sastri, the liberal leader felt that the country was losing faith in Gandhi's method of civil disobedience and it should be replaced by a new policy "aiming at constructive national good in legislation, finance and administration." He, therefore, suggested to him to retire from the Congress and leave it to evolve a new programme. On the other hand, J.L. Nehru urged him to give a more radical accent to Congress policies. However all such suggestion had no affect on him. But before he could renew his struggle he was arrested on the midnight of July 31, taken to Yeravada prison and served with an order to confine his Harijan movement to the Poona city municipal limits and take no part in civil disobedience. On his refusal to obey these orders, he was tried and sentenced to a year's imprisonment on August 4, 1933 and all the facilities to carry on his Harijan work from the jail were withdrawn. In protest he went on an indefinite fast on August 16. He was released on August 23 when his condition took a serious turn and was sent to Sasson hospital. For some time his life hanged in the balance. He himself lost hope of his survival. He gave the 'mritadan' (the charities given by a Hindu when he is near the hour of death). But he recovered soon and was removed to the house of Mrs. Thackersey. After hard thinking and praying, he came to the conclusion that he must take himself as a prisoner for one year and so must not indulge in any political activity during that period. The path was now clear to him. He must devote himself to Harijan work during this work. He did not even attend the funerals of Vithalbhai Patel on the grounds that though technically a free man, he considered himself as a prisoner since he was released only because of the deterioration of his condition on account of his fast. Very few could understand this logic and it created a lot of misunderstanding in the Patel family about his absence.

After taking necessary rest on doctors' advice after the fast, he undertook a whirlwind tour of the South and Central India for his anti-untouchability propaganda as well as for collecting money for the welfare programmes of the Harijans. It was interrupted by his brief visit to Delhi in December 1933 to attend the meeting of the Central Board of Harijan Seva Sangh.

Though his meetings were well-attended both by Svarna Hindus and the Harijans and his appeals for funds were well received, he had to face stiff opposition of orthodox Hindus whose leaders not only drew him in open debates which he welcomed but also tried to impede his movement by undesirable means. They burnt his effigies, lay down in front of his car and engage professional wrestlers to disturb his meetings. At Poona, an attempt was made on his life when a bomb was thrown at what the assailant believed to be the car carrying him on his way to the municipal building where a meeting was scheduled to be held. Several persons were injured as a result of this attack. At some places there were scuffles between the reformers and orthodox Sanatanists who, though in minority, were very aggressive. Once the leader of the Orthodox section Lal Nath was assaulted. On hearing this Gandhi decided to observe fast for a week. This was the Mahatma's way of communicating to his opponents and his critics that he had goodwill in his heart for them. The reformist in him was always very considerate towards those who were attached to the old order either out of ignorance or personal interest. For, he was ready to suffer to bring in the new order. At times the determined opposition of the orthodox section compelled him to carry on his campaign on foot, though this turned out to be a better method of communicating his message of the uplift of the Harijans to the world. Thus apprehending a violent demonstration by the orthodox sections, he converted his tour in Orissa into walking pilgrimage in May 1934. A new strategy for the communication of his message developed out of this situation. Since it was not possible for him to cover the whole of India on foot, he advised his co-workers to undertake similar tours in their respective areas. While touring South Bihar against untouchability, he heard that a strong demonstration was planned. He decided to face it in a novel way by going alone and on foot along the mile long route to the meeting. His followers begged to be allowed to accompany him or to have a car in readiness in the rear, but he was adamant and set off alone. Many thought that he would not return alive. But no untoward incident happened. To a British admirer of Gandhi who witnessed this incident, this was Gandhi's answer to all disarmament questions.[23]

During the nine months of his Harijan tour he travelled 12,000 miles of which 156 miles were covered on foot and collected about ten lakh ruppes. The response to his fund raising campaign was some time very touching. The poor would untie their rags to offer copper coins to the Mahatma. For they had never seen a silver rupee in their life.

His complete identification with the Harijan uplift work sometimes pushed him into an indefensible intellectual corner. Thus while on a tour, a natural calamity occurred in Bihar. A devastating earthquake flattened a substantial area of the province on January 15, 1934. Nearly 2500 persons died and thousands of people were rendered homeless. To Gandhi this was a divine chastisement for the sin of untouchability. "It is a curse brought upon ourselves by our own neglect of a portion of Hindu humanity."[24] He was on a weak wicket in an intellectual dual with his friend R.N. Tagore by making such pronouncements. For the latter argued that physical catastrophies have their inevitable and exclusive origin in certain combination of physical facts. If ethical phenomena are associated with cosmic phenomena "we shall have to admit that human nature is morally superior to providence that preaches its lessons in good behaviour in orgies of the worst behaviours possible." This kind of explanation, Tagore reminded him "would suit more his opponents who would hold him and his supporters responsible for the divine anger simply because of going against the traditions and Hindu Shastras."[25] Why was Bihar alone selected for divine anger when Hindus all over India were responsible for the curse of untouchability? Gandhi could be asked. His reply dressed in metaphysical and ethical language could not appeal to a rational mind. For, he evaded direct reply on the plea that human beings cannot know the laws of God and their working. So visitations like droughts, floods, earthquakes and the like "though they seem to have physical origins are for me, somehow connected with man's morals. For, there is indissoluble marriage between matter and spriti."[26] Nevertheless, this controversy made him more cautious in future. For, his explanation on the occurrence of earthquake at Quetta (now in Pakistan) a year later was better worded and thought-provoking in reply to a correspondent who asked him whether this, too, was a divine chastisement for the sin of untouchability. Such physical calamities he said, "brings a sensible man down on his knees",[27] and "humble us and prepare us to face our maker whenever the call comes and that we may be" ever ready to share the sufferings of our fellows whoever they may be. Prayer is the only course left to man, for it is a sign of "a desire to become better, purer."[28]

In other words such calamities remind man of his limitation and the existence of the mighty force governing this universe the purpose of which can be known through inward perfection.

However, the suffering of the people of Bihar as a result of earthquake interrupted his Harijan work in Orissa. He left for Bihar to co-ordinate the relief work. He also advised the inmates of the Ashram who were outside jail to go to Bihar for relief work. Besides collecting money for Harijan work, he started collecting money for relief work and within a short span of time he had twenty lakhs with him for this work.

A move by Ambedkar that all the scheduled caste give up Hinduism and join any other religious group that offered them equal status with other members of that group disturbed the Mahatma. For, it made Christian missionaries and Muslim proselytising agencies very active. He countered this move with all the power at his command since, for him, it was an irreligious act as the motive behind this move was not religious. It was absurd as the desire for the change of religion had not sprung from the yearning of the soul of the individual. It was purely a move by a leader of a group who had suffered at the hands of the caste Hindus because of their wrong attitude towards a section among them. But he could not claim on that account that all the members of the scheduled caste were anxious to be uprooted from their own religious background. Though the Mahatma had respect for all religions, he never wanted the destruction of Hinduism or disintegration of Hindu society by the exodus of a large section from it. Arguing with Andrews who pleaded that non-Christians should not be prevented from accepting Christianity if they found peace in it, he said, "It is absurd for a single individual to talk of taking all the Harijans with himself. Are they all bricks that they could be moved from one structure to another?"[29] At another occasion he stated that he could understand the anger of a high-soul and highly educated person like Ambedkar over atroicities "but religion is not like a house or a cloak which can be changed at will. It is a more integral part of one's own self than of one's body." When the Hindu Sabha leader proposed that all the scheduled caste might embrace Sikhism as it was close to Hinduism, Gandhi objected it on the grounds that it was also conversion as the Sikhs were holding on to separate electorate on the grounds that they were separate from the Hindus. In a letter to Birla he wrote, "If you can persuade the Sikhs to accept that Sikhism is a part of Hinduism and ready to give up separate electorate, I have no objection to Harijans calling themselves Sikhs."[30]

Ambedkar actively pursued the idea of his community embracing

Sikhism. He even sent his son and nephew to the Golden Temple in Amritsar where they lived for about a month to acquaint themselves with the tenets and traditions of Sikhism. But this move came a cropper for various reasons. Firstly, it was opposed by several Congress leaders. Secondly, some of the leaders especially the Akalis did not show much enthusiasm for this move as the joining of five crores scheduled castes to their faith could have some adverse affect on their leadership. Thirdly, and possibly this weighed heavily with Ambedkar that the gains in terms of reservations of seats for scheduled castes which Poona Pact had conferred on them might be lost on their conversion to another faith.

Notes and References

1. Quoted in S. Radhakrishnan, Hindu View of Life, p. 98.
2. *Ibid.*, p. 21.
3. *Young India*, 20-10. 27, Hindu Dharma.
4. *Harijan*, 3-10-36, Gandhi, Hinduism (Navajivan Publishing House, 1950), p. 177.
5. C.W., XXXIII, p. 430.
6. Gandhi, M.K., Hindu Dharma, *op. cit.*, p. 75.
7. *Ibid.*, pp. 297-98.
8. C.W., XXXIV, p. 26.
9. Hunt, Gandhi and the Non-Conformists, *op. cit.*, p. 19.
10. *Ibid.*, p. 43.
11. C.W., Vol. LII, p. 33.
12. Chopra, P.N. (ed), The Collected Works of S. Vallabhbhai Patel, Vol. V, pp. 166 and 194.
13. C.W., LIV, p. 336.
14. *Ibid.*
15. *Ibid.*, LII, pp. 165 and 169.
16. *Ibid.*, LIV, p. 323.
17. *Ibid.*, LV, p. 80.
18. *Ibid.*, Appendix, p. 441.
19. *Ibid.*, p. 120.
20. *Ibid.*, p. 255.
21. Chopra, Collected Works of Patel, Vol. IV, p. 21.
22. C.W., LVI, pp. 252, 428, 429.
23. Birla, G.D., Bapu (Bombay, Vidya Bhavan, 1977, Vol. I, p. 362).
24. C.W., LVII, p. 46.
25. *Ibid.*, Appendix.
26. *Ibid.*, LVII, pp. 164-65.
27. *Ibid.*, LXI, p. 161.
28. *Ibid.*, p. 136.
29. *Ibid.*, LXIV, p. 18.
30. *Ibid.*, LXIII, p. 267.

19

Withdrawal from the Congress

The voluntary withdrawal of the Mahatma from politics for a year had given him an insight into the working of the minds of Congressmen. He observed that a large number of them had become apathetic towards the civil disobedience movement as well as to their co-workers in jail. He, therefore, released them from the obligation of carrying on the struggle and had taken upon himself the sole responsibility of keeping the cauldron of civil disobedience boiling through individual Satyagraha. But this places the A.I.C.C. in an incongruous position, for it would mean one section of the Congress entering the council to make laws and the other for breaking them. It was only because of his impassioned appeal to them that they had agreed to allow him to carry on C.D. movement on behalf of the Congress. But this implied surrender of their conscience or reason in deference to the wishes of the Mahatma. Didn't it mean that the Mahatma's presence in the Congress has made most of its members hypocrites? For they were agreeing to certain decisions not out of convictions. This was certainly obstructing the growth of its members. No organization can develop if a leader has such a hold over the minds of its members. Expressing his mental agony on this account, he wrote to Patel that he could "think of no way of fighting the rot except by leaving it; for my doing so will rid it of hypocrisy."[1] A great organization in his view could not be governed by affections but by cold reason and so it was appropriate for him to retire from a field where his presence would result in arresting full play of reason.[2] For, he explained, "My policies fail to convince their (Congress intelligentsia) reason, though strange it may appear, I do nothing that does not satisfy my own reason. But my reason takes in a direction just the opposite of what many of the most intellectual Congressmen would gladly had enthusiastically taken if they were hampered by their unexampled loyalty to me." In fact, the intellectual section in the Congress could hardly understand his complete devotion to the spinning wheel and his total identification with the poor residing in the villages. He was shocked when he learnt that his devoted disciple was planning to buy a cloth mill which would ultimately push him out of the Khadi work.[3] The Socialists in the Congress were openly denouncing some of his policies, though most of them were bound with him by strong personal ties. To dominate Congress in such a situation was, for him, almost a species of violence. Even in 1924 while having a tussle with the Swarajists he was mentally prepared to step off the Congress stage.

However, before leaving the Congress, he proposed major changes in its structure which were moved in the form of resolutions at its annual session in October 1934. But these were not tamely accepted. Gandhi was no more messiah for the Congress leadership. All the resolutions were hotely debated. There was tremendous opposition to the clause stating the creed of the Congress as Gandhi wanted to replace peaceful and legitimate means by 'truthful and non-violent means.' So it could not be incorporated in the constitution. There was also opposition to the clause requiring habitual wearing of Khadi by the office bearers of the Congress. Similarly, his recommendation of reducing the number of delegates to the Congress session was accepted only when the number was raised to two thousand in place of one thousand that he had suggested.

However, his withdrawal did not mean break with the Congress. For he continued using his influence and moral authority in removing all the hurdles that impended its march towards freedom. As C.R. told an English friend that the Mahatma's withdrawal was more a judicial separation than a divorce. Commenting on Gandhi's withdrawal from the Congress, The Editor of the Tribune wrote, The Mahatma has gone out of the Congress, and yet he remains the master of the Congress — He is still the idol of the average Congressman — Though he was leaving the organization he was not leaving behind any rancour or bitterness. For he was ready to co-operate with those whose policies and methods he could not support. He, therefore, appealed to all Congressmen to allow all such persons who were inclined to Parliamentary work to carry on their work without hindrance as "in its own place it will be useful for the country." So he made efforts to bring into being the Congress Parliamentary Board and even offered his good offices in bringing about electoral adjustment between the Congress candidates and those put up by other parties who held him in high esteem. Thus, when Aney and Malaviya formed Congress Nationalist Party because of their differences with Congress Working Committee over the Communal Award, he dissuaded them from using the name of the Congress and advised them to consult the Congress leadership while putting up candidates for election.[4] The Congress could hardly afford to sever connection with him, for, not only he had hold over the Hindu masses, he alone could keep the Congress as one piece as he was its binding force. He still had power to weather any storm that could split the Congress. Thus, a schism was averted in the Congress by his tactful move of persuading J.L. Nehru to accept the presidentship of the Congress when the harangues of the Socialist leaders in the Congress alarmed the old Congressmen. Similarly, it was he who could prevail upon Nehru and the members of his Working Committee who were submitting their resignations because of their President's Socialist views, to subordinate their differences to the interest of their country.[5] He alone could advise the young president to win over his colleagues by affable manners as they dreaded him because of his irritability, impatience, magisterial manners and above all his arrogation which appeared to them as his infallibility and superior knowledge. Again, when the Congress was placed in a dilemma after the general election held under the Act of 1935 over the issue of office acceptance, he lifted it out of morass of conflicts and inactivity. For the Congress was committed to wrecking the Act. But the extension of the franchise to some 35 million people had changed the situation as it offered an opportunity to the Congress for mass contact. But the leadership was divided. Nehru had all along vehementally opposed the move for office acceptance while several other Congress leaders such as Rajagopalachari, Rajendra Prasad, V. Patel favoured office acceptance. It was left to Gandhi's practical insight to reconcile the two different points of view. Though a messiah of non-cooperation, he did not consider any opportunity to serve the people by going to the legislature, as violation of non-co-operation since even this programme was conceived in pursuit of the goal of 'Swarajya'. "We shall go there (legislatures), he told the workers of Gandhi Seva Sangh, "as servants and if the Congress gives the call. If we can form ministries on our own conditions, then we have found the way to Swaraj."[6] As a practical man, Gandhi readjusted his strategy to the changed circumstances. Defending the new move, he said, "I now strongly advising the Congress to send its representative to the legislatures and even to accept office, I have responded to the wholly new circumstances that have since come into being. I have never made a fetish of foolish consistency."[7] But the office had to be accepted with dignity which involved assurances from the Governors not to use their special powers in the normal day-to-day working of the Government. The demand for assurances led to a deadlock between the Government and the Congress and Gandhi virtually acting as a mediator between them displayed his skill and patience in breaking it. A climate of co-operation was created by both sides. A simple conciliatory speech by the Viceroy was viewed as no less than assurances that opened the way for office acceptance with dignity. However, the decision of acceptance of office by Gandhi was not sudden or plunge in the dark. Several persons close to Gandhi and the British authorities both in England and India had put in efforts to remove misunderstandings between the British and Gandhi. G.D. Birla who met several British statesmen and politicians in England and the Viceroy in India believed that his talks with them had something to do in making Gandhi to advise the CWC to accept office which, according to Birla, raised Gandhi's stock in the political market, though the Mahatma had a hearty laugh over it as he believed that political market was always shaky.[8]

Since office acceptance was not more than an opportunity to serve the people, the Mahatma advised the Ministers to set an example of simple living. Even rupees five hundred p.m. as a salary for a minister, for him, was luxury. But very few Congressmen were ready to act on his advice.

Even after the assumption of power by Congressmen in some provinces, many eyes turned towards him whenever there was a crisis in the Congress because of differences between the leaders. In most of the cases he was acting as a referee and his decisions were considered as binding.[9] The working of CWC was plagued by differences between its president and several members of the Working Committee and Gandhi had to advise Patel and some other members to resign leaving Nehru to select a new committee of his choice. Spurt in peasant marches, strikes, picketing and similar agitations besides lethargy and corruption among Congressmen put a heavy strain on his mind as a result of which his blood pressure rose alarmingly. Some of the teeth and the stumps of two old teeth were giving him a lot of trouble their removal in 1936 removed to some extent at least the physical cause of his blood pressure. He was removed to Juhu beach in Bombay for rest on doctor's advice. At times his health was so bad that it was feared that he might not live for a long time. An astrologer even forecast after studying his horoscope that the period between July 20 and August 27, 1936 was very critical for him. His secretary Mahadev Desai was deeply concerned about his health as he felt that he was overstraining himself and was taking great risks.[10]

Since the Congress was in power in several provinces, the Harijan lobby made a move that there must be a Harijan in the cabinet where the Congress was in power. A group of Harijans started a relay fast in Gandhi's Ashram at Sevagram to put pressure on him to persuade the Congress leadership to concede this demand. It was the political fallout of the awakening among the Harijan that he had brought about. The ambitious Harijan leaders tried to reap political harvest out of his campaigns for Harijan uplift. While admitting his inability to do so, he had to vacate a part of the Ashram to make room for their peaceful Satyagraha.[11]

Besides, there were conflicts between the Ministry and the party at several places. One glaring instance was that of Dr. N. Khare, Prime Minister of Central Provinces. The Congress Parliamentary Board had censured him for several allegations. In a bid to assert his independence of the Board, he took certain actions which invited the interference of the Governor. This hurt Gandhi as all such actions by Congress leaders in his view, impeded India's march towards freedom. For, in his view, "— the Congress conceived as a fighting machine has to (exercise) centralized control and guide every department and every Congressman, however highly placed and expect unquestioned obedience. The fight cannot be fought on any other term."[12] So, according to Gandhi's secretary, the Mahatma was not only responsible for the resolution of CWC over Khare's affair but even felt "that it might well have been stronger."[13] Khare might have been right if it is viewed on the basis of Parliamentary system in a free country. But from the point of view of Gandhi and Patel India was fighting for freedom and the parliamentary experience had to be treated as a means for attaining the goal.

In fact, the taste of political power surfaced the differences between Gandhi and several top Congress leaders. He felt distressed because of his differences with J.L. Nehru. "I can tell you, he wrote to him," how positively lonely I felt to know that now-a-days I can't carry you with me. I know that you would do much for affection. But in matters of state there can be no surrender to affection, when the intellect rebels."[14] The vociferous campaigns and propaganda of the Leftists in the Congress were sending dangerous signals to the old guards of the party and some of them felt that division in the Congress was inevitable. But the Mahatma tried to tame the Leftists by his tolerance of criticism, appreciation of their spirit of service, love of the country and their sympathy with the poverty stricken masses. He had put his weight for the election of one of the topmost among them as the president of the Congress for 1936 and 1937. It was a very tactical move revealing his political sagacity. For, while he tamed the revolutionary urge of J.L. Nehru, the majority in his Working Committee had Old Guards who could neutralize the effects of the revolutionary policies of their young president. In deference to the wishes of the Leftists, Gandhi did not oppose the election of Subhas Bose next year at Haripur Congress session in February 1938, though he did not consider him dependable. But the gulf between the two widened during the year Subhas was at the helm of affairs of the Congress. His differences with Gandhi over the release of prisoners, his abortive move to transfer the head office of the A.I.C.C. from Allahabad to Calcutta and his moves to overthrow coalition ministry of Krishak Praja Party in Bengal and most of all his readiness to carry on the struggle by any means if non-violence would not yield immediate results made Gandhi quite apprehensive of the unity in the Congress if he continued to hold a dominating position in it. Gandhi had learnt that Subhas had been in contact with the German Consul at Calcutta and was negotiating some arrangement.[15] Possibly some of the admirers of Subhas including Dilip Kumar Roy were feeling that their hero was ready to use questionable methods to achieve commendable ends.[16] In this situation a tug of war between the Mahatma and Subhas started when Subhas sought second term for presidentship of the Congress. Gandhi relied on Maulana Azad whose name was put up by some members of the CWC to oppose Subhas. Patel also had put up his candidature. But when Azad's name was proposed, he withdrew from the contest. The name of Sitaramayya was also proposed as a covering candidate. But Azad withdrew his name and Sitarammyya who was hardly known in northern India was left in the field to oppose Subhas whose career, sacrifices and radical views had greater appeal for the youth all over India. Gandhi put his weight on the side of Sitarammyya. But Subhas won by a majority of 200 votes. For, very few Congressmen were aware that the contest was not between Subhas and Sitarammyya but between Subhas and Gandhi. This was the first time the office of the president of the Congress was contested as earlier Gandhi's views generally prevailed and the contest was avoided. It was only when Gandhi admitted it as his defeat, the delegates or the voters became conscious of the real situation. As a result, 17 members of the Working Committee resigned leaving Subhas and his brother Sarat Chandra Bose alone as member of the Working Committee. Events moved fast. On a resolution of Pant the A.I.C.C. directed the president to appoint the members of the Working Committee in consultation with Gandhi. But the latter refused to nominate members of the CWC which compelled Subhas to resign. At another front Gandhi was pushed into an unseemly political situation only to save the honour of his close associate Patel. Faced with the agitation of his subjects, the Thakur of Rajkot on the advice of his Chief Minister Virawala, acted on a policy of repression that inflamed the people. To weather the storm Patel intervened and a compromise was effected between the Thakur and his subjects. But later on the Thakur, possibly on the instigation or support of the Resident repudiated the agreement which created a dangerous situation. Then Gandhi entered the scene and tried to persuade the Thakur to honour the pledge. But he failed in spite of Gandhi's fast. An appeal was made to the Viceroy. Gandhi agreed to the arbitration of the Chief Justice of India. The Mahatma, in fact, had been driven into an undesirable political situation where he had to depend upon the Viceroy for any support. Though the Viceroy Lord Linlithgow was very courteous to Gandhi in all his communications to him, he never wanted the Congress to acquire an upper hand in the disputes between the rulers and their subjects in the states and the Rajkot was the test case. To Gandhi's Secretary Mahadev who had meetings with Virawala and the Resident Gibson felt that the whole Rajkot agitation was a picture of our impatience.[17] While admitting that the Prime Minister of Rajkot was playing a game of chess the Congress leadership, too, were by no means lagging behind. He succeeded only in outwitting them or at least Vallabhbhai. Bapu out of his attachment for Vallabhbhai and weakness for Rajkot committed a blunder.[18] It looks the Mahatma himself had second thoughts over the consequences and nature of his fast. He felt that an appeal for the intervention of the paramount power added an element of 'himsa' (violence) and so his fast was tainted with 'himsa'. In a mood of repentence, he even offered to give up the advantages that the award had given. But it further caused hardships to the people of Rajkot. These unfortunate developments tarnished Gandhi's image as an impartial judge in the struggle for power in the Congress. Besides political matters especially after the assumption of political power by the Congress in several provinces, had diverted Gandhi's attention from the constructive programme which he thought would be his first love after the withdrawal from the Congress. On his initiative all India village Industries had been formed as an autonomous body of the Indian National Congress. It was a non-political body, the purpose of which was to rejuvenate the villages through the development of village industries. It aimed at freeing the villages from their dependence on the cities and from the tyranny of centralized production. His programme of village development anticipated Integrated Rural Development of independent India. For, the promotion of health and vigour of the villages was an integral part of his programme of village uplift. He invited medical men, biochemists, etc. to investigate and report on the methods for keeping the full nutritious value of food stuff. Some of the members of the Board of the A-I-V.I.A. were highly educated persons who had training in scientific methods of economics and law. He made efforts to identify articles of food which were easily available in the countryside with nutritious value. In a serious discussion with the scientists from Bengal, he appealed to them to devise a scientifically perfect diet for the villagers through biological experiments. He planned to set up a museum for the display of tools and machines useful for the villages. He prized every invention of science made for the benefit of all. To identify himself completely with the villagers, he decided to settle down in a village. In fact, he had been making efforts in this direction since his return from South Africa in 1915. In this process he had changed his dress, discarded all the trappings associated with the modern urban life, simplified his food habits and had advised his co-workers and followers to live among the villagers to share their woes and free them from all the evils and superstitions that impeded their progress. But he himself had not yet lived in a village where the modern civilization had not yet penetrated. So he gave up the comforts provided by the munificence of his disciple at Wardha and moved to a village which was not connected by any pucca road, having no post office, no store for food stuff of quality, no medical facility and accessible only with difficulty in the rainy season. This developed into his new Ashram after some time.

Notes and References

1. C.W., LVIII, p. 329.
2. *Ibid.*, p. 404.
3. *Ibid.*, LIX, p. 85.
4. *Ibid.*, LVIII, p. 371.
5. *Ibid.*, LXIII, pp. 127-28.
6. *Ibid.*, LXV, p. 106.
7. *Ibid.*, p. 422.
8. Birla, G.D., *op. cit.*, Vol. III, p. 38.

9. C.W., LXVII, p. 223.
10. Chaudhry, Valmit (ed.), Dr. Rajendra Prasad, correspondence select documents, Allied Pub., Vol. II, p. 30.
11. C.W., LXVII, pp. 289-90.
12. *Ibid.*, p. 226.
13. Birla, G.D., *op. cit.*, Vol. III, p. 180.
14. C.W., LXVII, p. 47.
15. Gandhi, Raj Mohan, Patel, 278.
16. Limaye, Madhu, *op. cit.*, 165.
17. Birla, *op. cit.*, Vol. III, p. 292.
18. *Ibid.*, p. 294.

20

Experiment with Community Living

Community living had become a necessity for the Mahatma. It was a part of his nature which possibly he inherited from his father. Call of the spirit, compulsion of circumstances, the impact of the ancient system of Ashram life, the influence of community living of the Mariam Hill Trappists community in South Africa, the concept of joint Hindu family system, his conviction that simple life was essential for spiritual attainment, all drew him towards Ashram life. So during his struggle both in South Africa and India, he set up four community settlements which came to be known as Ashramas. Two such settlements were in South Africa—the Phoenix and Tolstoy Farm. The other two were in India—Sabarmati Ashram and Sevagram. Wardha was a sort of transit camp where he settled down for sometime after winding up the Sabarmati Ashram in 1933. He stayed there for a short period before he moved to Seagaon, a small village at a distance of four miles from Wardha. Even before becoming a Mahatma, the young lawyer Mohandas rejoiced in sharing his apartment and comforts with his friends and companions. As soon as he had a house of his own, it became a sort of Ashram as many persons who joined him in social work started living with him. Thus while he was practising in Johannesburg his friend Polak and his wife Millie lived with him. The call of the spirit and his endeavour to live a life in accordance with his understanding of Ruskin's 'Unto This Last' led him to establish the Phoenix settlement. Precarious financial position of the 'Indian Opinion' also pressed on him to turn to the simple community life which besides reducing the cost of publishing the journal would improve the quality of life of the inmates. Similarly, responsibility of supporting the families of the Satyagrahis in South Africa with the minimum of expenses led him to set up the Tolstoy Farm. Both the settlements were based on the principles of simplicity, self-sufficiency, self-help and spiritual pursuits. These settlements offered its founder opportunities to make experiments in education, dietetics, nature cure community living, etc. Great emphasis was laid on manual labour and religious tolerance. Evening prayer and religious discourses were the regular features of these settlements. Hindus, Muslims, Christians and Parsis joined in their prayers where Hindu Bhajans (religious hymns) were sung by all sometimes with alterations of names of God in compliance with the sentiments of non-Hindu participants. Thus at the evening prayer at Phoenix the name Hormazd was said instead of Rama on the suggestion of Rustom Seth. Similarly on the suggestion of a Christian the word Vaishnava was replaced by the Christian when this hymn was sung. A few shalokas of Bhagavadgita selected by Gandhi were recited. Some changes in Gujarati Bhajans were made to suit the requirements of the religions of the inmates. For, the object of the settlement was purity of body and mind as well as economic equality. The co-workers were expected to live as one family. Brahmacharya was not considered essential for the inmates. Most of them were working for the 'Indian Opinion.' Gandhi put his heart and soul into this experiment of community living as Phoenix was the first step in this direction. He reminded his second son Manilal that "the progress of phoenix is our aim because through it we can search our souls and do service towards our country." Similarly, in a letter to Polak in April, 1909, he wrote, "Nothing has caused me so much worry as the financial question. I hate the idea of Phoenix being in debt." He was ready to sacrifice his law books, the jewellery, the large safe of his office to improve the financial position of the settlement.

Life in the Tolstoy Farm was on the pattern of Phoenix settlement. Self-reliance was the rule. All inmates dined together. There was common kitchen run by the women, though private kitchen was not totally forbidden. Just as in Phoenix, food in Tolstoy Farm was simple. Spices were avoided. The inmates were also required to have simple and inexpensive dress. Since all families had converted themselves into labourers and farmers, it was felt by Gandhi that they should use dress corresponding to their work, that is, labourer's trousers and shirt. These were imitated from prisoner's uniform. The ladies of the settlement undertook to stitch these clothes. Sandals required by the inmates were to be made at the farm. Kallenback learnt this art and taught it to Gandhi and other workers of the Farm. Fruit and vegetables were grown on the Farm. Of course, some provisions were obtained from Johannesburg. However life on the Tolstoy Farm was very hard like that of Phoenix.

A school was also set up for the children of the inmates of the Farm. Gandhi himself was the main teacher. At Phoenix he could not perform this function as he was most of the time absent from the settlement. Character building was the main objective of the education there. Gandhi made an experiment with co-education which quite often strained his nerves. He admitted that sometimes he burnt his fingers in the process. While at Phoenix, the prayer meetings were held in the evening, at the Farm prayer was held both in the morning and evening. The broad outlines of prayer were copied from Phoenix.

Both the settlements were viewed as the training centres for the Satyagrahis. Tolstoy Farm was closed in 1912 and the inmates were sent to Phoenix who started Satyagraha in 1913.

When Gandhi set up a settlement at Ahmedabad, he had the experiences of running two settlements in South Africa. In the Indian setting, the settlement was consecrated by the name Ashram and it acquired a religious connotation, though for Gandhi its objective was to train volunteers for the service of society through Satyagraha. According to Hindu tradition, 'Ashram' has several meanings. It means a place outside the town or in a forest where saints lived for the purpose of meditation. The Ashram was also a seat of learning. The students were admitted to an Ashram set up by a saint for education. An Ashram was also a place of refuge for high and low, who were tired of the routine of worldly life. A king losing his kingdom in war or a rich man losing his mental peace could find solace in an Ashram of a saint. Religious leaders in the modern times such as Arvindo Ghosh, Swami Shraddhananda, Swami Vivekananda, Swami Dayananda Saraswati have tried to revive the tradition of Ashram, though in a new form in accordance with the changed conditions of the times. Gandhi visited some of these 'Ashrams' that enriched his knowledge of the objectives and working of the Ashram in the modern times. The word 'Ashram' is re-interpreted in terms of his own view of an Ashram. It is not a place of refuge for tired and despondent persons. But a place of work or labour (Ashram) for those who were striving hard to build a new society based on truth and non-violence.

The regimen of Phoenix and Tolstoy Farm were introduced here with greater rigour. The 'Bapu' of Phoenix and Tolstoy Farm and the

'Bahi' (brother) of Indians living outside the settlement, had become a Mahatma. So greater emphasis was laid on the ideals of truth, non-violence, Brahmacharya, non-possession, etc. While at the Tolstoy Farm, the life of poverty had become a necessity because of lean financial resources of Gandhi, Voluntary poverty in the Satyagraha Ashram had become an ideal for an individual's spiritual unlift. The principle of manual labour, self-sufficiency, self-reliance led to the development of several industries in the Ashram, such as Khadi, dairy farming scientific scavanging, tanning, etc. The object was to serve the nation by making experiments in all such industries as could be set up in model villages. Removal of untouchability and Swadeshi became important in the Indian setting as, in Gandhi's view, these were the basic requirements for the reconstruction of Indian society since the Ashram, in his view, existed for the development of the nation.

The number of the inmates in his first Ashram in India varied from time to time. It rose from 33 at Kochrab to 200 souls at Sabarmati. At the time of disbanding of Satyagraha Ashram in July 1933, it had 107 inmates (42 men, 31 women, 12 boys and 22 girls).[1] Gandhi sometimes discouraged persons joining the Ashram because of the rigorous life in the Ashram. All the inmates were required to do some kind of manual work. Gandhi himself would participate in most of the activities of the Ashram in the beginning. No work was considered low. Visitors to the Ashram were sometimes surprised and even shocked when they found Gandhi engaged in menial work. When G.V. Mavalankar, secretary of Gujarat Sabha visited the Satyagraha Ashram in 1917 to discuss certain matters with Gandhi, who was the president of the Sabha, he was put up in a tent as there was not enough space in the building to accommodate all the inmates. In the morning he went to the main building to enquire as to where the bed had to be deposited. On his return he was shocked to find Gandhi carrying the bed on his shoulders.[2] Kanji Dwarkadas went to Gandhi's Ashram in 1921. After meeting him, he went for his bath. Some body put into his ears that he should wash his own clothes and dry them himself otherwise Gandhi would himself do it and he would feel embarrassed. After taking meals when every body was washing his plates Gandhi noticed that Kanji was not accustomed to doing so and he offered to wash his plates. But Kanji did not allow him to do so.[3] It was not unusual for Gandhi to help women working in the kitchen. Once the person incharge of the kitchen complained to him that all the inmates did not grind their share of wheat. Gandhi offered to grind the flour himself. Once it was an amusing sight for the inmates when they found

Gandhi and Kasturba cleaning big vessels of the kitchen.[4] The life at Sabarmati was purposely kept highly disciplined and hard. For if one could not stand it one was not of much use either for constructive work in the villages or for Satyagraha which involved hard life in jail. Daily routine started with the prayer between 4 and 4-15 a.m. and ended again with the prayer meeting from 7 to 7-30 p.m. All the inmates were expected to attend it. Initially Gandhi prepared Ashram prayer in Sanskrit. Later on, Gujarati and Hindi Bhajans were also sung. This suited the inmates as most of the Ashramites were Hindus. Subsequently Christian hymns, the well-known Fateh of the Muslims, some hymns from the Granth Sahib and Mazda of the Parsis were added to the Ashram Bhajnawali. Thus it became a sort of Compilation from Hindu, Muslim, Parsi, Christian and Sikh scriptures. Some of them were translated by Gandhi into English for the benefit of his devoted disciple Mira.[5] A Japanese Buddhist who stayed in the Ashram in Sevagram for some time left a mantra meaning 'I bow to the Buddha, the giver of true religion', which he used to recite with a beating of a drum. Gandhi assured him that the mantra would remain an integral part of the Ashram prayer. Verses from the Gita were recited daily and the whole Bhagavadgita was finished in a fortnight. At the evening prayer the last 19 verses of the second chapter that describe the characteristics of Sthitaprjna were recited which a Satyagrahi was required to cultivate. Whenever Gandhi was present in the Ashram, prayer would be followed by a discourse by him. For a long time if any one had no faith in the prayer he could not be admitted. But this rule was relaxed sometime in 1945 in favour of Ramachandra popularly known as Gora who was an atheist but was deeply devoted to Gandhi's drive against untouchability. When Narain Rao Shastri joined the Ashram, he started, 'Ram Dhun' along with Bhajans of other sages. He was a musician and was the pupil of Pandit Vishnu Digambar whom the master sent to the Ashram. He made hymn singing interesting and the Ashram Bhajanavali was mostly compiled by him.

The prayer was held in the open. Whenever there was rain, prayer was conducted in the Verandah of the main building. No idol was kept for the prayer. But the inmates could keep idols in their rooms if they so desired. Food in the Ashram received Gandhi's serious attention. He always favoured common kitchen as, in his view, it would bind the Ashramites into one family. But this created a lot of problems in all the settlements that he established because of the different food habits of the inmates. For, very few could follow Gandhi's dictum that food should be taken as a medicine for the maintenance of the body only and not for enjoyment. Control of the palate was a part of his Brahmacharya. So at Sabarmati, on his insistence the Ashramites agreed to cooking food in one kitchen. But it remained a source of great tension in the Ashram especially because many inmates were fond of spices and the common kitchen did not allow the use of spices. Ultimately Gandhi had to yield to the demand of those who liked spiced food and allowed the common kitchen at Sabarmati to prepare two varieties of food, one spiced and the other unspiced. Initially Gandhi was against the consumption of milk in the Ashram as his view of vegetarianism and the cruelty to which cows were subjected made him give up milk. But since he could not find a good substitute of milk from plant life, he not only allowed its use in the Ashram but also maintained a good dairy in the Ashram for the supply of milk to the inmates. Strict punctuality was observed for serving meals at the common kitchen. Lunch was served at 11 a.m. Late commers were to wait outside the hall and take food in the next session. Even per chance Gandhi himself was late, he had to wait outside the hall like any other ashramite. The Mahatma had a passion for cleanliness. So great effort was made to keep the premises of the Ashram clean. He himself would frequently visit the latrines in order to keep them clean. He, of course, had lost a sense of smell and so he was assisted by others, quite often by Mira (Miss Slade) in this task. Sanitary work was considered by him as an essential and sacred service. The members of the Ashram were assigned the sanitation work in turn. The new entrants to the Ashram were given three months' apprenticeship in the sanitary department of the Ashram. This was in a way their test for fitness for the service of society.

The sphere of the industries in the Ashram was extended to giving training to the workers engaged in the uplift of villages as well as for the promotion of Khadi. The Sabarmati Ashram trained one thousand Khadi workers.

Education of the children was an important activity of the Ashram. Gandhi had definite views about education and these became the bases of the Gujarat Vidyapith. Co-education upto the age of sixteen as far as possible covering two stages of a pupil's career was allowed. Manual training was to be given at second stage (9 to 16) and it should be self-supporting. English was to be taught only one of the several languages. Women were to be provided the same facilities as men for education.

Equality between men and women was one of chief characteristics of any settlement established by Gandhi. Women were not subjected to any other restraint which was not imposed on men. Even cooking was attended to by both. Men and women worked together. 'Purdah' was absolutely unknown in the Ashram. Special attention was paid to the sick persons in the Ashram. The Mahatma personally attended to the sick. Even in the midst of the most important meetings he remembered the treatment given to the patients in the Ashram. A person in the Ashram enjoyed a sort of royal treatment if he or she fell sick in Gandhi's Ashram. It was his daily practice to visit the patients in the Ashram twice a day and console them with the sympathetic words and prescribe them required treatment. He especially attended on Parchure Shastri, a well-known Sanskrit scholar who was suffering from wet leprosy. Parchure Shastri had participated in the Satyagraha and was released on March 8, 1933. Before admitting him to the Ashram Gandhi sought the opinion of the Ashramites through a letter to Narandas advising them to express their views frankly.[6] Even after being admitted, most of the members were not ready to go near him. Gandhi looked after him. Once a woman attending on Gandhi, fell ill in Calcutta. Gandhi sought the best treatment of a physician for her. But some of his co-workers felt that he was unnecessarily pampering the ailing disciple.

The Mahatma considered his Ashram as his best creation. He described Ashram as "group life lived in religious spirit." However, religion was taken in a broad sense. It did not mean enforcement of any kind of ritual. Nor did it mean belief in any kind of theological principle. All it meant purity of personal conduct. The success of the Ashram life was for him the real criterion for judging him. For, the strict observance of the principles of the Ashram, in his view, could raise an ordinary person to a great moral heights. The life that he planned for the inmates was the life that would make an individual seek his happiness in the happiness of others. However, the working of the Ashram in India or his settlements in South Africa gave him a lot of trouble. For they were not free from petty bickerings among the inmates. Sometimes moral lapses of the inmates led Gandhi to observe fasts, a sort of penance for the faults of others. Both at Phoenix and Tolstoy Farm boys and girls misbehaved that shocked him. He discovered such failings again in the Sabarmati ashram for which he had high hopes. Petty bickerings in the Ashram especially among the women compelled Gandhi's devoted follower Miss Slade to shun the Ashram. He once wrote to her that if she still retained the horror of return to the Ashram, she could meet him outside the Ashram.[7] She once wrote to her mentor Romain Rolland that there were never-ending series of clashes and friction in the Ashram which could be controlled by Bapur's firm hands.[8] The Mahatma sometimes felt that he had failed to take all the women in the Ashram towards his ideal. For, he had pinned high hopes in some of them but their conduct belied his expectations.[9] At times even earnest inmates such as Gangabehn, Mahadev Desai, Narandas Desai etc. thought of leaving the Ashram because of undesirable atmosphere there. Many in the Ashram did not observe the vow of non-possession. Gandhi was shocked to learn that his close relative Chhaganlal carried on systematic thieving for many years and when he was discovered he tried to hide his guilt by forgery. Of course, he had contributed ten thousand rupees to the Ashram but from Gandhi's point of view, it contained a part of the stolen money. In sheer anguish and remorse, he left the Ashram.[10] But a greater shock was in store for him when he found that his own wife Kasturba had accumulated a few hundred rupees as a result of the offerings made to her by the visitors to the Ashram. As a rule she was required to pass on that money to the Ashram fund. Possibly because of some misunderstanding she kept the money with her. But to the Mahatma this act, too, was nothing short of stealing. Sometimes new entrants committed acts which in ordinary life were not very unusual but were aberrations from the point of view of the founder of the Ashram.

The great source of tension and daily bickerings in Ashram was the working of the common kitchen since several members did not like the food prepared there. One major reason for the lapses and shortcomings of the Ashram inmates was that a number of them had not joined the Ashram or his settlements in South Africa on the call of the spirit or because of their enchantment with Gandhi's view of life. Women had generally followed their husbands to the settlements of Gandhi. They could not adjust themselves to the hard life of Gandhi's Ashram. So was the case with children. They had come with their parents. According to Mira the Ashram was a heterogeneous collection of one or two hundred people—men, women, children from fanatical ascetics to sceptical family women. The ascetics were few in number and the family type were in majority.[11] The Ashram was not at all of the monastic type but was miniature cross section of the every day world. Millie Polak who had great appreciation for Gandhi and had lived with him as a member of his household along with her husband in Johannesburg, could not adjust herself to the life at Phoenix. She confessed that "the impossibility of suitable food, the knowledge and fear of the snakes, spiders and other poisonous or unpleasant creatures—proved too much for her." Gandhi allowed her and her husband to live in Durban. The Tolstoy Farm had been established to provide shelter and food to the families of Satyagrahis, though Gandhi looked upon it as a laboratory for his experiments in community living. So if women did not follow the Ashram rules, it was nothing unusual. Sometimes persons of doubtful character joined the Ashram. Most of them were hypocrites as they tried to show that they were faithfully observing the principles of the Ashram when Gandhi was in the Ashram. Reginald Reynold, Gandhi's English follower who stayed in the Ashram for sometime found a number of such persons in the Sabarmati Ashram.[12] Such persons polluted the atmosphere of the Ashram. Once Gandhi even toyed with the idea of breaking up the Sabarmati Ashram. But as a practical step he decided to reduce his control over its management so that 'inmates themselves shape it in the manner they thought best'. For 'the Ashram' according to him 'was medium for conducting' an experiment in absolute democracy. But he desired the elimination of persons of doubtful character. However, to those who were sincere but desirous of leaving the Ashram because of undesirable atmosphere there, he offered them the option of living on the premises of the Ashram as tenants. In that capacity they would have the liberty to observe the Ashram rules to the best of their ability and could carry on occupations which were welcomed by the Ashram. That way they could shape the institution in the manner they thought best.[13] He assured that he "can tolerate every freedom being given, but I myself do not understand what freedom I should ask people to exercise."[14] Though a stickler with regard to the observance of rules in the Ashram, he never wanted the individuality of any person to be crushed as "it would harm the Ashram itself."[15] Since the 'Ashram' was not working in accordance with his concept, he decided to change its name from 'Satyagraha Ashram' to 'Udyog Mandir' as the Ashram had several industries which were useful for society.

The Ashram was a motley crowd. There were inmates who were making strange experiments which would make them appear eccentric or mad persons in the eyes of others. One person had virtually sealed his lips and was taking liquid food through a pipe. The same person was once a dandy but under the influence of Gandhi's discourses on Gita and his narration of Pilgrim's Progress in the Ashram, he behaved in a queer manner in his efforts towards self-restraint. Gandhi felt happy when he got his stitches of the lips removed and started taking normal food.[16] He was for some time professor in the Gujarat Vidyapith. Gandhi had great admiration for him for his selflessness and determination. In the Aga Khan detention camp in the course of a talk when Pyarelal remarked that in his opinion after Bapu, Bhansali had reached the greatest spiritual height, Gandhi said "I think he has gone higher than me. He is always fearless and that is the sign of a saint. What he can do I cannot."[17]

Once the Mahatma himself said, "cranks, faddists and mad find their way to the Ashram, I am the maddest of them all." In a lighter vein he described the Ashram as a 'shamboo mela' where all types of curious and abnormal persons were present who would ordinarily be regarded as cranks in society. Rajkumari Amritkaur who for sometime worked as his secretary asked him, "why do you waste so much of your time of the personal affairs of the mad inmates of the Ashram?" Quick came the reply, "I know mine is a mad house and I am maddest of the lot," but those that cannot see the good in these mad people are blind."[18] Similarly in reply to a letter of an inmate who had asked him as to why learned men did not join the Ashram, he said, "the reason is that I don't regard myself as a learned man. The few learned men who were drawn to the Ashram joined it not in order to pursue their learned callings but to receive and nurse something else altogether."[19]

It is true that Ashram was a unique institution. But it could not attract many persons who were trained in different fields of life. This was because of the nature and object of the Ashram itself. For, preparation for the identification with the poorest in the country did not require degrees in science or art but strong will to shed one's ego and direct one's energies to the service of others. The ideal was to reduce oneself to zero. Very few could come up to this ideal and the Mahatma was fully aware of it. But all had to be judged by their efforts. Undoubtedly there were some persons who deceived him. But to his knowledge their number was not large. He owned full responsibility for the deficiencies of the Ashram as he claimed they "are a reflection of my own deficiencies." Once a well-educated and wealthy youngman who stayed in the Ashram for sometime was amused by the strange observances of the inmates of the Ashram in the morning. For, one elderly person was deep in meditation, a youngman was standing on his head while practising Asnas and lady was talking in her sleep. In sheer amusement he chuckled to himself and thought 'what an entourage for the leader of the nation.' Just then Gandhi happened to come by and noticing the cause of his amusement, he said, "It does seem quite ridiculous. All the same these people are good, honest human beings, and that is all I ask." He did not need Mahatmas and took delight in his title of Mahatma and said, "The Mahatma I must leave to his fate—my friend never have anything to do with Mahatmas or those who use their names. Mahatmas are the most slippery customers treading on this overburdened earth."[20]

The Mahatma decided to disband the Sabarmati Ashram in 1933.

To some this decision was the result of his disappointment about the working of the Ashram. But he denied it, for "if despair had been the reason," he said "I would have declared it." Rather, it was an act of a sacrifice which in his view "was intended to add lustre to the great work it had done." At that time it had immovable property of 3,60,000 and moveable including cash of 2,00,000. While taking this decision what weighed on his mind was the oath that he had taken on the commencement of Salt Satyagraha that he would return to the Ashram only in free India. However, one cannot rule out his disappointment at the conduct of some of the inmates. When Gandhi was recovering from three weeks fast in May 1933, Patel warned all those connected with the Ashram, not to burden Gandhi with Ashram problems as it would give him shocks. In a letter to Mahadev dated 30 May 1933, he wrote, "if bit or small quarrels are brought to Bapur we will be in great trouble— let him not know anything for a week at least. Who can run the Ashram as it is today? I don't thing anybody can run, and Bapur finds it burdensome. Some way should be found out that also should be such that Bapu does not get shock—."[21]

When Gandhi decided to move to Seagaon (Sevagram) he had no mind to set up an Ashram. His main objective was to live among the villagers and improve their lives through selfless service. It was predominantly a Harijan village having a population of 600. Most of its inhabitants suffered from Malaria, Gandhi too, had an attack of the fever within a year of shifting to it and was hospitalised at Wardha for a few days. Before settling down there, he assured the villagers "I shall try to serve you by cleaning your roads and surroundings by trying to render such help as I can if there is illness in the village, and by teaching you self-help by way of helping you to revive your handicrafts, if you co-operate with me." He wanted to live there alone. So on April 30, 1936, he walked to Seagaon along with Mahadev Desai, Jamnalal Bajaj and Shriman Narayan with hot winds blowing all round, covering four miles on foot and one mile in a bullock cart. After reaching the proposed site for his dwelling place, he rested under an improvised bamboo hut by the side of a well in the midst of guava trees since there was no other dwelling place there. A cottage was built for him with the help of Mira and Jamnalal which had a large room of 29' × 14' with 7 feet varandah running all round. The entire building was constructed with purely local material. Here was a man who planned campaigns to destroy imperialism and thereby reconstruct human society on the foundations of justice, was ready to live in a small village sharing the woes of the people living there and offering to them the solutions to their day-to-day problems in order to lift them out of the degraded conditions. His secretary Mahadev Desai told Birla in August 1936 that being fully occupied in village work, Gandhi was loath to take up any other activity. In fact, he was turning his mind off from the Congress and all other activities. What was working in the mind of the Mahatma when he undertook this unattractive and arduous task? He must have thought that if he could find a solution of a problem at a small scale, it could serve the purpose at a bigger scale since big or small ultimately it is a human problem.

Mira built a hut for herself at a distance of one and a half mile from Gandhi's cottage since Gandhi wanted to live there alone. His secretary Mahadev Desai had to walk daily eleven miles to do his secretarial work. Gandhi himself walked daily to Wardha to attend the Congress Working Committee meeting for some time. But as it became difficult for Mahadeva to do his work efficiently by walking daily to Gandhi's hut, he was allowed to stay in Seagaon. Gandhi's wife Kasturba followed suit and one corner was given to each of them in the same cottage. After some time Khan Abdul Gaffar Khan came to Seagaon to see Gandhi. He was accommodated in the fourth corner of the same hut. As time passed, more followers joined them and the place virtually acquired the look of an 'Ashram', though Gandhi refused to admit that it was an 'Ashram' of his conception. More cottages were constructed. A separate cottage was constructed for Kasturba. Gandhi also shifted to a smaller cottage which Mira had constructed for herself. Gandhi stayed there till 1946 when he left for Noakhali and never returned to it. The cottage was decorated with two quotations. The first one was from Ruskin. It runs as follows:[22]

> "The essence of lying is deception and not in words. A lie may be told by silence, by equivocation, by the accent of a syllable, by the glance of the eye attaching particular significance to a sentence, and all these kinds of lies are worse and baser by many degrees than a lie plainly worded."

The other was from Larimar. It reads as:

> "When you are in the right, you can afford to keep your temper, and when you are in the wrong you cannot afford to lose it."

Many women joined Gandhi in this 'Ashram', Among them were Prabhawati, wife of Jayaprakash Narain, Amtus Slam, a devoted Muslim young woman, Sushila Nayyar and Rajkumari Amrit Kaur. A guest house was also constructed for visitors who would come to Sevagram to consult Gandhi. The name of Seagaon was changed to Sevagram as there was a town of the same name on Bombay-Nagpur line to avoid miscarriage of Gandhi's letters. In addition to the cottages of the inmates, big cottages were constructed for two training schools, that is, Technical Training School and Khadi Training School and a building for Basic Education Centre. Soon after the All India Spinners' Association shifted its headquarters to Sevagram. Thus a cluster of buildings came into existence. Later on a hospital building was constructed. Thus where there was only one hut a few years earlier, a sprawling rural township came into existence. Telephone was installed in the Ashram. With many persons coming to join Gandhi at Sevagram, it started functioning on the lines of Sabarmati 'Ashram'. Common Kitchen, dairy farming were undertaken. The daily routine would start at 4 a.m. and continued with regularity of a clock up to 8 p.m. The day would start with prayer meeting and in the beginning there were only two persons at the prayer meeting, Gandhi and his devotee Balwant Sinha. The former reciting the verses and the latter singing Bhajans. At times Gandhi would participate in the digging of a well for the Ashram. At night all would sleep on the ground at the place of the prayer meeting and it would look like a railway platform. An inmate was advised to maintain a diary which could be checked by Gandhi. When so many persons with different temperaments had to live together, naturally there would be irritants. Balwant Sinha who looked after the dairy was short tempered and this created a lot of problems for Gandhi who once advised him to leave the Ashram. But on his promise to reform himself, he continued staying.

The Mahatma entered on a period of silence on May 24, 1940 because of certain irritations in the Ashram. Complaints of partiality sometimes spoiled the atmosphere in the Ashram and the Mahatma felt that he and his wife were to be mainly blamed for this as his wife could not rise 'above mine and thine' and he could not leave her. The diary of Amritlal showed that he was very much concerned about his son who was staying in Ashram along with his father as the prevailing atmosphere there was not congenial to social, moral and spiritual growth of a person.

Though the Mahatma laid great emphasis on Brahmacharya, love making was not completely absent in the Ashram. Even his devoted follower Miss Slade could not avoid fascination for a revolutionary who stayed in the Ashram for some time. Similarly, a boy and a girl in whom Gandhi had full faith fell in love with each other and deceived the

Mahatma. In fact, the requirement of observance of Brahmacharya created both tension and hypocrisy in the Ashram. It deluded even his close disciples that they were observing Brahmacharya even when they were wishing company for young girls. Gandhi himself had to write to his nephew that his desire for companionship with a young girl was actuated by sexual desire and therefore he should decide to marry some girl. A nature cure doctor who was treating some inmates in the Ashram told another inmate that a few persons in the Ashram were suffering from venereal diseases. Gandhi held an enquiry and found that it was false. When Gandhi sent a copy of proposed rules of the Sabarmati Ashram to his friend Andrews, the latter objected to the inclusion of the vow of celibacy on the grounds that it would create a sort of moral hypocrisy.

Gandhi himself was not fully satisfied with the atmosphere in the Sevagram Ashram. He wrote to Kishorlal Mashruwala in May 1941 "I have experienced such disappointments regarding the Ashram that I have lost all interest in embarking on new ventures. I do wish that some of you should set up brotherhood during and even after my life time."

Did the Ashram serve any purpose? To the Mahatma it did serve the purpose for which it was set up. For, it created a spirit of service to society in most of its members. Both in South Africa and India, most of its members participated in the Satyagraha and underwent trials and tribulations in Gandhi's struggle against injustice or untruth. The Ashram provided him with a band of dedicated workers to support him in all his programmes for the political, social and economic uplift of the society. The Ashram served as a laboratory or a workshop to develop the tools for the development of village industries. The Khadi industry acquired a pre-eminent position both in Sabarmati and Sevagram Ashrams. Besides, dairy farming, bookeeping, tanning industries were developed in the Ashrams. Further, the Ashram life fostered the discipline for bearing the hardships of life in jail that Satyagraha involved or hardships of village life for the workers engaged in the constructive programme in the villages. The spirit of service that the Ashram generated in some of its inmates found expression in different fields of social life. For instance, Mira found her self-expression in the development of animal husbandry and Gandhi encouraged her to do so. During Gandhi's life as well as after his assassination she developed centres of animal husbandry in the United Province (Rishikesh) and Kashmir.

It is true that life in the Ashram was not free from tension generated by petty quarrels and undesirable incidents. But then most of the inmates were ordinary human beings who could not rise above normal human failings such as jealousy, ambitions, short temper, self-love immediately after joining the Ashram. Gandhi himself was conscious that the persons related to him could not rise above 'mine and thine' even after living with him for a long time. It is true that sometimes there was a commotion in the Ashram because of the conduct of an inmate which appeared to the management reprehensible. But the Mahatma sometimes made a mountain of a mole hill. A minor theft in the Ashram of a pen and a letter of a female inmate which might have been passed as a minor incident with any other head of an institution, extremely disturbed Gandhi, for, in his view, it showed his weakness or incompetence. So he decided to fast as a penance since the suspected person denied she had done it. But the suspicion was not well-founded and the disappearance of the letter remained a mystery for him. He, of course, abandoned the idea of fast on the insistence of other inmates. Similarly an inmate who had almost become a daughter to him lost control of herself, became insolent both to the manager and Gandhi and left the Ashram in a huff. It was a minor incident. The manager only drew her attention to her carelessness and reported the matter to Gandhi. He was busy writing when she appeared before him. He was trying to avoid having taken notice of her presence so that she could compose herself. But the lady sailed in when Gandhi made certain remarks. She raised her voice and unusually the Mahatma, too, did the same and asked her to leave. But he was sorry. For, if she had lost her temper, it was his duty to remain silent. He, then, asked his secretary to send her back to the Ashram.[23] Another incident which, though did not happen in the Ashram, created an uproar in the Ashram. It occurred when his wife along with two Ashram women visited the famous temple at Puri that had denied entry to the untouchables and Gandhi had taken the decision that he or his followers would not visit any such temple. Though his secretary, Mahadeva had full knowledge of the incident, he failed to report it to Gandhi. This upset him to such an extent that his blood pressure shot up to an alarming level. Mahadeva even threatened to leave. But Gandhi was not ready to part with him. Imploring him to stay on, he wrote, "—I will tolerate thousands of mistakes, but I can never part with you; even death at the hands of a 'bhakta' is preferable to salvation at the hands of those who have no love for one."[24]

In fact, the Mahatma fixed the target very high for those who were very close to him as he was trying to make them models for others. He was an experimenter and he was making experiments with all sorts of persons. In the process, whenever he found himself at fault, he modified his course. When he found that the wife of his devoted follower was anxious for family life, he directed him against his will to first satisfy the urge of his wife. Similarly boys and girls brought up in the Ashram were given the choice either to marry or accept strict celibacy on reaching the age of puberty. So several marriages were performed in the Ashram in the presence of the Mahatma. Undoubtedly there were a number of persons who deceived him. But it was the first principle of his life to trust a person who expressed faith in his ideals. Not that he did not know that he was being deceived. But he would give a long rope to the erring individual to reform himself. The Mahatma having full faith in the indwelling of the universal spirit in all human beings, believed that everyman was capable of rising like him to level of spiritual development. Once he was warned by a friend not to encourage immature and growing persons to take absolute vows. For, it would create an atmosphere of hypocrisy, inconsistency and tension in the Ashram. But the Mahatma was impelled by his own nature. He told the person incharge of the Ashram that "I act on the assumption that his co-workers particularly those close to him as matter of course do what I do."

Notes and References

1. C.W., LV, p. 301.
2. Shukla, *op. cit.*, p. 172.
3. Kanji Dwarkadas, *op. cit.*, 189.
4. Shukla, *op. cit.*, Kumarappa, narrates the incident.
5. C.W., LIV, p. 51.
6. *Ibid.*, XCVII, pp. 172-73.
7. *Ibid.*, XXXVIII, p. 43.
8. Romain Rolland, Gandhi, Correspondence, p. 199.
9. C.W., XL, pp. 250-54.
10. *Ibid.*, pp. 208-12.
11. Mira Behn, The Spirit's Pilgrimage, p. 70.
12. Reginald Reynold, To Live in Mankind, pp. 6-7.
13. C.W., XL.
14. *Ibid.*
15. *Ibid.*, LIII, p. 52.
16. *Ibid.*, LX, p. 402.
17. Nayyar, Sushila, *op. cit.*, p. 132.
18. Grover, Arora, Amrit Kaur, pp. 303-4.
19. C.W., XLIX, p. 105.
20. Jeangir and Sykes, *op. cit.*, p. 111.
21. Collected Works of S. Patel, Vol. III, p. 28.
22. C.W., LXXII, pp. 124, 151.
23. *Ibid.*, LXXIII, p. 166.
24. *Ibid.*, LXVII, p. 455.

21

An Indefatigable Experimenter

Gandhi claimed that the aim of his life was search for truth. That is also the objective of an earnest and adroit scientist. "Truth and non-violence," he observed "are as old as hills. All I have done is to try experiments in both as vast a scale as I could. In doing so I have sometimes erred and learnt by my errors. Life and its problems have thus become to me so many experiments in the practice of truth and non-violence." So the Mahatma endorsed the view of a group of foreign scientists that all scientists seek truth.[1] He was aware of the contributions of Western scientists such as Galileo, Newton, Darwin, T.H. Huxley, etc. to human knowledge. Once he had discussion with his associate Kalelkar over the question whether Galileo could be called a 'Rishi'. He had no objection to this appellation for Galileo from one point of view as he was a learned man and was a seeker of truth. But there was one objection. For 'Rishi' was used according to ancient Indian tradition for "those who depended upon the inner eye for their knowledge." But that was not the way of Galileo or for that matter of any modern scientist. Like any modern scientist the Mahatma believed that "no proposition can be called universal unless it is proved so by analysis and synthesis" and in support of it he quoted Darwin who applied it in his famous work 'The Descent of man.'[2] He read the works of T.H. Huxley in 1889 when he went to England for studies. Huxley was a biologist and a foremost exponent of Darwin's theory of evolution. Late in life Gandhi read with great interest the life and work of Madame Curie who worked on uranium and along with her husband discovered radium and polonium and pionered medicinal use of radioactivity winning Nobel Prize for chemistry (1911). In Gandhi's view she was a true devotee to scientific knowledge and suggested to Sushila Nayyar to translate the biography of Madame Curie written by Curie's daughter into Hindi.[3] The Mahatma paid tributes to the spirit of research that fired the Modern scientists. For, in their search for truth they were ready to discard well established ideas and theories and even suffer ridicule and punishment from those who held power in society.

In tune with the spirit of science Gandhi looked upon reason as his ally in his search for truth. Though faith was his bedrock for his belief in the presence of divine spirit in man and in the universe, he did not consider reason and faith as opposed to each other. Only their spheres are different. So faith, in his view, becomes lame when it ventures into matters pertaining to reason. For "a scientific mind will not be satisfied with having things scientific just on faith. He will insist on finding a basis in reason." In a discussion with an American clergyman about the solution of conflicting religious ideas, he suggested "that all matters which can be reasoned out, should be rejected if they are in conflict with reason." But all such matters which are beyond reason, he averred "we have to accept them on faith. It is a kind of sixth sense which works in cases which are without the purview of reason."[4] In short faith transcends reason in a particular sphere. But he vehemently opposed reliance on faith where rational study of facts and experience could take us nearer to truth. "In every matter he reminded his followers," faith must be supported by empirical knowledge. For, ultimately experience is the basis of faith and everyone who has faith must at some time pass through experience. . . ."[5] For him reason was the basis of morality. So any social norm or tradition which is opposed to reason and morality must be rejected. This involves re-interpretation of our 'Shastras' or religious books in the light of our new experiences and the demands of reason. He himself re-interpreted the message of the Bhagavadgita, the epics and the Puranas. In his theological warfare with orthodox sections of the Hindu society he exalted reason like the seventeenth and eighteenth centuries rationalists in Europe who challenged Christian theology and the Christian scheme of the world. He was certainly not on a sound footing when he claimed that untouchability had no support of the Hindu Shastras. But he was quite logical and convincing when he justified his opposition to untouchability on the grounds of reason and morality. However his interpretations of the 'Shastras' in the light of new demands of the time and situation did not appear very offensive to the majority of the Hindus as these had been subjected to various interpretations from time to time in the long course of the development of the Hindu society. But when he applied the same yard stick of reason to Muslim scriptures and traditions, he burnt his fingers. For, he was fiercely opposed by several Muslim leaders some of whom were his comrades-in-arms during his non-co-operation movement and he had to make a hasty retreat. Though he was logical, his interpretation could not be trusted by the Muslim masses and their leaders.

Similarly, it was because of his reliance on reason that he never paid any heed to astrology, palmistry or any system of sooth saying.[6] As a rationalist he had no faith in miracles. For God, in his view, "does not work through miracles, though the divine mind is revealed some time in a flash and it appears like a miracle to man."[7] So he never claimed any miraculous power, though the masses quite often assigned such powers to him. Thus during one of his tours the inhabitants of a village told him that his auspicious presence had made the village well miraculously filled with water. But to him, it was only an accident and he reproved the villagers for having such beliefs. In a light vein he told them, suppose a crow sits on a palm tree at the moment when the tree falls to the ground. "Will you imagine that the weight of the bird brought down the tree."[8] Once when he was travelling a person trying to have his 'darshan' fell from the train. But he remained unhurt. When he met him he told him that his escape was miraculous because of the Mahatma's presence in the train. The latter smiled and said, 'Then why did you fall?'

Similarly, he was opposed to communication with the spirits. For, in his view, 'contact with the spirits, even if true' is a hindrance between God and ourselves.[9] He warned a friend that a spiritualist had harmed man's search for truth. His main reason for not joining the Theosophical Society was its belief in occultism which Gandhi could not appreciate. Though he rejected astrology, he was drawn towards astronomy which he considered as science. He read three books by James Jeans, English Physcist and astronomer.[10] Maunder's 'Astronomy without a Telescope' appeared quite interesting to him and he liked author's definition of science as 'accurate measurement' and he applied this principle to spinning and allied processes. He acquired elementary knowledge of astronomy during his incarceration in 1930-31. Earlier he had encouraged Shankarlal Banker who was with him in Yeravada jail in 1922 to study this subject. During his imprisonment in 1932, he started a systematic study of this subject. He acquired from a lady friend two large sized telescopes which were placed in the open yard occupied by him in the jail to watch the stars at night. He told a lay inmate of the Ashram that astronomy had become a passion with him. So "every minute I get I devote myself to it." It is a wonderful subject; he added, "it impresses upon me the mystery of God and the majesty of the universe." It strengthened his faith in God.[11] One could not help becoming a worshipper of God, he averred, "while watching universe after universe on a starry night."[12]

The Mahatma claimed that all his activities though undertaken in good faith, had sound scientific foundation. He told his co-workers that he had made and was all the time making all possible experiments based on reason.[13] For, "scientific knowledge require constant probing into the why and wherefore of every little process that one performs." Mere affirmation that in 'charkha' there is Swaraj, 'he warned' is not enough."[14] Narrating his own experience with regard to the development of the spinning wheel, he pointed out that initially he confused it with handloom but later on with the help of his nephew Maganlal, he made all possible efforts to improve by experimenting with different types of spindles.[15] The spinning wheel, he reiterated, could not become power for the liberation of the country unless a deep study of various sciences related to it was made by all the workers engaged in this industry. The Mahatma wanted his associates and co-workers to cultivate scientific outlook in life. For, in his view, it is not true scientific outlook if it is confined to investigation in a specific field in a laboratory. Rather, it is reflected, "he affirms in every act of the person, in his eating, drinking, rest sleep." In other words, every thing should be 'scientifically regulated with a full appreciation of its why and wherefore.' Finally, a scientific mind must have detachment. Some of the members of the Board of All India Village Industries were selected by him for their knowledge of applied sciences. Besides, he was in touch with a number of experts in different fields of science and industry.[16] For, according to him, research in the technique and tools for village industries was one of the important functions of A.I.V.I.A. So he favoured the setting up of a museum of various instruments and machines used in village industries in different parts of the country. He sought the development of all industries such as tanning,[17] dairy farming, etc. which are relevant to rural reconstruction on scientific lines. At the Sevagram Ashram he started making a scientific study of snakes.[18] He consulted experts on the subject and read books on it in order to know the types of snakes that are poisonous and to share his knowledge with the villagers. Though he had been keeping a dairy in his Ashram in India, he always had the feeling that the person managing the cowpen lacked scientific knowledge of tending the animals. So on his request, the principal of agricultural college, Poona sent a good student to his Ashram to do the needful. He also wanted to send Balwant Sinha, the manager of dairy at Sevagram to Lahore for equipping himself with scientific knowledge of dairy farming.[19] Two highly educated persons, Jehangir and Marjorie Sykes who had stayed in Gandhi's Ashram for some time felt that the Mahatma mostly laid emphasis on the role of reason in his search for truth. They have recorded that Gandhi urged on them again and again the importance of "letting reason be our guiding star and of not allowing ourselves to be carried away by emotion."[20] They noted in Gandhi openness and readiness for change. For, the power of inward growth, in his view, is the mark of the life of the spirit. Once a journalist in a conference accused the Mahatma of contradicting "today, what he said yesterday."[21] In reply Gandhi said, "well if I contradict on Tuesday what I said on Monday it merely means that I have learned something in between."[22] Quite often the seeming contradictions in his statements given at different times is the result of his realism. For, as a leader of the nation he had to change his policies with the change of circumstances.

But it was in the field of dietetics Gandhi made special experiments throughout his life. For dietetic experiments were an integral part of his search for truth. The abandonment of this experiment he viewed as the worst evil. But its success he believed demanded complete detachment which he could not fully acquire. It was during his first visit to England that he initiated food reform for himself for economy, hygienic and observance of vow. Religious motive had not as yet consecrated such experiments. Contacts with English thinkers of vegetarianism and the study of its philosophy enlightened his view on this subject. He stopped taking sweets and condiments and started relishing boiled vegetables. Cocoa replaced tea and coffee which were considered harmful by some English vegetarians. With a view to avoid starchy food, he started living on fruits, bread, cheese, milk and eggs. But the last item he gave up after a few days on the grounds that while taking a vow before his mother for not taking meat, egg was included in her definition of meat, though an English school of vegetarianism did not object to the eating of eggs as their definition of meat denoted only flesh of birds and beasts.[23] For some time he lived entirely on fruits and became fruitarian. But it was in South Africa religious motive added a new dimension to his search because of his belief that passion in man "is generally co-existent with a hankering after the pleasures of the palate."[24] Some of his dietary and nature cure experiments were rooted in his physical needs. For a long time he was troubled with constipation and frequent headaches. At that time he was taking three meals besides afternoon tea every day. He gave up breakfast on reading a recommendation of 'No Breakfast Association of Manchester' as a result of which headache disappeared. This led him to conclude that he was eating more than his body needed. But his problem of constipation continued. On reading Just's book 'Return to Nature' he started taking fresh fruit and nuts besides applying a bandage of clean earth moistened with cold water on the abdomen at night. This had good results and he had less trouble for constipation.

On his return to India, the consciousness of the extreme poverty of the people of his country and the necessity of training Satyagrahis for the rigours of jail life added more objectives to his dietetics experiments. In short, these experiments had hygienic, spiritual and economic motives. For, throughout his life he was in search of a wholesome diet suitable to his own body as well as for his associates and the poor people of his country. He himself suffered from hookworms besides constipation and high blood pressure from time to time. Commitment to vegetarianism and abandonment of milk led him to alter his dietary articles frequently. He shifted from cow's milk to goat's milk only because of the need of his body. Throughout his life he was in search of a substitute for milk. He started living on fruits and nuts in pursuit of this objective. But he did not succeed. He tried cereals, and was anxious to take 'Jawar and Bajra' which was served to other prisoners as substitute of milk. But it did not suit his body. He tried soyabean but that too was not acceptable to his body. It was discovered later on that his stomach was good only for milk, dates and fruits. Addressing a meeting of Vegetarian Society in London in 1931, he confessed that he made experiments without number to give up milk but failed.[25] Later in his life he arrived at the conclusion that green leafy vegetables and the edible leaves of plants and fruits were more suitable for his body. Again to train his co-workers for a harder life as well as to obtain maximum food value from any article, he once made an experiment of taking uncooked food in his Ashram. But all the inmates had a bitter experience of this change. His devoted English follower Miss Slade was virtually on death's door because of her valiant continuance with this experiment.[26] He himself suffered while carrying on such experiments. He damaged most of his teeth while living on fruits and nut diet. Later on with a view to find cheap perfect diet for the poor in the country, he started taking 'neem' leaves and other non-poisonous leaves. He made marmalade from the skins of oranges. On learning the medicinal value of tamarind, he made sweet drink of it by adding 'gur' to it and made a concoction out of oil cakes by adding curd. The purpose was to reduce the cost of his own diet as he was feeling guilty that he was not able to bring down the cost of his diet to the level of the poor in the country.

Though the Mahatma was making all kinds of dietary experiments, he was not having a balanced diet because of lack of scientific knowledge of the calloric value of the articles he was taking. Once Birla noticed that his diet of honey and lemon in hot water followed by roasted ground almonds, dates in tomato juice was deficient in protein and fat while it was rich in vitamins, iron and lime. It could become a balanced diet if a pint of milk was added to it.[27] However, the Mahatma maintained scientific outlook by keeping his mind open. He once frankly stated that in his search after truth he had discarded many ideas and learnt new things "Old as I am in age, he added" I have no feeling that I have ceased to grow inwardly and that my growth will stop at the dissolution of the flesh."[28]

Though himself a stickler, he was no food faddist. For he wanted all the persons around him to take food to which their bodies were accustomed. He put his son Ramdas on unfertilized eggs as he was losing weight. Such eggs, in his view, were less objectionable than milk. Similarly, he advised his devoted lady follower to take coffee or tea if it was essential for her health.[29] He even suggested to a lady how tea was to be prepared in order to avoid its harmful effect. He suggested that tea leaves should be kept in a stainer and boiling water should be poured over it. Foreigners staying in the Ashram for a short while were served tea if thcy could not do without it. He encouraged a European friend to eat meat when he was ill.[30] For, discretion, in his view, is necessary in all such matters. He admitted that in the Boer War he himself served wine to the stone breakers in his corps and served 'bidis' to others.[31] Generosity to others, he argued, "is necessary as strictness with oneself." To the horror of many of his friends and followers he even suggested the eating of fish to those for whom it was their normal diet as a measure for overcoming food shortage in the country. So he argued that those "who have been habituated to eating meat from childhood and with whom meat eating has become a natural part of their diet, should give up the habit will be tantamount to committing violence upon them."[32] So when Dr. Syed Mahmud came to his Ashram as a sick person, he got chicken curry prepared for him.[33] His close friend Andrews used to take meat and he had no objection to it.[34] He was not opposed to providing non-vegetarian food to those who were accustomed to it even at the Congress session of 1938.[35]

Though himself not an expert dietitian, he valued the opinions of the experts on this subject. He agreed with the advice of some scientists of Bengal that mere calculations of vitamins and proteins should not be the only consideration for determining the quality of food. Rather biological experiment should determine the perfect food.[36] This opinion was given in reply to Gandhi's view that polished rice was not good for consumption as vitamin B would be removed in the polishing process.

On his return to India from South Africa in 1915, an enthusiast suggested to him saltless diet for the prevention of plague. In reply, he told him that he had made experiments with saltless diet for several years in South Africa. He claimed that by his own experience of saltless diet he could cure the hemorrhage of his wife in South Africa and he treated asthmatics and patients suffering from lung diseases with a saltless diet. Moreover his dietary experiments possibly of saltless diet had made his skin tender and delicate so much so that the soles of his feet were tough and hard in spite of walking bare foot.[37] However, he was ready to utilize his services both for plague research and for finding out the real value of salt as an article of human consumption "provided he had such a scientific mind as would refuse to swerve even by a hair's breadth from the path of truth."[38] Normally Gandhi used to seek the opinions of experts about the food value of any article of food before expressing his opinion on the subject. On learning that onions and garlic have some medicinal value, he included them in his dietary experiments. After making several experiments he arrived at the conclusion that cow's milk, fresh green vegetables including leaves of vegetables and fruits, onion, garlic, wheat or any other grain gur or unclarified sugar constituted perfect food. In fact, dietetics experiments were as important to him as any political action for the freedom of the country. Thus while the Congress leaders were busy in the elections of provincial assemblies in 1936-37, he was absorbed in experiments relating to the nutritional needs of the people in his country 'Four ozs. of wheat, two ozs of rice, so many ozs. of vegetables, these and other problems' fully occupied the time of India's most important leader,[39] wrote Rajagopalachari to Gandhi's son Devadas.

Gandhi's dietetic experiments were closely related to his fascination for nature cure. In a way this catered to his latent ambition of joining the medical profession which initially he could not do because of the sentiments of his parents and later on because of his commitment to non-violence as it could not be reconciled to the vivisection which learning of allopathic science involved. However, throughout his life he entertained great appreciation for allopathy because of its scientific approach to the subject. While explaining the superiority of allopathy over other systems such as Ayurveda, he said, "At present it commands enterprise, industry and knowledge. It is a developing science. It has many defects. Its pharmacopoeia is vast and yet very restricted. But it is systematic and so can draw upon whatever is special in Ayurveda."[40] His major complaint against the practitioners of ancient Indian system of medicine or Ayurveda was that their approach to the subject was not scientific. For, they did not test whatever was given in the ancient texts. However he revised his opinion about this subject after a discussion with the president of All India Vaidya Sammelan Dr. Lakshmipati in 1940-41 and found the Ayurveda system akin to nature cure system.[41] A proposal was mooted to open a research centre of Ayurveda. But it did not materialize. He was quite uncomfortable when he learnt that Patel was thinking of seeking Ayurvedic treatment for his ailment. For, their remedies, in his view "were like black magic— they are just a shot in the dark."[42] The reason was obvious. They lacked sufficient knowledge of human body which the allopathy doctors possessed. Gandhi asked a naturopath Dr. Sharma to acquire the knowledge of anatomy and physiology and recommended him to Dr. Ansari, an allopathy, to seek guidance on this subject and finally made arrangements for his studies on the subject in the United States.

Gandhi developed interest in nature cure quite early in his life. He started observing its principles from 1901. He not only applied nature cure treatment to himself whenever he suffered from any physical ailment, but also to his children and his wife even at great risk to their lives. He cured his wife of haemorrhage by hydropathic and dietetic treatment. But his mud plastic treatment when applied to six weeks baby of Mrs. Polak aggravated the condition of the baby. She tore the plaster off the body of the baby and the child recovered on receiving the warmth of the body of the mother.

Nature cure, for Gandhi, was relevant to his major objective in life, that is, to render service to the poor. It is not a drug cure. Rather it is a way of life. It lays greater emphasis on the prevention of the disease. So cleanliness of environment and simple and nutritious diet are its two remedies for avoiding any disease. For cleanliness, he followed the English definition of dirt, that is, "anything out of place is dirt." Explaining it, he aside "If urine reaches fields, it would make the soil yield gold. If it keeps puddled here and there it produces disease."[43] In other words, orderliness and neatness are its main characteristics.

In this system the physician has to depend upon earth, air, water and sun to overcome any ailment. Besides, Gandhi laid great emphasis on the recitation of the name of God or Ramnam as a Cure for the disease. In his view it was not merely faith healing. For, the recitation of the name of God with pure heart shows that one is filled with the presence of God within, and with this kind of consciousness one is free from all ailments, physical, mental or moral. Psychotherapists, he argues, can bear witness to the truth that recitation of name with faith can help a person to put up with suffering bravely.[44] But he recognized the limitation of the 'nam therapy'. "For where a surgical operation is needed, it cannot be avoided. 'Ramnam' cannot restore a leg that is cut off."[45] In fact, the main principle underlying nature cure is that most of our ailments are due to the violation of natural laws. This means that real road to health is returning to nature. For, Gandhi, it means conquest of animality, spiritual discipline and control of the palate. Faith in God helps in this process. Gandhi's view of nature cure goes beyond merely treating the disease of an individual. For nature cure, according to him, means teaching the hygiene of the body, mind and soul of the individual and society. A naturopathy physician has also to keep in view the social environment of the individuals suffering from a particular disease. So he advised his co-workers attending to the improvised hospital set up by him at the village of Uruli-Kanchan near Poona that in addition to cleaning the streets of the village and attending to their bodily ailments, they should also investigate the causes of poverty of the inhabitants there. Though he set up nature cure centre at Poona which was to be developed as a nature cure university, he later on changed his plans on realizing that he had committed a grievous mistake by setting up a centre in a city since the main objective of his nature cure was to serve the poor who were mostly living in the villages. So he shifted his nature cure activities to a village near Poona. He proposed to stay there at least four months in a year in order to treat the patients. On the first day there were thirty patients and their number increased to forty-three on the third day. He normally examined five to six patients in a day and the treatment that he recommended was sun bath, friction both, simple diet of milk, sour butter milk, fruit and fruit juices with plenty of clean water to drink. Though he had faith in the nature-cure treatment, he was fully aware that nature cure science was in a nascent stage of development. It required more research and knowledge as the contemporary state of this science was choatic because of the narrow view of nature cure physicians as each one of them considered himself an authority and did not care to develop it. He himself had his own view of nature cure treatment. But he never tried to impose his view on other nature cure doctors some of whom depended upon him for financial support. He had differences with doctor Dinshaw Wacha who was incharge of the nature cure hospital at Poona which was set up with former's support. But he never interfered in his treatment. He even learnt that beef was served there. But he did not object to it. Similarly, he could not endorse Dr. Dinshaw's view about vaccination.[46] Though firm, he was not obsinate. For, without firmness, in his view, one cannot pursue truth.

Nevertheless, the Mahatma's views and actions do not always bear scientific outlook. It is not even possible for any person howsoever great who is deeply involved in seeking solutions of social problems to work out his solutions with a detached mind. His strong commitments to certain ideals, imperfect knowledge of some subjects on which he was called upon to express his views, his faith in the indwelling of God in man, the superiority of spirit over matter, his religious pursuits, the rush of work and his involvement in several fields of social reconstruction made a dent into his scientific approach. He could not justify his observations about Bihar earthquake on rational grounds. At that time he was in the thick of a battle against untouchability and the opposition that he received from the orthodox sections of the Hindu society for this noble task made him look to divine authority for support. For, he believed that there was some divine purpose behind every physical calamity. However, he admitted while commenting on Quetta earthquake "that perfected science may tell us before hand when it will occur and it will be a triumph of human mind."[47] To a great extent he is right that such triumphs cannot bring about purification of self. To attain it what man requires is spiritual and moral uplift. Similarly, it looks that in his preference for cow milk over buffalo milk, the hold of tradition and sentiments had taken precedence over him though he tried to justify his preference for cow milk on rational grounds. Likewise his opposition to vaccination for the prevention of small pox cannot be explained on rational grounds. For he considered vaccination as a filthy process which is little short of taking beef."[48]

Some of his observations made in the 'Hind Swaraj' are viewed in some quarters as an indictment against the progress of science. It looks that in order to push his arguments into the mind of his opponent he brushed aside several good aspects of modern western civilization. He was stating his case like a lawyer who would either brush aside or understate the arguments of the other side. Most of the arguments in the 'Hind Swaraj' were the record of his discussion with his friend and benefactor in England Dr. Mehta who failed to appreciate the strange outburst of a youngman against western civilization who had his higher education in England which was considered as the centre of modern civilization. However with experience Gandhi realized that his language in the 'Hind Swaraj' did not communicate his real view about the western civilization. Possibly he was identifying the modern civilization with capitalism and whatever dark spots he found in it could be attributed to capitalism. Once he told Jawaharlal Nehru who could not appreciate his views expressed in 'Hind Swaraj' that the "sum and substance of what I want to say is that the individual person should have control over the things that are necessary for the sustenance of life. If he cannot have such a control the individual cannot survive. Ultimately the world is made of individuals. If there were no drops there would be no ocean."[49]

The Mahatma's reliance on inner voice or the little voice within, the call of God from within, at certain moments for taking crucial decisions especially for undertaking fasts, appeared to many including his close friends as an attitude contrary to rational approach to life. Though at the time of taking such decisions he did not take recourse to reason nor did he make out his case on rational grounds, he later on pointed out that all such decisions were affirmed by his reasons, too. He admitted that he was moved by intuition but intuition in his view was not opposed to reason. According to Radhakrishnan intuition supplemented reason and did not supplant it. "In moving from intellect to intuition, he observes" we are not moving in the direction of unreason but getting into the deepest rationality of which human nature is capable. "When the Mahatma was confronted with a situation that challenged his basic values, the main purport of his life and struggle, he put his whole being against that challenge. Reason could not fathom the intensity of his commitment and so he refused to listen to the arguments of his friends against his decision which to him was the call of the spirit, though his mind or intellect was not lying dormant in the process of taking that decision. It is science that makes us believe that no man can be cent per cent scientific in his behaviour always. For, in the process of his development several impressions and emanations following from his cultural heritage, family traits and environment accumulate on his mind that determine his behaviour for which he has no scientific explanation. That behaviour becomes a part of his nature. Once in the Yeravada jail Patel complained to Gandhi thus: "You keep putting forward proposals frequently without ever consulting your colleagues—At times this habit of yours makes their position extremely awkward." Bupu (Gandhi) Do you think I behave in this way deliberately.—There is no remedy for my nature.[50]

NOTES AND REFERENCES

1. C.W., LXII, pp. 387-88.
2. *Ibid.*
3. Nayyar, Sushila, The Last Imprisonment, *op. cit.*, p. 122.
4. *Ibid.*, LXIV, p. 398.
5. *Ibid.*, XLI, p. 436.
6. *Ibid.*, L, p. 2.
7. *Ibid.*, LXXXIII, p. 305.
8. Radhakrishnan (ed.), Mahatma Gandhi—100 years (Gandhi Peace Foundation, 1968), p. 153.
9. C.W., LXIV, p. 6.
10. *Ibid.*, LI, p. 113.
11. *Ibid.*, LIV, p. 235.
12. *Ibid.*, p. 236.
13. *Ibid.*, LXXIV.
14. *Ibid.*, LXXXII, p. 368.
15. *Ibid.*,
16. *Ibid.*, LXI, p. 166.
17. *Ibid.*, LIII, pp. 214-15.
18. *Ibid.*, LXIII, pp. 255-56.
19. Sinha, Balwant, Under the Shelter of Bapu, p. 119.
20. Jehangir and Sykes. *op. cit,*, p. 139.
21. *Ibid.*, p. 138.
22. *Ibid.*, p. 114.
23. Gandhi, M.K., Autobiography, p. 49.
24. *Ibid.*
25. C.W., XLVIII, p. 328.
26. *Ibid.*, LV, p. 231.
27. Ross, Alan, The Emissary-G.D. Birla (London: Collins Harvill, 1986), p. 78.
28. C.W., LV, pp. 60-61.
29. *Ibid.*, LIX, p. 200.
30. *Ibid.*, LXIII, p. 379.
31. *Ibid.*
32. Chaudhary, Ramnarayan, Bapu As I saw Him (Navajivan Publishing House 1954), pp. 146-47.
33. *Ibid.*, p. 147.
34. C.W., LXVI, p. 132.
35. *Ibid.*, p. 207.
36. *Ibid.*, LX, pp. 311-12.
37. Desai, M., *op. cit.*, Vol. I, p. 14.

38. C.W., XIV, pp. 171-72.
39. Gandhi, Rajmohan, Rajaji's Story, p. 274.
40. C.W., Vol. LXXVI, p. 202.
41. Chaudhary Ramnarayan, *op. cit.*, pp. 166-67.
42. C.W., LXI, p. 184.
43. Chaudhary, *op. cit.*, p. 45.
44. C.W., Vol. LXXXIV, p. 24.
45. *Ibid.*, p. 237.
46. *Ibid.*, Vol. LXXXII, p. 350.
47. *Ibid.*, LXI, p. 135.
48. Gandhi, M.K., Essence of Hinduism, p. 96. year 12.3.30, p. 95.
49. C.W., LXXXI, p. 314.
50. Collected Works of Patel, Vol. IV, p. 276.

22

Aesthetics of an Ascetic

The Mahatma's great stress on self-restraint and puritanic and religious outlook may leave the impression that he was a man without emotions or of a lighter side of life. But as Nehru noticed that people "who did not know Gandhiji's personally and had only read his writings were apt to think that he was a priestly type. But he was the very opposite of the calvinist priestly type. His smile was delightful, his laughter infectious and he radiated light heartedness."[1] Humour was natural to him. Once he told an interviewer that if he had not the gift of humour he might have committed suicide or something to this effect."[2] He would laugh away if any of his co-workers teased him for his strange habits. His close workers could make fun of him for his dietary experiments. Sarojini Naidu could amuse his co-workers by her remark "If only Gandhiji knew how much it costs to keep him in poverty." His experiment with neem leaves and other non-poisonous leaves as an item of cheap and healthy food invited a banter from Patel who addressing Kumarappa said, "You see—Bapur started with drinking goat's milk and how he has come to goat's food."[3] He would laugh away his anger or annoyance by a witty remark. While going to Vinayashram in Andhra he felt uncomfortable when his car was climbing and descending little mounds and diches. But he removed the embarrassment of his host by a humorous remark, "well this is a fine macadamized road. Going over it will improve any body's digestion."[4] His sense of humour did not spare his own self. Once an artist presented him with his portrait. He looked at it and inquired "But who is this monstrosity please?" The artist said 'yourself sir.'[5] At another place, he got another caricature of himself and he said, "Is this a goat? A co-worker remarked 'it has the ears of one'. Then this is a goat man or a man-goat."[6] Some times he would enjoy a humorous rapartee from a friend. Andrews addressed Gandhi by his Christian name Mohan and Gandhi addressed him as Charlie. Once on a visit to Sevagram, he was wearing a long kurta's with upper butten open and a 'dhoti' with wide black border. The person who went to receive him told Bapur that Andrew was wearing a 'sari'. When he appeared before Gandhi, the latter remarked 'Why is this make-up to-day' Bewildered Andrews said' Why, what has happened, Gandhi said such 'dhotis' are worn by women. Andrews gave a saucy reply "Because I was coming to my Mohan."[7] Once an artist pleaded for a short sitting, Gandhi asked "But can you make an ugly man beautiful."[8]

The Mahatma, in fact, was not a 'dreadful' and dry old man. In his own words he was a very jolly fellow. Once he told a lady devotee of the Ashram that he had interest in art but he had to renounce many such interests in his search for truth and his endeavour to dedicate all his faculties to the service of humanity.[9] Another time he disclosed that if he had not taken the vow of Satyagraha for the deliverance of his country he would probably have occupied himself only with songs.[10] For, he considered art as an essential aspect of human life as it distinguishes man from the beast and elevates the human spirit.[11] He had reverence for beautiful things of the earth, of its flowers, plants, etc. How deeply it pains me "he would say that people should pluck masses of delicate blossoms to fling in my face or hand or around my neck." He protested when a friend brought in a handful of babul leaves after dark to clean his carding bow. "Look all these are folded up, asleep, he said, trees need sleep as we."[12] He himself enjoyed the beauty of nature "No drama, he wrote" while watching the constellations in the sky at night, "composed or acted by human beings can ever equal the great spectacle which nature has arranged for us on the stage of the sky." Thus whenever his mind was free from political and social problems, the poet in him would come forth and he would enjoy watching the beauty of nature. While at Almora where he had gone for rest, he enjoyed watching the beauty of Himalayan peaks wrapped in snow. But beauty, for him, lies in the eyes of the beholder. He told Agatha Harrison, who suggested that people should grow flowers, that beauty is also in vegetables. He opposed the current view that beautiful need not be useful." Rather, in his view, "what is useful is beautiful."[13] For that matter "art is skill in work". For him, beauty lies in purity, the purity of environment, in cleanliness. His ideal village is beautiful because it is free from dirt disease and poverty. "The dazzling light of inner purity, 'according to him', outshines the outward ugliness." In a discussion with Ramchandran in 1924, he laid stress on the true purpose of art, "All true art 'he affirmed' must help the soul to realize its inner self."

The concern of aesthetics is with all fine arts, that is, music, poetry, drama, painting, sculpture, architecture, dance, literature. The young Mohan had ears for music, though in England as a student initially he could not follow the piano and failed to keep time. If he could not continue his lessons in violin, it was not because of lack of sensibility to music. But because of his awareness of the purpose for which he had come to London.[14] Once he told a friend that Bengali music had great charm for him. For it had "a most soothing effect upon his nerves which were otherwise always on trial." He felt enraptured on watching the play of Tagore 'The Post Office' performed by the poet himself and his party in January 1918.[15] Similarly while he was convalescing in the hospital after the operation of appendicitis, the Bhajans sung by Dilip Kumar Roy not only thrilled him but also removed some of the misconceptions about him in the mind of the singer who had pictured him as a dry saint who was positively against music. Stung by this impression, the Mahatma exclaimed, 'well, I know, I know', "he added resignedly, there are so many superstitions rife about me."[16] When the singer put the whole blame of all such superstitions on his asceticism, he asserted that he considered asceticism as the greatest of all arts.[17] India's religious life, he believed, was inextricably related to music.[18] He liked melodious recitation of the Gita. In the Ashram, an arrangement was made for the singing of Bhajan with the accompaniment of musical instruments. A trained musician, a pupil of Pandit Vishnu Digambar made the singing of religious hymns in the Ashram fascinating. He endorsed the view of Pandit Khare of Gandharva Mahavidyalya that music was a sort of tranquilizer as it helped him in overcoming anger.[19] He, therefore, wanted that music of all lands be blended. Commenting on the music that he heard in the Santiniketan, he observed that it was charming. But at the same time advised that the professor of music should not confine himself to the Bengali music. Rather both Hindustani and western music which had made immense strides should have place in the Santiniketan. In a discussion with Romain Rolland on the subject of music in 1931, the latter noticed that the Mahatma had sufficient knowledge of Indian music. To him (Gandhi) there was music in life, music in the march of the soldiers or of walk which should also be studied. He developed taste for western music with the passage of time, though earlier it bored him.

The Mahatma was not devoid of interest in drama and poetry. He liked Shakespear's plays and he used to attend the Lyceum while he was in England. If he could not attend theaters in London during the Round Table Conference in 1931, it was only because of lack of time.[20] In the Agha Khan palace prison, he renewed his interest in the plays of Shakespeare. He appears to be familiar with the language and the characters of some of the plays of Shakespeare. He wound up his lecture in June 1891 to a meeting of the members of the Society for the prevention of cruelty to animals in London with a quotation from Shakespeare.[21] Expounding his view about the historicity of the Mahabharata, he stated that the characters of the Mahabharata, like Krishna and Pandavas, might be historical like Caesar or Henry of the Shakespeare's plays, but not the story of the Mahabharata could be conceived as historical like Shakespeare's plays.[22] He compared some of the characters of the plays of Gujarati writer Manilal Nabhubhai with Shakespeare's Richard III and Macbeth. Again Shakespeare's counsel to a character in Hamlet echoes in his advice to a correspondent in a slightly different language "Give thy ear to every one, thy voice to none."[23]

Though he did not write any drama, he rejoiced in creating a dramatic situation before launching a political and social movement to create a powerful effect on the participants, symathisers and even his opponents. At the Amritsar Congress where the topmost leaders such as Tilak and C.R. Das were arrayed against him, he threw his cap before Tilak for the acceptance of the compromise. It was a dramatic act and Tilak succumbed to it. The Mahatma's decision to observe twenty-one day fast in the house of Mohammed Ali—a Muslim to make an appeal to the hearts of Hindus and Muslims to refrain from flying at each other's throat had the ingredients of a drama. It was a move to keep the eyes of both Hindus and Muslims on an act of sacrifice by a Hindu in the house of a Muslim. Again when the voluntary registration of certificates by the Indians in Transvaal as a result of Gandhi-Smuts Pact did not produce any favourable result his plan of mass burning of the certificates generated great enthusiasm among the Indians present there. It was a master stroke to quicken the flagging zeal of the Indians in a foreign country. Similarly, the burning of the foreign clothes as a joint venture on July 31, 1921 under the non-co-operation movement had the same effect on the participants and the spectators. When Gandhi lighted the fire a sort of frenzy seized the whole crown. Again the whole episode of Dandi March was a drama enacted for 24 days which stirred the people all over India and kept the eyes of Viceroy and the British administration in India and the statesmen in England fixed on his deeds and programmes.

Poetry, too, fascinated him. Possibly Arnold's translation of the Gita attracted him because of its rhythmic music. Sometimes he would write a charming letter in a poetic language. A letter written to Mrs. M.H. Morrison of the Green Cross Society for protection of wild life and nature echoes Wordswoth's expression, "That there is spirit in the wood."[24] In a letter to a poet friend once he wrote that he would "come over to Mahabaleshwar just to hear his poem."[25] Dance and music communicated to him a disposition to create sweetness in life or to create sweetness in whatever one does." In 1915, he told Kalelkar, "If I have given up anything for national service, it is my interest in English literature. Renouncing wealth and career was no sacrifice.

Religious paintings and architecture, too, captivated him. He showed his interest in Indian architecture, the design and beauty of Taj Mahal and the paintings of Ajanta in a short article in 1893 in the Indian Opinion. But underlying his interest was his patriotism. His object was only to tell his South African readers both European and Indian that India, as was often believed in South Africa, was not a place dotted merely with huts inhabited by savages. "Indian rulers like enlightened potentate of Mysore were encouraging Indian art."[26] On his return from London after attending the RTC he visited the famous Cathedral in Rome and enjoyed seeing the paintings and sculptures. The sculpture of Jesus on the Cross attracted him most. But he expressed his inability to give his opinion on these works of art as he stayed there hardly for two hours. For, their right appreciation according to him, required two to three months attentive and serious study.[27]

The purpose of an artist is communication or 'infecting' other people with his or her feelings through lines, colours, music or poetry. But Gandhi could create this kind of effect through his prose full of metaphors such as cow as the 'poem of pity' or India is 'a house on fire.'

Nevertheless, his view of art transcended the current concept of art. For, him, even search for truth comes under the domain of art. To him, 'ascetism is the greatest of all arts' and for that matter the practice of Yoga is an art. Possibly he was thinking that any rhythmic movement demanded control over the body, self-restraint or even self-abnigation. A musician or a singer has to discipline himself before he acquires proficiency in his art. It is not merely an outburst of emotions. Rather it is an effort to bring forth certain aspects of reality or truth. A seeker of truth has a vision of beauty. So he observed, I see and find beauty in truth or through truth. All truth, not merely true ideas but truthful faces, truthful pictures, or songs are highly beautiful. People generally fail to see beauty in truth, the ordinary man runs away from it and becomes blind to the beauty in it.[28]

But the Mahatma in Gandhi opposed the theory 'art for art's sake'. For he firmly believed that like religion the purpose of art is moral and spiritual elevation of the individual. Art, in his view, has a place in life to the extent that it promotes harmony in individual and society. Commenting on K.M. Munshi's presidential address to the Hindi Sahitya Sammelan in 1945, he said, 'It has always seemed to me a terrible thought that the 'end of art is for it to be made interesting'. Leaving aside debauchary, even hypocrisy, violence and untruth can easily be made interesting. Would such writing be called art.[29] To cultivate art for art's sake from his point of view "is a lamentable aberration of the human mind."[30] Rather art is an ally of religion "in as much as the fundamental experience in both of them 'belongs to the domain of man's relationship' with God."[31] It is an instrument for understanding the works of God. The Mahatma was not alone in making a demand upon the artist to make his art as an instrument for the service of society. The French Socialist Sociologists of the nineteenth century worked out a theory that the artist has a social responsibility. Saint-Simon, Aguste Comte, Charles Fourier and Proudhon attacked the idea that art can be an end in itself. In England John Ruskin and William Morris held similar views. They insisted on the social conditions and effects on art on society. Morris argued in his "Art and Socialism" that radical changes were needed in the social and economic order to make art what it should be. Leo Tolstoy in his essay 'What is Art'? asked whether all the social costs of art could be rationally justified. Great art, in his view, is that which transmits either simple feelings, drawing men together for the feeling of brotherhood.[32] In other words, the purpose of art is to serve mankind. As a man of the masses, the Mahatma looked upon that art merely as self-indulgence in which "the masses cannot participate, whether it concerns the voice or clothes or stone."[33] He is echoing Tolstoy's view that unless the emotion that transmits is shared by men in general, it is no art or it is pseudo art. Good art is not a preserve of a few.

Great art is for the good of all. So for Gandhi, a large number of persons singing Ramdhun in unison is art, which ought to be cultivated.[34] Once he admonished his grand niece Manu who had been devotedly attending on him during the last and difficult days of his life, for being out of tune while singing a bhajan and taking lightly of the misconduct at the prayer meeting in Delhi. He felt like weeping at her conduct. So he asked Manu to make a public apology of the misconduct which he himself drafted.[35] He told Dilip Kumar Roy that art "is acceptable to him only to the extent that it tends to the welfare of the people at large." For his aim of life "is ever and always that of public weal."[36] He, therefore, admired the artists of the olden days for having lavished their art on the walls of temples and caves and thus making their creation unreservedly open to the public especially to the poor who "can resort to these placers and get all the enjoyment and inspiration they want."[37] In the same vein he said at the meeting of Gujarat Sahitya Parishad "I want art and literature that can speak to the millions." "Real work of art 'he added,' should appeal to all. It must be joy for all." From this point of view that literature is 'a miserable affair if it cannot raise the life of the common people living in the villages to a higher level'.[38] Thus to him art is a means for ameliorating the condition of the people. It is not merely the affaïr of the elite. The Mahatma was exploring the art of right living, not for a few but for all. Keeping villages free from dirt, disciplined personal life and transparent honesty in individuals, and relation with others, are the attributes of art.

However, Gandhi's great western admirer and friend Romain Rolland who was well known in Europe for his devotion to music and literature observed that "Gandhi's view of art stopped in the middle of his artistic profession of faith." For while admiring the beauty of nature, he should have said, "Let man be an artist like her. He, too, should create beautiful harmonic relationships with lines, colours, sound and thoughts. His conception seems to remain passive in face of Nature or the divine principle hidden in her, which alone is active and creative. If God is in each of us, then we should seek within our means to be in the image of the Master of Beauty."[39]

Romain Rolland could not conceive God or truth without joy and for him it was in art and beauty one could find that joy. In his view "great art has harmony as its essence and it brings peace, health and equilibrium to the soul. Beauty manifests itself in many ways and there is hidden harmony in it which is in essence moral. It was on this issue the Nobel Laureate found himself in opposition to Tolstoy[40] in spite of his great admiration for him and possibly to the Mahatma, too.

Notes and References

1. Nehru, J.L., An Autobiography, *op. cit.*, p. 515.
2. Nehru, *op. cit.*, p. 207.
3. Shukla, Incidents of Gandhi's life.
4. Malkani, N.R., *op. cit.*, p. 54.

5. *Ibid.*
6. *Ibid.*
7. *Ibid.*
8. Chaudhary, *op. cit.*, p. 169.
9. Malkani, *op. cit.*, p. 56.
10. C.W., Vol. XLIX, p. 37.
11. Quoted in Martin Green, The Challenge of the Mahatmas (Basic Books Publishers, New York, 1978), p. 181.
12. Marjoie Sykes, *op. cit.*, p. 60.
13. CW., Vol. LXXXIII, p. 257.
14. Gandhi, M.K., Autobiography, p. 44.
15. Desai, M., *op. cit.*, Vol. I, p. 8.
16. *Ibid.*, Vol. IV, p. 27.
17. *Ibid.*
18. *Ibid.*
19. *Ibid.*, LXVI, p. 121.
20. *Ibid.*, XL VIII, p. 2.
21. *Ibid.*, Vol. I, p. 216.
22. *Ibid.*, XLV, p. 95.
23. Desai, M., Vol. I, p. 216.
24. C.W., LXXXI, p. 433.
25. *Ibid.*
26. *Ibid.*, Vol. III, p. 447.
27. *Ibid.*, XLIX, p. 37.
28. *Ibid.*, Vol. XV, p. 249.
29. *Ibid.*, LXXXII, p. 9.
30. *Ibid.*, XLVIII.
31. *Ibid.*
32. Encyclopaedia of Philosophy, Vol. I, pp. 30-31.
33. C.W., Vol. XLV, p. 7.
34. *Ibid.*
35. *Ibid.*, LXXXIX, pp. 211-12.
36. Desai, M., *op. cit.*, Vol. IV, p. 287.
37. *Ibid.*
38. Romain Rolland, Gandhi's Correspondence, p. 23.
39. *Ibid.*, p. 208.

23

From World War to Gandhi-Jinnah Talks

The outbreak of the war on 1st September, 1939 after the invasion of Poland by Germany, put the Congress in a predicament; for, it could either support the war efforts because of the non-committal attitude of England about the Indian demand for independence nor could impede them as that policy would have been construed as a support to an aggressor who had no regard for democracy. Thus, the constitutional experiment which the Congress had begun in July 1937 came to an abrupt end as the Congress ministries in the provinces resigned to get out of this dilemmatic situation. The Mahatma, too, was placed in a quandary. For, his commitment to non-violence prevented him from giving any active and material support to Britain with which he had sympathies. Nor could he sit still and watch this diabolical drama calmly. For, he viewed Hitler as an aggressor. Even before the outbreak of the war he had written a letter to Hitler appealing to him to abstain from a situation that "may reduce humanity to the savage state". But this letter was not forwarded to the addressee by the British authorities. So he advised the Congress to give moral support to the Allies in the war. This was the only practical solution to the ticklish problem which the Congress and the Mahatma faced. For, the material support was already at the disposal of the Government while the moral support could make a material difference in the prosecution of war as "it will lift the Allied cause to a high moral plane." In his interview with the Viceroy on 4th September, Gandhi was unusually sentimental on visualising the possible destruction of London. He, thus, wrote, "As visible between Gandhi and several Congress leaders including Rajagopalachari, Nehru, Patel, etc. over the question of starting a movement against the British. But the Mahatma remained undisturbed. When Rajagopalachari moved the alternative resolution to that of Gandhi in the working committee meeting offering to the Government co-operation in war efforts abandoning any commitment to non-violence, the latter in place of dissuading the former encouraged him to follow his course. Explaining his reaction to this resolution which had the support of Nehru and Patel, he said, "It was in my power to stop him from seceding from me. But it did not seem to be proper to do so. And it would have been morally wrong to strive with Rajaji in what he firmly regarded as his clear duty."[6] Possibly as a good strategist, the Mahatma allowed the Congress leadership to try any other course for winning Swaraj knowing fully well that the British would not accept the demands of the Congress at that time. This policy did yield good results as the Congress leadership after their failure to carry the British statesmen with them, moved into the arms of the Mahatma without questioning his authority to carry on the struggle against the Government in the light of his own assessment of the situation. He outlined a new strategy to meet the demands of various sections in the country and the needs of the hour. The younger elements in the Congress were pressing for an aggressive action against the British. But several other leaders in the country were against obstructing the British war efforts as it would be construed as assisting the Nazis who were represented as anti-democratic. So any move for mass Satyagraha did not appear to be desirable or feasible. The Mahatma himself had declared several times that India did not seek "independence out of British ruin." So his objective at that time was to offer only a token protest without seriously hindering the war efforts. Initially he thought of embarking on 'limited or unlimited fast' in order to prick the conscience of the British people and to focus the world opinion on the problem of Indian independence. But he abandoned the idea on the unanimous decision of the CWC against it. Even after the arrest of Vinoba who inaugurated the Individual Satyagraha the idea of going on fast again griped his mind about which he wrote to the Viceroy. But he was dissuaded by the CWC from taking any such action.[7]

The issue underlying his Satyagraha at that time was limited to the demand for carrying on anti-war propaganda and preaching non-co-operation with the government in their war efforts. In order to avoid mass excitement volunteers were instructed to offer Satyagraha singly and not in groups by simply raising anti-war slogans or by delivering an anti-war speech. Demonstrations and public meetings had to be avoided. Only persons having faith in non-violence and constructive programme were eligible for offering Satyagraha. They were to seek Gandhi's permission before offering Satyagraha. Instructions were issued and fresh restrictions were imposed from time to time by Gandhi to keep the movement on the right track. Significantly the movement was inaugurated by Vinoba Bhave, a member of Gandhi's Ashram engaged in constructive programme and known in Gandhian circle for his faith in Gandhian ideals but practically unknown in the political circles of the country, by his speech protesting against the British policy of dragging India into the war. By selecting Vinoba, the Mahatma communicated to all Congress workers that the real test for joining his non-violent army was faith in his ideals and programmes, especially Hindu-Muslim unity eradication of untouchability, promotion of Khadi. Vinoba was to be followed by J.L. Nehru on November 7, after giving due notice to the authorities. But he was arrested a week in advance and was sentenced to four years imprisonment for speeches delivered early in October. The progress of the movement was so designed as to remain under the control of its author. In the first stage only very select persons were to offer Satyagraha. It could be described as representative Satyagraha and it lasted till the end of the year. Under this category important leaders such as the president of the Congress Abul Kalam Azad, Rajendra Prasad, Kriplani, were arrested. The second stage was planned to begin about January 5, 1941, after the expiry of Christmas truce unilaterly proclaimed by Gandhi. It was supposed to last about three months. The third stage began early in April and continued until the movement came to a virtual end with the release of the Satyagrahis in December 1941.

The movement appeared to be ineffective as it only hardened the attitude of the Government. It did not create any mass resurgence as against the effect of earlier Satyagrahas. However, its planner could argue that it was not the aim of the movement this time. Such arguments cut no ice with his critics. But he stood his ground. For he was sure that it served the purpose for which it was started. To a correspondent of a daily he said that it was not started to create an appreciable impression upon the war efforts. It was only a moral protest against the conduct of the war in the name of free people. Once Tottenham, Viceroy's secretary, asked Gandhi's secretary Desai, who used to meet Viceroy's secretaries while Individual Satyagraha was in progress, as to what the Mahatma gained by his limited individual Satyagraha. The latter replied self-satisfaction, that is, it was a gesture of protest against being dragged into the war against our will.''[8]

However, its major gain was that it made the position of the British uncomfortable in the United States as it made it clear that India was not happy with the British policy of dragging India into war.[9] The policy of non-embarrassment, Gandhi reiterated, was logical consequence of non-violence and in that way a political necessity.[10]

But there was no doubt that a large number of his followers were crest fallen because of the failure of the movement to produce any tangible results. He tried to raise their spirits by arguing that in the scheme there "is no scope of miracles, for, Ahimsa does not admit of sudden spurts. But those who will, can always see the miracles of Ahimsa. We watch the sky every day but we see no miracles there. But those who have an eye for it are spell bound by the spectacle. They see new miracles every moment."[11] But such arguments did not produce the desired results. Rather some of his close associates felt that he was unnecessarily becoming argumentative and recapitulating his experiences of Satyagraha in South Africa only to reassure himself the efficacy of new technique of fighting an opponent. But to the Mahatma it was not true. "My past experiences, 'he told a faithful lady follower,' are no valid arguments. They may give me strength but as arguments their value is limited."[12]

The release of the prisoners created an unpleasant and poignant situation for the Congress. For, most of the leaders had become disillusioned with its policy because of Gandhi's strict adherence to non-violence loaded with meanings which were not comprehensible to them. Change of policy appeared to be the need of the hour. But any change without the consent of Gandhi could lead to a split in the Congress; for, very few could muster enough strength and courage to oppose him in his experiments with non-violence despite their lack of faith in it. But the Mahatma on reading the minds of his co-workers saved them from embarrassment by encouraging them to consider the change of the policy in accordance with the call of their conscience. Addressing the members of the A.I.C.C., he said, "I do not want it to be said that in order to retain my leadership, you bade good-bye to your senses because you had no courage to give me up."[13] He also asked the CWC to relieve him of the leadership and responsibility for pursuing his non-violent course to which the CWC agreed at its meeting at Bardoli in the last week of December 1941 and reiterated its earlier decision that only free India "can be in a position to undertaking the defence of the country on a national basis." This implied that the Congress was ready to assist the British in the war efforts provided India was granted full freedom. This meant giving up non-violence which was not acceptable to Gandhi. But he would not like to divide the Congress on this issue.

There was some talk of resumption of parliamentary activity by some Congress leaders to ease the situation. But it could not be pursued because of absence of response from the Government. All the eyes were now riveted on international situation that had brought the war at the doorsteps of India. The entry of Japan on the side of Axis powers and its spectacular victories in South-East Asia against the Allies had not only raised its prestige as a military power but had threatened the invasion of India as was evident from the fall of Rangoon and Andaman. The gravity of the situation compelled England to send Cripps to settle the Indian question. He stayed in India about two weeks during which all eyes were fixed on his negotiations with Indian leaders. But his mission did not evoke any hope in Gandhi. However, on his persuasion, he came to Delhi and met him on 25 March 1942. On seeing the draft that Cripps had brought, he rejected it summarily as it involved the possibility of the dismemberment of the country and the participation of India in war without any immediate significant change in the structure of the Indian Government. It contemplated the splitting up of India into three parts each having a different idea of government. It envisaged Pakistan and yet not the Pakistan of Muslim League conception. So he left for Sevagram leaving the CWC to make up its own mind. The CWC rejected the proposals but certainly not for its adherence to Gandhi's view of non-violence as Cripps tried to make the Allies believe. For, a number of times since the outbreak of the war most of the top leaders of the Congress had given out that their commitment to non-violence could not take precedence over their goal of independence. However, the failure of the Cripps mission widened the breach between the Congress and the Government. It placed the leadership in a very difficult situation. They had not only to mobilize the country for resisting the threatened Japanese invasion but also to wrest freedom from the unwilling powerful foreign government without which resistance to Japanese was not possible. Gandhi, therefore, insisted on the orderly withdrawal of the British from India. This, he argued, was not only in the interest of India but was also for the good of the British and the Allies since this, in his view, was the only way whereby they could avoid the repetition of the situation of humiliating withdrawal from Singapore, Malaya and Burma. So he told the Chinese leader Chiang-Kai-Shek in a letter that only free India could help the British in war.[14] On his visit to India in February 1942, the Generalissimo and his wife were very anxious to meet Gandhi at Wardha.

The proposed visit upset the Viceroy Lord Linlithgow, the Secretary of State Amery and the Prime Minister Churchill. The Viceroy even told Amery that for good political reasons he could not tolerate this kind of visit and was ready to prevent it even at the risk of offending the Chinese leader. For, he believed that the Chinese leader to go to Wardha to meet Gandhi would not only raise the stature of the Mahatma in the international sphere but would also create the impression that in India there was another centre of power different from that of the British or rival headquarters of authority.[15] However, the Secretary of State, the Viceroy and the Prime Minister did not object to Chiang-Kai-shek meeting Gandhi at Santiniketan where he had gone to see Tagore's centre of education since before this meeting the Chinese leader had met Jinnah.[16]

The advance of the Japanese had compelled Gandhi to think of starting a powerful mass movement to force the British to leave India. But the odds this time for launching an all-India movement were great as the majority of the Muslims had not sympathy with the Congress because of the propaganda of the League that the Congress was a Hindu body aiming at Hindu raj and eminent Congress leaders had showed scant regard for Gandhi's policies. Moreover, the atmosphere was favourable for the eruption of violence in the country because of the policies of the government. In a way the country was heading towards anarchy. So the need of the hour was a strong mass movement for bringing together all sections of the Congress on a common platform. It was the only way to raise the spirits of his colleagues in the Congress who had been overcome by a sense of helplessness and despair as well as to knit the various threads of thought in the Congress. The differences were sometimes so acute that it appeared that there were two organizations in the Congress, one siding with Gandhi and the other opposing him. Moreover, in his view, there was no other way of controlling the pent up violent feelings of the people. "The people' he observed," do not have any Ahimsa. And, therefore, I have to take a risk, if I cannot control their violence. I cannot remain inactive. I will prefer anarchy to the present system of administration because the ordered anarchy is worse than real anarchy."

The Congress again rallied round him to launch a vigorous attack on British imperialism in spite of several risks and dangers. His draft outlining his programme of the movement was sent to the Congress Working Committee meeting at Allahabad through Mira (Miss Slade). It had the following points:

(i) A demand to the British to withdraw from India.
(ii) India was a zone of war because of British imperialism.
(iii) After the withdrawal of the British Japan would not invade India as India had no quarrel with Japan and so India could have peaceful relations with Japan.
(iv) If Japan did not agree with peaceful relations with India and invaded India, she would resist with non-violent non-co-operation.
(v) India did not need foreign troops.

The draft was debated for hours as members expressed conflicting views. Nehru felt that if Bapu's approach was accepted we would become passive partners of the Axis powers. For, even if Japanese offered civil administration to the Indians, they would demand certain strategic advantages for the purpose of war which would make India as the theatre of war. Rajagopalachari and Bholabhai Desai generally took Nehru's view. Rajagopalachari also felt that at the back of Bapu's mind was the impression that Japan and Germany would win. Rajendra Prasad and Patel endorsed Gandhi's view. The president then asked Nehru to prepare his own draft in the light of discussion in order to have unanimous view. This draft was finally accepted by CWC. In the final draft only that part was omitted which could be interpreted that India would be passive spectator or passive partner of Axis powers.[17] The document of discussion was sent by Sir M. Hallett to the Viceroy which he found in the course of a search of the office of Congress at Allahabad. To the Viceroy and the various British statesmen it was an important document showing various strains inside the Congress. But that could not help the authorities as Gandhi had so much influence in the country that he could launch any movement alone.[18]

However, the Government was in no mood to listen to Gandhi or the Congress. For its attitude had hardened under the impression that the Congress movement had fizzled out. In fact, Gandhi's policy of non-embarrassment and symbolic Satyagraha had left the impression of the weakness of the Congress in the Government circles against Gandhi's calculation that it would win for the Congress goodwill of the Allies and the general public in England and America. Thus Linlithgow reported to Amery in May 1942, "We have reduced them (Congress) to pulp and destroyed the national spirit, the Mahatma did not know what to do."[19] He further reported that the Congress had lost a great deal of ground as a result of its attitude towards the Cripps proposals, the onset of the

Japanese, the obvious inadequacy of the non-violent programmes and Rajagopalachari's campaign in favour of cooperation over the war and compromise with the Muslims over Pakistan. In this atmosphere the bureaucracy was considering steps to wipe out the Congress. The Muslim League had stepped up its activities to dissuade the Muslim from joining hands with Congress. On the other hand, the extremist sections in the Congress were in no mood to wait and watch. Under these circumstances the CWC met on 14th July 1942 at Wardha and passed the resolution demanding the immediate withdrawal of the British from India which came to be known as the Quit India resolution. Gandhi himself did not use the expression 'Quit India'. It emerged while discussing with an American journalist 'the ordered withdrawal of the British from India' and then it was taken up by all. A meeting of the A.I.C.C. was called at Bombay on 7 and 8 August to consider this resolution. It was viewed by the British authorities as a blend of Nehru and Gandhi aiming at befogging opinion in America and elsewhere. It allowed the presence of United Nations troops to resist Japanese aggression. The Congress was only reluctantly compelled to utilize all the non-violent strength it might have gathered since 1920.[20]

The Congress started making preparations for launching the movement. The decision-making power shifted to Gandhi. Any one who could not follow his programme of non-violent non-co-operation was advised to step aside and resign from any office holding in the Congress organization. The resolution of the A.I.C.C. was endorsed on 8 August. It inaugurated the last battle of India's war against imperialism. Now every soldier of India's freedom was to consider himself free. Addressing the members of the A.I.C.C., he said, "you have to cultivate the spirit of freedom before it comes physically. The chains of a slave are broken the moment he considers himself a free man." Anticipating it to be a fight to the finish, he told the people that after the arrest of the leaders each person would be his own general and expected to do or die in the implementation of 'Quit India' resolution keeping himself 'within the four corners of non-violence'. As a leader Gandhi could create a psychological atmosphere in favour of his moves. So the question of freedom was not left with the opponents. Rather it was the prerogative of the person who was seeking it or fighting for it. This is what he did when he asked the people to consider themselves free the moment they raised their voice against their alien rulers. His speech at the A.I.C.C. meeting after the acceptance of this resolution was well thought out statement of the rationale and urgency of a mass movement. Its purpose was to carry with him even those groups and interests in the country which were opposed to the Congress. Thus while giving assurance to the League leadership that free India would admit all the claims of the Muslims based on equity and justice, he told them that he could not wait for total Hindu-Muslim unity as a condition for starting a movement.[21] Similarly he assured the princes that they would occupy an honourable place in free India if they remained faithful to the country. He advised them to derive their power from their people and not from the foreign government.[22] To the English he said that he was not actuated by any hostility or ill feeling. "The spirit of Andrews, he assured them," hovers over me. He recalled his friendship with the Viceroy Lord Linlithgow. But the call of the conscience prevailed upon him launch a movement against the Empire at that moment.[23] However in spite of making all preparations for the final assault on the citadel of imperialism, he did not lose hope of arriving at some kind of understanding with the Viceroy without compromising over the question of full freedom. So he wanted his followers to wait and watch till he had talks with the Viceroy whose friendship he claimed. But the Government was ready with its plan to smash the movement. They had even toyed with the idea of depositing Gandhi and members of CWC outside India. The idea was abandoned only when it did not receive the approval of the majority of members of Viceroy's council. So the Mahatma and all the Congress leaders present in Bombay were arrested in the small hours of 9th August. Gandhi realised only a day after his arrest that the Government was in no mood to show any special consideration to most of the top leaders of the Congress. For, all of them were put in two lorries like ordinary prisoners when they alighted from the train at Chinchwara. Only one car was arranged to carry Gandhi, Mira, Sarojini Naidu and M. Desai. The Mahatma felt humiliated at the treatment meted out to other members of the CWC. In his view it would have been better if all of them had been asked to occupy the prison van.[24] In a letter to the Viceroy of 10th August he wrote "I propose this time to accept no privileges and comforts which my comrades may not receive except for the special food so long as the Government allow it for my bodily needs."[25] Gandhi was lodged in the Agha Khan palace which was converted into a prison. But he desired that all be treated as ordinary prisoners and no privilege be extended to any one of them. But the Government brushed aside such views. The CWC members were immured in the old fort at Ahmednagar.

The events after the arrest of topmost leaders started moving fast. There were arrests of Congress leaders at all levels. The leaderless masses replied to the repressive measures of the Government with the means which they thought fit. They showed their anger through hartals, processions, picketing and several types of acts of disobedience. At places efforts were made to paralyse the local administration by destroying and damaging public property. Railways suffered a great loss as a result of sabotage. The disturbances though widespread lacked planning. All such occurrences gave an excuse to the Government to suppress the movement with heavy hands and put the whole blame of the happenings at the door of the Congress on the plea that all such acts of violence and destruction were preplanned.

On his arrest the Mahatma suffered a great personal loss. Only a week after his arrest his close associate and devoted secretary Mahadev Desai suddenly collapsed and died. All the inmates of the Agha Khan palace were thrown into deep distress. Gandhi's wife even felt that Desai's death at that moment was an evil omen and for a moment felt that "God was against them." But the Mahatma remained unnerved. For, Desai's death he considered as one of the noblest sacrifices on the altar of freedom. It was a Yogi's death, he felt. So it was bound to bring the day of deliverance for India nearer. Frequent visits to the place where Desai was cremated reminded the rest of the party the sacrifice made by Desai.

Mira tried to break the monotony and gloomy atmosphere of the prison life by introducing the games of badminton and carom. The Mahatma and his wife were persuaded to inaugurate the badminton but to the amusement of all their shuttle cock did not cross the net. Kasturba enjoyed playing carom as Mira's partner, though she could not play well and Mira had to play mostly for her in any game. But all this did not happen for a long time as Kasturba fell ill and after a long struggle died. In spite of all the limitations that he and his wife had as state prisoners, he and his devoted fellow-workers who had been with him in jail looked after her with loving care to reduce her agony. But the Mahatma was sorry for the cold and unsympathetic attitude of the bureaucracy that left a deep scar on his mind. For, he had entertained great regard for the British as civilized and cultured people. Through the two deaths created a void in his life for some time, he was meeting the new situation through philosophical detachment and continuous work for the country. He could not sit still when his co-workers were languishing in jails and many outside were facing bullets and batton charges. He entered into correspondence with the Government in order to open a new channel for talks. He put the whole blame on the government for the eruption of violence in the country. In his view the government had acted in haste by arresting all the leaders of the Congress and thereby destroying all channels for talks as well as removing from the scene all those persons who could keep the movement on non-violent course. For him the mass movement and violence were avoidable as he had left room for talks with the Viceroy. In his view, had the government waited his contemplated letter to the Viceroy and its result thereafter, no calamity would have overtaken the country and the deplorable destruction could be avoided.

But the perception of the Government was entirely different. For, Gandhi had declared that he would not compromise over the issue of complete independence. It could be interpreted that he had left no scope for arriving at understanding with the Government. But the Mahatma had the knack of giving new meanings to his words if any offer by the opponent ensured the substance of the demand. He had done this earlier, too, whenever there was an opportunity for an honourable settlement. Even before making a move for Quit India, he had sent Mira to meet the Viceroy to open before him the working of the mind of the Mahatma and convey to him his commitment to the good of both England and India. The Viceroy avoided meeting her. But advised her to see his secretary Laithwaite. After a long discussion with him, she only warned him the evil consequences of not listening to the voice of Gandhi's conscience. She told him, "This time it will be impossible for you to hold him — The more you crush him, the more his power will spread. You are faced with two alternatives; one to declare India's independence and the other to kill him and once you kill him, you kill for ever all hope of friendship between India and England." Sapru confirmed that Gandhi had hoped in the beginning of August to avoid a crisis and even at the A.I.C.C. session he had publicly declared that he intended to contact the Viceroy before launching the movement. He refused to believe even a few hours before his arrest that the police was coming to arrest him. Though truth and non-violence were the mainstay of his movements, the strategy for each was determined by the situation. This time he was confronted with a situation which had been complicated by the possibility of an aggression by an Asiatic power. Any defence against that power, whether non-violent or violent involved reconsideration of the strategy against the original imperialist power. He, therefore, thought that an appropriate strategy would evolve after having a discussion with the Viceroy. That also may be the reason for not giving any thought to the detailed programme of the movement which he would do before launching it. Whenever his colleagues or correspondents asked him, he would only refer to non-violent non-co-operation, the term that he used for the movements launched earlier.

However, the British statesmen both in England and India were in no mood to arrive at an understanding with him as they thought that they were on a strong wicket and could suppress the movement easily. For the non-Hindus especially the Muslims and a section of the Sikhs had not joined hands with the Congress. The depressed classes under Ambedkar were equally opposed to any move of the Mahatma. The Government had given instructions to the local authorities to mobilise all the forces opposed to the Congress.[26] It means that the Government was in no mood to give a long rope to Gandhi and the Congress. They planned to make the movement abortive by immediately arresting all the leaders. Both the conservative and labour leaders in England put the whole blame on the Congress and Gandhi for the disturbances and violence in country. That gave the impression to the Allies that the Congress had abandoned the policy of non-violence which Gandhi had so long inculcated in theory and had come into the open as a revolutionary or violent movement to paralyse the administration by destroying rail and telegraphy systems and sporadic attacks on the police. But the Mahatma reiterated that he was still committed to non-violence and this he could say from the housetop.[27] He pointed out that whenever Congressmen committed any act of violence, he not only condemned it openly and unequivocally but had done public penance for it. But this time whatever violence the people had committed was done on their own behalf because of their belief in violence. The Government goaded them to the point of madness. But the government was not ready to accept Gandhi's plea. The reply of the Viceroy to his letter was courteous but contained firm denial of unfairness on the part of the Government and so he exhorted him to make amends by denouncing the movement.

Undoubtedly Gandhi used very powerful language to exhort the people to make sacrifices for the freedom of their motherland. It was the language of war as he always contemplated his non-violent struggle as a war without violence. By such expression as "wade through sea of blood" or "leave India to God — or anarchy." "This is open rebellion," he was expressing the intensity of his feelings. But these expressions were pressed by the Government to mean exhortation for violence. Possibly the leaders at the lower levels, did not fully comprehend the meaning and scope of Gandhi's view of non-violence and therefore committed acts which could not be endorsed by Gandhi. R.R. Diwakar who had led the Karnatak group to the A.I.C.C. meeting at Bombay was perplexed as to 'what to do' and 'how to die' in pursuance of Gandhi's call 'Do or Die'. He consulted Gandhi's two close associates K.L. Mashruwala and Kaka Kalelkar, about the meaning of non-violence in the situation after the arrest of Gandhi and the members of the Working Committee. 'The answer was', no violence to the person was permitted during the struggle. From this the idea emerged that attack on Government property and administrative machinery was permitted. Jai Prakash Narayan after jumping the Hazaribagh jail, recommended the Karnatak pattern to the whole of India. But Diwakar was still doubtful about the new interpretation of non-violence. He referred the matter to Gandhi through his son Devadas who had been allowed to attend on Gandhi during his 'Capacity Fast' in the Agha Khan Palace from February 10, 1943 to March 3, Gandhi's reply was that violence to property is sure to lead to violence to person.[28] Similarly when he met Gandhi after his release in 1944, the latter firmly told him that "underground life is taboo as secrecy is sin."[29] Undoubtedly those who resorted to violence or secrecy in the name of Gandhi during the movement had misunderstood Gandhi's view of non-violence and truth. Was this the fault of Gandhi as he was not there to guide the movement?

When the Government refused to listen to him, the Mahatma decided to "make an appeal to the Highest Tribunal for justice by announcing his fast from 9th February. Some of his friends and associates inside and outside the jails did not want him to take this risk at this time when the country was passing through very difficult times and a large number of his followers were languishing in jails. Sarojini Naidu who was looking after him at the Detention Camp, frankly told him that his earlier fasts, too, put his colleagues in the Congress in difficult situations. But fasting at this time he would be doing violence to the soul of the people. For "you are bound by certain contract with you colleagues. You cannot break that contract behind their back. History will find you guilty."[30]

The Government interpreted the proposed fast as political blackmail. But offered temporary release because of their apprehension that his death in prison would damage their image among the Allies who would blame them for weakening their cause among the Indians. But Gandhi refused his release on the grounds that the impending fast was not conceived to be taken as a freeman. So it was commenced on February 10, 1943. It kept the Government of India, all the Provincial Governments and the British Government at Home on tenterhook during the period of fast. Special instructions were issued daily to the Provincial Governments as to the steps they had to take in case of Gandhi's death during the period of the fast. Daily communications were exchanged between the

S.S. and the Viceroy about all the developments relating to Gandhi's fast. Bombay Government which had special responsibility for tackling the problem issued instructions to District Magistrates to remain at their Headquarters, police force was reinforced and troops movements maintained when Gandhi's condition became serious. In fact, the fast had become the main preoccupation of the Government of India, all the Provincial Governments and the Secretary of State in England. However, the possibility had been long contemplated by the Government of India about the policy to be adopted in that event as this was considered as the most powerful weapon in the armoury of the Mahatma. A suggestion had been made to set him on liberty as soon as the fast reached the danger point. But the war Cabinet headed by Churchill rejected this policy on the grounds that Gandhi must not secure his release by a threat of fast.[31] When the Mahatma began his fast the Government became nervous as all the doctors both official and non-official reported that Gandhi would not last longer than further five days from February 16th. For, his death could occur any time as a result of heart attack. On 19th decisions were taken as to whether flag was to be kept at half-mast or courts to be closed in case of his death. His condition became very serious on 21st as he entered a crisis in the evening. He was seized with severe nausea and he almost fainted. His pulse became imperceptible. But he soon rallied from crisis and took water with sweet lime juice. And after this his condition became stable. He was served orange juice. The Government even suspected that the crisis was deliberately arranged to coincide with the conference of the leaders who were demanding his unconditional release.[32] Churchill even suspected the *bona fides* of the fast on the grounds that the Hindu doctors could slip glucose or other nourishments. The finger was towards Sushila Nayyar.[33] She not only denied this charge but even warned General Candy who was looking after Gandhi that it would shock Gandhi if glucose was given to him surreptitiously.[34] Doctor Roy and Dr. Gilder agreed with her. In fact, the British bureaucracy and doctors did not keep in view Gandhi's control over his body which he had acquired after incessant effort and rigorous discipline. It was also his will to live that sustained him. However after this the Government had become certain that Gandhi would survive the fast. He was taking more orange juice than even necessary. In Dr. Miss Nayyar's opinion the addition of sweet lime juice saved his life as the fluid that went into the system enabled the kidneys to function as a result of which blood urea came down.[35] Khare who formerly headed the Congress Government in the M.P. even observed that Gandhi's fast really ended on 21st February and not 3rd March as after that he was taking orange juice. The Mahatma himself referred to it as fraudulent fast, of course playfully, as he was taking more juice than even necessary. However one point which was missed by his critics and observers was that this was not fast unto death. It was only fast to capacity, that is, he would keep it so long as his body could bear it.

Gandhi's detention in the Agha Khan Palace gave him sufficient rest to recuperate. He was not burdened with writing letters as he had taken a vow not to write any letter as a protest against the order of the Government not to allow him to write letters to the members of his Ashram on the plea that they were not the members of his family. Miss Slade (Mira), Manu, Pyarelal, and Sushila Nayyar were giving him company. There was some change in his schedule of leaving the bed in the morning. He would get up at 6-30 instead of 4 a.m. After finishing morning ablutions and breakfast he would have a walk for about 45 minutes accompanied by other detnues of Agha Khan Palace during which they could have talks on public and other matters. After this he would take his food while Miss Slade would read books to him. Some time he would teach Sanskrit to Miss Nayyar. After Siesta for an hour Pyarelal would read papers to him and would discuss several matters while he would go on spinning. He would teach Manu from 3 to 4 p.m. and then examine the newspapers cuttings or Miss Slade would read newspapers to him. The evening was spent in walk and another bout of spinning. Then all would gather for prayer before going to sleep.

While the Government was jubilant for having nullified the effect of Gandhi's fast, the Mahatma made another move to keep the political ball moving. On reading Jinnah's speech appearing in League's paper *Dawn*, which Gandhi had been receiving regularly during his detention, wherein he had invited Gandhi to write to him directly for political settlement with League. Gandhi immediately wrote a letter to Jinnah for a face to face talk with him hoping that the letter would be sent to him by the Government. The letter was non-committal on the issue of Pakistan. But the issue of delivery of the letter to Jinnah put the authorities both in India and England in a tight corner. For while the Viceroy and his advisers were in favour of delivering this letter, the War Cabinet in England was opposed to it and finally directed the Viceroy not to deliver this letter. The difficulty which this letter created was summed up by the Viceroy to the Secretary of State as follow:

"Gandhi hopes no doubt also that if we decide not to forward the letter we shall play into Jinnah's hands and make ourselves a target of Jinnah. If on the other hand we do forward it, it may place Jinnah in an awkward position and it is certainly likely to present Government with difficult questions and tactics whether Jinnah responds it not."[36]

However, finally it was decided to communicate the receipt of this letter but its contents were withheld. The League leader took a safer course by declaring publicly that the letter was only a move to embroil Muslim League with Government. He had taken full advantage of Congress struggle against the Government and was therefore in no mood to offend the authorities.[37]

But in spite of the rest available to him, he was not keeping good health. He suffered from low blood pressure, hook worms and amoebic infection. All these troubles had caused acute anaemia. But he refused to take any drug in the detention camp. He had living faith in God whom he considered as the Master physician. His illness virtually brought him to death's door. The British foreign office had even issued a directive in anticipation of his death over the signature of Anthony Eden, the Foreign Secretary, as to how his obituaries to be written.[38] In view of his deteriorating health, he declared on May 14, 1944 to observe silence for a fortnight. But he was released before that date on grounds of health. However, his unconditional release was no humanitarian act. It was a political move. For, Wavell had informed the authorities in England that Gandhi was dangerously ill making it impossible for him to remain active in politics if released.[39] The Government doctors as well as B.C. Roy had reported that the Mahatma was suffering from anaemia and low blood pressure as a result of attack of Malaria. The Prime Minister agreed for his release because of this situation. But he was very much disappointed when he learnt that a few days after his release Gandhi had a remarkable recovery and he became the prime mover. The Prime Minister questioned the doctors' reports. In view of this situation the SOS in a light moment quoted Byron's letter to a friend wherein he had said, "My mother-in-law had been dangerously ill; she is now dangerously well."[40]

Though emerging from the detention camp as a shattered man he would not rest so long as the fight for freedom was continuing and the Congress leaders were behind the bars. He was in search of an opportunity to break the political deadlock in order to reinvigorate the Congress which had spearheaded the fight for freedom. He first tried to open a dialogue with the Viceroy by making some offers without compromising the stand of the Congress taken before the launching of the movement. In an interview to Gilder, he had agreed that in case the national government was formed, Congress would join and help the war efforts and he himself would stand aside. He did not withdraw the Quit India resolution but only re-interpreted it in the light of changed circumstances. According to him, direct action was a necessity in 1942 because the British Government had shown itself to be interested only in draining India of its material resources and man power while it was preparing to allow large parts of the country to be overrun by the Japanese. But in 1944 C.D. movement was not a necessity nor practicable as the spectre of famine was staring the land and the people had committed mistakes in the practice of non-violence.[41] But all this reasoning cut no ice and the Government remained unmoved. Gandhi then turned to Jinnah to keep the political cauldron boiling. During his fast in jail in 1943, he had already given his consent for Rajagopalachari formula for opening a dialogue between the Congress and the League for a settlement which could deprive the British of their trump card in the political game. Though earlier the League leader had showed contempt for the Rajagopalachari formula, he was ready to talk on its basis if it was sent direct to him by Gandhi. Each leader had some thing in view by agreeing to the talks. While the Mahatma thought that he would be able to make the League leader concede that Pakistan was not a rational demand by subjecting it to sympathetic but critical analysis Jinnah had in mind to boost his dwindling popularity among the Muslims in India by acquiring a central place in the political stage of the country. For, he had not as yet been able to establish his dominance in the Muslim majority provinces. He had received a rebuff from Khizr Hayat Khan, the premier of the Punjab, who had refused to convert the Unionist Ministry into Muslim League coalition ministry as desired by Jinnah. Nor was the league leader putting on well with Fazl-ul-Huq in Bengal and the Khan Brothers in the North West Frontier province. But by the announcement of the talks, it was publicly recognized that Jinnah was the foremost leader of the Muslims of India while all other Muslim leaders were only provincial leaders.

Gandhi and Jinnah were not unknown to each other. Their acquaintance dated back to the time when Gandhi was fighting for the rights of Indians in South Africa and Jinnah showed sympathy with Gandhi's struggle in South Africa and supported Gandhi's cause in his first speech after election to the Imperial Council in 1909. He attended several meetings that were convened to honour Gandhi after his return from South Africa. Both participated in the Muslim League meeting held in Bombay on December 30, 1915. In 1918 both led Home Rule Day celebrations in Bombay. Gandhi sought his support in his recruitment campaign. At the Congress session at Amritsar Jinnah seconded a motion by Gandhi supporting Montagu Chelmsford Reforms. But the differences between the two leaders appeared when Gandhi planned a mass movement against the British for the realisation of his objectives. The legalistic and aristocratic mind of Jinnah could not endorse this method as a result of which he left the Congress. But he did not throw overboard all the liberal and constitutional idioms and practices of the Congress. On his visit to England in 1921, he lobbied for a constitutional response to Gandhi's programmes and campaigns. He warned the British public of the dangers of driving the Indian intelligentsia to rebellion. He pointed out that "if the Punjab wrongs were righted and the constitution amended for provincial autonomy and dyarchy in the Central Government, India might be restored to an even keel."[42] When the Swarajists entered the legislatures after the withdrawal of the NCO, Jinnah found an opportunity to offer his legal and constitutional acumen to his erstwhile colleagues in the Congress for the political progress of the country. When the Congress leadership was occupied in producing a constitution for free India, Motilal felt that if Jinnah could be won over for Nehru Report, it would acquire great prestige. So he deputed Purshotamdas Thakurdas to rope in Jinnah before Shaukat Ali got to him. In fact, during the talks leading to Nehru Report, a large number of Congress men believed that Jinnah was "the only man to deliver the goods on behalf of the Muslim League." So his departure for Europe in May 1928 was viewed by them as unfortunate.[43] Some of them even wanted the postponement of All Parties Conference to be convened at Lucknow on 28 August in order to enable Jinnah to participate in it. In spite of their differences both Gandhi and Jinnah remained on speaking terms. It was not for the first time they were meeting. Earlier they met several times to solve the Hindu-Muslim problem. On December 12, 1929 Jinnah went to Gandhi's Ashram at Sabarmati to discuss Viceroy's announcement of R.T.C. A few days later both met the Viceroy in Delhi concerning this conference. Both had a dialogue over the question of two-nation theory and Jinnah's insistence on a separate homeland for Muslims did not cut much ice with Gandhi. He not only opposed the two-nation theory but believed that the advocacy of the two-nation theory by Jinnah was only a temporary phase in Jinnah's political career since prior to 1937 he had full faith in Hindu-Muslim unity and before 1920 he was a leader of the Congress. Both had met on

April 28, 1938 to solve the communal problem. Subhas also attended that meeting. But the meeting did not produce any result as Jinnah insisted that he be recognized as the sole spokesman for the Muslims which both Subhas and Gandhi were not ready to admit. So it was not unusual for Gandhi to make another effort to arrive at an understanding with the League leader to solve the Hindu-Muslim problem.

Though the move for the talks started in July, these were held from September 9 to 27, because of the indisposition of Jinnah. In all 14 interviews took place between them. But they also exchanged views through correspondence during this period. The talks started in a cordial atmosphere. On the first day when Gandhi reached Jinnah's house, the League leader came out into his porch to receive him. They shook hands and embraced each other. He escorted him back at the time of leaving and posed with him for a photograph. The talks initially moved on the basis of Rajagopalachari formula but later on efforts were made to explore new avenues for arriving at an amicable settlement.

In spite of Gandhi's efforts to bridge the gulf between the Congress and the league by conceding some demands of the League even at the risk of annoying several Hindu and Sikh leaders, he failed to carry the League leader with him. For, there was sea difference between their attitudes and approaches to the political problem. The main hurdle was the two-nation theory of Jinnah which challenged Gandhi's fundamental religious and political beliefs. For, he could not accept that a change in the way of worshipping God could change the nationality of a person. Even a few decades earlier Jinnahs were Hindus. The name Jinnah is of Hindu origin, translated from Gujarati, it means lean. Jinnah's father was a successful businessman and belonged to the Khojas, a Hindu sect of recent converts to Islam. So without compromising his fundamental beliefs, Gandhi was ready to meet the demand of the League halfway by admitting the separation of certain parts on the basis of self-determination to be decided by all the inhabitants of the area as against Jinnah's plea that it should be decided by the Muslims alone. In fact, Jinnah was pleading that only two million Muslim voters had the right of deciding the fate of twenty-eight million inhabitants of Punjab. It was a clever move. For, the Muslim leader knew the weakness of his case in a province where the Muslims held only marginal majority and where a decade earlier the League had the minimum influence. So on rational grounds, Gandhi's case was strong and it was natural for him to believe that he could convince any reasonable person that the demand for Pakistan lacked historical and logical foundations. But the issue was not before two rational persons. Rather it was before two lawyers and political leaders. Jinnah was clever enough to know the weakness of his case on historical or logical grounds. Being a good lawyer and a clever politician, he stood his ground. He never aimed at any settlement. For any settlement at that stage could weaken his hold over the Muslim masses by exposing his concept of Pakistan to critical examination by politicians of different hues and shades as well as of intellectuals. But most of all it would reduce his importance in the eyes of the British who had been building him up as a counterpoise to the Congress. So Gandhi's dialectical skill fell flat on him. The new Viceroy Wavell after examining the implications of the two-nation theory felt that Jinnha himself was not sincere about the two-nation theory and so he had not thought out the implications of Pakistan.[44] His only strong point was that he could afford to say 'No' to any formula which did not square well with his demand. For he knew very well that at his back was the British Conservative Party led by Churchill. During the negotiations for settlement under Mountbatten the Viceroy admitted that he failed with Jinnah. But added that nobody else would have been any more successful. For in his view Jinnah had a closed mind, closed ears. He did not want to be persuaded. It was only when the Viceroy passed on to Jinnah Churchill's message that it was a matter of life and death for him to accept Mountbatten plan that he agreed.[45] In fact, the League leader gained some political mileage by the failure of the talks. For, he emerged as the saviour of the Muslim interests by holding on to the demand which had great emotional appeal for the Muslim masses who were in no mood to know its reality. For, any dissection of the nature of Pakistan could create dissensions among the Muslim League supporters especially in Muslim majority areas. The League leader was aware of the fact that his own logic of two-nation theory would not be able to maintain peace and unity in his Pakistan. No wonder, after the attainment of his goal he used Gandhi's language and logic in his first speech to the new Constituent Assembly of Pakistan when he said, "You may belong to any religion or caste or creed that has nothing to do with the fundamental that we are all citizens and equal citizens of one state and that you will find in course of time Hindus would cease to be Hindus Muslim would cease to be Muslims in the political sense as citizens of the state."

The non-Congress Hindu leadership heaved a sigh of relief on the failure of the talks as there was apprehension among them that Gandhi might concede many things inimical to the interests of the Hindus in order to placate Jinnah. They were averse to the talks right from the beginning. Several Hindu Sabha volunteers picketed his hut at Sevagram to prevent him from going to Bombay for talks. But they were arrested. The talks also tarnished Gandhi's image in the Congress as some of the Congress leaders felt that by associating himself with the Rajagopalachari formula Gandhi had gone against the general feeling of Congressmen that Rajagopalachari formula did not represent the Congress approach, to the communal problem.

However, the Hindu leaders failed to understand the implications of Gandhi's consent to the talks with Jinnah. The British, both in England and India, believed that Gandhi never had in mind to subordinate the Hindu interests to placate the Muslims. Viceroy Lord Wavell even believed that Gandhi's idea of united India was in which Hindus would dominate though he was careful not to express it.[46] The Governor of C.P. reported to the Viceroy that the talks were designed to trap Jinnah into an exhibition of unreasonableness which would be beneficial to the Hindu case in the eyes of the world.

After the failure of the talks, Gandhi pinned his hope on Bholabhai Desai-Liaquat Khan talks. The former was the leader of the Congress party in the Central Legislative Assembly. He was negotiating with the League leader for Congress-League coalition at the centre. Gandhi blessed Bholabhai's move. The agreement between the two assured equal representation to both the parties in central executive. But the pact was neither endorsed by the League nor by the Congress. Jinnah frowned upon it. The Congress leaders who were in Jail were furious on learning about it. They condemned it as a stab in their back as it was arrived at without their knowledge. It blasted the political career of Desai. Gandhi tried to raise the attenuated spirit of Desai but of no avail. Rather the acrimony of the Congress leaders against Desai stuck to Gandhi as he had blessed the move. However, the formula was welcomed by the Viceroy Lord Wavell as it formed the basis of his recommendations for the reconstitutions of the Executive Council.

Notes and References

1. C.W., LXX, p. 162.
2. *Ibid.*, p. 181.
3. *Ibid.*, p. 257.
4. Birla, Bapu, *op. cit.*, Vol. IV, p. 41.
5. C.W., LXXII, pp. 229-31.
6. *Ibid.*
7. Nanda, In Gandhi's Footsteps, pp. 340-42.

8. Birla, Bapu, Vol. IV, p. 144.
9. C.W., LXXIV, p. 281.
10. *Ibid.*
11. *Ibid.*, LXXV, p. 8.
12. *Ibid.*, LXXV, p. 27.
13. *Ibid.*, p. 221.
14. *Ibid.*, LXXVI, pp. 223-24.
15. Transfer of Power, Vol. I, p. 190.
16. *Ibid.*, p. 191.
17. Collected Works of Dr. Rajendra Prasad, Vol. 5, pp. 217-23.
18. Transfer of Power, Vol. II, p. 191.
19. *Ibid.*, p. 123.
20. *Ibid.*, pp. 386-87.
21. C.W., LXXVI, p. 289.
22. *Ibid.*, p. 393.
23. *Ibid.*, p. 398.
24. *Ibid.*, p. 404.
25. Gandhiji's Correspondence with Govt., 1942-44, p. 1.
26. Transfer of Power, Vol. II, p. 396.
27. C.W., LXXVII, p. 52.
28. Diwakar, R.R., My Encounter with Gandhi, *op. cit.*, p. 53.
29. *Ibid.*, p. 54.
30. Sushila Nayyar, *op. cit.*, pp. 190-91.
31. Transfer of Power, Vol. III, p. 467.
32. *Ibid.*, p. 724.
33. *Ibid.*, p. 789.
34. Nayyar, Sushila, *op. cit.*, pp. 226-27.
35. *Ibid.*, p. 230.
36. Transfer of Power, Vol. III, p. 97.
37. *Ibid.*, p. 1031.
38. Pyarelal, The Last Phase, Vol. I, p. 12.
39. T.P., Vol. IV, p. 949.
40. *Ibid.*, p. 965.
41. Pyarelal, The Last Phase, Vol. I, p. 30.
42. *The Times*, 29 June, 1921, quoted in David Page, Prelude to Partition, p. 107.
43. *Ibid.*, p. 167.
44. T.P., Vol. V, p. 75.
45. Collins, *op. cit.*, p. 102.
46. T.P., Vol. V, p. 75.

24

Loneliness Amidst Great Changes

The Congress leadership could not realize the significance of Gandhi's moves of breaking the deadlock during their detention. For, he not only wanted to keep the political ball rolling but also tried to snatch the initiative for breaking the political deadlock both from the ruling authority and the Indian political leadership. Nevertheless, his moves did not produce the desired results so far as the Congress was concerned. But the Viceroy took cue from the Bholabhai-Liaquat Pact and persuaded the British statesmen to allow him to start negotiations in order to break the political deadlock. In his broadcast on June 6, 1945, he invited the Indian leaders to take counsel with him with a view to the formation of a new executive council representative of organized political opinion. The proposed new council would represent the main communities and would include equal number of caste Hindus and Muslims. It would work if formed under the existing constitution. But it would be entirely an Indian council except for the Viceroy and the Commander-in-Chief who would retain his position as a war member. Orders were issued for the release of the members of the C.W.C. who were in detention. Invitations were issued to 21 persons for attending the conference at Simla from Junce 21, 1945. The President Maulana Abul Kalam Azad was invited only on Gandhi's insistence. The Mahatma refused to be a delegate on the grounds that he did not represent any political organization. But he agreed to be present in Simla during the period of conference on Wavell's insistence since, according to the Viceroy, he still wielded enormous influence, though he had learnt from several sources that his position was not as strong as before launching the Quit India movement. Gandhi had several reservations about the approach of the Viceroy to the Indian problem. He expressed his anguish over the use of the term caste Hindus as in his opinion it would not only exacerbate the communal division but would seriously damage the national character of the Congress. For, the parity between the Congress and the League in the Bholabhai-Liaquat Pact which was blessed by him was parity between two political parties and the Congress could be represented by a Muslim, Sikh or a Parsi. But, according to Wavell's plan Congress would be completely identified with the Hindus and that is what Jinnah wanted. The Viceroy explained that by Caste-Hindus he only meant Hindus other than the scheduled castes. This was another attack on the national character of the Congress since under Gandhi's leadership it was engaged in breaking the barrier between the caste Hindus and the scheduled castes. The Congress leadership, too, did not realize the significance of Gandhi's objection to parity between caste Hindus and the Muslims and were in a mood to accept Wavell's offer as a temporary measure.

Gandhi remained in Simla during the conference but he did not attend any meeting. The Viceroy had a talk with him as well as with Jinnah a day before the conference separately. On his meeting with Jinnah, the Viceroy felt that the League leader was depressed as he was not sure of his position.[1] For, he was having a difficult time with his followers. On learning that Gandhi was not attending the meeting on the plea that he represented no body, Jinnah was upset and remarked that it was another trick of Gandhi. For, he pretended not to belong to the Congress when it suited him, but when necessary appeared as the "Dictator of the Congress which every one knew he was."

In his inaugural speech the Viceroy explained that the purpose of the conference was not a constitutional settlement nor a final solution of India's problems. But "If it succeeds it will pave the way towards the settlement." But the conference failed mainly because of the insistence of Jinnah that the League alone be recognized as the representative of all the Muslims and so must have the right to nominate all Muslim members of the council. He also claimed that the Muslims were not a minority but a nation and so must be accorded equality of members in the executive that is, half the total membership of the council. These conditions were not acceptable to the Viceroy not because of his soft corner for the Congress but for saving the prestige of the Unionist Party in the Punjab which had been locked in a fierce struggle with the League for supremacy in the Punjab. For, the Unionist leadership had extended unstinted support to the British war efforts. Though the failure of the conference was owned by the Viceroy, it was evident that the plans and efforts were torpedoed by Jinnah supported by several high British bureaucrats and statesmen. While the British conservative statesmen were putting pressure from England on the Viceroy to make every possible effort to conciliate Jinnah, British bureaucracy in India were making moves to help Jinnah. The leader of the Muslim League party in the Council of State in a talk with V.P. Menon suggested that the Viceroy was not aware that a member of his own executive council was advising Jinnah to stand firm and possibly this member was in touch with the Secretary of State, Amery.[2] Several contemporary observers felt that the League supremo was adamant only because the Viceroy was not allowed to show his teeth to Jinnah or twist his arm. Gandhi advised that in view of the disagreement the Government should decide between the two parties. But the Viceroy was not willing to go to that length. An off hand remark by Churchill in a discussion with Mountbatten clarifies the difficulty of the Viceroy. For, he said, "By God he is the one man (Jinnah) who cannot do without British help."

The immediate effect of Wavell's surrender to Jinnah was that it raised the prestige of the Muslim leader very high in the eyes of the Muslims especially in the areas which were crucial for Pakistan notably Punjab where the League was struggling hard to acquire foothold because of the hold of the Unionist Party over the Muslims which was holding the fort against Pakistan. Further, in the NWFP Congress had taken over control. In Bengal Nazimuddin had been defeated in the Assembly and in Assam and Sind the league ministries were in power on Congress sufferance. It is possible that if the Viceroy had not capitulated over the issue of the inclusion of a Muslim member in the council presumably from the Punjab it would have been difficult for the League to carry the majority of the Muslims in the Assembly of the Punjab with them as they were already in power. The League leader now could afford to expel Khizer from the League. In fact, Jinnah's strength demonstrated at the Simla Conference was a shot in the arm of the League. It was a move towards the creation of Pakistan.

The failure of the conference made it clear that no constitutional advancement was possible in India without coming to an understanding with the League leadership especially Jinnah. The British, in fact, handed over key to India's political progress to him. This means that he was head and shoulders above all Muslim leaders. The acceptance of parity between Hindus and Muslims in the executive council by the Congress added strength to his demand for Pakistan. It also revealed that the Congress leaders were tired of the struggle and were not obliged to toe Gandhi's line of thinking, though always conferring with him whenever they were faced with a serious political problem.

Acute food shortage and economic distress all over the country equally demanded Mahatma's immediate attention. Much of the time between November 1945 and the middle of January, he remained in Bengal where famine had caused great suffering to the people. As the Government was equally occupied in tackling this problem, he received good response from the provincial administration as well as from the Viceroy for his efforts in alleviating the suffering of the people. He had six meetings with the Governor of Bengal, Mr. Casey who showed considerable interest in Gandhi's solutions to the economic problems. There was a ring of practicability around his solutions the significance of which were not realized either by the Government or by the Indians. The Governor of Bengal even felt that his political reasoning lacked realism and balance.[3] While appreciating Casey's suggestion for the utilization of the water of the rivers of Bengal as solution to the food problem, he stated that what was more important was the utilization of the human labour of the millions in India which was going waste because of lack of opportunity to the masses. The tens of millions of farmers of Bengal, he said "are idle more than half the time. They constitute the biggest problem of unemployment in the world and the biggest of the potential human effort." So in this context he brought to the notice of Casey the value of All India Spinners' Association which apart from providing a large number of people with gainful employment and increased confidence in these employed in this work.[4]

The immediate measures that he suggested for overcoming the food shortage were distribution of food through co-operative societies, stoppage of the export of articles of food even to relatives and friends, cultivation of vegetables by all public gardens by law, utilization of abundance of fish as food and the release of all food stuff stocks lying with the military.

The Viceroy also sought Gandhi's help in tackling the problem of food shortage. He sent his private secretary Abell to Bombay to seek his consent to the membership of the proposed advisory committee to regulate the food distribution of which Jinnah and possibly the Nawab of Bhopal were proposed to be other members. It was to function under the Chairmanship of the Viceroy. But Gandhi declined its membership on the grounds that he did not represent any party. In his view the only person who could represent the Congress was its president Abul Kalam Azad. It was an intelligent move to blast the two-nation theory as well as to demolish the claim of the League to represent all the Muslims of India. The move failed as Jinnah refused to work on any committee where Azad a Muslim claimed to represent the Indians. However, the move showed that the British administrators were aware that the Mahatma had his finger on the pulse of the nation and his appeal could galvanize the people for any action or adventure. Abell left the Mahatma with the impression that the latter had made up his mind to 'play'. It was Gandhi's day of silence when the interview took place. Gandhi asked Abell to write down his ideas 'as a man' for tackling the food problem. Gandhi nodded his consent to his suggestions such as sacrifice by both rich and poor in this situation, encouragement to thrift by the housewives, treating hoarding as a criminally wicked act etc.[5]

He made use of his long stay in Bengal to visit Assam for a few days. He had to face a lot of difficulty during this journey as at every station people thronged the train by which he was travelling to have his 'darshan'. He could hardly snatch a wink of sleep. But the love of people for him was enough for him to put up with this hardship.

When the Congress leadership came out of the jail, great changes had taken place in Europe which were sure to have their effect on Indian political system. Though Germany had been defeated and Japan was on the run, the economy of England was completely shattered and it depended upon the aid of the United States. It was no more a super power. New balance of power was emerging which was beyond the control of Britain. It was, therefore, becoming clear that the erstwhile imperial authority had to arrive at some kind of understanding with its colonial people. The majority of the people in England desired some change in order to meet new challenges. The Government of Churchill resigned and the leader of the Labour Party was installed in office. The election results clearly demonstrated that the people in England were not enamoured of the policies of the Conservative Party. For the first time the Labour Party secured majority in the House of Commons. This created some hope in the minds of the nationalists in India that great changes with regard to Britain's relationship with India were round the corner as the Labour Party had been in sympathy with India's aspirations for self-government. The Mahatma, too, smelled change in the British attitude towards India. He was, therefore, reminding the people about their new responsibilities that demanded disciplined behaviour. For, the behaviour of the crowd thronging to his meetings was unruly. Most of the people were least interested in listening to what he said. They had come only for his 'darshan'.

At the political level, too, the atmosphere was not favourable to a smooth transfer of power. The public trials of Subhas Bose' Indian National Army Officers had created ill-will in the minds of the Indians against the British. These officers were lionized by the people and so violent disturbances broke out at several places. The rebellious spirit had its effect on the Royal Indian Navy and in February 1946 an open mutiny of the ratings broke out which could be controlled only with the help of Sardar Patel. Gandhi, too, did not approve of this act of the ratings as it demonstrated lack of discipline in the armed forces which was not a good portent for India standing on the threshold of freedom.[6]

In this atmosphere of hope and fear, elections to the Central Assembly and the provincial legislatures were held which clearly showed that the Congress and the Muslim League were the two major political parties that held key to all the political problems of the country which transfer of power could raise. For the Congress secured 91.3 per cent of votes in the non-Muslim constituencies. It won 57 seats as against 44 which it held in the Assembly elected in 1934. The Muslim League annexed all the 30 seats reserved for the Muslims in the Assembly. In the election to the provincial assemblies, too, the two parties improved their position. The Congress won 923 general seats as against 714 won in 1937. The representation of the League went up to 86% as against 25% in 1937.

The Mahatma, of course, did not play any active role in the elections. Sometimes his attitude appeared irksome to Congress leaders engaged in election campaigns. Thus when Patel on Azad's advice, sought Gandhi's help in persuading Gopichand Bhargava to contest a seat for the Punjab provincial assembly, he replied in his characteristic manner that it was for Gopichand to decide whether the interest of his province lay in his going to the assembly or not. Patel was not surprised by this reply of Gandhi as it was in keeping with his attitude towards elections in the past.

However, the elections refuted the wishful thinking in the Conservative camp in England that the Congress had been reduced to dust as a result of the suppression of the Quit India movement and its leader Gandhi had become a non-entity. But, in fact, the sufferings endured by the volunteers on the call of the Mahatma had raised the image of the Congress. Thus when the Cabinet Mission came to India on March 23, 1946 to speed up the transfer of power, its members were very keen to meet Gandhi as early as possible to seek his help in finding the solution of the Indian people.

The Mission consisted of Lord Pethic Lawrence, the Secretary of State for India, Sir Stafford Cripps, the President of the Board of Trade and A.V. Alexander, the first Lord of Admirality. The Viceroy Lord Wavell also played an important role in the negotiations carried on by the Mission. On the arrival of the Mission, he told the Secretary of State that he did not intend to be a lay figure in these negotiations and it appears from his journal that he played an active role in them throughout. According to Gandhi's secretary, Pyarelal, the first two shared with Gandhi a distinct life style and religious outlook. Stafford Cripps with his austere simplicity, vegetarianism and faith in the healing power of the spirit was close to Gandhi's mental make-up. Pethic Lawrence was the friend of Gandhi's close friend C.F. Andrews and was deeply religious.[7] The deference shown by these two members of the Mission to Gandhi irked Wavell. Once at a meeting of the Mission with Gandhi, the latter expressed a wish for a glass of water. The Secretary was sent to fetch himself instead of sending for a 'chaprasi' and when it did not come at once Cripps hustle off himself to see about it.[8] This exercise horrified the Viceroy who considered Gandhi a very tough politician and not a saint. He noted that Gandhi "is a remarkable old man, certainly and the most formidable of three opponents who have detached portions of the British Empire in recent years: Zaghlul and de Valera being the other two."[9] He considered him at heart implacable enemy of Great Britain.

When the Mission arrived, the Mahatma was at his nature cure centre at Urulikanchan, offering simple nature cure remedies to the poor villagers suffering from various diseases. According to the official schedule, the Delegation was to meet Gandhi after the first week of April. But Cripps and Pethic Lawrence wanted to see him even earlier and conveyed to him through Sudhir Ghosh, who claimed to be Gandhi's emissary during that period, to come to Delhi immediately. Cripps made a special request to him on meeting him to stay on "especially at the time of the formulations of the possibilities as 'he would be able to influence all kinds of persons'. He reminded the Indian leader that 'it is not I but India that needs you in Delhi.' On the initiative of SOS and Cripps, special arrangement was made to take Gandhi and his party from his nature cure centre to Delhi. The journey in the special train and the cancellation of viceregal arrangement aroused intense interest in political circles as it revealed the position the Mahatma held among those who had come to transfer power to India. On reaching Delhi a comic controversy showed the differences of outlook between Gandhi and the British hierarchy close to the Viceroy. Gandhi wanted to pay third class fare of his 13 member party as he did not want to be under any obligation of the Viceroy for this journey. The fare at the rate of Rs 27/16 came to Rs. 355/14 which was sent to the Private Secretary of the Viceroy. The latter felt offended as no one had asked Gandhi to pay the fare. But when Gandhi insisted, the PVC said that Gandhi should pay Rs. 18,000 for the special train. Gandhi refused as he did not want to travel by special train and the P.V.C. accepted the fare.[10]

Gandhi claimed that his main objective in all the negotiations was to help all the parties to arrive at a settlement which would ensure independence of culture and satisfaction of legitimate ambitions of all the parties while maintaining the Unity of India. But the Viceroy and to some extent members of the Delegation and the League leadership believed that his role was to promote the interest of the Congress. As usual, he vehemently opposed the two-nation theory on the basis of which Jinnah demanded Pakistan. In the first meeting with the Delegation he showed the irrationality of the two-nation theory by the example of his son becoming a Muslim for a while in support of his argument that the change of religion had nothing to do with the change of nationality. He also referred to his efforts to meet the demands of Jinnah by Rajagopalchari's formula and his Bombay talks. Besides, he pressed on the Viceroy for the abolition of salt tax. He made this demand in several other meetings with the Delegation and the Viceroy. The Delegation met him several times jointly. The SOS and Cripps also consulted him several times individually as they believed that he alone could solve the political problem because of his hold over the Congress. But the Viceroy completely distrusted him. In his diary he wrote after meeting him on September 26, "The more I see of that old man the more I regard him as an unscrupulous old hypocrite; he would shrink from no violence and blood-letting to achieve his ends, though he would naturally prefer to do so by chicanery and a false show of mildness and friendship."[11] In a letter to the king the Viceroy while giving his assessment of the character of Gandhi said, "He is an odd mixture of benevolence (outward) and malevolence (inward). I should put the composition of his character as, he added, 70% extremely astute politician with a fixed dislike of the British and the determination to rid India of them, 15% saint, 15% charlatan. I am always pretty clear about the first of these."[12] Later on while making full assessment of the problems facing him during the period of his Viceroyalty he told the king "that Mr. Gandhi was a most inveterate enemy of the British and did not desire a peaceful transfer of power; he wished the British to be finally driven from India by the force of popular rising. I think he still does."[13]

Possibly on this account Wavell had sympathy with the League which was evident during the negotiations. Gandhi even said that in his talks with him, Wavell had admitted that his leanings were towards the Muslim League. But the Viceroy denied it. Nevertheless the Viceroy was convinced that the Congress was using all their powers to destroy the League and so unconsciously he was trying to outwit the Congress leadership to save the interest of the League. The Viceroy being a soldier did not fully understand the political problems of India and could not fully appreciate Gandhi's motives and moves to prevent the partition of the country which the Muslim League under the leadership of Jinnah was demanding. Since Jinnah stuck to his demand which the Congress or Gandhi could not concede, the Mission recommended its own solution. It envisaged a loose federation mainly having three subjects that is, foreign affairs, defence and communication with necessary powers to raise the finances for these subjects. It recommended a three-tier constitution, that is a central government with limited powers, the groups of provinces or states. It offered a limited scope for Pakistan by its recommendation that the provinces would be free to form groups with executives and legislatures with the powers to determine the provincial subjects to be taken in common. NWFP was grouped with Punjab and in the North-East, Assam which was not a Muslim majority area was grouped with Bengal which was a Muslim majority area. That way NWFP which was Congress stronghold and Assam were placed under the domination of Muslim majority areas. While in Simla the Cabinet Mission had given an assurance to the Muslim League, which had not been made known to the Congress at that time, that decisions in the sections would be by a majority vote and the constitution for the provinces would be framed by the sections. That way the province which was unwilling to join a group was compelled to join it. That way the Mission had accepted *de facto* Pakistan. The Mission recommended only one Constituent Assembly composed of the representatives of provincial assemblies and of the states. It also recommended the formation of an interim government having the support of the major political parties during the period when the constituent making body was proceeding.

It was a sort of compromise plan which offered something to each party but not conceding complete demand of any party. So no party was fully satisfied with its recommendations. But Gandhi did congratulate the Mission for its act of renunciation though he did not consider the recommendations best either from the British or Indian point of view. The League, too, was dissatisfied with the plan of the Mission as it did not concede its demand of full Pakistan. But after much dithering and challenges accepted it while reiterating the attainment of Pakistan as their unalterable objective.

During the negotiations with the Mission Gandhi showed his legal and forensic skill while interpreting the offers of the Mission in terms of the ideas, interest and claims of the Congress. His Secretary, Pyarelal, noted two stages in the process of negotiations so far as the Congress was concerned. In the early phase of the negotiations practically all important resolutions and the drafts of the Working Committee were first conceived in Gandhi's brain and subsequently adopted by the CWC. The Mahatma even corresponded with members of the Mission for clarification of points. The members had several meetings with him where the questions of parity in the Central Government and provincial governments and procedure of Constituent Assembly were discussed. But a stage did come when the leadership could not fully subscribe to his thinking. Why did it happen so? The Mahatma himself supplied the answer. For, when all these negotiations and parleys were going on, he was experiencing great crisis more inside than outside. His instinct and reason were at loggerheads. The former was the call of his inner being which was, for him, nothing short of the voice of God and the latter the product of disciplined and unattached mind normally supporting each other whenever a crucial decision had to be taken by him. Thus while his reason could not find fault with the efforts of the Cabinet Mission to work out a formula for the transfer of power to both the major parties, his instinct was grouping in dark as it apprehended trouble of great magnitude which might shatter all his dreams of a united India freed from the clutches of imperialism and virus of communal hatred. His article in the *Harijan* on June 10, 1946 entitled the 'Unknown' shows the state of his mind. He talks of political moves and political decisions in the language of a mystic. He says, "—in spite of my irrepressible optimism I am unable to say decisively that at least in political parlance the thing is safe. All I can say, therefore, is that, if—the unsafe happens, I would invite them to join with me in saying it was as well that safety lay in unsafety."[14] So his advice to the Congress leadership lacked force of convictions. He laid before them only his misgivings and apprehensions about all the plans and schemes of settlement suggested by the Mission. But he did not insist on the acceptance of his advice. For, it could be a plunge in the dark and the seasoned politicians must not take any such risk. His advice was that of a lawyer who would state the consequences of any act to his client leaving the choice to him to follow it or not. In his interview with Louise Fischer he explains the situation thus:

L. 'If the Working Committee had reacted to your grouping in the dark, they would have rejected the Cabinet Mission Plan'.

G. 'Yes, but I did not let them'.

L. "You mean, you did not insist."

G. More than that, I prevented them from following my instinct also, they also felt likewise. Dr. Rajendra Prasad asked me "does your instinct go so far that you will prevent us from accepting the long-term proposals, whether we understand you or not. I said no, follow your reason since my own reason does not support my instinct. I myself have not followed my instinct unless reason backed it."[15]

Such an attitude was rare in the case of a leader who held sway over the masses and received deference both from friends and foes for his judgement and uncanny intuition. He kept his ego under control which was essential for a person who kept his eye on Gita's ideal of Stithaprajya. May be, he was becoming conscious of the fact that political situation was beyond his control. There were inexorable forces at work which were compelling him to reconsider the importance of his old methods and technique to meet the existing situation. So his endeavour was to approach the political situation with an open mind.

However, this kind of internal struggle created a piquant situation embarrassing to him as well as to those who were engaged in helping him in the performance of his daily functions. Thus when the Viceroy and the Mission asked him to be available at Simla for advice, he decided to go there accompanied by all the persons attending on him. The Government had made all the arrangements for the stay of his large party during the course of the negotiations. The house 'Chadwick' on Summer Hill, which was the residence of the Governor of Burma during the war when the Japanese had occupied Burma, was placed at his disposal.[16] But to be the guest of the Government agitated his mind. For, it was a moral question for him. It was a burden on the money of the people. So on reaching Simla he sent back most of the members of his large party and decided to perform all the functions with the minimum assistance from others. This *volte face* let loose several rumours in the country. Some believed that this was the result of a quarrel among some of his close associates attending on him. Others felt that the negotiations had failed and the Mahatma was taking steps to return. To scotch all such rumours he had to explain in a press statement that he had no time to carry convictions with members of his party to stay back in Delhi. It was a difficult decision for him as he was used to human aids and it was not easy for him to tear himself away from all of a sudden. Here was a man who would spend half a day in searching for a small bit of pencil which had been with him for a long time as he could not reconcile himself to its loss. And here he was deciding to send away most of the members of his party who had been trained and seasoned for his work for years. To a casual onlooker he appears to be a theatrical figure. But if one delves deep into his mind one may find that this strange behaviour was the result of the disturbed state of mind resulting from the behaviour of some of his colleagues during the course of negotiations. He was not keen to go to Simla to be associated with the negotiations in any way. For he had come to know that his very close associate, Azad had written a letter to the members of the Mission at the back of his colleagues in the Working Committee which found favour with the thinking of the Mission, though Azad as the president of the Congress honestly believed that it would help in finding the difficult solution. The question was not what the Congress president felt. But what disturbed Gandhi was that he had told a lie that he had not written any such letter while the original was lying before him. In such an atmosphere of distrust he felt like withdrawing from the negotiations. But under the pressure of SOS and Cripps he suddenly decided to go to Simla. On reaching there, he realized that he and his party would be the guest of the Government as Manorville where he used to stay as the guest of Amrit Kaur could not accommodate such a large party accompanying him. Possibly he felt that he could not perform his task as a self-appointed adviser to all the parties concerned in the negotiations. The differences with his colleagues started developing over the issue of grouping and joining of the provinces in the sections. Initially both Gandhi and the topmost Congress leaders believed that provinces must not be forced to join the groups but the Viceroy and the League believed that grouping was the crux of the Mission's plan. But later on when the Mission held that in the case of grouping the provinces were not entirely free and the Congress leadership was ready to accept it, Gandhi opposed it. He even gave advice to Assam Congress leaders that Assam should not go into sections if there was no clear guidance from CWC. For, according to him it will be a kind of Satyagraha against Congress for the good of the Congress as Congress had committed itself to the judgement of Federal Court.[17] The Viceroy even reported that a draft which he drafted for AICC about HMG's declaration of Dec. 6, amounted to its complete rejection and it was mainly on Patel's instance that this was not accepted.[18] Gandhi admitted in a letter to Cripps dated 24th June 1946 that "I—propose to advise the working committee not to accept the long-term proposition without its being connected with Interim Government. I must not act against my instinct and shall advise them to be guided by their own judgement."[19] According to Sudhir who was close to Patel that in the meeting of the CWC next day Vallabhbhai vigorously pleaded that the prestige of the Congress would be severely damaged if the acceptance of the proposal for constitution making was withheld any further and he carried the day. The Mahatma stoutly defended the CWC's action in accepting the proposal of constitution making although his colleagues had taken the decision against his will. It was characteristic of the Mahatma that he did not part company with his colleagues because of his differences with them.

Not only in the political field, the Indian leaders were hesitant to go along with the Mahatma in several other fields, too. Thus when his view of national language changed from Hindi to Hindustani, other leaders of Hindi Sahitya Sammelan including K.M. Munshi and Tandon could not commit themselves to his concept of national language. For Hindustani meant a language which was commonly spoken and understood in northern India and written in both Devnagri and Persian scripts. Gandhi, therefore, had no choice but to resign from the Hindi Sahitya Sammelan,[20] the body entrusted with the task of propagation of national language.

Notes and References

1. Moon, Penderel (ed.), Wavell, the Viceroy's Journal (London: Oxford Uni. Press, 1973), p. 147.
2. Quoted in Tarachand, History of the Freedom Movement, Vol. IV, p. 450.
3. T.P., Vol. VI, pp. 588-589.
4. *Ibid.*, p. 178.
5. *Ibid.*, p. 934.
6. Moon, Penderel, *op. cit.*, p. 228.
7. *Ibid.*
8. Pyarelal, The Last Phase, *op. cit.*, Vol. I, p. 172.
9. Moon, *op. cit.*, p. 236.
10. Ghosha, Sudhir, Gandhi's Emissary, p. 86.
11. Moon, *op. cit.*, p. 240.
12. T.P., Vol. VI, p. 714.

13. *Ibid.*, Vol. IX, p. 807.
14. T.P., Vol. VII, p. 861.
15. Pyarelal, The Last Phase, Vol. I, p. 230, also C.W., LXXXV, p. 17.
16. Ghosh, *op. cit.*, p. 111.
17. T.P., Vol. IX, p. 403.
18. *Ibid.*, p. 499.
19. Ghosh, *op. cit.*, p. 175.
20. C.W., LXXXII, p. 9.

25

Opponents, Friends and Followers

The differences between the Mahatma and the top brass in the Congress were not sudden. It was not a new development in their relationship. For, their differences started showing their heads as soon as he appeared on the Indian political scene. But these were sometimes open, sometimes subdued and sometimes pushed under the carpet in view of the exigencies of the situation. The differences were natural as the persons around him had different outlook in life born of different experiences and different mental development. There were accomplished and uncultivated persons around him. What was the secret of his success in carrying with him persons of varied temperaments? Or to keep his opponents and critics in good humour and maintain normal relationship with them? The secret of his success was the training of his own mind resulting from his view of truth. For, he earnestly believed that differences of opinion between two persons should not stand in the way of union of hearts as honest differences may follow from looking at truth from different angles. According to him truth like God is infinite and multifaceted. But man is finite and therefore no man can claim the possession of complete knowledge of truth. This implies that everyone can claim to be true from his own point of view. There is no room for such a person to break relations with a person holding different views on any issue. For him, "there is nothing in the world equal to an understanding of those from whom you differ." Each individual who came in contact with him meant so much to him that he never wanted to lose him in spite of his differences with him. So when Reginold Reynold developed differences with him over the Gandhi-Irwin Pact, he appealed to him 'Don't desert the cause or give me up."[1] Once Gandhi told Birla that the secret of his carrying with him persons of different temperaments was that he cared only for good qualities in people and ignored their shortcomings.

"By doing this, he added" I neither harm myself nor the people nor those either who have earned my admiration.[2] In a discussion with his secretary Mahadev Desai, Gandhi told him that in spite of the fact that Annie Besant had been spitting venom against him, there was no trace of hatred for her in him.[3] He appreciated her service to India. It was in 1889, the young Gandhi saw Besant and was impressed by her oratory and her sincere devotion to truth. So he followed her career with unabated interest and admiration for her boundless energy and her organising ability. When Gandhi returned from South Africa in 1915, the venerable lady paid compliment to him for his self-sacrificing spirit at a reception given in his honour. But Gandhi's speech on the occasion of the opening of the Banaras Hindu University raised an acrimonious controversy between them. Both developed differences over several issues and their methods of work. But Gandhi never wavered in his belief for her devotion to the good of the country and excellent work she did in popularising Home Rule League.

Gandhi, in fact, maintained cordial relations with all leaders who did not agree with him in public affairs. For, he kept personal relations apart from his public activities. He never wanted anyone to surrender his own judgement in deference to a friend or a leader. For, it only means blind following which not only hampers the search for truth but also signifies one's disregard of one's inner being. So he himself never allowed his own judgement to be coloured by his loyalty to a friend. This is evident from his relations with the Moderates or Liberal leaders who raised his image in the Indian National Congress Gopal Krishna Gokhale virtually introduced him to the Congress leadership, helped him during his struggle in South Africa and showed great consideration to him when he returned to India in 1915. Though he admitted Gokhale as his political Guru, he did not follow him blindly. So it was no surprise when he told Lady Minto in 1931 at a party in London that Gokhale committed a mistake by agreeing to separate electorates. Gokhale was succeeded by Srinivas Sastri as a leader of the Servants of India Society. Though only ten days older than him, Gandhi treated him as his elder brother and paid due regard to him in spite of deep differences with him on several political issues and methods of his work. Born of a poor Brahmin parents,

Sastri, gradually rose from a school teacher to a Privy Councillor. He believed in India's emancipation through constitutional methods. Though both Gandhi and Sastri were fellow disciples of Gokhale, it was Sastri who virtually prevented Gandhi from joining the Servants of India Society and he made it clear in one of his later speeches: "Mr. Gandhi, having completed the year of travel prescribed by Gokhale, knocked at our door for admission—We saw deep differences between him and us and felt, though none could have given clear expression to it, that his political evolution would take him farther from us. Still our hearts trembled as well as grieved when we told him that it was best for both of us to remain apart and pursue our several courses. "So Sastri vehemently opposed all the political movements launched by Gandhi. But on January 12, 1924, when Gandhi was asked by the attending doctors if he wished to see anybody before he was put under chloroform he wished to see Sastri who was at Poona at that time. During the operation Sastri sat outside the operation room "marvelling at the exhibition I had witnessed of high mindedness, forgiveness, chivalry and love transcending ordinary human nature."[4] Sastri played the role of a peace-maker between the British authorities and the Mahatma whenever the Congress movement got boggled or stuck up. Lord Irwin thanked him for his role in Gandhi-Irwin Pact. When Sastri was appointed agent of the Indian Government in 1927 for South Africa he relied on Gandhi's advice in tackling the problem of Indians in South Africa. Sastri extolled the ideals of the British Empire in South Africa which Gandhi's son Manilal who was editing Indian Opinion did not like. He complained to his father that Sastri's reference to the British Empire was very embarrassing to the Indians in South Africa. Gandhi while passing this letter on to Sastri wrote that knowing my later views about the Empire "I am not surprised at his mentality. He has not the faculty of discrimination to see that we are like blood brothers."[5] Similarly, presiding over Gandhi's birth day in 1929 when Gandhi was preparing to make a final assault on the Empire, Sastri described the Mahatma as "one of those rare souls who are born from time to time—all too rarely it may be—to redeem mankind from their sins and failings."[6] Sastri was perhaps one person outside the circle of Gandhi's disciples and friends whom Gandhi consulted on critical occasions and whose advise he valued though often he found himself unable to accept it. In a letter to Sastri on November 24, 1932 from Yeravada prison, Gandhi wrote, "Your criticism soothes, your silence makes me nervous. Time only deepens my love for you; our differences appear to be superficial. Deep down I feel and touch the meeting ground that is precious."[7] Sastri did not appreciate Gandhi's work at the Round Table Conference calling it as another Himalayan blunder. These differences in their approach to the Indian problems continued till Sastri's death in April 1946 but without impairing their personal relationship. In a letter written in 1936 Sastri said of Gandhi, "His faculty of keeping private friendships alive amidst public differences is marvellous and one wishes his followers learnt that virtue."[8] While touring the country Gandhi went to Madras where his first priority was to meet Sastri who was ailing. He called on him thrice and all these meetings revealed the soft cords between the two disciples of Gokhale that knit their hearts in deep affection. The following conversation between them at the second meeting shows Shastri's regard for Gandhi":

Sastri: You have been blessing me in a hundred ways.

Gandhi: What nonsense, Sastri.

Sastri: Ah, don't I know, Gandhi, you are the greatest fellow alive in the world today. Let your 'Kataksha' fall on them.

In good humour, he quoted Valmiki Ramayana "He who does not see Rama and whom Rama does not see is despised by everyone in this world."[9]

Sastri died on April 17, 1946. To Gandhi his death had removed from the world one of the best sons of India. He wrote, "Though we differed in politics our hearts were one and I could never think that his patriotism was less than that of the tallest patriot."[10]

Like Gokhale, S.N. Bannerjee and Pherozeshah Mehta, Madan Mohan Malaviya was one of the old guards of the Congress. He attended practically all the sessions of the Congress from 1886 till his death in 1946. He presided over the sessions of the Congress four times. Though an orthodox Hindu, he abjured untouchability as a curse on Hinduism. He showed great consideration to Gandhi when very few in the Congress circles were aware of his high character and political ability. He supported Gandhi's drive against untouchability. But he opposed his non-co-operation movement and the boycott of Councils. However, he was an ardent supporter of Swadeshi and Gandhi's programme of Hindu-Muslim unity. But he never wanted Hindus to be browbeaten by Muslim hooligans. He was horrified at the Moplah and communal outbursts in which Hindus suffered. So the Hindu Mahasabha found in him a good supporter. In spite of all such differences Gandhi held him in high esteem. On reaching Delhi in 1946, Gandhi learnt that Malaviya was very anxious to see him and was getting ready to meet him in his Bhangi colony in New Delhi. But Gandhi surprised him by going to Malaviya's place at

5, Canning Road. When asked, he replied, "You would have covered me with shame if you had come to me instead of my going to you."[11]

Gandhi also maintained good relations with the extremist leadership of the Congress in spite of his political differences with them. He admired Tilak for his scholarship, his love of the country, purity of his private life and his indomitable will. He expressed regret at the exclusion of Tilak from the war conference presided over by the Viceroy Lord Willington. Tilak equally admired Gandhi for his high character. At the Lucknow Congress, Gandhi was elected to the Subjects Committee with the help of Tilak.[12] In the preface to the biography of Gandhi written by Mrs Avantikabai Gokhale, Tilak observed that the path of passive resistance discovered by Gandhi and sanctified by his penance had great potentialities although he was sceptical about its universal applicability.[13] At the time of writing his autobiography, the Mahatma had firm faith that had the Lokamany been alive he would have given his benediction at the time of moving his resolution on non-co-operation. How far is Gandhi's calculation true, it is difficult to answer. But Tilak had prophesied that there would be a battle royal at Calcutta Congress over the question of non-co-operation and he would have to work hard to avert the rift in the Congress. He believed that Gandhi's movement would spread. Possibly Tilak was planning to leave for England to allow Gandhi to work out his programme without any hindrance from his side.[14] On Tilak's death, Gandhi paid homage to Tilak by associating Tilak's name to the Swaraj fund of one crore. In his obituary article in *Young India*, he wrote "no man of our times had the hold on the masses that Mr. Tilak had, the devotion that he commanded from thousands of his country men was extraordinary. He was unquestionably the idol of the people—for us he will go down to the generations yet unborn as a maker of modern India."

The Mahatma gave to his opponents and his critics whatever was their due and thereby made a niche for himself in their hearts. He appreciated Lajpat Rai's devotion to his country in spite of strong differences that developed between them immediately after the withdrawal of the non-co-operation movement. The lion of the Punjab as he was addressed by both the elite and the laity during the freedom movement, stood between the Moderates and the Extremists. For, ideologically he was with the latter admiring Tilak's political vision, his view of nationalism and his reliance on mass awakening for the freedom of the country. But he was the friend of the Moderate leaders especially Gokhale and so he did not break connection with the Congress at the time of the split in 1907, though the split slackened his interest in Congress activities. In 1913, he collected money in the Punjab for helping the South African Satyagraha and invited Gokhale to Lahore for this purpose. In 1914 he went to England as a member of the Congress delegation. But did not return and went to the U.S.A. where he stayed for five years. He watched with amazement and joy, the progress of Gandhi's movement in India following the declaration of the Rowlatt Bills. He wrote to Gandhi from New York on June 20, 1919 telling him that he was in substantial agreement with his method.[15] On his return to India he told both the Extremists and the Moderates that the masses of India had been able to realize their strength as a result of Gandhi's Satyagraha. But the two had differences over the programme of non-co-operation. For, Lajpat Rai felt that the programme be introduced gradually as the masses were not fully trained for it. Also he did not favour the indiscriminate withdrawal of children from Government or Government-aided schools and colleges. The withdrawal of the non-co-operation movement infuriated Lajpat Rai and he wrote a lengthy letter to Gandhi in protest against the decision. The differences went on multiplying after that event. But this did not affect their personal relations. Gandhi admired Lajpat Rai for his sincerity, patriotism and self-sacrifice. "Let me not conceal, 'said Gandhi,' my regard for Lalaji. I hold him to be brave, self-sacrificing, generous, truthful and God-fearing. His patriotism is of purest type—." He paid high tributes to the 'Punjab Kesari' on hearing the assault made on him by the police while leading demonstration against the Simon Commission. After Lajpat Rai's death, he took great pains to establish Lajpat Rai Memorial Fund for strengthening the institutions founded by the Punjab leader.

Gandhi-Subhas controversy is an interesting episode in the history of the Congress as well as in the history of India's struggle for freedom. It reveals the way Gandhi kept the Congress as a united party in spite of the emergence of several forces in the country that could split the Congress on grounds of ideology and methods for the attainment of freedom. Nehru and Subhas represented the leftist group that had no patience with the Gandhian methods and ideology which were stigmatized by their opponents as Rightist. Gandhi made an effort to steer clear of the controversy by adopting some of the ideas and catch words of the leftists. He tried to tame their leaders and to some extent he was successful by moving a few steps with them in order to restrain them from pushing the Congress towards an unknown terrain. The Mahatma chided Patel for being aggressive towards the Socialists at the Congress session of 1938 and advised him to seek Subhas's permission to go up to the dais and wipe out their tears and make them smile.[16] For some time even the fiery petrel Subhas who scoffed at Gandhi's ideas and methods was tamed. For, Gandhi secured his election as the Congress President at Haripur in Gujarat in 1938. Then why did he oppose his second term? Possibly Subhas's opponents in the Congress had dinned into the ears of Gandhi that the leadership of Subhas for a longer period would divide the Congress and might take it towards the path of violence. Bose himself did not make any effort to remove this kind of propaganda against him. He had cast aspersion on the motives of the old guards whom he had called old reactionaries and had taunted them as compromisers. Nehru felt that Subhas was surrounded by odd individuals whom he called as adventurists in the technical political sense.[17] These persons obfuscated his vision and he failed to judge the real power of Gandhi. Though elected second term in spite of Gandhi's opposition, he could not carry the majority of the Congress with him and was forced to leave the Congress. Though Gandhi admitted that the defeat of Sitarammya was his defeat, the fact was the withdrawal of Maulana Azad at the last moment created a difficult situation for the opponents of Subhas as Sitarammaya was only a covering candidate and was hardly known in the North. The pattern of voting shows that Subhas won mostly because he received overwhelming support in his own province, U.P. and Punjab.[18] It is not correct to say that Bose had differences only with those whom he called Rightist. Even Nehru did not favour second term for Subhas as most of the members of the CWC felt that it was difficult for them to work with Subhas. According to some of the members of the CWC the continuation of Subhas was a threat to the unity of the Congress. Patel had told Rajendra Prasad that it was impossible for him and most of the members of the old CWC to work with Subhas. Even as the President of the Congress during his first term he had criticized the prohibition policy of the Congress Government of Bombay.[19] In some quarters it is believed that Gandhi could not carry Subhas with him only because Subhas was a socialist and Gandhi was opposed to socialism. But, in fact, there were several other forces at work that prevented them from getting closer. There were several other socialists in the Congress who were tamed by Gandhi. He made their opposition of his leadership sterile by love, tact, accommodation and exposition of his ideas through socialist idioms. He virtually treated Jai Prakash Narayan, one of the topmost leaders of the Congress Socialist Party, as his son-in-law. For he treated, his wife, Prabhavati, who lived in the Ashram for several years, as his daughter. He found a job for Jai Prakash when he was in dire financial difficulty.

Both the Mahatma and the Young Marxist J.P. were bound by some kind of personal relationship in spite of ideological differences. While the latter criticized the former on the platform, his wife would go on plying the Gandhian wheel. The Mahatma did not stifle opposition. He only explained his ideals and methods through the language that his opponents understood. As a result, slowly but imperceptibly Gandhian ideas flowed into the sub-conscious mind of the young convert to Marxism and gushed out after Gandhi's death transforming him as a topmost Gandhian in the post-Gandhian era. Similarly, Acharya Narendra Dev's fascination for Marxism and Socialism did not distance him from Gandhi as the latter did not allow ideological differences to intervene in their personal relations. In the process Gandhian and socialist ideals penetrated into each other. This attitude liberated the leadership from narrow partisan thinking. The Mahatma even claimed pleasant relationship with Savarkar Brothers despite his fundamental differences with them.

The faithfuls, that is, those who were close to Gandhi, also had moments of anguish and embarrassment over master's decisions. Gandhi tried to satisfy them by his skill as a lawyer. He did not stifle criticism. Rather he encouraged them to open their hearts to him so that he could place his own cards before them. This device quite often yielded good results as his friends had not to carry the burden of their conscience while following him. Most of them had gathered round him only because of his performance in the national field. He had raised the spirits of the Indians. But it was not necessary for them to approve of every idea or act of the master. This is evident from the relationship between Gandhi and Nehru.

Gandhi was deeply religious. But Nehru was agnostic, though late in his life he was drawn towards non-dualism of the Vedanta. But since the time Nehru saw Gandhi working at the Congress Enquiry Committee in 1919 till his assassination in January 1948, both worked together in spite of their differences on several vital issues. Young Nehru was drawn towards Gandhi because his method and technique assured great results for the political enlightenment and mobilisation of the masses. But he did not agree with all the ideas and acts of Gandhi. His first dis-illusionment with Gandhi's policies came over the withdrawal of the non-co-operation movement. The clash of ideas between the two became more frequent after that as the euphoria of Gandhi's powers to deliver the goods started evaporating. Nehru criticized Gandhi's view of 'Ramraj', his complete reliance on Khadi his distrust of machinery and industrialisation, his surrender to inner voice, his views expressed in the

Hind Swaraj, his fasts, his concept of trusteeship etc. In his autobiography, Nehru highlights several paradoxes in Gandhi's view of social life. He considers Gandhi's concept of village self-sufficiency as narrowest autarchy which is an impossible objective in the modern times. But the old man took all this criticism in its stride. Rather he advised him to resist him whenever his suggestions did not appeal to him. When the two did not see eye to eye at a critical juncture in 1938, the old man wrote thus:

> "I can't tell you how positively lonely I feel to know that now-a-days I can't carry you with me.—I know that you would do much for affection. But in matters of state there can be no surrender to affection, when the intellect rebels. My regard for you is deeper for your revolt."[20]

Only the Mahatma could write this. Realising that both held strong views on certain matters which could not be easily reconciled, Gandhi advised Nehru to take full charge and lead the country, "leaving me free to voice my opinion." But all these differences did not prevent Gandhi to declare in 1942 that Jawahar was his political heir. For, he had full faith that the interest of the poor masses were safe in his hands.

V.B. Patel was considered as a Mahatma's loyalist. It is true that he stood by the leader through thick and thin for a long time. While the two were together in the Yeravada jail in 1932-33, Sardar served Gandhi with motherly care which the Mahatma acknowledged on May 8, 1933 "One of the greatest joys of my life was that I had an opportunity of staying in prison with Sardar. I knew of his invincible courage and of his burning love of his country but never before had I had the good fortune of spending so much time with him as I was able to do during these sixteen months. His affection and love overwhelmed me and reminded me of my dear mother."[21]

But the relationship between the two were not always of a master and a disciple. The Sardar quite often showed courage to oppose some of the decisions of Gandhi. There were sharp differences between the two on payment of land revenue in Bardoli and Borsad. The matter even came to a breaking point.—There was heated discussion which caused some offence to Gandhi. But next day Gandhi revised his opinion acknowledging that Sardar was right.[22] When the CWC had to take certain hard decisions with regard to its attitude towards war, Gandhi pressed Patel to act according to his own lights. Patel differed with Gandhi over their attitude towards war and he spoke frankly about such differences.

Gandhi publically backed Patel's independence over this issue. So he wrote, "All honour to Sardar for holding fast his convictions." Quite often Gandhi than his own judgement or his inner voice.[23] He was conscious of the indomitable spirit of his comrade that won for him the battle in Bardoli. After attending the Second Round Table Conference, he sought Patel's advice for extending his stay in Europe for a month more after the conference. Gandhi shared his personal troubles with his friend. But when Patel was ailing, he abandoned all his public activities to look after him like a father at his nature cure centre. However in the public life, there were moments when Patel took a different line of action which caused pain to Gandhi. But the later did not lose trust in his comrade and frankly expressed his opinion on the controversial issue which removed some of the misunderstandings between them. Several letters were exchanged between the two from 1945 till Gandhi's death that showed the extent of their differences. But it was not because Patel's regard for Gandhi had worn off. In fact, the two were working at different planes. Patel had to take certain decisions as an administrator while Gandhi had to listen to the grievances of the people who were adversely affected by such decisions. But in spite of their differences, Gandhi liked the company of Patel and enjoyed his banters. According to Rajagopalachari, Patel as a blind follower of Gandhi is a class himself. For "his eyes are clear and bright. He can see every thing but he deliberately allows his eyes to be blinkered and attempts to see with Gandhiji's eyes."[24]

C.R. Rajagopalachari, popularly known as Rajaji, the name given to him by Gandhi's Secretary Mahadev Desai, was one of the earliest comrades of Gandhi from the South when Gandhi turned non-co-operator from a co-operator over the issue of Rowlatt Act. However, he was aware of the heroic fight Gandhi had carried on in South Africa. He had read Gandhi's Indian Home Rule sent to him by a friend in 1910, Doke's biography of Gandhi and an account of his three terms in prison in South Africa published in the Modern Review in 1913. So he wrote a paper on Gandhi in 1916 wherein while appreciating his role, he said, "led by him (Gandhi) our brothers and sisters of South Africa had so acted that Indians may forget their unworthiness for a time and walk proudly in the world." He played host to the author of Satyagraha in Madras when Gandhi was in search of an effective programme for protesting against Rowlatt Act. Rajaji was known for sharp intellect and practical insight. He had been practising as a lawyer since 1900. In the year 1920, we find him addressing Gandhi as 'My dearest Master'. He had become an all-out Gandhi man and during the non-co-operation movement he displayed great zeal in promoting non-co-operation in the Madras Presidency. He virtually became Gandhi's conscience keeper and when Gandhi decided that he would reduce his raiment to a length of cloth covering the body from the waist to the knee, he showed his statement for making this announcement on the train between Trichy and Madura. During Gandhi's incarceration after the withdrawal of non-co-operation movement, he led the no-changers against the formidable leaders such as Das and Motilal who stood for council-entry. He pleaded for constructive programme which for him did not mean merely social reform but a deliberate preparation for political action. Because of his faith in Gandhi's programme, he was even satirised in the South by his opponents as the Deputy Mahatma. Following in the footsteps of the Mahatma, he established an Ashram at Pudupolagam on Feb. 6, 1925 where he "would attempt to live out with willing co-workers the gospel of constructive programme." But the relationship that developed between them during the decades after the withdrawal of the non-co-operation movement was not of a master and a disciple. For Rajaji had a strong mind of his own of which Gandhi was fully aware and would not therefore, embarrass him by insisting on something which he did not like. When Gandhi agreed to making Khadi franchise optional, C.R. wrote a searing letter to him saying, "I wish I had been a private gentleman, pure and simple and I should then have been less of a fool than I am now." But probably anticipating C.R.'s reaction, Gandhi wrote 'My soul is living in a world physically away from me and yet a world by which I am and want to be affected. You are a part of that world and perhaps the nearest to me. My innermost being wants your approbation of what I am doing and thinking. To this C.R. said to Gandhi's son Devadas "My soul had been surrendered long ago and I cannot but agree."[25] In view of C.R.'s strong mind of his own, Gandhi did not like to disturb him by insisting on the acceptance of his own view. On July 5, 1942 he wrote to C.R. thus, "Mahadev was telling me how sad you were over my obstinacy in not appreciating what was plain to you. All that I can say is there is no want of will about me. Once an idea possesses me I can't get rid of the possession. I suppose you are of the same build. Therefore, there seems to be no escape but to suffer each other's limitation."

In view of C.R.'s sharp differences with the Congress in 1942, Gandhi even advised him to resign from the Congress as well as from the Assembly since he was elected on the Congress ticket. But all this had no effect on their personal relations. Even in June 1942, Gandhi invited him to his place for rest. He wrote, 'Nonsense—These differences mean nothing — I shall no longer enter into a controversy with you—you should come here for rest, jokes and in search of strength and joy."[26] On several occasions both of them would strike hard on each other. But the heat of the controversy would not produce any animosity. They differed and yet they depended on each other. It was the realistic approach of C.R. that cleared the way for Gandhi-Jinnah talks. When riots broke out in the West Bengal after the partition, only C.R. as the Governor had the courage to tell Gandhi in plain words that his fast would have no effect on the trouble-makers.

A classic example of deep love and regard between two persons in spite their deep differences over certain political moves, is the relationship between Tagore and Gandhi. They adored each other. Both believed in self-realization through service to mankind. Both held the supremacy of the spirit over matter. Tagore held Gandhi in high esteem for introducing spiritual force in politics. So he popularised him as a Mahatma while Gandhi addressed Tagore as Gurudev. But the latter denounced Gandhi's non-co-operation movement because of its negative foundations. He protested against the burning of clothes. Also he criticized Gandhi's complete faith in the spinning wheel as the only solution to India's economic problems. But it had no effect on their personal relations. In reply to Tagore's criticism Gandhi said, "The frank criticism (of Rabindranath) pleases me. For our friendship becomes all the richer for our disagreements. Friends to be friends are not called upon to agree even on most points. Only disagreements must not have sharpness much less bitterness about them. And I gratefully admit that there is none about the poet's criticism

Thus before undertaking the epic fast in 1932, Gandhi sought Tagore's blessing and the latter not only congratulated the former on his heroic stand but went to Yeravada undertaking three day's journey in his eighties to be present besides him at this difficult time for his friend. In his old age when the poet was undertaking tours with ballet troupe to collect money to tide over the financial difficulties of his institution, the Mahatma was perturbed and sent a cheque of Rs. 60,000 and asked him to relax.

The Mahatma did not like to impose his views on his comrades especially when he himself was not sure of his own position or the correctness of his view. He "claimed to be of the earth, earthy, prone to as many weaknesses as any other human beings. He was, therefore, slow to see the blemishes in others." In 1940 when the Congress Working

Committee renewed its demand for the formation of the Provisional National government as a condition for supporting the British war efforts, Rajaji brought his own resolution which was not in accord with that of Gandhi. The latter responded to it as follows: "Rajaji was the framer of the resolution. He is as certain of his position as I was of mine. He would not have even thought of bringing up his resolution if I had chosen to prevent him. But I give my comrade the same credit for earnestness and self-confidence that I claim for myself—."

In fact, the nature of Gandhi's leadership was unique. For, he treated any person associated with him as his fellow traveller striding with him towards the common goal without losing his or her own personality. So he told a devoted lady inmate of the Ashram, "—I do not wish to make everybody like me. My teaching is that everybody should be true to himself. Anybody who has digested my teaching will never fall into doubt but will ever go forward."[27] Kriplani probably was echoing the same idea when he told the delegates to the Peace Conference at Santiniketan after Gandhi's death "not copy Gandhi but to use their own initiative. What they needed was Gandhi's spirit and sense of urgency."[28]

The Mahatma was allergic to blind imitation which he considered as "an evidence of paralysis of the mind or sport of little minds." He felt distressed when he learnt that some women in Maharashtra had done his 'arti' which is done in case of a god. He considered it sinful. He allowed them to do so on a mistaken belief that they were only blessing him.[29] He had advised his followers that "none should take from him as gospel truth."[30] He should take it only if it appeals to his head and heart." Once a co-worker in his articles was found to be very critical of Gandhi's views. The latter asked him to come over to discuss the matter concerned. The co-worker showed great respect for the master. But said, "Bapu my heart opens to you but my mind closes against you and I am sorely grieved at this. Tell me what should I do." Gandhi said, "Set the dictates of your heart aside for the time being and only follow the promptings of your mind."[31] He discouraged his lady admirer from keeping his sandals "as it was nothing short of idolatry" which he did not like. Andre Philip, a French man who had lived in Gandhi's Ashram for some time, told Romain Rolland that he noticed among the members of his Ashram "that though they venerate Gandhi, they don't hesitate to express their opinion if they disagree with him and Gandhi likes people who contradict him."[32]

However, there were some followers especially women in his Ashram for whom it was a spiritual necessity to be attached to his person. This attitude apart from generating tension in the Ashram, embarrassed the Mahatma who expected from his followers devotion to his cause and not to his person when Madeleine Slade (Mira) joined his Ashram, he had no idea that she obtained spiritual comfort by serving his person and so it was her intense desire to remain close to him. She belonged to the aristocratic family of England. Her father Sir Edward Slade, K.A.I.E. was the admiral. When he was made Commander-in-Chief in the East Indies, she accompanied her father and had the experience of living among the topmost administrators of India. So the Mahatma warned her of the hard life of his Ashram before taking the plunge. But that did not deter her. She was no more a young girl but a woman in her early thirties when she took this decision. Her parents did not stand in her way as they felt that it was her spiritual necessity to serve the Mahatma. For, they knew that she was no ordinary girl. She had been moving from one interest another in search of her own 'self.' Her interest in music especially of the German composer Beethoven drove her towards Romain Rolland whose series the novel Jean Christophe was inspired by the life of Beethoven. When she met him sometime in 1924, the French Nobel Laureate had just finished his short biography of Gandhi in which he had portrayed the Indian leader as a saint who was demonstrating the real strength of all the Christian virtues. During their talk, Romain Rolland casually mentioned Gandhi as a living Christ. That gave Miss Slade her mission. She wrote to Gandhi and he permitted her to join his Ashram. But while Miss Slade wanted to remain near him in order to serve his person, Gandhi wanted her to serve his cause and therefore arranged a programme for her training which involved separation from him. Quite often that created a void in the life of Mira, her Indian name given by the Mahatma. She overcame the wrench of parting with him through correspondence with him as her letters in reply were a great source of spiritual comfort to her. Though her devotion to the Mahatma appeared to a large number of her countrymen as an abnormal behaviour, the Mahatma impressed upon her to retain her individuality. He never wanted her to treat him as her 'guru'. She had the freedom to discuss several matters with him and even to advise him on certain problems.[33]

There were many persons working in varied fields and holding different political and economic views who were drawn towards the Mahatma for spiritual comforts. The Mahatma carried them along with him to the extent they could go with him. Vallabhbhai's elder brother Vithalbhai could not join Gandhi's movement to the extent his brother could do because of his mental make-up and the training of his mind. He was interested in council work. So Gandhi told Vallabhbhai that he well appreciated the qualities of his brother as such qualities "are needed for the good of the country."

Similarly a business magnate G.D. Birla had long association with Gandhi, though he could not endorse his economic philosophy and political programmes. He was 22 years of age when he first met Gandhi in 1916 and this meeting developed into close relationship till Gandhi's death in Birla's palatial mansion on January 30, 1948. The spiritual aspect of Gandhi's personality and non-violent approach to all problems of social life drew him close to him. So he declared, "My point is that Gandhiji's influence over me was more through his religious character—his sincerity and search for truth than his power as a political leader." Birla made liberal financial contribution to Gandhi's constructive programme of anti-untouchability and Khadi. Gandhi appointed him president of All-India anti-untouchability league which later on came to be known as All India Harijan Sewak Sangh and under his guidance it created a net work of educational and training institutions in the country for raising the economic and social status of the Harijans in society. Though Birla was no convert to Gandhi's economic programmes, he gave liberal donations to them on the demand made by Gandhi. For, Gandhi was father figure for him. However, he never claimed to be a Congressman nor participated in any of civil disobedience movements. His eyes were on the economic interests of Indian industrialists. The struggle of the Congress was viewed by him favourable to the Indian industrialists as it would eliminate the unhealthy competition of Indians with the British industrialists who could obtain favours from the British administrators. Though he did not participate in any political movement, he maintained good relations between the Congress leaders and the British administrators and statesmen. He kept the channel of communication with the Congress leaders and the British high officials and tried to act as 'go between' in any conflict between the Congress and the Government. Gandhi knew this and used Birla's services whenever it was in the interests of the country and the Congress. However, Gandhi never allowed his personal relations to affect his views. In fact, Gandhi had the knack of finding work for different kinds of persons, work that would give satisfaction to the person concerned and serve the cause of nation. His relations with another capitalist, Jamnalal Bajaj and his family were on a different plane. It was a spiritual necessity for Jamnalal to be associated with Gandhi like a family member. He was adopted by a rich man Seth Bechhraj whose adopted son Ramdhandas died in the prime of his life. He was deprived of the natural affection of his parents and this created a void in his life. For, he could not get rid of the feeling that he was discarded by his parents. So his first request to Gandhi when he met him to treat him as his fifth son. He, therefore, completely identified himself with all the programmes of Gandhi and as the treasurer of the Congress played an important role in its organization and programmes.[34]

One important trait in Gandhi's leadership was his concern for the individual. Even when his activities increased and he was called upon to tackle bigger problems of the country and of the world, he never lost sight of the needs of the individuals who were bound to him. According to Reginald Reynold who had stayed with him and carried on correspondence with him after his return to England, "He (Gandhi) gives to each individual who comes in contact with him the impression of real personal impression but he can sever every attachment without sign of pain."[35] So a large portion of the hundred volumes of his collected works is covered by his correspondence with individuals who sought his advice for their personal problems, varying from their family relations to physical ailments and Gandhi in reply offering them comfort on the basis of his personal experiences or suggesting nature-cure remedies. For him no individual was small or insignificant. So he affirmed, "For me the smallest work is as important as the biggest. For me whatever is in the atoms and molecules is in the universe." Sudhir Ghosh who claimed to be Gandhi's emissary during the period of negotiations carried on by the Cabinet Mission for the transfer of power, observes in reply to a question as to the clue of Gandhi's great power over other men and women that "he (Gandhi) loved you as an individual and quickened to your singular sorrows, your particular happiness. He always had time for you—."

However, Gandhi's co-workers, friends, sympathisers and disciples had one great difficulty while working with him. They could not easily judge the working of the mind of the Mahatma when they were faced with a crucial situation. For, quite often the Mahatma stood at different plane and so the factors that determined his decision were beyond the comprehension of even those who were close to him. Thus when the discussion was going on in the Yeravada jail between Gandhi and Patel who was with him at that time in August 1932, about the views of leaders of different groups in India about the Communal Award, Patel asked Gandhi as to why Malaviya had as yet not expressed his view on this crucial issue, the Mahatma replied that he must be confused as he had no idea of his (Gandhi's) views on this subject. Patel then opened his mind and said "that, of course, is the real trouble in working with you. You never let us know right till the end how your mind is working, with the result that the position of your colleagues and companions becomes extremely awkward. This is our main quarrel with you."[36] In a similar vein Patel wrote to his daughter Manibehn who was in the Belgaum jail in May 1933 and was seriously disturbed on hearing the 21-day Gandhi's fast undertaken for his own purification as well as of his co-workers "— But when we follow Bapur we must realize that there are times when his actions and decisions are incomprehensible to us when judged by our ordinary standards. There is so great a difference between our worldly outlook and his that it is quite impossible for us fully to understand all his actions. Therefore, it is as well for us just to place our trust in God and assume that whatever he is doing is for our good."[37]

Notes and References

1. Reginald Reynold, To Live in Mankind, *op. cit.*, 87.
2. Birla, G.D., Bapur, *op. cit.*, Vol. I, p. 11.
3. Desai, *op. cit.*, Vol. II, p. 34.
4. Rao, Kodanda, P., V.S. Srinivas Sastri, A Political Biography, p. 160.
5. *Ibid.*, p. 268.
6. *Ibid.*, p. 287.
7. C.W., Lii, p. 52.
8. Rao, *op. cit.*, p. 379.
9. C.W., Vol. LXXXIII, p. 62.
10. *Ibid.*, LXXXIV, p. 19.
11. *Ibid.*, p. 20.
12. Keer, Dhananjay, Lokamanya Tilak, p. 374.
13. *Ibid.*, p. 393.
14. *Ibid.*, p. 436.
15. Lajpat Rai, Writings and Speeches, Vol. I, p. 327. Also C.W., Vol. XVI, Appendix III.
16. Quoted in, Gorden, Leonard A., Brothers Against the Raj—A Biography of Sarat & Subhash, p. 353.
17. *Ibid.*, p. 382.
18. Dr. Rajendra Prasad, Correspondence, Vol. III, p. 369.
19. *Ibid.*, p. 174.
20. C.W., LXVII, also Bunch of Letters, p. 276.
21. Collected Works of Patel, Vol. IV, p. 22.
22. *Ibid.*, Vol. III, p. 209.
23. Quoted in Gandhi, Rajmohan, Patel, p. 294.
24. *Ibid.*, p. 246.
25. Gandhi, Rajmohan, Rajaji Story, *op. cit.*, p. 144.
26. C.W., LXXV, p. 199.
27. *Ibid.*, LXXX, p. 306.
28. Reginald, Reynold, *op. cit.*, pp. 143-44.
29. C.W., XCV, p. 214.

30. *Ibid.*, LXXXIII, p. 218.
31. Ramnarayan, *op. cit.*, p. 143.
32. C.W., XLIV, p. 192.
33. R.R. & Gandhi's Correspondence, p. 135, from R.R.'s Diary.
34. Birla, In the Shadow of the Mahatma, p. 2.
35. Reginald Reynold, *op. cit.*, p. 41.
36. Parikh Narhari, Sardar Vallabhbhai Patel, Vol. II, p. 110.
37. *Ibid.*, p. 153.

26

Ploughing a Lonely Furrow

The Cabinet Mission Plan did not remove the differences between the League and the Congress as it was subjected to various interpretations. Both the parties held different views over the issue of grouping of provinces and the scope of the powers of the Constituent Assembly. The negotiations between the two parties having failed, the League refused to co-operate in the formation of the Indian Government as provided in the plan. The Viceroy, though having sympathies with the League, had no choice but to invite the Congress to form the ministry at the centre partly under the advice of the Secretary of State and partly apprehending fierce communal trouble resulting from aggressive attitude of the League leadership that declared 16th August as the 'Direct Action Day'. Ostensibly it was the day of protests and meetings to propagate the Muslim demand, to explain the Muslim attitude towards the Cabinet Mission's offer and to condemn the conduct of the Congress. Jinnah refused the offer of Nehru to participate in the Interim Government on his invitation. The Government of Suhrawardhy in Bengal declared 16th August as a public holiday and thus made it possible for students, office staff and others to join the crowd. In Calcutta, the demonstrations and processions of the Muslims led to rioting and looting which spread all over the city. This mad fury continued for four days. As a result, 5000 persons were killed and about 1500 were seriously injured. The fury of Calcutta riots marked a watershed in the political developments that clinched the issue for the partition of the country. For, it became a powerful argument for those who held the view that the British could not leave India by handing it over only to one of the parties.

The Congress assumed office on September 2 under the leadership of Nehru. The Muslim League declared it as a day of mourning. Violence broke out in Bombay, Punjab, Bengal and Bihar. It appeared to the Mahatma that the situation was pushing India to the brink of a civil war. To escape such an heinous fratricidal war he acceded to the formula of the Nawab of Bhopal which required the Congress to recognize the Muslim League as the authoritative representative of an overwhelming majority of the Muslims of India without giving up its right to choose any representative it thought proper for the interim government or the Constituent Assembly. The Viceroy reported to the SOS that there were two stories current about the framing of this formula. One that it was drafted by Gandhi and objected to by Jinnah and the other that it was drafted by Nehru and objected to by Gandhi on the grounds that it went too far in the direction of satisfying the Muslim league.[2] The first story appears to be more plausible as Nehru at that time was reluctant to go out of the way to accommodate the League. However, the acceptance of this formula broke the deadlock and paved way for the League to join the interim government, without any commitment of joining the Constituent Assembly. The League list of five members for the interim government had a surprise for the Congress as it included the name of Jogendra Nath Mandal, a schedule caste, whereby the League challenged the right of the Congress to represent the schedule caste.

Nevertheless, the formation of the coalition government did not reduce the tension between the parties as it rested on distrust and mutual acrimony. For, one of the League representatives of the council openly declared "we are going into the interim government to get a foothold to fight for our cherished goal of Pakistan." So the conflict between the two wings of the council fuelled the communal fire raging in the country. Even when it was smouldering in Calcutta, it broke out with greater force in Noakhali, a district in East Bengal, that caused great suffering to the Hindu minority. Forcible conversion of the Hindus, rape and kidnapping of Hindu women and the destruction of the property of the Hindus on a large scale stunned the Mahatma. The cry of the outraged womanhood peremptorily called him to Noakhali. Equally disturbing to him was the outbreak of riots in Bihar as a retaliatory measure. He, therefore, decided either restore the communal peace both in Bengal and Bihar or die if he failed to do so. It was again the 'do or die mission' before him. But this time he alone was involved in it though assisted by some of his close associates. So he mentally disengaged himself from all responsibilities with regard to the Congress, Sevagram Ashram or the nature-cure centre of Uruli-Kanchan which was his latest love. He was even prepared for fast unto death if the situation so demanded. He no longer desired to live for 125 years which he wished only a few years earlier. He started living on spare diet[1], partly for reasons of health and partly as a preparation for fast unto death which virtually took him to death's door. Events agitated his mind to such an extent that he lost his self-control and equanimity essential for living for 125 years. Even a small unintentional lapse on the part of his admirer or a loyal colleague would make him 'flare up madly'. Thus on his birth day according to the Hindu calendar which fell in 1946 ten days in advance of the ordinary calendar, a function was held which was presided over by Dr. Rajendra Prasad who at that time held the portfolio of food in the Central Ministry, where raisin and monkey nuts were served to Harijan children and volunteers in the camp. This disturbed him so much that he called this act as an insult to the Food Minister since food was served needlessly when every morsel of food had to be husbanded because of acute food shortage in the country.[2]

In this state of mind he moved to Noakhali. The decision in this regard, he said, came from within. "Why should you be witness to the slaughter" his inner being asked him. For some time he was a prey to despondency as he felt that there must be some fault in his technique of non-violence. Otherwise why should there be so much violence in spite of all his efforts to solve all the problems through this technique of non-violence. He, therefore, planned to tackle the communal problem in Noakhali by a new technique which involved great risk to his own life as well as to the lives of his associates who had accompanied him to East Bengal. Each member of the party, including women, was required to settle down in one affected village and make himself or herself hostage for the safety and security of the Hindu minority of that village. All such volunteers were pledged to protect with their lives, if necessary, the Hindu population of the villages under their charge. A non-Bengali volunteer was to be accompanied by a Bengali interpreter for communication with the local population that could understand Bengali alone. He deprived himself of the services of all his companions except two or three who could assist him in carrying on the heavy load of daily work, especially correspondence. According to the plan, he would stay as far as possible in the house of a Muslim of the village that he would visit. For some time he was assisted by Parsuram, who was a good stenographer and

Nirmal Kumar Bose, a professor of Calcutta University as his interpreter. At the same time he made a request to the League Ministry of Bengal to give him one honest and brave Muslim and one Hindu of the same character to accompany him to each effected village. They should guarantee at the cost of their lives the safety of the Hindus who would return to their homes.[3] The Government was hardly in a position and mood to meet this demand. His own programme, of course, was to go every morning to the houses of the local Muslims and talk to them to ascertain their real views on the contemporary situation. He was determined to bury himself in East Bengal till Hindus returned to their homes and the two communities learnt to live together in harmony and peace. Settling down in the village Srirampur for some time, he decided to visit other villages around it. Normally he would walk barefooted just as Hindus do while going to a holy shrine. For, it was a sort of a pilgrimage for him. With Tagore's song 'walk alone' on his lips "he moved from one village to another. Broken glass pieces and filth were deliberately strewn in his path by some Muslim miscreants as a result of which his feet were sometimes hurt. At great risk he had to move quite often on swaying bamboo bridges ten or fifteen high from the ground. Because of his poor health, he would plan his movement in such a way that he had not to walk for more than one hour and fifteen minutes at a stretch. In the evening he would hold prayer meetings to which both Hindus and Muslims were invited. The burden of most of his speeches was that Hindus should trust the local Muslims in place of insisting on the protection of the military and the police because of his conviction that normalcy would not return so long as Hindus depended upon outside help.[4] However, this argument did not appeal to the local Hindus because of their bad experience of Muslim officers and League volunteers who were mainly responsible for creating a hell for the Hindus in their programme of forcing the Congress leadership to concede their demand for Pakistan. Moreover, the outbreak of riots in Bihar in retaliation to the suffering of the Hindus in Noakhali, reduced the efficacy of Gandhi's mission and all his arguments for mutual understanding between the two communities. For the Muslim leaders asked him to go to Bihar to alleviate the condition of the Muslims who had been subjected to the wrath of the Bihar Hindus. Though Gandhi did not deny the suffering caused to the Muslims in Bihar, he was in no mood to leave Noakhali as he was sure that he could do the needful without personally visiting Bihar through Congress leadership that was in power there. Moreover, he was aware that riots in Bihar were of retaliatory nature and consequently as soon as normalcy was restored in East Bengal, Hindus in Bihar would automatically create conditions for the safety of the Muslims living there. However, to speed up the process of restoration of peace in Bihar, he impressed upon the Congress ministers of Bihar to take effective measures immediately for the return of the Muslims to their homes. He even suggested the appointment of an impartial commission to enquire about the causes of the riots to assess the damage done to a particular community during the riots, to identify the guilty and to suggest measures for the prevention of the recurrence of such events. But this did not satisfy the League leadership of Bengal. For, this suggestion could not be carried out mostly because of the opposition of the Governor of Bihar and the Viceroy though some body put into Gandhi's ears that it was Patel who had opposed this move.[5]

The Mahatma had to face many more difficulties in Noakhali in his efforts to carry the Muslim leadership with him for the restoration of peace there. His prayer meetings were becoming counter-productive. Several Muslims objected to the coupling of Ram with Rahim or Krishna with Karim by him at the prayer meetings on the grounds that while Rama and Krishna were mere kings Rahim and Karim were the names of God. None was satisfied by his explanation that his Rama and Krishna were not human beings but only the different names of one God. But much more offensive appeared to the Muslims was his advice to the Muslim women to discard 'Purdah' which was interpreted as an attack on the tenets of Islam by a non-Muslim. Several Muslims, therefore, asked him not to dwell upon matters relating to Islam in his speeches. It looks that odds were so formidable against his mission that sometimes he lost control over himself. Once he was extremely worked up when Sushila Nayyar, his old co-worker and his physician suggested to him to take along with him persons like her who knew him better than new persons like N.K. Bose or Parsuram. It irritated him so much that he raised his voice and slapped his forehead in anguish which was against the basic principle of his mission in Noakhali as in his view, it was 'tapascharya' or penance and so a person undertaking it must be free from anguish, anger or any kind of feeling of lust. This was Gandhi's old habit which he probably inherited from his father. As narrated by him, he once as a child went to the theatre against the will of his father. He was called back and he stood by the side of his father. He saw his father weeping and striking his forehead in grief. Once while returning from Calcutta in 1921, on his way to Varanasi, he was harassed by Darshan seekers. His secretary requested to the people not to disturb him but of no avail. Gandhi in sheer angush beat his forehead thrice and this had the desired effect on the Darshan seekers. Gandhi later on explained that at Noakhli it was the fourth time that he beat his head to overcome his anger or anguish. On three occasions his grief was due to the misdeeds of those dear to him which he could not bear. On one occasion he atoned for his own lapse.[6]

Because of the difficulties in Noakhali, he was sometimes overcome by a feeling of despondency and dismay. To his English admirer Agatha Harrison, he wrote, "I have never been in such darkness as I am in today. And the darkness does not come from outside. It is due to my limitations. My faith in Ahimsa has never burned brighter and Yet I feel that there is something wanting in my technique of it that I feel as though I were on an unbeaten track."[7] Writing in the same vein to another person, he said, I cannot see my path in the thick darkness of the night."[8]

In this state of mind, he turned searchlight inward and discovered that the force of the challenge to his ideals was far greater than his own power. But he was sure that no power on earth could subdue the spirit abiding in him. So the real problem with him at that time was how to draw that powei out of the spirit. The reply came from within. Complete purity was the only way to make the spirit manifest itself in social life. But without complete Brahmacharya purity was not possible. That was his faith.

What was his ideal of Brahmacharya? In his view a real Brahmachari becomes mentally eunuch, that is, he loses distinction between a man and a woman. Indian tradition relates the story of a young saint who acquired so much control over his passions that even when he was nude, young women would not hesitate to come before him to pay their obeisance. Once his father, fully attired as a 'Sanyasin' was passing by tank where women were taking bath. As he came near them they covered themselves with their clothes. But he was followed by his son who was nude. When he came near them, they all came out to salute him. His father looked back and was surprised by the behaviour of the women. He came back and asked them about their strange behaviour. The women replied, sir, although you are a saint, you are still aware of the distinction between a man and a woman. But your son had lost even that distinction and so we were not ashamed of coming before him. The Mahatma had been making efforts to attain this state of mind since the day he took the vow of Brahmacharya while offering his services to the Natal Government engaged in the suppression of Zulu Rebellion. The nature of the work set him thinking that procreation of children was inconsistent with public service. Even earlier he had made an attempt to observe self-control to avoid more children as he detested the use of contraceptives. But he had failed in spite of taking all kinds of precautions such as retiring to a separate bed after complete exhaustion from a day's work. Brahmacharya for him was a condition for complete devotion to public work. It was also a condition for his experiment with community living as in his scheme of social life there was no segregation between men and women. Rather the latter had to play an important role not only in the struggle for freedom but also in his programme of national reconstruction. Consequently both had to observe strict self-control in order to avoid dissipation of their energies in love making. Sexual indulgence appeared to him as a serious impediment to his view of nation building. Brahmacharya, therefore, was considered as one of the important observances for the inmates of his Ashram. It was one of the five props of his spiritual striving which, in his view, constituted an indivisible whole. "If one of them is broken, all are broken."[9] So even married couples were required to avoid sexual indigence in his Ashram. He could visualise a healthy social system wherein men and women could work together without any lustful intention. For, it was essential for the freedom of women in society. However, Gandhi did not totally oppose sexual union. For nature, according to him, wanted it only for procreation and not for pleasure. Sexual indulgence, in his view, was unnatural if committed for pleasure alone. He was, therefore, not against marriage if one followed this norm. He himself performed several marriages in his Ashram. Nor did he like a married person to observe celibacy if the other partner desired sexual act. However, a number of his disciples and his sons could not observe Brahmacharya and some of them who tried to observe it strictly later on faced psychological problems.

However, Gandhi's view of Brahmacharya was not merely a condition for a healthy social life. It was rooted in his belief of the identity of the essence man and that in the universe. The spiritual aspect of Brahmacharya acquired greater prominence as the consciousness of the identity of the soul with the universal spirit acquired greater hold over him. It led him to believe that one could overcome all odds by invoking the spiritual power pervading the universe through perfect purity of mind by acquiring 'complete mastery over all senses.' He started making experiments to test the extent of his control over sexual passions. He used to sleep with young women in the Ashram. But he would take precautions that such women were also motivated by Brahmacharya. Thus, as soon as he came to know that these women had no such motive and were ready to sleep with him out of regard for him, he stopped the experiment with them.[10] But the significance of such experiments could not be realized by several inmates of the Ashram who were shocked by such acts of the Mahatma. He put off such experiments for the time being in the Ashram on their plea that such acts would be exploited by persons of impure motives which would vitiate the atmosphere in the Ashram. But he did not give up the idea of resuming such experiments if the situation demanded it. For, he believed that a real Brahmachari would not think of sexual pleasure even in his dreams as for him Brahmacharya did not mean merely preservation of vital fluid, for, according to him, 'can save it through an operation and enjoy sexual pleasure without losing it.[11] So the Mahatma was extremely disturbed when he had discharge at the age of 66. Of course, he had involuntary discharges in dreams even in South Africa when he took the vow of Brahmacharya. But this time he was not dreaming. So it made him feel that his Brahmacharya was not completely pure. It put him on a mood of self-introspection with regard to his relations with young women. On the suggestion of Mira he decided to avoid physical contact with women as an experiment. His secretary was amazed rather bewildered at his way of going to extremes in his conduct. For, earlier he was allowing women to be in the bath room when he was on the commode or in the bath. But now he was not allowing them to touch him.[12] Even before this event, he put off for some time the practice of placing his hands on the shoulders of women. But resumed it when he settled down in Sevagram as this practice appeared to him quite innocuous since it did not create any difficulty in his observance of Brahmacharya. For, in his view, Brahmacharya was a mental state and was not limited to external conditions. He could take bath naked in the presence of women which did not appear unusual to any person present there. He told a confidant that he always touched the girls with pure feelings. But the discharge at this age created a doubt in his mind. For, he felt that there might be impure feelings in his heart quite unknown to him. His confidence was shaken. It appeared to him as if he was "hurled by God from imaginary paradise."[13] He was overtaken by despondency which was affecting his public life. This was the time when he was to conduct crucial talks with Jinnah. So in a letter to Nehru he wrote, "I am carrying, but it is galling to me to think that I have lost the self-confidence that I possessed only a month ago."[14] In a statement to the press about the forthcoming talks, he said, I find myself for the first time during the past fifty years in a slough of despond, the cause is purely personal, it is purely internal."[15] Thus for the Mahatma personal character and public life were interdependent. It means that lasting solutions of social problems can be found only when there is corresponding purity of character in the individuals. That way the failure of his talks with Jinnah could be traced to his imperfect Brahmacharya.

The Mahatma was in this state of mind when he was in search of a solution to the communal problem in Noakhali 'Kya Karon' 'Kya Karon' (what should I do), such words quite often slipped from his lips. His own wits and resources were no match to the new challenge. He viewed his present undertaking as a 'Yajna' or highest kind of self-sacrifice for the good of humanity. It demanded complete purity which was not possible without perfect Brahmacharya. He therefore, resumed the practice of sharing his bed with a young woman. The only woman attending on him at that time was his grand niece Manu. She was the daughter of his nephew Jaisukhlal. She was extremely attached to his wife who treated her as her own daughter. She was transferred from Nagpur jail to Agha Khan Palace where Gandhi and Kasturba were interned during the Quit India Movement to look after Kasturba who was ailing. She was fourteen at that time. The death of Kasturba was a big shock to her. So Gandhi took upon himself the task of bringing her up. She received from him motherly love. She herself recorded that she regarded Gandhi both father and mother and so it was not unusual for her to share the bed with Gandhi. Thus when the Mahatma asked her to sleep with him in Noakhali in nude for his experiment in Brahmacharya, it did not surprise her and so she yielded without ado or excitement. He did not hide this fact. He made it known to all in his post prayer speeches in Noakhali as well as through personal letters to his co-workers, members of his family and inmates of the Ashram. But few could appreciate the importance of this act. Some of his closest and earliest associates like Kishorilal and Moshruwala, Narhari Parekh, etc. were to part company with him on this issue.[16] It also perturbed his sons. But this did not dishearten him. Explaining its purport in one of his letters, he said, "My mind, however, is becoming firmer than ever, for it has been my belief that alone is true Brahmacharya which requires no hedges. My experiment arose from this belief. I did make mistakes in them—Manu's sleeping with me is not a part of my experiment but it is a part of the present 'yajna'. My mind daily sleeps in an innocent manner with millions of women and Manu also who is a blood relation to me, sleeps with me as one of those millions. If she stops doing that out of deference to customs or to please co-workers, would I not be a hypocrit.[17] Writing to Kriplani, the president of the Congress, he said, "this has cost me dearest associates. You as one of the dearest and earliest comrades—should reconsider your position in the light of what I have to say—I have given deepest thought to the matter. The whole world may forsake me but I dare not leave what I hold is the truth for me. It may be a delusion and a snare. If so, I must realize it myself. I have risked perdition before. Now let this be the reality if it has to be."[18] He also sought the opinion of Vinoba, his most trusted disciple who was well versed in Indian philosophy and like his master dedicated to constructive programme and was of spiritual disposition. The latter while withholding his definite opinion on the subject warned him that this experiment was contrary to the ideal of Brahmacharya so long as a person had consciousness of the distinction between a man and a woman.[19]

But the Mahatma was firm on this issue as it was undertaken on the call of the spirit. To his son Manilal, who was perturbed on hearing this, he wrote, "—it is God who has prompted me to take this step." Indian mythology is replete with stories of great ascetics attaining tremendous power through Brahmacharya, self-control and penance as a result of which they could acquire control over heaven and earth. Possibly these stories left their mark on Gandhi's sub-conscious mind and determined his conduct. Nevertheless, he could justify the validity of his experiment even on rational and pragmatic grounds. In a discussion with Swami Anand and Kedar Nath, he argued that this experiment was in conformity with the latest researches on sex-relations both in the West and the East. He quoted Havelock Ellis and Bertrand Russell who were believers in the possibility and desirability of purity of life independently of the institution of marriage and the customs and urges governing it. My research, he added runs somewhat in that direction."[20] He disdained Brahmacharya which had reduced itself to a system of prescriptive do's and don't's as it had lowered the ideal and robbed it of its true contents.[21] So as a reformer holding a distinct view of relations between men and women, he could not wait till others were converted to his view. He "must take the lead and venture forth alone even in the teeth of universal opposition." For, his aim was "to test, enlarge and revise the current definition of Brahmacharya."[22] However this practice was abandoned when Thakkar Bapa, an esteemed co-worker of Gandhi, prevailed upon Manu not to participate in this controversial practice at a time when the Mahatma was engaged in the great task of extinguishing the communal conflagration. Though it was done with Gandhi's approval, he never admitted any flaw in this venture. Similarly, none of his co-workers who were alarmed at this experiment, believed that Gandhi had any lustful motive behind this practice. Though some of them did not rule out the possibility of containing in it the remnant of his sensuality of which he was not conscious. Manu herself does not throw light on this controversial act while narrating incidents of Gandhi's life of which she was a partner. Possibly either she did not give any importance to it or did not want to add any thing to this controversy as she published her account when the embers of this fire of controversy were red. However none could understand the state of Gandhi's mind. He wanted adequate strength to face an alarming situation which posed a challenge to all his ideals. May be it was an illusion or a myth. But every society creates certain myths or illusions to sustain its ideals and to strengthen the social bonds. Gandhi had created a myth for himself that the purity of mind attainable only through Brahmacharya would illumine the path of a man who had no choice but to walk alone to save his life-long work and his ideals when most of his co-workers had overcome by despondency and had parted company with him.

Further, the Mahatma was also contemplating the possibility of a new view of social life wherein sensual motive is not the only factor behind contacts between men and women. He believed that sexual pleasure was not the real objective of life. For nature's objective for sexual union, in his view, was procreation. This means it should be resorted to only when a child was needed. He favoured birth control through self-control. He opposed the indiscriminate use of contraceptives on the grounds that it would cause incalculable harm to society. He was aware of the existing literature on the subject and asked Kaka Kalelkar to study and collect facts about the effects of the use of contraceptives. It looks that sometimes Gandhi entertained wrong notions about sex relations. For he believed that men excite women for sexual acts. It was difficult for him to accept that it was the wife of a youngman who wanted him to satisfy here sexual urge. It was quite late in his life that he was confronted with the problem where actually the wife of his close disciple wanted her sexual satisfaction and Gandhi had to advise the former to submit to her desire and later on blessed their first child. It was equally disappointing to him that his own sons were not giving due considerations to his views on sex relations after their marriage. He was not happy when he learnt that his second son Manilal was expecting another child shortly after the birth of the first. In sheer anguish he wrote to Patel: "I have lost interest in the growth of the family tree. My only feeling is one of profound sadness. However, who can thwart nature?—Or we can adopt the European way (birth control)—and sing come let us enjoy ourselves—

I can't help feeling that we shall not gain spiritual knowledge if we follow that path."[23] Gandhi's road to perfect Brahmacharya were covered with pitfalls, hazards and traps. Some times his ceaseless effort in this direction created misgivings in his own mind and confusion in his dealings with women who came in contact with him in his public life. For, at no stage in his life he had reached the state of perfect Brahmachari or bisexual state which, it is believed, Ramakrishan Parmahansa had reached. So it became difficult for him or for his associates to decide as to how far his contact with a particular woman with whom he had become very close was motivated by lust or by love of his cause. Thus when he turned fifty and was deeply involved in the Rowlatt Act agitation, he came in contact with Sarladevi, wife of Rambhuj Dutt Chaudhry, a man of substance in Lahore. She was the grand niece of Rabindranath Tagore and the daughter of Ghosal, once secretary of Indian National Congress. Born in 1872, she completed her B.A. at the age of seventeen (according to Gandhi 19) and then onwards she had been engaged in public service in one form or the other. Her participation in the Congress commenced quite early in her life. She edited the Bengali monthly 'Bharati', through the columns of which she demonstrated the power of her pen. She was also a poetess and, according to Gandhi, her poetic power was of high order. She was married to Rambhuj Dutt in 1905 and onwards her public life covered Punjab, too. When Martial Law separated her from her husband, Gandhi came to Lahore and stayed with her. She accompanied him to various places in the province. She devoted herself to the promotion of Swedeshi movement in the Punjab. Gandhi was impressed by her poetic and literary genius and her devotion to his principles. He felt that she carried on fearless and vigorous struggle against Dyerism in the Punjab. Her poetic and literary genius added colour and force to Gandhi's pleas for handspinning. She continued her correspondence with Gandhi during the non-co-operation movement. Gandhi's secretary recorded several letters by her to Gandhi during his tour of the country which he replied. Her son Deepak was with Gandhi for some time.[24] It appears that Gandhi was so much impressed by her personality, accomplishment and commitment to his ideals and principles that he even imagined that both of them were bound by some kind of special relationship which he described as spiritual marriage. Possibly he was wishing a life-long companionship with her in the pursuit of his goal. Was there an element of lust in his thinking? Possibly Gandhi became conscious of it and discouraged Sarla Devi from getting close to him. His secretary records that this decision disheartened Sarla Devi who "put in one pan all the joys of life and pleasures of the world and in the other Bapur and his laws and committed the folly of choosing the latter." She looked upon Gandhi as the law-giver. Her words rather show that she had probably thought of some kind of companionship with Gandhi in his fight for the freedom of the country and not any kind of marriage or physical union motivated by lust. Gandhi, in reply, wrote to her "I am unworthy to have companionship with you, I require in me an infinitely higher purity than I possess." Possibly Gandhi was becoming conscious of an element of lust in his relationship with this gifted lady. Very likely he felt that his endeavour to attain perfect Brahmacharya was at stake. Only a few months after his first visit to Lahore when he met this lady, that he abandoned the idea of getting close to her and said that the thought of his wife and the love of his son Devadas and the persuasion of his secretary and his nephew saved him from rushing into the hellfire. Rajmohan Gandhi, the Mahatma's grand son quotes this as an admission of the element of lust in this kind of relationship which he expressed later on. Fifteen years later he told Margaret Sanger that he had "nearly slipped after meeting a woman with broad cultural education but had fortunately been freed from a trance." It is argued that the reference was undoubtedly to the 1920 relationship with Sarla Devi. Similarly, in March 1947 Gandhi wrote to Amrit Kaur with "one solitary exception I have never looked upon a woman with lustful eye.—Even the one solitary instance referred to by me was never with the intention of despoiling her.

Possibly the Mahatma in Gandhi was overstating an iota of guilt in his relations with the gifted lady. Very likely he was pointing out that the path to Brahmacharya was not straight and easy. For, one has to be very careful in the pursuit of this goal. If Gandhi decided to withdraw from having permanent companionship with her, it was only because he was not sure that both of them had perfect purity of character essential for companionship without any lustful motive.

There could be another reason for abandoning the idea of having permanent relations with this gifted lady. He started feeling that the persons around him, his friends and followers, were quite confused about the behaviour of Sarla Devi in the Ashram. Once the person incharge of the Ashram, questioned as to why Gandhi and Sarla Devi were not taking meals in the common kitchen.[25]

Notes and References

1. T.P., Vol. VII, p. 683.
2. C.W., LXXXVI, p. 72.
3. *Ibid.*, p. 138.
4. *Ibid.*, p. 149.
5. *Ibid.*, pp. 431-32.
6. *Ibid.*, pp. 374-75.
7. *Ibid.*, p. 196.
8. *Ibid.*, pp. 197-98.
9. C.W., Vol. LXXXVII, p. 14.
10. *Ibid.*, Vol. LXXIX, p. 212.
11. *Ibid.*, XXXIII, p. 430.
12. Birla, *op. cit.*, Vol. III, p. 170.
13. C.W., LXVII, p. 116.
14. *Ibid.*, LXVII, p. 56.
15. C.W., LXVII, p. 38.
16. *Ibid.*, LXXXVI, pp. 452-53.
17. *Ibid.*
18. *Ibid.*, LXXXVII, pp. 13-14.
19. *Ibid.*, LXXXVI, p. 453 f.n.
20. *Ibid.*, LXXXVII, pp. 106-08.
21. *Ibid.*, p. 91.
22. *Ibid.*
23. *Ibid.*, LVIII, p. 17.
24. *Ibid.*, XVII, p. 29 f.n.
25. *Ibid.*, XVII, pp. 384-88.

27

Father and Sons

Mohandas Gandhi had four sons, Harilal, Manilal, Ramdas and Devadas. The eldest was only of a few months when Mohandas went to England for higher studies. On his return he was getting attached to his family, though his love for his wife was not free from lust. So before he started off to South Africa, he had added another son to his family. He returned to his country in 1896 to take his family to South Africa as he did not know how long his public work would require his presence there. As a father, the barrister Mohandas liked his sons to pick up his life style so that the family appeared civilized in the eyes of the Europeans. For, without it, he believed, it was not possible for an Indian to serve his community and to build up his practice in South Africa. So he selected an appropriate dress for his children and his wife which caused some inconvenience to them. For, the shoes cramped their feet and their toes often got sore. They agreed to the change because their father's wish was a law to them. In their new home in South Africa they were made to use knives and forks as the barrister had acquired a taste for European life style. But unfortunately as soon as they got accustomed to it, their father had lost charm for it. It must have been hard on them to give it up. This was the most impressionable age of the first two children. The eldest son was nine and the next was five years of age. Their education was a big problem for their father mostly because of his view of education, the non-availability of good schools for Indians in South Africa and his sense of honour. There were good schools for European children which as a rule did not admit Indian children. Barrister Gandhi's children, of course, could be admitted as a matter of favour and exception. But he did not like it. There were schools established by Christian missions which were open to the Indian children. But Gandhi did not like the type of education imparted in those schools as their medium of instruction was only English or perhaps 'incorrect Tamil or Hindi.' He engaged an English governess for some time and imparted the knowledge of Gujarati to the children himself through conversation. But his teaching was at best irregular because of his deep involvement in public activities and his legal practice. He was reluctant to send the children to India for education as he believed that the education which the children naturally imbibed "in a well-ordered household was impossible to obtain in hostels".[1] As Mohandas moved towards 'Mahatmahood', he lost interest in the conventional system of education because of his conviction that this system did not equip a person for the selfless service of the community which in his view should be the real aim of education. So his sons were given education mostly at home by Gandhi himself. While practising at Johannesburg, the children were required to walk with their father from the house to his office, a distance of six miles, to obtain some knowledge of their mother tongue and their culture through conversation. What kind of education he was imparting to his sons while hurriedly walking towards his office or on his return? Possibly he was narrating stories from the Mahabharata, Ramayana, or from the Bhagavata. For he liked to impart education through didactic stories since, in his view, they aided in character building. Writing a letter to his nephew Chhaganlal in 1902, who was looking after his children in India, he advised him to read from 'Kavyadohan, a collection of story-poems in Gujarati from the Mahabharata, Bhagavata, etc. or narrate the stories of Sudama, Nala, Angada, Harishchandra, etc. He did not feel the necessity of reading out to them the plays of English poets as there was not much morals to be drawn from them. He was especially instructed to see that the children under his charge did not pick up bad habits. A semblance of regular schooling was also arranged for the children when he set up an improvised school in Phoenix and Tolstoy Farm for the Satyagraha children. But the education impacted there was different from conventional system of education that prepared the children for degrees. So his eldest son virtually broke away from his father as he was under a spell of the glamour of degrees. He was extremely unhappy when his father encouraged Sorabji Parsi to become a barrister but did not like Harilal to go in for legal profession. It was more disheartening to Harilal because Gandhi's friend Pranjivan Mehta had offered a scholarship intending for the use of Harilal or Manilal for studies in England. But Gandhi first selected Chhaganlal for this scholarship who stayed there only for a few months and came back. Eventually it was given to Sorabji. By this act Gandhi was setting an example of breaking the traditional practice which placed family welfare above public welfare. Moreover, he wanted his sons to be trained for public service. But such ideas did not appeal to his sons. Once there was a heated exchange of arguments between the father and his eldest son over the importance of conventional degrees. The later argued that if Bapu had not become a barrister, he would not have been able to do the work that he was doing. To some extent the son was right. But the lawyer father could cite the examples of Shivaji, Rana Partap, Rama Krishna Paramhansa, Dayananda—none of whom had English education and who were yet among the greatest Indians of their times. But the son could cite the examples of Gokhale, Tilak, Malaviya and Lajpat Rai who could serve the nation because they had equipped themselves with higher English education. The father yielded and sent his son to India to pursue his studies. But he could not carry on his studies partly because of the opposition of his father and partly because of his love for the daughter of the lawyer friend of his father, whom he wanted to marry. When Gandhi learnt about it he wrote in anger a letter to his elder brother Laxmidas, "it is well if Harilal is married, it is also well if he is not: For the present at any rate I have ceased to think of him as a son."[2] When Harilal returned to South Africa with his wife Gulab, the father showed his annoyance by not receiving his son's bride. But he mellowed down when his son showed his zeal for the cause of his father and offered Satyagraha. In a letter to Tolstoy, Gandhi proudly stated that his eldest son was undergoing imprisonment with hard labour for six months. This was fourth imprisonment in the course of the struggle.[3] When the third phase of the struggle in South Africa started, Gandhi wanted Harilal to join the struggle. But Gokhale detained him in India to continue his studies. In 1911, when Passive Resistance was temporarily postponed, Harilal disappeared. He had left a very pathetic letter for his father. A search was made in Johannesburg but all in vain. But Harilal was found in another town where he had changed his name. However Kallenback brought him back to Tolstoy Farm. All night father and son walked and talked till it was decided that Harilal would leave for India to carry on his studies. When the train was about to start, the father kissed Harilal and gave a gentle slap on his cheek and said, "forgive your father if you think he has done you wrong." It was a touching scene and tears rolled down the cheeks of Harilal's friends. When Gandhi returned to India the

event, Gandhi's euphoria of his son's transformation was over. He left his job and disappeared. The father routed all letters addressed to his son through the manager of the Ashram as the latter was feeding him and providing him work. Harilal conceived a new plan for overcoming his financial difficulties. He made an offer to all proslytishing agencies that he would accept the religion of the highest bidder. Gandhi's admirer offered him a job to prevent him from adopting this policy. But that did not satisfy him and he secretly embraced Islam. It was then the father realized that there was no change in his son. He only pretended change to overcome his financial difficulties. He was completely a broken man. He had practically no family life. His son was left under the care of Gandhi and his daughter was being brought up by another relative against whom Harilal was threatening some action to the annoyance of Gandhi. In sheer disgust he wrote to her to expose the misdeeds of Harilal.[17] On his son's conversion to Islam, Gandhi made a statement that his son had only sold his religion to the highest bidder as he was heavily in debt to a Pathan. He, therefore, warned all the proselytisers that his son's conversion to any religion would be no gain to that religious community. So he did not encourage some Arya Samaj enthusiasts who were trying to bring Harilal back to Hinduism. The pain that it caused to the Mahatma while giving this statement can be judged from his reply to a Muslim correspondent. "Every word that he wrote," he said, "while giving the statement against his son was with his pen dipped in heart's blood."[18] However, he told the Governor of Bengal in an interview on 22nd Dec., 1945 that he had "not put any impediment in the way of his son becoming a Muslim. For, if this change in his religion could result in his giving up drinking, he (Gandhi) would be glad."[19] It was only a wishful thinking of the father who had lost control over his son. Was there any possibility of Harilal listening to his father? The shock of the conversion was greater to Harilal's mother. In a lengthy letter which she dictated to her youngest son, she implored him to mend his ways at least for the peace of the old weak woman like her "who finds it difficult to suffer patiently the mental torture caused by his regrettable way of life, though his father was bearing it bravely." Rajagopalachari was moved by the text of the letter which he described as "liquid mother lava or ancient pathos pouring out from the volcano of maternal anguish."

However, the Mahatma looked after Harilal's children with fatherly care and affection, though certain actions and the ambition of Harilal's son Kanti caused some embarrassment to him as he was drawn towards the daughter of the sister of his co-worker with whom he (Kanti) was staying. Gandhi, of course, assured his approval of the match on girl's consent on attaining maturity. Possibly Harilal tried to create some misunderstanding between his son and his father by putting into his ears that by such actions Kanti had lost value in Gandhi's eyes. But Gandhi removed his suspicion by telling him that he had been tending him "carefully like a flower."[20] Kanti wanted to go in for formal education in the field of medicine. Though Gandhi was against this career for his grandson as he wanted to prepare him for public service, he yielded to it on his persistence and asked his three sons to contribute money for the education of Kanti. For, it was against his principle to pay money out of public funds, for the education of the members of his family. Kanti was married to Saraswati, daughter of Ramachandran's sister and they tried to reform Harilal which pleased Gandhi. He, therefore, advised Saraswati to continue with her efforts as it was possible that the love of their daughter Shanti might hold him (Harilal) to the right course. But all this remained a pipe dream for the Mahatma. Harilal again disappeared and possibly managed to obtain some money from the Maharaja of Mysore.[21] Earlier Gandhi had met Harilal in April 1942. He must have met with some accident. He had a fracture in the hand. Gandhi sent him to the hospital for treatment. He again talked of coming back to his fold. But this time the father was more realistic and careful. He knew that all this talk of returning to him was only a ruse for getting money out of him. For, he had realized that his eldest son was devoid of all human feelings. He thought of sending him to some asylum to which his son did not agree. The Mahatma was not devoid of fatherly love. In a letter dated Dec. 29, 1945, addressed to a lady, Gandhi wrote, "it is good that Harilal has reached there at last. Both you husband and wife should now redeem him. If he is saved. I will consider him as your property."[22] Even a year before his assassination, the father wrote to his eldest son, "How delighted I shall be to find that you have turned over a new leaf. Just think of the affection I have lavished upon you. Mine is an arduous pilgrimage. I invite you to join me in it if you can. If you purify yourself no matter where you are, you will have fully shared it."[23] Harilal attended the funerals of his father without being recognized and spent the night with his youngest brother. He died in a hospital after a few months.

The conduct of Gandhi's second son, Manilal too, caused some concern and embarrassment to Gandhi at times though he never followed in the footsteps of Harilal. Like the eldest son, he also felt that the neglect of the development of the children by his father was nothing short of cruelty. Gandhi appears to have been hurt by this charge of his son and wrote to him that he had sinned without knowing in charging him with cruelty. For, in his view, "a son should have devotion enough to his father not to notice his shortcomings but think only of his virtues."[24] He reminded him again and again that he was motivated by the purest love whenever he did anything against his wishes. So he wrote, "It should not be difficult for you to say that you were sent away to live by yourself because father did not like your ways. You should realize that in releasing you from attendance on Ba and asking you to go, without thinking of my personal convenience I must have acted with the purest of love."[25] Gandhi had great hopes in Manilal. But was sorry that "he had taken to the evil ways of pleasure."[26] In reply to his son's letter, he wrote, " I am a father who is prejudiced against you. I do not approve of your ways at all." He was once shocked to learn that his son had an affair with a married woman who turned out to be a schemer. Gandhi observed fast as a penance for the sins of both.

When Gandhi returned to India, Manilal was sent to South Africa to look after the 'Indian Opinion' and the Phoenix settlement. But Manilal at times felt lonely because of separation from the family. He yearned for marriage. He fell in love with a Muslim girl Fatima whom he wanted to marry. But Gandhi did not agree to it as, in his view, it would be counter-productive in his drive towards Hindu-Muslim unity as a result of which his son would neither be able to serve India nor run Indian Opinion in South Africa. However, he assured him that his marriage would be arranged in India. So it was fixed with Sushila, daughter of Gandhi's friend and co-worker Mashruwala. He asked the girl to write to Manilal so that some understanding could develop between them even before marriage.[27]

Differences also developed between the son and the father over the management of the Indian Opinion and the Phoenix Settlement. The latter was unhappy on learning from the West that even after five years of Gandhi's departure from South Africa, his son had no developed the habit of writing the editorial himself. He, therefore, asked West to stop writing editorial for Manilal.[28] Moreover the son had a different view about the running of the Indian Opinion. For he wanted to accept advertisements to make it a profitable business concern which was contrary to his father's principles. He even thought of shifting the paper and the press from Phoenix to Durban. The father protested against this plan and asked him to leave the place and resign from the trusteeship of the settlement if he could not follow its ideals.[29] Manilal also desired to go to America for training in nature cure and sought help from his father.

But the latter expressed his helplessness as he could not arrange money for this plan.[30]

Nevertheless, despite differences over certain matters, the two continued to maintain good relations. Not only they corresponded with each other frequently, the son sometimes came to India to see his parents and his brothers. He participated in Satyagrahas both in India and South Africa. The father quite often tried to assuage the ruffled feelings of his son resulting from former's decision by soothing words. Thus when Manilal was sad on account of his failure to obtain the approval of his marriage, Gandhi wrote to him, "You are not my prisoner but my friend— I want you not to stand in awe of me or any one else—."[31] The son also surrendered to the advice of his father and promised not to marry without his permission. While staying in the Ashram on his visit to India he would take pleasure in massaging his father. But Gandhi did not show any appreciation for this devotion to his father. Jehangir, a wealthy admirer of the Mahatma noticed this and said bluntly to the Mahatma" I think you are unkind and unfair to Manilal." "I don't think so" Gandhi replied. "On the contrary I have to struggle continually against the temptation to show partiality for my own family."[32] In December-January 1945 when Gandhi was staying in Bengal, Manilal came to India to see his father. A girl in Gandhi's entourage fell sick. Manilal noticed that everybody was anxious to go out of his way to pay attention to her and to all members of his entourage which the Mahatma called his family. Manilal then gave a long lecture on the way Gandhi had failed to take care of his real family and commented that life with Bapu was comfortable and cosy. The father listening patiently to his son's discourse remarked in a soft voice, "Manilal if life with me was so comfortable then all my sons would not have left me."[33]

Gandhi's relations with his third and fourth sons were on even keel, though not without a feeling of deprivations in life, at least in the mind of the third son because of the change in the life style and ideals of their father. Ramdas had to struggle throughout his life in search of his own identity and sometimes livelihood. He was born and brought up in South Africa. He was seventeen when he came to India on the return of his father to his country. It was hard time for him to adjust himself to the climate of India and the new environment of the Ashram. He started learning tailoring when his father established an Ashram to pursue the life of poverty. His father explained it to the Ashramites that his son had not left the Ashram in a pique.[34] But had purposely joined the tailor's as he wanted to earn a little and also to have some experience of unpleasant condition. So he was pleased as his "son would get seasoned since he could not expect any monetary help from his father." Ramdas also went to South Africa to try his luck there in business. There he assisted his brother in managing the Indian Opinion for some time. When tailoring business started giving him some return, the father felt that his son was well-fixed, well cared for and happy. For "he is at least earning something without doing violence to his conscience. He took to Khadi work and was supposed to go to Khadi school to have training in the manufacture and sale of Khadi. Gandhi arranged his marriage with the daughter of a co-worker which was performed at the end of January 1928. The engagement had taken place nearly two years before. But Gandhi would not consent to the marriage until the bride had completed her sixteen years. Ramdas was thirty at that time. Gandhi blessed the couple in a solemn speech. He was proud to tell the guests invited to the function that his third and fourth sons had been brought up under his care and he was sure that they had never deceived him. Addressing the sons he said, "you have confessed your faults to me, but they had never alarmed me, for your frank confession has exonerated you in my eyes. I am glad that you would rather be deceived by the whole world than deceive any one."[35] A few years latter when Ramdas suffered from physical ailment and was getting weaker, he was given both allopathic and nature cure treatment. He advised him to take cod liver oil and eggs if necessary.[36] Ramdas was keen to earn his livelihood to look after his family. For, some time he looked for an opening in Bombay.[37] He asked his father for some financial help to stay in a rented room. Though this request appeared wrong to Gandhi on account of his principles, the nature of the health of his son "made wrong as right."[38] For some time he battled with his fate in Bombay.[39] Later on he joined the Tatas but without any peace of mind.[40] The lack of formal conventional education, for which he blamed his father, had deprived him of any opportunity of getting a good job. According to his wife, he was happy go-lucky person. He had a generous extravagant nature. Father's ideal of Brahmacharya had no attraction for him.[41]

Devadas was Gandhi's youngest son. After his birth the Mahatma claimed that he had conquered the animal in him as he could not afford another addition in the family because of intense public activity. He was brought up under his father's care and possibly his father had greater attachment with him. He was five when Gandhi's wife came to Johannesburg in 1905 where Gandhi had decided to settle down. Even after his return to India Devadas mostly remained with his father to assist him in public work. He went to Champaran to help his father in the constructive work. He was sent to Madras to learn Tamil in order to teach Tamilians Hindi. When riots broke out in Bombay in November 1921, the father decided to send him out as a sacrifice "for slaughter by the rioters should a fresh outbreak occur in some neighbouring locality." After Gandhi's first imprisonment in India, Devadas and Rajagopalachari had first interview with Gandhi in April 1922 and the son virtually made a scene as he burst into tears on seeing his father standing in the superintendent's room like an ordinary prisoner since according to the rules a prisoner was not offered a seat in the presence of the superintendent of the jail. He attended on his father while he was convalescing after the operation in 1924. He was sent to hawk Khaddar during the National week in 1927. For some time in 1928, Devadas taught spinning in Jama Milia. However Devadas' love with Rajagopalachari's daughter Lakshmi created some tension and misgiving between the father and the son. In a letter Gandhi explained the situation thus: "Rajaji is not likely to let Devadas marry his daughter Lakshmi—and Devedas is mad after her, while Lakshmi is cheerful and she would not take any step against the wishes of her father. Devadas wishes to obey me. But his soul rebels against him. He seems to believe that I stand in the way of his marriage with Lakshmi and so feels angry with me."[42] In fact, both the fathers were surprised when 27 years old Devadas asked for the hand of 15 years old Lakshmi. Was it infatuation or love? The wise fathers could not decide. Time alone could answer. So they advised the two lovers to remain separate for some time without writing letters to each other, to which they agreed. Four years' separation proved that it was not mere infatuation. Possibly the two fathers apprehended a political fallout of this marriage in the South as Rajaji was a Brahmin and Gandhis' were Banias. However, Gandhi was not only looking forward to intercaste and interprovincial marriages but also marriage between the higher castes and the Schedule Castes. In an interview with Ved Mehta Rajaji was reported to have said that he and Gandhi felt that "our political association should not be cemented by a marriage alliance."[48] However their love overcame all difficulties and age-old prejudices and the marriage was solemnized on June 16, 1933 at Lady Thackeray's house in Poona where Gandhi was convalescing after the fast.[44] Dr. Syed Mahmud and Birla presented Silken saris to the bride. But Gandhi refused them as he wanted the marriage to be a simple affair.[45] As Gandhi wanted his sons to earn their livelihood themselves, Devadas joined service in Delhi on a salary of Rs. 250.

development of his sons, he wrote to Manilal "I still maintain now as before that no father could have discharged his duty towards his sons and served them as well as I have. I made you partners and inheritors of my spiritual experiences—."[49] The sons, too, could not realize the difficulties and compulsions of their father as a leader of the nation. When he considered the conventional system of education and the current view of life with all its values as harmful to the life of the nation, there was no course left to him but to restrain his children from following that course. Tension in the family arose when the sons or the persons around them judged their abilities and competence according to the current standards. Judged by Gandhi's standards most of them were much better than many young men of his age. But the children and the grand children did not look at the world around them from Gandhi's point of view. So the Mahatma had sometimes to yield to the aspirations of his grand children when Harilal's son insisted on medical career for himself he arranged to support him financially. Ramdas' eldest daughter, too, desired formal Western type of education with degrees. She had her way in spite of her grand father's opposition as he wanted her to be associated with his work.[50] The aspirations of his grand children disappointed him. On Kanti's insistence on medical career, he wrote, "Of course, Kanti has fallen from the ideal which I had hope he would live up to. What does his fall matter in the debris of many of my hopes. I do not blame him, for he could not go against his fundamental being."[51] Possibly he realized that the forces operating against his own life style and world view were so powerful that his children and grand children had no choice but to yield to them. So in a mood of self-assurance he once said, "I am not worried that Radha, Keshu, Shankar, Bal, Jayant rebelled against it. I see in it the force of current stream and not any defect in my thinking."[52]

Notes and References

1. Gandhi, M.K., Autobiography, pp. 166-67.
2. C.W., May 27, 1906.
3. C.W., Vol. IX, pp. 528-29; also (Nayyar, Sushila, Satyagraha at Work, pp. 321, 403.
4. C.W., p. 368.
5. *Ibid.*, Vol. XIII, p. 36.
6. *Ibid.*, Vol. L, p. 92.
7. *Ibid.*, XVII, p. 365.
8. Desai, M., *op. cit.*, Vol. I, pp. 144-45.
9. *Ibid.*, pp. 183-84.
10. Fischer, Louise, The Life of M. Gandhi Paperback, p. 210.

11. C.W., XXXVI, p. 56.
12. *Ibid.*
13. *Ibid.*
14. *Ibid.*
15. *Ibid.*, LX, p. 226.
16. *Ibid.*, p. 456.
17. *Ibid.*, LXI, p. 215.
18. *Ibid.*, LXIII, p. 48.
19. T.P., Vol. VI, p. 679.
20. C.W., LXI, p. 34.
21. *Ibid.*, LXXXI, p. 76.
22. *Ibid.*, LXXXII, p. 301.
23. *Ibid.*, LXXXVI, p. 376.
24. *Ibid.*, XII, p. 351.
25. *Ibid.*, p. 362.
26. *Ibid.*, p. 368.
27. *Ibid.*
28. *Ibid.*, XVI, p. 9.
29. *Ibid.*, LIV, pp. 419-20.
30. *Ibid.*,
31. *Ibid.*, XIV, p. 178.
32. Jehangir & Marjorie, *op. cit.*, p. 140.
33. Ghosh, Sudhir, *op. cit.*, pp. 68-69.
34. C.W., XIV, p. 157.
35. Tendulkar, *op. cit.*, Vol. II, p. 306.
36. C.W., LIX, pp. 211, 274.
37. *Ibid.*, LX, p. 41.
38. *Ibid.*
39. *Ibid.*
40. C.W., Vol. LXXII, p. 89.
41. Ved Mehta, Mahatma Gandhi and His Apostles (Indian Book Co., 1977), p. 51.
42. C.W., XXXV, p. 339.
43. Ved Mehta, *op. cit.*, p. 48.
44. C.W., LX, p. 212.
45. *Ibid.*, pp. 218-19.
46. *Ibid.*, LIX, p. 118.
47. *Ibid.*, XIV, p. 157.
48. *Ibid.*, LIX, p. 145.
49. Desai, *op. cit.*, Vol. I, p. 209.
50. Mehta, *op. cit.*, p. 54.
51. C.W., LX, p. 224.
52. *Ibid.*, LXIII, p. 378.

28

Mahatma and the Partition

The shocking news of the outbreak of riots in Bihar in retaliation to the riots in Bengal compelled the Mahatma to suspend his personal efforts to restore communal peace in Noakhali. He left for Bihar to wipe the tears of the Muslims in Bihar. He reproached the Hindus of Bihar for resorting to violence for their false notion that their revengeful attitude would teach a lesson to the Muslims of Bengal who would cease causing harm to the Hindus of their areas because of the suffering of the Muslims in Hindu dominated provinces. For, in his view, this policy would engulf the whole country in endless communal bloodshed. As the Congress was in power in Bihar, his word carried greater weight and so he was able to restore peace in Bihar for some time. But even here his programme of restoring peace had to be suspended because of the far-reaching changes in the country and the world. For, on February 24, the Prime Minister of England, declared the intention of the His Majesty's Government to withdraw British authority from India by June 1948 and the appointment of Lord Mountbatten as Viceroy in place of Lord Wavell to carry out the operation.

The new Viceroy immediately on his arrival expressed his desire to see Gandhi and so invited him to Delhi offering his own plane to carry him. But the latter while accepting the invitation chose to travel by train like any ordinary person. He was rather disturbed when he discovered that his grand niece Manu who was looking after him got two compartments booked for him, one for preparing food and the other for his rest and other activities. When she came to his compartment to serve food, he found him looking outside the window. In his characteristic way he had communicated to her that she had committed a serious harm to a large number of poor passengers who were hanging to the train simply because the Mahatma had reserved two compartments. Was it right for him to occupy two compartment when he claimed to live like a poor man? This thought troubled him. Even those who were close to him and were looking after him could not fathom into the working of his mind. He immediately called the station master and surrendered one compartment who reluctantly agreed to his decision since he had been specially instructed to provide all comforts to the Mahatma during the journey.[1] A similar incident had happened when he was going to Bengal in 1945. Two compartments were reserved for him and his party. But on realising that his party could be accommodated in one compartment, he instructed his grandson to surrender one compartment. When the latter told him that payment had been made to the Railway authorities for two compartments, Gandhi replied, "it does not matter. We are going for the service of the poor and starving millions. It does not behove us to enjoy comforts on the train."[2] In fact, since the time young Mohandas resolved to seek his salvation through service to humanity, he had been deliberately shedding his own comforts to have an access to the hearts of the poor.

On reaching Delhi, his immediate task was to meet the new Viceroy. He had no secretariat worth the name as his staff had been left behind either in Noakhali or Bihar to help in extinguishing the communal fire. So he went to see the Viceroy without any consultation with his colleagues. It was an informal meeting. On the first day Gandhi narrated the story of his life after exchanging the pleasantries. That was his way of giving an idea about himself to the man who had been sent by the British to implement their policy of surrendering their most precious jewel of their empire to the Indians. This was not the first time that Gandhi introduced himself to a Viceroy or a high dignitary of the British Empire. He was generally autobiographical in the first meeting. The object was to develop friendly relationship with him and equip him with his approach to life. Mountbatten listened to him attentively. He was sizing up the man. He was following Catlin's advice who had informed him to 'let Gandhi expound a doctrine which is really a psychologial escapism from what the Raj has symbolised and then to fasten him with a question that brings him to earth.'[3] The Viceroy, on his part tried to show him his sincerity to the cause of the Indians, told him that he made an effort to bring about a meeting between him and the Prince of Wales when he (Gandhi) was in prison.

The next day he was up around 3 a.m., though he had gone to bed very late the preceding night. The day started with hectic activities and so he had hardly any time to go through his normal routine.[4] Possibly his mind was in search of a solution of the communal problem which had acquired greater complexity as a result of communal disturbances and the political events in the country. It defied simple solutions. So in the next meeting he surprised the Viceroy by his proposal that at first Jinnah be invited to form a Government at the centre of his choice with freedom to select his colleagues from any group or party or form coalition with Nehru and other Congress leaders. On his refusal the offer be made to the Congress to form the Government to whom the power be handed over. He assured the Viceroy with full sincerity that he would make every possible effort to seek the support of the Congress leadership as well as of the masses of the country for the success of Jinnah's Government in case he agreed to this plan. He also had some meetings with the secretaries of the Viceroy to work out its details. According to the Mahatma, the initial response from the Congress leadership was encouraging to this plan. But he had not as yet consulted Nehru and Patel. But Jinnah turned it down by describing it "a wily move of Gandhi." For he always considered Gandhi as a clever politician making subtle moves to frustrate all his efforts to attain his goal of Pakistan. The Viceroy, too, did not show much enthusiasm for this plan. He considered it far-fetched but potentially feasible. His staff described it as "old kite flown without disguise" and advised the Viceroy not to be drawn into negotiations with the Mahatma and only listen to his advice. They came to the conclusion that the scheme was not only unworkable but would also put the Viceroy in an impossible position as Jinnah's Government would be at the mercy of the Congress majority. Both Nehru and Patel, too, were sceptical about the feasibility of the plan. Nehru told the Viceroy that this offer was made during the Cabinet Mission negotiations but was turned down as impracticable.[5] The Mahatma then realized the wide gap between his approach and that of the Congress leadership. He therefore, informed the Viceroy to conduct the future negotiations with Congress leaders in the interim government who, in his opinion, "were stalwarts and seasoned servants of the nation."[6] In this way the Mahatma was eliminated from the negotiations for the transfer of power. This was a tragedy as Gandhi was the only influential leader who was opposed to the partition of the country. Gandhi was equally opposed to the partition of the Punjab and Bengal as it was demanded on religious basis which not only cut at the root of the view of nationalism of the Congress but also carried the seeds of disintegration of the country. For, it logically implied that Congress could claim allegiance of the people of the area where non-Muslims were in majority. So it could weaken the hold of the Congress Ministry in the N.W.F.P. where the decision had yet to be taken through referendum whether the people would like to join the dominion of Pakistan or not. It could encourage any area where the Muslims were in majority to demand secession from the Indian Union. In fact, logic or reason was the only casualty in the parleys for the transfer of power. For, carrying the two-nation theory to its logical conclusion, as Azad pointed out during the Cabinet Mission negotiations, that on the basis of this theory Non-Muslims in Pakistan and Muslims in India would be aliens as one religion alone would determine the claim of an individual to citizenship both in India and Pakistan. In other words, exchange of population on religious grounds was the only logical course of this theory. But neither the League nor Congress leadership were ready to go so far. Theories and principles were kept aside and each party was busy in oneupmanship. The Congress leadership was demanding the partition of Bengal and the Punjab on the same principle on the basis of which the League had demanded the partition of the country. They were trying to beat the League leader with his own stick. They did not notice that they had surrendered their own view of nationalism on the basis of which they hoped to raise a secular, democratic nation. The Mahatma warned them of the consequences of their decision. Unfortunately the breakdown of the machinery of the Government as a result of communal riots, the prospects of freedom of the country and escape from continuous struggle and prospect of going to prison in the event of rejecting all the plans of the transfer of power involving partition clouded the minds of the Congress leadership. Possibly the leadership suffered from double think or amnesia. They justified the reversal of their policy by arguing that partition was accepted only as a lesser evil. So Nehru observed "—I suppose it was the compulsion of events and the feeling that we couldn't get out of that deadlock or morass by pursuing the way we had done; it became worse and worse."[7] On another occasion, he said: "We saw the fires burning in the Punjab and heard every day of the killings. The plan for partition offered a way out and we took it—." The Congress president, J.B. Kriplani, said, "The Mountbatten plan offered us freedom from the British rule at the price of division of India. We agreed to pay the price because freedom was the prime necessity of our national existence and the British were bent upon extorting the price to secure for the Muslim League its pound of flesh...."[8]

Nehru later on admitted in an interview that the Congress leadership accepted partition because "—we were tired men and were getting on in years too. Few of us could stand the prospect of going to prison again—and if we had stood out for a united India, as we wished it, prison obviously awaited us."[9]

Jinnah, too, felt that the Pakistan of his dream would go to pieces if his two-nation theory was applied in full scale in the Indian situation. When Lord Mountbatten carried Jinnah's argument to its logical end by arguing that it would mean partition of the Punjab and Bengal, the League leader was extremely distressed and displeased and so complained that the Viceroy was ruining his Pakistan. So in one of the interviews he said, "If you persist in chasing me with your ruthless logic we shall get no where."[10]

The Congress leadership was in no mood to listen to the Mahatma. This was a new development. To Gandhi's secretary Pyarelal this development in the relations between the Mahatma and the Congress was unusual as it was inconceivable in the olden days. No doubt, differences were there between the two earlier, too. But the leadership did not stretch them to the breaking point as there was hardly any opportunity to frame a policy of the Government in the light of their approach to any problem. But now they had to take a decision which in their view vitally affected not only their future but the destiny of the country. The Mahatma was left alone. He was sticking to the logic of his view of nationalism which stood on the bedrock of secularism and religious tolerance. He turned to both the Viceroy and the League leader to avert partition whether of the country or any of its provinces on religious basis. He suggested to Viceroy to impress upon Jinnah to win over Bengal and Eastern Punjab through persuasion and by speaking to the people directly. For, he believed that this would help in removing the virus of communalism in the Politics of the two dominions and would strengthen the bonds between the two communities in spite of administrative and political changes on the withdrawal of the British and would in due course bring to the surface the weakness and irrational aspects of the two-nation theory. He made a similar suggestion for avoiding referendum in N.W.F.P., which, in his view, would intensify communalism resulting in Bloodshed. He told Isamy that Jinnah should talk to the Chief Minister of N.W.F.P. in a friendly manner and convert him to his point of view.[11] When the suggestion was made to Jinnah he readily agreed to it on the condition that Gandhi should give assurance that Congress would not intervene in this task. Gandhi wrote a letter to Jinnah on the suggestion of Viceroy in this connection and Jinnah in reply wanted undertaking from the Congress for non-interference and so the matter ended there as the idea did not commend itself to Nehru.[12] In fact, all the three parties involved in the transfer of power—the Viceroy, Congress, and the League were in a hurry for the accomplishment of their plans and so the logical consequences of their decisions did not receive their attention. The Viceroy had a passion for speed and for him this was the gateway to success. He had created a feeling among the Indian leadership that if they did not act quickly they would lose the battle. Partition was announced in May 1947. But the commission to decide the boundaries along which the two states would be divided was not appointed until the end of the June. Hardly there was a month and a half left for the British to leave India and the new state of Pakistan. The Congress was in a quandry. For, most of the Congress leaders believed that if the Conservative Party came to power under Churchill it would become difficult for them to attain freedom as the Conservative leader was not only opposed to India's freedom but also had sympathy with the League. There was another danger in the existing situation. If the Congress failed to accept the solution of the Viceroy, there was the possibility of the British leaving India by giving the provinces and the states Dominion Status. This could split India into several independent political units. Thus they reconciled themselves to the division of the country. Further, the Viceroy and his staff were making several plans as an alternative to partition and united India. The Viceroy had sympathy with the move of Suhrawardhy and some Hindu leaders for an independent united Bengal. There was also a move to make Calcutta a free city. There was another danger. Acceptance of Cabinet Mission plan meant acceptance of weak centre with only limited powers such as Defence, Foreign Affairs and Communication which would be incapable of controlling fissiparous tendencies resulting from strong provinces. In such a situation even the Mahatma could not give a clear and definite lead. For he had been pursuing two goals which could not be reconciled at this moment, that is, freedom of the country and united India. He had to select one keeping in view the mood of his colleagues. Probably he hoped to reconcile both in the distant future and the present was only an occasion to create the ground for that future. He started taking some steps in that direction. He did not favour division in the army.[13] This implied common defence which could prevent the two dominions from squandering their resources and energies in mutual warfare. Another step that he contemplated to reduce the tension between the two dominions was the return of the refugees to their homes. He sent a proposal to Jinnah through Suhrawardhy that involved the convening of a conference at the highest level for this purpose.[14] When the Congress had agreed to the partition, he made another attempt to avert it by calling at Jinnah's house at Delhi. They had a cordial talk for about three hours but Jinnah remained adamant. Disclosing the results of his talk, Gandhi wrote to the Viceroy, "We did talk about Pakistan-*cum*-partition. I told him my opposition to Pakistan persisted as before and suggested that in view of his declaration of faith in non-violence he should try to convert his opponents by reasoning with them and not to show force. He was, however, quite firm that the question of Pakistan was not open to discussion.

In a prayer meeting on May 31, 1947 Gandhi repeated the same idea, that is, convincing India of the rationale of his conception of Pakistan. However, all his efforts to avert partition proved futile. The Congress Working Committee accepted the Mountbatten Plan on June 3, 1947 that involved partition of the country. When this news was conveyed to him he was extremely unhappy as he saw nothing but evil in the partition. It is reported that the Viceroy received from Krishna Menon an unusual letter on 4 June, 1947 warning him that Mr. Gandhi was in a very unhappy and emotional mood and he feared that he might denounce the plan and its acceptance at his prayer meeting that very evening. The Viceroy sent a message to him to see him before the prayer meeting. For, the Viceroy was afraid that the only Indian who could upset his apple cart was Gandhi. The Mahatma came but that was the day of his silence. He wrote his replies on the back of separate old envelops with the stub of a pencil which was not properly sharpened. He did not give any indication that he was opposed to his plan. But only advised him to remove the Governor of NWFP who, in his view, was not impartial in his conduct. The Viceroy immediately wrote to the Secretary of state that "God must be on our side since Gandhi who had the power to stop the agreement was afflicted by a day of silence."[15] The Viceroy tried to assuage his feeling that it was not Mountbatten Plan but Gandhi Plan as he tried to follow his advice in framing this plan since on his failure to carry the parties for the acceptance of the Cabinet Mission Plan to which Gandhi had given top priority, he framed the plan that involved no coercion and acceptance by the representatives of the people.[16]

The Mahatma did not oppose the Working Committee resolution in the meeting of the A.I.C.C. which had the power of rejecting the decision of the Working Committee. Rather he appealed to the members not to take any step which would stand in the way of the Working Committee in implementing its previous decision.

Why didn't the Mahatma put his weight on the side of those who were bent upon opposing the partition in the A.I.C.C. meeting? Does this show his helplessness or was it a calculated move to build bridges between the two neighbours which the partition was going to create? Some of his speeches of course, give the impression of his helplessness. For, in most of the speeches that he delivered after the acceptance of the partition resolution by the Congress, his oft-repeated argument was that "no one listens to me." Or that he opposed partition because people were with him but now they had turned their back on him which was evident from the acceptance of partition by the Congress which represented the overwhelming majority of the people. There may be some truth in this view. For, the Secretary of State wrote to the Viceroy after 17th June 1947 that "Gandhi will continue to require careful handling though it is to be hoped that the stage has now passed when it was within his power to sabotage the whole plan."[17] Gandhi's admirers in England such as Horace Alexander felt that the Mahatma had failed to convince his Congress colleagues not to accept the division of the country on communal grounds. In a letter to Agatha Harrison he wrote that one should not be worried about Gandhi's statement of 5 May 1947 that he had always said that communal division of India was not inevitable and would not solve the communal problem.[18] Rao Bahadur Menon told the Viceroy that in Sardar Patel's opinion not too much account should be taken of the recent utterances of Gandhi in favour of a united India.[19] Even Jinnah told Mountbatten that while his word ran supreme in the League, Gandhi's word was valueless as other leaders such as Nehru and Patel had important position in the Congress.[20] According to Azad, after meeting Patel during negotiations started by Mountbatten, Gandhi's opposition to partition does not remain as vehement as it was before meeting him.[21] The reason for this change is evident. Leaders like Patel and Nehru and for that matter many more in the Congress hierarchy were the people who were his backbone in all his struggles. They were old and tried servants of the nation. It was not easy to replace them. Rejection of the partition plan by the A.I.C.C. implied that he was to take over the leadership of the Congress single-handed for which he was not prepared. For, in the absence of the old colleagues he had to launch a struggle against those who had accepted the partition and had become part and parcel of the Government. They were the people who had been with him through thick and thin. The very idea of starting any movement of non-co-operation against them made him shudder. Of course, there were leaders of different hues and colours such as some socialists, a few Hindu Congress men, some Hindu Sabha men, who were opposing partition. Could Gandhi rely on them for any prolonged struggle for the annulment of the decision of partition? For, they had no faith in his technique and ideals. The Mahatma knew his powers and limitations. Possibly Patel, Nehru and Kriplani had told him in plain words that the alternative to partition was civil war which made him acquiesce in the partition. When he met the Viceroy on 4th June he was fully aware of his position in the Congress. Very likely it had occurred to him that the partition was not the end of the road for him. He could still think of ways and means for healing the wounds that partition was likely to cause. The first step in this direction was to reduce tension between the two communities. If the two could live together in both the dominions happily on the basis of equality, geographical division would lose meaning. In his words, "If Hindus in the union provinces regarded the Muslims, as their brothers and sisters, Pakistan will be wholly inoperative—if the hearts of the non-Muslims were sound, the physical partition could produce no ill-effects."

Possibly he believed that after the departure of the British from India on August 15, 1947 the leadership of the two communities in both the dominions would realize the mistake of the division of the country and would arrive at some kind of political and administrative arrangement to undo the wrongs done by the geographical division. May be underlying this approach was his suggestion to the Viceroy on 4 May, 1947 that the British should immediately give dominion status, strengthen the interim government for thirteen months and leave the country after handing over power either to the League or the Congress.[22] Then it would be the people of this country to decide whether to partition the country or to keep India as united. In the present situation the partition was being imposed on the people. Since this view was not acceptable to the Government he devoted himself to creating suitable atmosphere for that objective. He set out on a mission to wipe out the hatred between the two communities which the communal riots had generated in several parts of both the dominions. It was an herculian attempt of an individual to reduce to the minimum the effects of the partition. Though he was surrounded by the communal fire, he did not surrender to weakness and despair. The movement in Kashmir led by Sheikh Abdulla appeared to him as a negation of the two-nation theory. It created some hope in him that the

Muslim leaders and the masses would realize the logical weakness of the two-nation theory in the Indian context and the ill-effects of the partition would be removed. He spent three days in Jammu and Kashmir to assess the situation. He appreciated the role of Sheikh Abdullah in protecting Kashmir when it was attacked by marauders supported by the Pakistan Government.

Later on he decided to return to Noakhali to take up his unfinished task of restoring communal peace through contact with the people. But on his way to Noakhali, serious communal disturbances broke out in Calcutta that detained him there. Since this time the Hindus were aggressive and Muslims suffered more, the League leaders especially Suhrawardhy were very solicitous towards him. Suhrawardhy had flown to Karachi where he found no future in Pakistan. For Jinnah had no liking for him and so he had appointed his rival Nazimuddin as Governor designate of East Pakistan. It was in Karachi that Suhrawardhy read in *Dawn* that Gandhi was going to Noakhali and so he immediately returned to Calcutta. The League leaders wanted Gandhi's presence in Calcutta to end the disturbances. The Mahatma agreed to their request on the condition that Suhrawardhy would actively participate in his programme of restoring peace in the city even at the risk of his life and Muslim leadership would put in all their efforts to save the lives of Hindus in Noakhali. It was no horse trading. It was the Mahatma's way and technique of restoring peace single handedly in a vast area. The idea was to involve the leadership of both the communities in restoring peace. Suhrawardhy was entirely opposite of the self-denying and ascetic Mahatma in mental make up. The league leader loved money, champagne, night clubs and was known for engineering communal riots in Calcutta that created political climate for the division of the country. Wavell considered Suhrawardhy as one of the most inefficient, conceited and crooked politician in India. But the Mahatma was known for making use of any person for the fulfilment of any good cause. The Hindus even felt that Suhrawardhy was a sort of hostage for maintaining peace in Noakhali. Mountbatten claimed that he sent Gandhi to Calcutta to act as one man boundary force. But Gandhi was on his way to Noakhali to carry on his mission of Hindu-Muslim unity which he had announced earlier while addressing the Congress workers who saw him at Lahore, "My present place is in Noakhali, 'he said' and I would go there even if I have to die. But as soon as I am free from Noakhali, I will come to the Punjab."[23] Possibly it was on the Viceroy's advice that Suhrawardhy agreed to join hands with Gandhi to restore peace in Calcutta. For the

Viceroy believed that Gandhi had tremendous influence over the Hindus and Suhrawardhy had influence over the Muslims and the two would be able to carry both the communities with them.[24] There was a strain of self-preservation in Suhrawardhy's decision to join hands with Gandhi as he had lost confidence of Jinnah. It was decided that both Gandhi and Suhrawardhy would stay together in the same house. An old abandoned Muslim house known as the Hydari Mansion was selected and cleared up for this purpose. It was a ramshackle building open on all sides to the crowd in a riot prone locality. It was filthy and it was an uphill task to clear the floors of dirt and excrement.[25] Rats and snakes infested the corners of the building. There was all round foul smell. The Sardar, who was the Home Minister at that time, felt that it was a great risk for the Mahatma to stay in the building which was veritable shambles and a den of notorious den of gangsers and hooligans.

The Mahatma had to alter his programme of going to Noakhali and the Punjab as he believed that if the fury of communal violence did not abate in Calcutta, his going to the Punjab or to Noakhali would be of no avail. This move had some good results as the killings of the Hindus in Noakhali abated. The plan in Calcutta worked well for some time. Peace was restored, Hindus and Muslims embraced each other and an atmosphere of communal harmony of Khilafat days prevailed in the city for a few days as Hindus were welcomed in the Muslim mosques and the Muslims in the Hindus temples. What could not be done by thousands of soldiers and police men, was done by one man. But that was only a lull before the storm. The whole India stood on a live volcano because of the fierce struggle between the two communities for existence and Calcutta or for that matter no city of India where the two communities lived side by side could not remain unaffected by tension and violence in the country following the partition of the country. The outbreak of serious riots in the Punjab immediately before and after the partition causing immense suffering to the Hindus and Sikhs of Western Punjab disturbed the Hindus all over India especially those who had been forced to leave their hearths and homes as a result of communal riots. The peace sermons of the Mahatma were drowned in the cries of the suffering humanity. As a result, there was outbreak of violence again in Calcutta with greater fury. This time even Gandhi was not spared. The house where Gandhi and Suhrawardhy were staying was attacked by the enraged mob and Gandhi narrowly escaped a lathi blow and a brick aimed at him hit a Muslim standing beside him when he came out to pacify the crowd. He stood before the enraged crowd with hands folded. So did the policeman who were posted there to protect him. The window panes of the house were smashed. Fortunately Suhrawardhy was not there as he had gone home to make preparations for accompanying Gandhi to Noakhali. The crowd was in a mood to lynch him since he was looked upon by the Hindus as mainly responsible for their sufferings when he headed the Ministry in Bengal. The Calcutta miracle proved to be a nine days wonder. The Mahatma felt that it demanded supreme sacrifice. So he decided to go on a fast unto death to quench the wrath of those who cried blood for blood. The administration of independent India was embarrassed by this decision. For the fast could raise new problems for them. So Rajagopalachari, who was the Governor of Bengal at that time asked him, "But must you launch your fast at this stage. Why not wait and watch a little." Gandhi replied, "It would be too late afterwards—the minority Muslims cannot be left in a perilous state. My fast has to be preventive, if it is to be any good. I know that I shall be able to tackle the Punjab too, if I can control Calcutta. But, if I falter, the conflagration may spread—." But supposing you die, then the conflagration would be worse, remarked Rajaji.

"At least I wont be there to witness it," replied Gandhi, "I shall have done my bit. More is not given a man to do."[26]

In fact, when Gandhi had made a decision, it was very difficult for any body to persuade him to change it. What pained him most was that the riots were taking a heavy toll of innocent lives. There was hardly any attempt on the part of the Congress workers to risk their lives in order to save the lives and property of innocent people whether Hindus or Muslims.

The fast began from 8.15 p.m. on 1st September. He permitted himself to add salt and soda bicarb to the water that he wished to drink. In the earlier statement he allowed himself sour lemon juice. But he cancelled it when Rajaji pointed out the impropriety of this latitude if one had decided to put oneself entirely in God's hands. During the first twenty-four hours of the fast, he was resting most of the time. He looked a bit tired and spoke rather slowly. The fast stirred up the leaders of all the parties to restore peace with a view to saving the precious life. Hindu Sabha leaders headed by Dr. Shyama Prasad Mookerjee met him on the first day of the fast and pleaded with him to break the fast. Next day a Muslim League leader made a similar request to him. All the leaders assured him that peace had been restored in the city fulfilling his condition for breaking the fast. Some volunteers were sent to ascertain for themselves the truth of the statements made by the leaders. 500 strong police force of North Calcutta including British and Anglo-Indian officers observed 24 hours sympathetic fast while remaining on duty. The fast was broken on the night of September 5 after the leaders had given in writing, on Gandhi's insistence, assurance that in case there was recrudescence of riots, they would give their lives in the attempt to quell the riots. The fast lasted seventy three hours. Leaders from all walks of life paid tribute to him for his achievement in Calcutta. Rajagopalachari said, "Gandhiji has achieved many things but there has been nothing, not even independence which is so truly, wonderful, as his victory over evil in Calcutta."[27] Lord Mountbatten paid tribute to him by attributing to him as "the one man boundary force."[28] On receiving the reports from the Punjab, Gandhi realized that there was no meaning in staying in Noakhali or in Bihar so long as the Punjab was burning and Hindus and Sikhs were suffering. So he left for Delhi on September 7, on his way to Punjab. But the communal fire that broke out in Delhi tied him to this city till his death.

Notes and References

1. Gandhi, Manubehn, Bapu—My Mother (Translated from Gujarati by Chitra Desai) (Navajivan Publishing House, 1955).
2. Shukla, *op. cit.*, p. 3.
3. George Catlin to Mountbatten, 27 March, 1947, quoted in Manmath Nat Das, Partition to Independence (New Delhi, 1982), p. 30.
4. Pyarelal, The Last Phase, Vol. II, p. 77.
5. Hodson, H.V., The Great Divede (Oxford University Press, 1988), p. 221.
6. T.P., Vol. X, p. 103.
7. Breacher, Michael, Nehru, A Political Biography (London, Oxford University, 1959), p. 377.
8. Kriplani, J.B., Gandhi—His Life and Thought (New Delhi: Publication Division), p. 279.
9. Mosley, Leonard, The Last Days of British Raj, (London: Weidenfeld & Nicoloson, 1961), p. 248.
10. Hodson, *op. cit.*
11. T.P., Vol. XI, p. 182.
12. *Ibid.*, pp. 261-62.
13. C.W., LXXXVIII, p. 335.
14. *Ibid.*, LXXXIX, pp. 318-19.
15. T.P., Vol. XI, p. 53.
16. *Ibid.*, p. 131.
17. *Ibid.*, p. 538.
18. *Ibid.*, Vol. X, p. 616.
19. *Ibid.*, XI. p. 4.
20. *Ibid.*, X, p. 139.

21. Azad, Maulana Abul Kalam, India Wins Freedom, p. 203.
22. T.P., XI, pp. 610-11.
23. Tendulkar, *op. cit.,* Vol. VIII, p. 70.
24. Larry Collin, Mountbatten and Independent India, Vol. II, pp. 27-28.
25. Pyarelal, *op. cit.*, Vol. II, p. 410.
26. Tendulkar, *op. cit.*, Vol. VIII, p. 102.
27. *Ibid.*, p. 111.
28. *Ibid.*

29

The Great Sacrifice

"It is by my Cross that I can climb into the heart of humanity, Let me magnify my Cross, O, God.''

On reaching Delhi he was shocked to hear that the health of the capital of the Indian Union was in a deplorable state because of the suffering of the Hindu and Sikh refugees, driven out of Pakistan and the hardship of the Muslims of Delhi taking shelter in the improvised camps as a result of communal riots. This situation had reduced the gay and vivacious city into a dead city. It was an agonising experience for him to hear the tales of woes of the suffering humanity. He could not sit comfortably in the Birla House where his stay had been arranged this time as the area around Bhangi colony, where he stayed last time, had been occupied by the refugees. He immediately went to the camps of both non-Muslims and Muslims. Initially he was greeted by hostile slogans of the occupants of the camps. But, according to his secretary, his agonised looked and his words of sympathy touched their hearts and their hostility and scolding ceased. It was a matter of great anguish and sorrow for him that his old colleague Dr. Zakir Hussain who had shaped the institution of Jamia Millia was attacked by a group of angry Sikhs at Jullunder and he escaped death only by the timely aid of a Sikh captain and a Hindu railway employee. His experience of the refugee camps of Hindus and Sikhs were very agonising. For, their kith and kin had been mercilessly killed, their women raped and kidnapped and their property was looted in Pakistan. They were moving into Delhi for shelter with hatred for Muslims in their hearts. It was no easy task to wash out this hatred. His words of sympathy and the great heritage of their religion and the noble deeds of their ancestors which he recounted in his speeches were not enough to mollify them. The Mahatma knew it and he, therefore, addressed himself to satisfying their minimum physical needs. He directed his co-workers to devote themselves to providing comforts to the refugees. He made appeals for funds, clothes and blankets which received good response. But he vehemently opposed the efforts of the refugees to occupy forcibly the houses and business premises of the Muslims. For, it ran counter to his plan of creating conditions for the safety of the minorities both in Indian union and Pakistan. This implied exchange of population on religious basis which not only meant acceptance of two-nation theory of Jinnah but also involved uprooting of millions of people both in India and Pakistan besides creating two hostile neighbours with enough resources to cause harm to each other. He sent Suhrawardhy to Jinnah to create conditions for the protection of the rights of the minorities in Pakistan. But Suhrawardhy at that time was not in the good books of Jinnah and was in eclipse politically in Pakistan. Though Jinnah was not averse to his proposal as he too, had no plan of total exchange of population, he had not given full thought to the political implication and practical consequences of his two-nation theory. It was a slogan or a war cry so long as the British had not decided to quit India. But as soon as they decided to divide and quit, its logical and harsh aspects came to the surface and the leadership both in India and Pakistan completely failed to give right direction to the people. So the mob rule became the order of the day in certain parts of India and Pakistan where the two communities had been living together for ages peacefully. The Mahatma shudered at the thought of the horrible consequences of the mob rule. For, it meant the prevalence of lynch law which was worse than war. So in one of the speeches he appealed to the people not to take law into their own hands and seek justice through their Government. If one party persisted, in doing wrong, the only way open was war. This created a scare in both India and Pakistan as well as in the West. However, it did not mean that Gandhi had abandoned his principle of non-violence. All that he meant was that the insensible murder, loot and arson by the people would make any decent government impossible. The situation, in fact, revealed his feeling of helplessness in creating peace and security. So the congratulations showered on him on his 78th birthday jarred on his ears. For, his was a lone voice now. So he had lost all desire to live long. In reply to a birth day felicitation he wrote, "And if I had the impertinence openly to declare my wish to live 125 years, I must have the humility under changed circumstances, openly to shed that wish—that has not been done in a spirit of depression. The more apt term perhaps is helplessness."

But Gandhi's advice to the Hindus and Sikhs, especially the refugees from Pakistan, that they should refrain from any revengeful attitude towards the Muslims equally jarred on their ears. For, they held Congress leaders including Gandhi responsible for their misery and sorrows as they had time and again assured them that they would never agree to the partition of the country. Had there been proper planning for the present political arrangement, they would not have suffered so much. The words of the Mahatma fell flat on their ears. Didn't the same Mahatma assure them that Pakistan would be created on his dead body. How many of the refugees would trust him if he told them that he would be able to create conditions for their rehabilitation in Pakistan if he was able to rehabilitate the Muslims in Delhi? There was some logic and force in the assurance. For, much of the carnage and looting that followed the partition was the result of retaliation. But most of the refugees were not in a mood to understand that fact. So Gandhi's prayer meetings were quite often disturbed by some members of the audience who objected to the recitation of the passages from Koran. Initially he tried to pacify such persons by his offer that the would not hold prayer meetings even if one person objected to such recitations. But later on he only requested such protesters not to attend his prayer meetings. However, he forbade the police from using any force against them in accordance with his principle of non-violence. When some angry persons denounced him for his approach to the communal problem, he only turned to them with sympathy and affection. As reported by his secretary, one day two young men twitted him, during his morning walk, that he was no Mahatma but was only misguiding the Hindus by his doctrine of Ahimsa. He immediately pushed aside the girls who were serving as his walking sticks and affectionately put his hand on the shoulders of those youngmen. Possibly they were surprised by this gesture of the Mahatma and begged an apology for their remarks.[1] In fact, patience and affection appeared to Gandhi as the only answer to the anger of those who were suffering because of the lack of foresight of the leadership both of the Congress and the League. However, in spite of all the efforts of Gandhi and the government headed by Nehru and Patel, peace could not be restored in Delhi, as the refugees could not reconcile themselves to the policy of the Congress and Gandhi of the return of the Muslims to their houses while they had been pushed out of their homes in Pakistan. For, Gandhi had assured the Muslims in Delhi that he would no rest till every Muslim in the Indian Union who wished to live as a loyal citizen of the union, was back in his home living in peace and Hindus and Sikhs returned likewise to their homes. But Hindu and Sikh refugees could not imagine that they would ever be able to return to their homes for Jinnah was no Gandhi who could stake his life to restore pece in his new dominion. The League leadership that had worked up the sentiments of Muslim masses for the attainment of Pakistan could not direct their energies to any constructive purpose. They were busy in grabbing power. So the non-Muslims in Pakistan could not expect any protection from their new rulers. Consequently the refugees in India carried the impression that the Mahatma was showing favour to the Muslims at the cost of the interest of Hindu and Sikh refugees. When no body heard his counsel of sanity, he was left with no choice but to use his 'Brahmastra' of fast unto death. For, he was sure that this act of self-suffering would have the desired effect. But most of his friends and colleagues felt that it was not the right time for his fast as there would be a backlash of the killings of Hindus and Sikhs in Pakistan. Patel told the Viceroy that there was massacre of Hindus and Sikhs at Karachi and in the refugee train from the frontier. But the Mahatma thought otherwise. He felt that this was the most opportune time as it would test the strength of his appeal to the hearts of the Hindus and Sikhs who would listen to the call of the spirit amidst suffering. The object was not merely to save the Muslims from the wrath of the Hindus and Sikhs in the Indian dominion but to create an atmosphere of peace and reconciliation both in India and Pakistan. However, those who held the reins of the government did not respond unanimously to his decision. It was the unilateral decision of the Mahatma. He told the Viceroy that he had taken this decision without consulting the Prime Minister or the Deputy Prime Minister. While Mountbatten tried to cheer him up and Nehru felt happy for this courageous decision, Sardar felt that it would aggravate the relations between the two communities.[2] Conceding Gandhi's point of view reluctantly, he said, "We take a short range view, he takes a long range view."[3]

The fast began from 13 January at noon. It was preceded by a prayer on the lawns adjoining his room in the Birla House. To his youngest son Devadas this decision was nothing but surrender to impatience. But to the Mahatma his decision was the last word on patience. In reply, he wrote, "It was only when in terms of human effort, I had exhausted all resources and realized my utter helplessness, I put my head in God's lap. "This, in fact, was an appeal to the hearts of the Hindu and Sikh masses most of whom shared Gandhi's religious and spiritual sentiments and deified him for his self-sacrifice and concern for humanity. But the decision to undertake fast this time involved a great risk to his life. For, his health was not in good shape as for a few days before he had been running temperature and had severe attack of whooping cough which was worst at night. According to his secretary, the seizures were sometimes so frequent and prolonged that words came through with great difficulty. As a result of persistent coughing there was tenderness in the abdoman and streaks of blood appeared in the sputum.[4]

A health bulletin issued on the third day stated that Gandhi was considerately weak. His voice was feeble and acetone bodies had appeared in the urine. He had, in fact, entering the danger zone. For he had been taking water rather freely but it was not being eliminated which meant that his kidney was not properly functioning.[5] Since he was too weak to walk to the prayer ground a microphone was placed alongside his bed so that he could speak directly to the people. In his written message he admitted that his fast was for the protection of minorities both in India and Pakistan. He emphatically denied that it had been undertaken as a protest against the policy of the Home Government which was headed by Sardar Patel. However, one immediate political effect of the fast was that the government of India decided to pay to Pakistan fifty-five crores of rupees which it had been withholding because of a dispute in Kashmir in order to remove a cause of suspicion and friction between the two countries. This step was in accord with Gandhi's thinking of creating a congenial atmosphere for permanent settlement between the two neighbours which could pave way for the return of the refugees, whether Hindus, Sikhs or Muslims to their homes. In a written message to the prayer gathering, he said: "—The Cabinet deserves the warmest thanks from the whole country—And I know that all the nations of the earth will proclaim the present gesture as one which only a large hearted cabinet like ours could rise to—what then was the actuating motive. It was my fast. It changed the whole outlook—the present gesture, on the part of the Government of India, is one of unmixed goodwill. It has put the Government of Pakistan on its honour. It ought to lead to an honourable settlement not only of the Kashmir question, but of all the differences between the two dominions.[6] The Viceroy Mountbatten claimed that he suggested to Gandhi to take some steps for the return of 55 crores to Pakistan.[7] Before the commencement of his fast Gandhi met the Viceroy who told him that he considered it to be unstatesman like and unwise and dishonourable the decision of Indian Government to refuse payment of 55 crores as Pakistan's share of the balances as this figure was settled at the first series of Partition Council and Steering Committee meetings. Gandhi while agreeding to it narrated instances of his own life when honour bound he had to accept certain decisions which were harmful to him. He remembered an occasion in prison when he had signed a foolish letter which had been handed over to the prison authorities to post but which had not yet been posted. His request for the return of the letter was turned down since the Governor regarded it as 'in the post' since it had been handed over to his office. Gandhi did not find any fault in the Governor's decision and he had to stand by an awkward arrangement being unable to withdraw that letter. So he thought that his fast would do the needful.[8]

However, to Patel and the Indian Cabinet there was nothing dishonourable in their decision to refuse payment till all the issues including that of Kashmir was settled amicably. Sardar Baldev Singh, the Defence Minister, considered it a slap on the Indian Government and said that had there been an opposition party in the legislative assembly, they would undoubtedly have brought about the downfall of the Government on this issue.[9] The Mahatma was not in the Government. But he exercised tremendous influence over those who held reins of the Government as well as over the people. The Viceroy, now a constitutional head, tried to make use of the power of Mahatma to give directions to a policy which he considered useful for both the dominions. On Gandhi's assassination, the Viceroy in his heart of heart felt that he was partly responsible for this heinous act as the murderer held Gandhi responsible for the payment of 55 crores to Pakistan which the Viceroy felt he had in a way induced the Mahatma to take recourse to fast for reverting their decision to withhold the payment.

Nevertheless, Gandhi did not terminate the fast at the gesture of Government of making payment to Pakistan. For, he had undertaken fast for the restoration of communal peace especially in Delhi and not merely for the payment to Pakistan which the Viceroy claimed. His condition started worsening. The body became water logged because of the malfunctioning of the kidney. The doctors' bulletin sounded a grave note on the 17th. On the suggestion of Maulana Azad, Gandhi put severe conditions for ending the fast. A Central Committee consisting of 130 members representing all communities was formed under Dr. Rajendra Prasad to persuade people for the fulfilment of the conditions laid down by Gandhi for ending the fast. Next day he broke his fast when the important persons put their signatures to the seven conditions. Muslims were given assurances that they could return to their homes in Delhi.

one another."[11] Again on Nehru's suggestion that Rajagopalachari should take over as Governor General after Mountbatten, Patel wrote to unwilling Rajaji, "After Bapu's death it is all the more essential that the remnant of his circle should pull its weight together."[12]

The Mahatma, in fact, never believed that with the attainment of freedom his mission was fulfilled. In a way it had given rise to several new problems which could be tackled only by the concerted efforts of dedicated men and women. His major ideals and programmes were at stake.

The fast was just a prelude to his efforts to reduce the pernicious effects of the partition. For, he believed that the assurances given to him by the leaders of various groups and communities for terminating the fast was the beginning of the endeavour of the saner elements in the country to create an atmosphere of peace and harmony both in India and Pakistan. There still appeared a glimmering hope in his mind that the situation was developing that would enable him to live up to 125 years in order to establish a non-violent society. He was waiting for some positive gesture from the rulers of Pakistan in response to his suffering for the safety of the Muslims in India. But no such thing happened and he was dismayed for a moment. However, his faith in God raised his spirits for he had full faith in the mysterious ways of God of doing good to mankind. News and telegrams continued pouring in announcing the killing of Hindus and Sikhs in Pakistan that weakened the faith of the non-Muslims especially the refugees from West Pakistan in Gandhi's solution to the problem. Some of them even felt that the Mahatma alone was a bulwark against any effective action against those who had been responsible for the partition of the country which was the main cause of their suffering. It is estimated that 95 per cent of his mail in the summer of 1947 was hostile. The atmosphere in the country especially in the North was surcharged with anger against the policy of the Congress. It was a dangerous situation as the Mahatma could become a target of the anger of the refugees. He was fully conscious of it. He frankly told a Muslim gathering that several Hindus were extremely furious with him and he could any day become a prey to this fury.[13] Several times his grand daughter who was mainly attending on him received letters and telephone calls threatening her life. But such threats were not a novel experience for him. During his struggle in South Africa he was twice attacked by those who differed with him and was saved by the timely help of liberal Whites. When he was in the thick of his struggle he came to know of a conspiracy to eliminate him. But it did not deter him. He virtually wrote his Will instructing his nephew how to discharge his responsibilities after his death. In India, too, an attempt was made on his life during his campaign against untouchability and he was saved from a bomb attack only because the car carrying him was detained at the railway crossing as the train was late. During the Second World War an announcement was made by the German radio that the British were planning Gandhi's assassination. The Viceroy found in it German design of killing the Mahatma. He offered police protection. But Gandhi declined it with thanks on the plea that "having lived under the threat of assassination for a generation he had come to learn by experience that not a blade of grass moves except by His will and no assassin can curtail any body's life or a friend protect it."[14]

So he carried on his activities without any fear. As usual he had meetings with ministers, had his lessons in Bengali, sat over spinning wheel, had his normal massage, addressed prayer meetings, etc. His only reply to the threats was his wish to die with Ramnam on his lips and no anger against his killer in his heart.[15]

The plot to kill him was being hatched by a small group of determined conspirators in Poona. Its leader was Nathuram Godse, an editor of the Poona newspaper 'Hindi Rashtra'. One of the members of the groups was Madanlal Pahwa, who had suffered a lot as a result of the partition. He had seen his father and aunt being killed by the Muslim mob. By the third week of January all the conspirators had reached Delhi and had gone round the lawns of the Birla House where the Mahatma was holding his prayer meetings in the evening daily. The first attempt was made on 20th January. The plan was to explode a guncotton slab which would cause panic and confusion in the meeting giving opportunity to one of the conspirators to fire at the Mahatma. The task of igniting the guncotton slab was assigned to Madanlal Pahwa, a youngman of twenty. The prayer meeting was going on when the explosion took place 75 feet away from where Gandhi was addressing the meeting. But the disorder and confusion which the conspirators expected did not occur. Only a small group of people rushed to the spot where it happened and surrounded Madanlal and handed him over to the police. Gandhi remained unruffled, though his grand daughter Manu was visibly shaken. He reproached her for being so scared. He tried to pacify the people and resumed his speech. Other conspirators fled the scene. There were many persons who extolled the Mahatma for the way he conducted himself with tranquillity. But truthfully speaking there was no such occasion for giving him credit for his conduct. For, he really believed that the explosion was only the result of some military exercise going on nearby. It was later on he discovered that it was a ruse to divert the attention of the people to throw a hand grenade at Gandhi. But at the last moment the courage of the conspirator failed and the conspiracy ended in a fiasco. However, the Home Minister became more wary as he had received information from the Bombay Government about the conspiracy to assassinate the Mahatma. So security measures at the Birla house were tightened by posting army and police personnel along with plain clothes men. The Mahatma yielded to this arrangement as he did not want to embarrass Patel. But he refused permission for the search of every person entering the compound as he earnestly believed that his life was in the hands of God and if he (Rama) willed him to give up this body "no one could save him." So his normal routine went on. He had bouts of cough which worried the girls attending on him. For, the Mahatma was not yielding to any alopathic medicine for the treatment of his ailment. He was rather sorry that his close associates did not have as much faith in 'Rama' therapy as he had. He remained unperturbed. For, he believed that he had enough to do to alleviate the suffering humanity as well as to reorganize the Congress for a new role in the independent country. He was planning to go to Pakistan in pursuit of his peace mission. He sent his emissaries to have talks with Jinnah and Liaquat Ali to create a suitable climate for his projected visit. Dinshaw and Jehangir, Patel both Parsis went to Karachi, then the interim capital of Pakistan on 7th January to make arrangements for his visit. There they contacted Sri Prakasa, the Indian High Commissioner, and Suharawardhy, Ghulam Mahammed, the Finance Minister of Pakistan, who appeared to be friendly. They also met Abdul Rab, Nishtar and Fazli Rahman, the two cabinet ministers who appreciated Gandhi's mission. During the negotiations, the most valuable part was played by Jamshed Mehta, a Karachi citizen who was great admirer of Gandhi and habitual wearer of homespun Khadi. He was close to Jinnah whom he met frequently during this period in connection with the refugee problem of Pakistan. He became their go-between. This was the time when Gandhi undertook fast in Delhi for the protection of the Muslims. Jinnah appreciated Gandhi's good-will mission. The two emissaries returned to Delhi accompanied by Jamshed Mehta and reported to Gandhi. It is reported that February 8th or 9th was fixed as the tentative dates for his visit to Pakistan.[16]

Both the Mahatma and the Viceroy Lord Mountbatten hoped that conditions favourable to the co-operation between the two sovereign states could be created. The Mahatma was working at the psychological level while the Viceroy and his aides were working at the institutional level. They were relying on the Joint Defence Council for the realisation of his end. It was by means of this institution that the two Prime Ministers were able to meet at regular intervals to take decisions for the interests of the people of the two countries. However, their hopes were blasted by the disorder in Punjab and struggle over Junagad and Kashmir.

Gandhi had planned to leave for Wardha on 2nd February and return to Delhi as early as possible to pursue his peace mission in Pakistan. Even an hour before his assassination, he told a Sindhi Congress leader who had been assigned the task of helping the Hindus desirous of migrating from Sindh to India to convey the following message to the premier of Sindh on his return to Sindh, "I am willing to come to Sindh if he will allow me and then I will try to remove the tension between Hindus and Muslims."[17] He was advised to write to Jinnah and take his permission. But conditions in Pakistan for non-Muslims were so bad that all such plans appeared to many around him as merely 'day dreaming'. Things were not very encouraging for the Muslims in India, too. Even three days before his assassination he was disappointed to learn that only one Muslim attended his prayer meeting though he had several times earlier urged Hindus and Sikhs attending his prayer meetings to bring along with them their Muslim friends.[18] His close colleagues could not understand how they would be able to hold India non-violently. But Gandhi's faith was unshaken. He told Kingsley Martin, a British Press Correspondent, only three days before his murder that non-violence had greater chance of success in our contemporary democratic system since a non-violent man derived power through service to the people and for such a man or for such a government a non-violent army was a possibility. For 'the voters would themselves say, we do not want any military for our defence. A non-violent army would fight against all injustice or attack with clean weapons.' He asserted that he could even win over even the people of tribal areas of Pakistan through service. But all this talk lacked reality in the contemporary situation. For, the Indian Government had not adopted this course when Pakistan marauders attacked Kashmir. He lamented that there was no such leader in Kashmir who could create such a non-violent army to resist aggression.

Explaining the conduct of a non-violent person in a democratic set up to Vincent Sheean, an American journalist during the same period he said that "a non-violent person will not himself hold power as power corrupts but will keep check on those who hold power by educating and guiding the voters."

The Mahatma, thus, was contemplating a new role for his constructive workers or Congress volunteers and that motivated him to recast the constitution of the Indian National Congress. So he wrote to R.R. Diwakar on January 19, 1947, that the Congress should be co-extensive with the whole nation by extending membership to the whole population of the country. He even wanted the Congress to dissolve itself as a political party voluntarily. So even two days before his death his mind had been all the time working on drafting a new constitution for the Congress. The whole of the "29th January had been so cramful with work that at the end of the day the Mahatma felt utterly fagged out. But he was determined to finish the draft of the constitution for the Congress even working late hours, though his hand was reeling because of fatigue. Next morning he handed over the revised draft to his secretary Pyarelal "to go though it carefully and fill in any gaps he thought that there might be." He wanted the Congress to transform itself as a Lok Sevak Sangh for the social and economic uplift of the country. It was not the first time Gandhi thought of a unique role of the Congress in free India. As early as 1931 in a discussion with Nehru, he observed that after the attainment of freedom the Congress would pass a "self-denying ordinance, laying it down that none of its members could accept a paid job under the state and if any one wanted such a post of authority in the state he would have to leave the Congress. In other words, Congress would not work as a political party but only as a social force exercising moral pressure on the Government to keep it on the right track."[19]

The Mahatma had his usual massage and bath. But his mind was occupied with the threatened food crisis in Madras and he asked his secretary to prepare a note on how to meet it in the light of his experiences in Noakhali, for, he believed that a province which was blessed by nature with coconut, palm, ground nut and banana in such plenty need not starve if people were made conscious, how to husband their resources in food.[20]

He saw visitors after his mid-day nap and dissolved a very hard remark by a refugee into a laughter by his characteristic humour. The former had advised him to retire to Himalayas as he had failed to solve any problem. In reply the Mahatma said that nothing would be better for him to retire as this would raise the stature of his 'Mahatmahood by attracting larger crowds.' In the evening before his prayer meeting he had a talk with Patel for about an hour mostly over the question of reconciling his differences with Nehru. The conversation between them came to an end when Patel's daughter who accompanied his father, reminded Gandhi that he was getting late for prayer meeting.

Accompanied by Manu and Abha, he moved towards the prayer ground swiftly leaning on the two girls whom he termed as his 'walking sticks'. As he faced the congregation, he took his hands off the shoulders of the girls, folded his palms to acknowledge the greetings of the people. Then suddenly a man wearing a Khaki jacket pushed his way through the crowd. Manu thinking that he was coming to touch Bapu's feet remonstrated that they were already late and tried to stop him by holding his hand. But he 'violently jerked her off' and the spectacle case, the rosary, note book and the spittoon which she was carrying fell from her hand. The man bent down before the Mahatma as if in the act of making obeissence, took out his revolver and fired three shots in quick succession. In utter confusion, a feeble voice 'He Ram' escaped from the lips of the Mahatma before his body dropped on the ground.

The assassin, Nathuram Godse was overpowered by the people and taken to a nearby police station. Death was instantaneous. The body was carried inside and laid on the mattress where he used to sit and work.

Notes and References

1. Pyarelal, Last Phase, Vol. II, p. 247.
2. Collins, Mountbatten and Independent India, Vol. II, p. 82.
3. Gandhi, Rajmohan, Patel, p. 463.
4. Pyarelal, *op. cit.*, Vol. II, p. 454.
5. *Ibid.*
6. Tendulkar, Vol. VIII, p. 261.
7. Collins, *op. cit.*, Vol. I, p. 50.
8. *Ibid.*, Vol. II, p. 140.
9. *Ibid.*
10. Pyarelal, *op. cit.*, Vol. II, p. 775.
11. Gandhi, Rajmohan, Patel: A Life, p. 470.
12. *Ibid.*
13. C.W., Vol. LXXXIX, p. 384.
14. Birla, *op. cit.*, Vol. IV, p. 69; C.W., XC 273.
15. C.W., XC, p. 489
16. Jehangir & Marjorie Sykes, Gandhi, His Gift of the Fight, pp. 185-91.
17. Malkani, N.R., *op. cit.*, p. 37.
18. C.W., Vol. XC, p. 507.
19. Nehru, Autobiography, p. 252.
20. Tendulkar, Vol. XVIII, p. 287.

food to them, but personally worked as a consultant to the patients in a rural nature cure centre established by him. He was constantly expanding the sphere of his self because of his belief that it was the only road to see God face to face or to have the glimpse of the universal spirit. He was true to himself when he claimed that the main aim of his life was to seek 'moksha'. But he was sure that it could be realized only by serving others. Logically by serving others he was catering to the demands of his own self or say greater self. This approach changed his life style which left a deep scar on his relations with his family members as they were deprived of his sole personal attention for their development. If a son felt that he was deprived of his father when the latter became a Mahatma or the father of the nation he was justified. The differences between the two were the result of the compulsions of the father and the natural needs of the son.

As a youngman, Mohan was ambitious like all other youngmen, though he was not blessed with exceptional natural faculties and worldly resources. But he had rocklike determination. In the service of the community it made him tenacious though to his critics, he sometimes appeared very obstinate. By his nature he would 'do whatever was the demand of his inner being' which later on he considered as the voice of God. No argument or an advice of a friend could deflect him from the course he had adopted. He sincerely believed that he was in the hands of God when his particular action or decision was unwelcome to both his friends and opponents.

Self-respect was another trait in his character. This brought him in confrontation with the authorities in South Africa. He was ready to forgo all comforts to maintain his self-respect. Wasn't it the moral duty of all Indians in South Africa not to compromise over the issue of self-respect? Freedom from the British rule follows from it as self-determination is the first condition for maintaining self-respect and dignity.

It was part of his nature to trust others. He was very slow in relinquishing friendship which sometimes placed him in an awkward position in public life or put him in dual relationship with some of his opponents in public life with whom he was reluctant to sever personal relations. The man in the Mahatma was his leading light that cleared his way in his search for his true self which was truth for him. His greatness lay in expanding the sphere of his self.

The journey of Mohandas towards Mahatmahood was long arduous and painful. For, while the masses felt spiritual solace simply by looking at him and his friends and colleagues performed great deeds while working with him, he himself lacked self-fulfilment as he kept his ideals too high. However, the Mahatma in him has left for us a set of ideals and rules of conduct in public life which would serve as a lodestar for the generations to come in their search for enduring peace, happiness and human dignity.

Index